EFFECTIVE SPEECH–LANGUAGE PATHOLOGY: A COGNITIVE SOCIALIZATION APPROACH

EFFECTIVE SPEECH–LANGUAGE PATHOLOGY: A COGNITIVE SOCIALIZATION APPROACH

John R. Muma

 LAWRENCE ERLBAUM ASSOCIATES, PUBLISHERS
1998   Mahwah, New Jersey   London

KH

Lawrence Erlbaum Associates, Inc., Publishers
10 Industrial Avenue
Mahwah, New Jersey 07430

Library of Congress Cataloging-in-Publication-Data

Muma, John R., 1938-
Effective speech–language pathology: A cognitive socialization approach / John R. Muma.
p. cm.
Includes bibliographical reference and index.
ISBN 0-8058-2094-9 (hardcover : alk. paper). — ISBN
0-8058-2095-7 (pbk. : alk. paper)
1. Language disorders in children. 2. Cognition in children.
3. Language acquisition. 4. Socialization. I. Title.
RJ496.L35M86 1997
618.92'855—dc21   97-30925
                                                   CIP

Books published by Lawrence Erlbaum Associates are printed on
acid-free paper, and their bindings are chosen for strength and
durability.

Printed in the United States of America
10 9 8 7 6 5 4 3 2 1

7/15/15

CONTENTS

PREFACE

Brown (1956) indicated that language acquisition is, "a process of cognitive socialization" (p. 247).

The literature over the past four decades has elaborated on this theme. Accordingly, the field of cognitive socialization, with its attendant philosophical views and theoretical perspectives, has emerged to offer a viable perspective not only of language acquisition per se, but also of the acquisition of cognition, codification and language, communication, and expression and affect (CCCE). This literature offers the clinical fields a substantive base for rendering appropriate services.

Based on cognitive socialization, chapter 1 begins with the basic premise of this volume, the twofold principle of appropriateness of clinical practice. It is twofold because appropriate clinical practice in language and cognition should be both supportable by the relevant scholarly CCCE literatures, and relevant to a client's repertoire of available skills. With this bidimensional principle, those clinical fields interested in cognition in general and language in particular could make legitimate claims for disciplined and scholarly expertise in cognition and language and for rendering appropriate clinical services.

A TRIBUTE: CAROL PRUTTING

Carol Prutting championed such messages. Therefore, it would be appropriate to begin with a tribute to her. This tribute is extended for three reasons. First, Prutting was instrumental in drawing clinical implications from the Gricean model of communication (Prutting, 1982, 1983; Prutting & Kirchner, 1983, 1987). This constituted a major substantive advancement for the clinical fields interested in language because it carried a very important message: Philosophical views and theoretical perspectives not only have direct implications for the clinical fields, but define appropriate services.

Gallagher (1991) also reified the importance of a strong theoretical base for clinical endeavors in accordance with the *1983 ASHA Task Force on Training Standards* (Rees & Snope, 1983). These standards called for increased assurance of a strong scientific and scholarly base in training speech–language pathologists and audiologists. To reaffirm this concern, Minifie (1996) held a meeting with directors of graduate training programs in communication science and disorders in which he expressed the concern that scholarship and discipline may be eroding in the clinical fields.

Second, Prutting's contributions indicated that a paradigm shift occurred whereby behaviorism and reinforcement theory became replaced by mentalism, constructionism, functionalism, experiential realism, and experiential cognition with the centrality of intention (Searle, 1992). In so doing, intent replaced reinforcement as a viable account of language acquisition (Bruner, 1978, 1986; K. Nelson, 1985, 1986, 1996; Searle, 1992).

Third, Prutting's students are one in their appreciation of philosophical views and theoretical perspectives as comprising the substantive base of the clinical fields. They are disciplined yet constructively critical of philosophical views and theoretical perspectives. Prutting's legacy is not only substantive in advancing the clinical applications of the Gricean model, but it is a living legacy via her students. Thus, Prutting exemplified true scholarship for the clinical fields. The clinical fields and the clients who receive services from applications of the Gricean model are the beneficiaries.

SCHOLARS AND SCHOLARSHIP

Jerome Bruner has contributed mightily to our understanding of CCCE. His now classic books *Actual Minds, Possible Worlds* (1986) and *Acts of Meaning* (1990) provide centerpieces of scholarship for many of the issues raised throughout this book. I hope that I have done him justice because his contributions resonate in many clinical principles and practices derived from the cognitive socialization literature. I guess he would chuckle in appreciation for my salute to the cognitive socialization literature as the source of my virtual world renderings derived in large measure from his virtual world renderings of cognition, language, communication, education, and philosophy of science. This literature offers reasonably (reasonable in the sense of human affairs rather than formal logic) good opportunities to address appropriateness.

Known for his humility, I am sure that Bruner would give steadfast assurance that others, such as the "titans" he cited (Freud, Piaget, and Vygotsky) are significant players in understanding the pith of human affairs.

As a significant player, I would like to include Katherine Nelson in my tribute to Bruner, not because she has been a colleague of Bruner's, but because her contributions (K. Nelson, 1985, 1986, 1996) on script theory, making sense (shared meaning), and language as a means of knowing toward obtaining a situated mind (experiential cognition: biological, psychological, emotional, social, cultural) greatly advance the understanding of cognitive socialization in ways that are comfortably compatible with so much of Bruner's work. They dance the same dance.

Just as quickly, as though haste has its virtue, I want to acknowledge Roger Brown because his works reverberate as well, for the same reasons, throughout this volume, and other books, I have done. It is evident that the field of cognitive socialization took him at his word when he commented that language acquisition is, "a process of cognitive socialization" (Brown, 1956, p. 247).

The psycholinguistic literature over the past four decades has come to realize what cognitive socialization means and it continues to provide important new accounts of CCCE. Thus, due in large measure to Brown and his colleagues, cognitive socialization has become a bona fide field of study with great promise.

I would like to include Catherine Snow in my recognition of Brown. Snow and others, such as Courtney Cazden, have wrestled with various aspects of cognitive socialization, especially the centrality of communicative intent. Communicative intent is a running theme throughout this book and much of the cognitive socialization literature.

Brown, as so many true scholars, has been humble about his mighty impact. Is it fair to say that the study of human affairs makes one humble? Or is humility in the likes of Brown and Bruner another personal attribute worthy of admiration? Whatever, it is understandable that Brown has been regarded as the father of psycholinguistics—which has become the field of cognitive socialization—with his urging (Brown, 1986). Bruner may be regarded as a titan among titans in cognitive socialization or social cognition.

Thus, I am especially proud of Brown's (personal communication, October 9, 1986) comment about my 1986 book *Language Acquisition: A Functionalistic Perspective*: "I have been sampling it and want to congratulate you on an exceptionally well written and sensible book that seems ideal for your intended mark." I am thrilled that J. Bruner (personal communication, August 18, 1993) made a similar comment about it: "I also admired your earlier book as a very sensible and clear presentation, in agreement with Roger."

In both my 1978 and 1986 books and elsewhere, I have urged that the most viable approach to clinical assessment, in view of the *heterogeneous* nature of clinical populations and the *seven basic assessment issues*, is descriptive assessment predicated on the standardized procedures issuing from the contemporary CCCE literature. Furthermore, I have urged a facilitation approach for intervention predicated on an individual's available repertoire of skills, progress in acquisition sequences, available learning strategies, and evidence of active loci of learning in social context (Bruner, 1981, 1990; K. Nelson, 1985, 1986, 1996). This view of facilitation is in keeping with the facilitation model espoused by Bloom and Lahey (1978) and Lahey (1988).

Regarding the present volume, Brown (personal communication, September 14, 1993) commented, "Your book will be important and controversial" and he continued, "Your book speaks eloquently on its own." Needless to say, I would hope that it is important, controversial, and provides an eloquent message.

To all of the cognitive socialization scholars whose works are drawn on, I extend a salute. It is a simple but important salute; It is simple because the clinical fields are in constant need of substantive issues on which clinical principles and practices may be founded. The cognitive socialization literature is constantly providing such information.

It is important to import clinical implications from this literature because they are importable; that is, principles of normal language acquisition are applicable to the language impaired (Leonard, 1989); fundamental issues concerning dualism, monism, materialism, positivism, connectionism, behaviorism, and reductionism are undergoing close scrutiny (Searle, 1992); developments in cognition (Anderson, 1983; Karmiloff-Smith, 1992; K. Nelson, 1996; Rosch, 1973, 1978; Schacter & Tulving, 1994) and in neuroscience

(Fodor, 1983; Gunnar & Maratsos, 1992) have raised some fundamental issues with major clinical implications for understanding the nature of language impairment (Locke, 1994); delimitation is necessary for grammatical and pragmatic rules to work appropriately (Bowerman, 1987; Fodor & Crain, 1987; Macken, 1987); intent has pervasive implications for clinical assessment and intervention (Bloom, Beckwith, Capatides, & Hafitz, 1988; Bruner, 1981, 1986; Muma, 1986a; K. Nelson, 1985, 1986, 1991; Wetherby, 1991); attribution criteria (Bloom et al., 1988; Muma, 1983b, 1986a, 1987, 1991; K. E. Nelson, 1981, 1989; Prutting, 1979) are applicable to anyone acquiring grammatical and pragmatic systems; experiential cognition makes sense as a viable account of both cognitive and language acquisition (K. Nelson, 1996); mental functioning has social origins (Bruner, 1981, 1990; Hagstrom, 1994; Mandler, 1979, 1983; K. Nelson, 1996; Rogoff, 1990; Vygotsky, 1962; Wertsch, 1991), and so on. Thus, the clinical fields in CCCE are indeed indebted to the field of cognitive socialization.

It should be abundantly clear that this literature is not just for its own sake but it yields an end in the form of a substantive base for appropriate clinical assessment and intervention. Thus, the clinical fields are important consumers of the cognitive socialization literature and the salute to cognitive socialization is in recognition of the fact that its clinical implications constitute the substantive base for CCCE in the applied fields. By the same token, the field of cognitive socialization is flattered that its substantive outcomes are so beneficial.

SCHOLARSHIP: NEED TO CRITICIZE

In a scholarly arena, it is necessary to be vigilant and intelligently criticize. In doing so, the substantive issues become scrutinized toward a fuller and disciplined appreciation.

Perhaps a note should be inserted concerning the nature of criticism and disagreement among scholars. K. E. Nelson (1991) indicated that:

> It is essential to recognize that many key questions are open rather than settled ... Premature closure, the treatment of important questions as if a little bit of rhetoric and data settle them when neither argumentation nor data have been conclusive, can seriously hamper progress in intervention and theory. (p. 399)

Some of the many issues that are unresolved and open to alternative views include hypothesis testing versus discovery; richly evident input versus degree-0 learnability; modularity or integrated processes; assisted versus sovereign learning; fragile versus hearty learning; reinforcement or intent; mind and brain; generalization or abstraction; issues concerning dualism, monism, positivism, materialism, quantification, and reductionism; spontaneous speech providing prima facie evidence of grammatical and pragmatic skills; brute and institutional facts; centrality of construct validity; definitions of language impairment; teaching versus facilitation; acquisition sequences; alternative strategies of learning; active loci of learning; alternative attribution criteria; language sampling; becoming a situated mind, and so on.

It is most impressive that rigorous debates and challenges are frequently raised about such issues, but they are rarely personalized. Such is the work of scholarship. Personalizing has the devastating effect of gutting scholarship. In the end, it is issues, not people espousing the issues, that live or die in a scholarly arena.

The general thrust of this volume is constructive criticism toward advancing the clinical fields. And, the primary source of issues is the cognitive socialization literature, especially developments that have occurred in the past decade. In raising these issues, it becomes necessary to criticize various views, perspectives, and practices in the clinical fields. In doing so, remember that it is the issues, rather than the people espousing the issues, that are of concern. Needless to say, issues that undergo careful scrutiny are useful for conceptualizing and implementing appropriate clinical services.

PHILOSOPHICAL–THEORETICAL STANCE

As a positive stance, an explicit philosophical-theoretical base is laid out in this volume from which legitimate clinical assessment and intervention issues and practices are derived. Clinicians appreciate such an undertaking because they know that it is exceedingly important that clinical assessment and intervention not only have continuity with their underlying philosophical-theoretical bases, but each respective underlying base itself should be well supported by the current literature. Accordingly, a philosophical-theoretical base underlying appropriate clinical services is enunciated and supported by the contemporary cognitive socialization literature.

Some issues in the cognitive socialization literature have multiple clinical implications for rendering appropriate clinical services. Accordingly, some issues appear more than once. For example, Brown's (1956) comment that language acquisition is "a process of cognitive socialization" (p. 247) and Bruner's (1981) comment that "context is all" (p. 172) appear in the text several times.

COGNITIVE SOCIALIZATION

Perhaps it is useful to cite another of Brown's (1977) comments about cognitive socialization, "If you concentrate on communicating, everything else will follow" (p. 26). The cognitive socialization literature is replete with such comments, which make it quite clear that the study of language and language acquisition is about cognitive socialization. Such comments underlie the contemporary functionalistic perspectives of language and they comprise the cornerstones of my three previous books (Muma, 1978b, 1981c, 1986a).

This volume may be considered logical extensions of my earlier works. The thrusts of the previous books were issues attendant to cognitive socialization, especially the centrality of intent in pragmatic theory (Bloom et al., 1988; Bruner, 1981, 1986; Cazden, 1977; Grice, 1975; K. Nelson, 1985, 1986, 1991, 1996; Ninio, 1995; Ninio & Snow, 1988; Searle, 1979, 1983, 1992; Sperber & Wilson, 1986). These thrusts are reiterated and amplified in this volume. New developments are added. Essentially the same philosophical-theoretical views are espoused simply because the contemporary literature not only reflects these views but has amplified and clarified them further (K. Nelson, 1996). Consequently, these views provide a substantive base for appropriate clinical services.

This is a new effort incorporating new developments in the literature and presumably drawing legitimate clinical implications. Needless to say, it will stand on its own. Because it is a new effort, I have obtained feedback on this volume from many scholars and clinicians across the clinical fields. Much of this feedback was for selected aspects of the manuscript. Rather than acknowledge each individual for their particular input, perhaps a general "thank you" will suffice. However, three nationally known and highly regarded clinicians and scholars—and individuals with utmost integrity—deserve special mention because they provided useful detailed feedback over most of the volume. They are Sister Marie Kopin, Ronald Laeder, and Colin McPherson, three of the finest clinicians anywhere. I, of course, am responsible for these virtual renditions of the cognitive socialization literature and their clinical implications.

Hopefully, clinicians, like scholars, in the clinical fields will find it provocative; and hopefully, technicians will find information that will be useful in the effort to become clinicians.

Because the clinical fields have so many disconnections with the cognitive socialization literature and because these fields lack adequate training in the philosophy of science and scholarship, I have begun a series of seminar workshops on cognitive socialization and scholarship. Some are a few days and some are one year to provide academic credit.

—*John R. Muma*

1

SETTING THE STAGE

APPROPRIATENESS

Please permit me the basic premise of this book. Taken from the United States' federal policies, specifically P.L. 94-142 and P.L. 99-457, it is simply that individuals needing clinical services are entitled to the most appropriate services. Most appropriate is taken to mean that which is most supportable by the contemporary scholarly literature. Because clinical services are rendered to individuals, it is desirable to extend the meaning of appropriateness to relevance to an individual's presumed repertoire of skills.

In identifying patterns of impairment, Brinton and Fujiki (1994) held a similar perspective by relying on the literature on the one hand and local cohort performance on the other, "in identifying patterns of impairment, specific behaviors are compared with developmental expectations drawn from the literature and from the child's community cohort" (p. 61).

Thus, appropriateness in this book usually has two connotations: relevance to the contemporary scholarly literature and relevance to an individual's presumed repertoire of skills.

Inasmuch as this volume is about clinical services in cognition, codification and language, communication, and expression (CCCE), the scholarly literature that provides the most supportable information for rendering appropriate clinical services is the contemporary cognitive socialization literature with its attendant influences from philosophy, psychology, linguistics, psycholinguistics, and assessment. At once, reference to these literatures, rather than the clinical fields per se, raises a provocative issue: The clinical fields may be somewhat disconnected from the relevant cognitive socialization literature in understanding and dealing with many aspects of CCCE, especially the behavioristic applications, the reliance on frequency counts as presumed measures of acquisition, and the use of tests that lack construct validity.

Such disconnections might be somewhat justifiable if they substantiate theoretical positions that are uniquely clinical. However, Ringel, Trachtman, and Prutting (1984) observed that the clinical fields lack adequate theories for predicting, explaining, and understanding clinical impairments. Rather, the clinical fields that deal with cognition and language rely on the normal acquisition literature for three fundamental reasons. First, the kinds of impairments usually seen clinically "fit" the nature of normal acquisition with the exception that such problems persist. To this extent, the normal acquisition literature provides an attractive substantive base for understanding clinical conditions and rendering appropriate clinical services. Second, if it were true that clinical conditions are aberrant from the nature of the normal acquisition process, the clinical fields would be faced with a very perplexing situation. In this case it would be necessary to step outside of the normal human condition and reconnoiter the foreign terrain to appreciate what is taking place and what should be done to render appropriate clinical services. Then, we are faced with the very unpleasant recognition that such clients are not "one of us" and for us to deal appropriately with such individuals in becoming one of us, we are utterly naked in understanding and knowing what to do. In these cases, the socialized-based perspective, which is very attractive in dealing with both normal and other clinical conditions, is even more attractive (Hagstrom, 1994; K. Nelson, 1996). Third, the normal acquisition literature in the field of cognitive socialization has many attractive theoretical perspectives that offer viable perspectives for rendering appropriate clinical services.

NEED FOR PHILOSOPHICAL VIEWS AND THEORETICAL PERSPECTIVES

The basic message from the philosophy of science literature (Bruner, 1986; Crick, 1988; Kuhn, 1962; Medawar, 1984) is that it behooves scholars to have explicit philosophical views and theoretical perspectives in order to achieve a disciplined understanding of what they are striving to explain, predict, understand, or do. Such perspectives establish coherence. Theories provide coherent explanations, predictions, and understandings (Kaplan, 1964; Kerlinger, 1973); said differently, theories provide a means of organizing what is known into a coherent understanding.

Accordingly, professions strive to be solidly grounded on recognized philosophical views and theoretical perspectives simply because a great deal needs to be explained, predicted, and understood. Lacking such under-pinnings, a profession is likely to become the product of authoritarianism, elitism, anarchy, dogma, hearsay, hype, and misused eclecticism.

To reiterate, Ringel et al. (1984) made a telling observation of speech-lan-guage pathology and audiology. They held that this field lacked its own coherent theories. This is serious because the literature on the philosophy of science explicitly defines the roles of philosophical views and theoretical perspectives as the substantive base of scholarship.

It is all the more serious because a survey by Prutting, Mentis, and Myles-Zitzer (1989) showed that a very small percentage of the training programs in speech-language pathology and audiology include readings (3.6%) or subject matter in a course (11.3%) on the theory of science. This means that the field is largely unaware of the significance of philosophical views and theoretical perspectives as its substantive base. Such naivete would go a long way toward appreciating:

1. Why various disconnections have occurred between the clinical fields and the scholarly fields in CCCE.
2. Why reliance is often placed on authoritarian pronouncements and dogma thereby evidencing a political orientation.
3. Why technicians may disdain theoretical perspectives.

Surprisingly, there are advocates in the clinical fields who take the view that theories may be dismissible. For example, Kamhi (1993), Perkins (1986), and Starkweather (1992) decreed that theories may be unnecessary for the clinical fields. Starkweather (1992) cushioned this view by saying:

> There is a certain sense in which theoretical beliefs should influence therapy— one should have a good understanding of the disorder so as to make good judgments and choices when confronting an individual—but to allow a theo-retical belief to restrain one's therapeutic practice is thoroughly irresponsible. (p. 95)

Kamhi (1993) indicated that "providing clinical services that are theoretically coherent is not only impractical, but also unrealistic" (p. 59). Such decrees are very dangerous because they invite elitism, anarchy, dogma, hype, authoritarianism, and so on. Fortunately, Perkins has since become an ad-vocate of theories.

The *1983 ASHA Task Force on Training Standards* (Rees & Snope, 1983) recognized the lack of philosophical views and theoretical perspectives as possible major reasons that the field may have become technician (atheoretical, ascholarly) rather than clinician (theoretical, scholarly) ori-ented. In order to rectify this problem, *Resolution II-B* was passed, calling for courses to be solidly based on theoretical perspectives in an effort to overcome technicianship and promote clinicianship.

Because theoretical perspectives are predicated on philosophical views, according to the literature on the philosophy of science, it is necessary to expand this resolution to the philosophy of science in general and recognized philosophical views in particular. By doing so, philosophical views and theoretical perspectives constitute the most fundamental underpinnings of the field. Such underpinnings provide rational evidence for holding particular views and taking particular actions in the clinical arena. Thus, philosophical views and theoretical perspectives define what may be viable (appropriate) for a field and in so doing define what is practical (Muma, 1986a, 1991; Prutting & Kirchner, 1983, 1987).

Cruickshank (1972) raised a telling issue about the field of learning disabilities. He was concerned that this field claims to deal with learning disabilities but it is not predicated on theories of learning. It is utterly ironic that the field of learning disabilities continues to be atheoretical, especially in view of the fact that major theoretical advancements have occurred in the scholarly literature on cognition (K. Nelson, 1996). Such disconnections not only point to the atheoretical nature of the field but bring to the fore the vulnerability of this field and related fields to authoritarianism, elitism, anarchy, dogma, hype, and misused eclecticism.

There are two major symptoms of this circumstance: (a) Atheoretical and exclusionary definitions, and (b) Authoritarianism with attendant dogma. Both the national and federal definitions of learning disabilities and language impairment are atheoretical and exclusionary. When such definitions are atheoretical, clinical entities may be defined in virtually any way. That is precisely what has happened. For example, Gillespie, Miller, and Fielder (1975) reviewed state legislation concerning learning disabilities and found that there was very little, if any, agreement as to an operational definition of learning disabilities. Similarly, McCauley and Demetras (1990) showed that there was little consensus as to how individuals were identified as language impaired in studies with these participants.

Furthermore, the atheoretical nature of the field of learning disabilities is evidenced by yet another major issue: Definitions of learning disabilities are definitions of exclusion. Such definitions indicate that if a child does not have a hearing loss, mental retardation, or emotional disturbance, then a learning disability may be evident. This might be viewed as a "washed" definition but, unfortunately, substantive considerations of recognized theories of learning are what have been "whitewashed" in favor of normative tests that lack construct validity with theories of learning. Such a circumstance invites dogma at the expense of scholarship.

Three special issues of the *Harvard Educational Review* (Harvard School of Education, 1971, 1973, 1974) raised a similar concern about assessment practices in the schools. In short, the concern was that assessment practices have relied on brute empiricism whereby an individual's performance is compared to a norm and inferences are made about presumed skills, resulting in assessment practices that merely categorize and label individuals, missing the more important issues concerning the nature of a problem. This practice has become so accepted and pervasive that it has attained a level of acceptability as a bona fide practice of educational institutions. Yet it is little more than a mechanism for labeling children rather than assessing what they can do. It is what Mercer (1972a, 1972b) called "the lethal label" problem.

Messick (1980a, 1989a, 1989b) echoed this concern but from a different vantage point. He and other scholars in assessment were concerned that assessment practices may lack construct validity. This is a fundamental concern because they indicated that the traditional "holy trinity" for validity (content, criteria, construct) is no longer viable simply because all aspects of validity are derived from construct validity. Thus, it is imperative to establish construct validity for all assessment: "*All measurement should be construct referenced*" (Messick, 1980, p. 1015). "*All* validity is at its base some form of construct validity. . . . It *is* the basic meaning of validity" (Guion, 1977, p. 410).

Unfortunately, a survey (Muma & Brannon, 1986) of the most frequently used language tests in speech-language pathology revealed a general lack of construct validity, which means that the results for these tests are open to any interpretation—an ethical dilemma. Furthermore, it means that the interpretation of performances on these tests may be mere dogma under the sponsorship of norms. To be relieved of this ethical dilemma, it would be necessary to establish construct validity either derived directly from theoretical premises or indirectly via factor analytic procedures governed by theoretical perspectives. Either way, theory is needed to explain, predict, and understand.

In subtle ways, a call for improved scholarship may be in the form of questioning what a field is about. In audiology and speech-language pathology this question has arisen: Does a field want a research doctorate or a professional doctorate? At the heart of this question is a subtle one concerning scholarship on the one hand and the art of the field on the other. When discussions surface concerning the limits of a profession or what a profession is about, the issues invariably turn to definitions and theoretical perspectives. Here is where philosophical views and theoretical perspectives realize their greatest importance.

The clinical fields in general need to have a firmer grounding on philosophical views and theoretical perspectives as unifying constructs. The field of learning disabilities has already taken the lead in appreciating traditional philosophical views (Heshusius, 1989; Poplin, 1988; Weaver, 1985). The next steps, of course, are to consider the developments that have occurred in the contemporary philosophical literature, especially concerning the nature of science and human affairs (Bruner, 1986), brute and institutional facts (Lakoff, 1987), and the contemporary theoretical perspectives, especially experiential cognition (K. Nelson, 1996).

Professions are continuously realigning to particular views and perspectives, but the process is not an arbitrary one if scholarship and discipline have anything to do with it. It is a natural process of scientific evolution. Those issues and practices that lack support from the scholarly literature fall by the wayside, whereas those that have been substantiated, or show potential, are advanced.

COGNITIVE SOCIALIZATION

The cognitive socialization literature over the past few decades has given fuller meaning to Brown's (1956) perspective that language acquisition is "a process of cognitive socialization" (p. 247). Some particular theoretical perspectives have had major influences on this literature or show promise for doing so; for example, speech acts or relevance theory, representational theories, functionalist theories, shared meaning for knowledge of events, expression theory, rare-event learning mechanism theory, experiential realism, experiential cognition, social origins of the mind, and informativeness theory.

Perera (1994) identified the most influential theoretical perspectives in language acquisition since the early 1970s. They were the following:

1. *Government binding and parameter setting* (Atkinson, 1992; Chomsky, 1986)—Perhaps the most elegant innatist views of language acquisition.
2. *Modularity* (Fodor, 1983)—A provocative notion.
3. *Speech acts or relevance* (Austin, 1962; Clark & Clark, 1977; Grice, 1975; Sperber & Wilson, 1986)—A broad-based view of cognitive social communication.
4. *Bootstrapping* (Bruner, 1981; Gleitman, 1994; Pinker, 1984)—Semantic, syntactic, prosodic, pragmatic contexts of language acquisition.
5. *Connectionism or parallel distributed processing* (McClelland & Rumelhart, 1986)—Perhaps the most elegant computer analog perspective.

It should be noted that behaviorism and reinforcement theory did not make the list simply because they have not held up as viable accounts in acquiring cognition and language.

The functionalistic movement, especially from the theoretical perspectives of representation (Karmiloff-Smith, 1992; Mandler, 1983) in cognition, which is a contemporary version of Bruner's (1973) book entitled *Going Beyond the Information Given* (edited by Anglin), in establishing possible worlds (Bruner, 1986) and speech acts or relevance in communication, has been a preeminent influence. Moreover, the literatures on experiential realism (Lakoff, 1987) and social-cultural influences as enunciated in the Vygotskian perspective (Bruner, 1986; Hagstrom, 1994; K. Nelson, 1985, 1986, 1996; Rogoff, 1990; Wertsch, 1991) have had major impacts on the cognitive socialization literature.

It should be emphasized that two major developments have occurred that have, and will have, resounding ramifications for the entire field of cognitive socialization. These are:

1. Bruner's (1986) distinctions between science and human affairs or narrative.
2. K. Nelson's (1996) conceptualization of experiential cognition toward appreciating the situated mind.

The philosophical and theoretical developments reflected in the contemporary cognitive socialization literature have contributed substantially to the clinical fields that have vested interests in them. My own work has also drawn heavily from these developments (Muma, 1971a, 1971b, 1973a, 1973b, 1975a, 1975b, 1977a, 1977b, 1978a, 1978b, 1980, 1981a, 1981b, 1981c, 1983a, 1983b, 1984a, 1984b, 1985, 1986a, 1986b, 1987a, 1987b, 1991, 1993, 1994).

In recent years, there has been another movement in education in general, and the clinical fields in particular, that has attained a considerable following. It is the whole language movement. Shapiro (1992), Chall (Toch, 1992), and others, including myself, are not impressed with this movement, and the related movement concerning so-called school language, simply because such movements have very loud assertions about language learning, cognitive learning, and curriculum development but they lack appropriate evidence and ignore the relevant cognitive socialization literature.

Furthermore, the whole language approach makes claims and lists of criteria for ease of language acquisition (Goodman, 1986). Although intuitively attractive, they lack continuity with much of the cognitive socialization literature. The whole language approach has been impressive in dealing with learning to read and write (Athey, 1970; Goodman, 1967; Smith, 1971). However, its extension into presumed accounts of language acquisition and learning has resulted in some perplexing notions about ease of learning in general and language acquisition in particular. The notions are perplexing simply because of a lack of continuity with the available scholarly literature on CCCE. Without this continuity, the two literatures appear to be tangential to each other with little prospect of complementation. Yet, it is desirable for them to complement each other because they both claim to address language acquisition.

In contrast, speech act theory (Grice, 1975), relevance theory (Sperber & Wilson, 1986), theory of expression (Bloom, 1991a, 1991b; Bloom & Beckwith, 1989), representation theory (Mandler, 1983, 1990), representational redescription theory (Karmiloff-Smith, 1984, 1992), experiential realism (Lakoff, 1987), experiential cognition (K. Nelson, 1985, 1986, 1996), shared meaning for knowledge of events (K. Nelson, 1985, 1986, 1996), social mediation (Bruner, 1981; Hagstrom, 1994; K. Nelson, 1996; Rogoff, 1990; Wertsch, 1991), and rare-event learning mechanism theory (RELM; K. E. Nelson, 1981, 1991) have considerably more to offer the clinical fields than the loud whole language and school language perspectives and claims. The cognitive socialization perspectives have more to offer simply because they are more firmly grounded on the attendant scholarly literature and because they are more fully developed. Consequently, clinicians appreciate them more. On the other hand, technicians merely looking for hands-on approaches are likely to find the whole language and school language perspectives more attractive.

INTENTIONALITY

Paramount to cognitive socialization, and therefore this volume, is the centrality of communicative intent. Intent has emerged from the scholarly literatures in cognition, codification, communication, and expression as the central issue. It is what Bruner (1986) regarded as the irreducible nucleus of human affairs or narrative. The centrality of intent is the basic issue in the contemporary constructionist and functionalistic movements and speech act and relevance theories (Austin, 1962; Bruner, 1981, 1986; Greenfield, 1980; Grice, 1975; K. Nelson, 1985, 1986, 1996; Searle, 1969, 1975, 1977, 1979, 1983, 1992; Sperber & Wilson, 1986).

> In short, the personal and social world is inherently complex and interactive. More importantly, human action is intentional and thus demands interpretation. (K. Nelson, 1985, p. 37)

> Any successful effort toward an understanding of language development must be grounded in a theory which takes an intentional stance (Dennett, 1978), that is, a theory that explains behaviors as expressions of beliefs and desires. . . . This stance is already implicit in child language research. (Bloom et al., 1988, p. 101)

> A theoretical model of Intentionality and language development (Bloom & Beckwith, 1986), . . . proposes that children acquire language in order to express

what they are thinking about in their consciously active, mental states. We are calling these states of mind intentional states in the philosophical tradition of Brentano, as followed by Dennett (1978), and Searle (1983), among others. (Bloom et al., 1988, p. 100)

The role of situational structure is relative to the child's communicative intention. It is the child's communicative intention within which uncertainty or alternatives are perceived. (Greenfield, 1980, p. 217)

Describing speaker's repertoires of communicative intents and rules for expressing those intents is crucial to any complete description of the language capacity. (Ninio, Snow, Pan, & Rollins, 1994, p. 157)

Indeed, in referring to Searle's (1992) book *The Rediscovery of the Mind*, Block (1992) commented that Searle's fundamental message is that "there can be no study of mind that leaves out consciousness" (back cover). Consciousness both as declarative knowledge (Mandler, 1983) and as intent (Bruner, 1986) have arisen as crucial issues for cognition. In keeping with Bruner, Grice, K. Nelson, Searle, and many other major scholars, all clinical enterprises about the CCCE should be centered on intent.

Generally speaking, intent is usually passed over or merely implicated in the clinical fields (Duchan, 1991; Fey, 1986; Paul, 1995). However, there has been an increased clinical interest in intent (Lahey, 1988; Muma, 1978b, 1981c, 1986a; Prizant & Wetherby, 1989, 1990; Prutting, 1982; Wetherby, 1991).

The centrality of intent is a running theme throughout this volume, and my 1986 book. This theme reflects the contemporary developments in cognitive socialization, especially in regard to shared meaning in event knowledge (K. Nelson, 1985, 1986, 1991, 1996). For example, K. Nelson (1985) said, "The subjective meaning system is a complex of interactive component systems used to express intentions and interpret the intentions of others" (p. 9).

It should become abundantly clear that intent has replaced the notion of reinforcement in viable accounts of language acquisition. Yet, behaviorism has waged the counter view. Thus, Bruner (1986) wrote, "radical behaviorism is another: attributing cause and denying the role of intention in the realm of human events" (p. 88; "another" referred to another philosophical view). He also wrote, "the new approach to language has sparked a revolt against traditional 'cause-effect' psychology and raised deep questions about the adequacy of positivist theories" (Bruner, 1978, p. viii). Behaviorism is the "cause and effect" psychology and reinforcement theory is the positivist theory that Bruner was referring to in this quote. This and other literature centering on speech act and relevance theories have provided compelling reasons that behaviorism in general, and reinforcement and generalization in particular, give inadequate accounts of language acquisition.

Yet, there are various claimed accounts of language acquisition and clinical approaches based on behaviorism, reinforcement theory, and generalization (Bollinger & Stout, 1976; Connell, 1986, 1990; Costello, 1983; Goldstein, 1984; Guess, Keogh, & Sailor, 1978; Guess, Sailor, Rutherford, & Baer, 1968; Hart & Risley, 1975; Hegde & McConn, 1981; Hegde, Noll, & Pecora, 1979; Hester & Hendrickson, 1977; Kaiser, Alpert, & Warren, 1987; Kamhi, 1988; Mulac & Tomlinson, 1977; Rogers-Warren & Warren, 1980; Warren, McQuarter, & Rogers-Warren, 1984; Zwitman & Sonderman, 1979).

SCOPE

In an attempt to address substantive aspects of the bidimensional view of appropriateness, this volume is organized on the cognitive socialization literature with its attendant philosophical views and theoretical perspectives. Accordingly, a clinical model is established that is derived from these views and perspectives. In large measure, this clinical model reflects speech act theory, relevance theory, shared meaning for events theory, experiential realm, social mediation theory, and experiential cognition. The running theme in these theories and this clinical model is the centrality of intent in actual social commerce.

Accordingly, the clinical assessment model is oriented on descriptive assessment because it addresses best the heterogeneity of clinical populations and the seven basic clinical assessment issues (Muma, 1983b, 1986a). Heterogeneity haunts the clinical fields to the core. The clinical intervention model is facilitation as contrasted to teaching or instruction (Muma, 1978b, 1986a).

Various substantive issues in the cognitive socialization literature pertaining to CCCE are raised. These issues constitute the substantive base of appropriate clinical assessment and intervention.

It should be acknowledged that the conceptual strength of this clinical model is the degree to which it has continuity with the underlying philosophical views and theoretical perspectives issuing from the cognitive socialization literature. Thus, continuity counts in deriving appropriate clinical implications from the available scholarly CCCE literatures. Furthermore, this enterprise demonstrates that philosophical views and theoretical perspectives make things practical.

To this extent, the scholarly fields in CCCE have provided a service—a viable application. The clinical fields as disciplined consumers of this literature strive to uphold their end of scholarship by virtue of disciplined applications of it.

TONE

Aligning the clinical fields to recognized philosophical views and theoretical perspectives provides a means of rectifying difficulties with authoritarianism, elitism, anarchy, dogma, hype, hearsay, misused eclecticism, and intuition. Thus, continuity with available philosophical views and theoretical perspectives constitutes a scholarly substantive base for the clinical fields, casting aside other deleterious influences. The extent to which this clinical model with its attendant substantive dimensions achieves continuity with the available CCCE literatures is the extent to which legitimate claims can be made for rendering appropriate clinical services.

Unfortunately, it is not difficult to find examples of issues in the clinical fields that are disconnected from the relevant scholarly CCCE literatures, thereby constituting threats to philosophical and theoretical continuity. The following are high on the list:

1. The lack of construct validity for most psychometric normative tests used in the clinical fields.
2. The reliance on language samples of 50 or 100 utterances for grammatical analyses. Such samples have been shown to have excessive error rates (see Appendix D) and poor reliabilities (Gavin & Giles, 1996).
3. The subtle ways in which behaviorists used frequency of behavior as evidence of acquisition both in intervention and claims of efficacy. Yet, the CCCE literatures turn to context as a more viable account of acquisition.
4. The reliance on "continua" as a way of remaining silent about substantive issues in cognitive socialization.

Regarding the later, virtually all of the major scholars in cognition and language acquisition acknowledge that reinforcement theory does not provide viable accounts of acquisition in either cognition or language (see Appendix C). In short, intent has replaced reinforcement as a more viable account. Yet, some individuals in the clinical fields hold on tenaciously to the notions of reinforcement, generalization, and stimulation (Fey, 1986; Fey, Windsor, & Warren, 1995; Kamhi, 1988; Paul, 1995) in accounts of language acquisition. The way this is done is to posit continua of "intrusiveness" or of "child-directed/hybrid/clinician-directed approaches" with one end being the highly structured behavioristic perspective and the other being a naturalistic perspective (Fey, 1986; Fey, Windsor, & Warren, 1995; Paul, 1995). Unfortunately, these two ends are philosophically incompatible (see Johnston, 1988; Muma, 1986a).

Perhaps we should be reminded that according to the research design literature incompatible variables do not belong on the same continua. If the distinction between nominal and ordinal variables is considered with regard to the two ends of this continuum (behaviorism and natural approaches), it becomes apparent (because of their incompatibilities) that they are nominal rather than ordinal; and, therefore they should not share the same continuum. Placing them on a continuum of intrusiveness (a service delivery notion) merely serves to ignore their substantive incompatibilities. Thus, such continua are not only inappropriate, but they provide a disservice by virtue of silence about their substantive incompatibilities. With such illusionary continua and the related silence about substantive issues, the clinical fields become vulnerable to technicianship rather than clinicianship with its attendant scholarship.

TWO GREAT IMPLICIT GOALS

Clinicians can take pride in two great achievements:

1. Rendering services that have coherence across philosophical views and theoretical perspectives, thereby establishing a disciplined rationale for appropriate services.
2. Obtaining desirable effects of assessment and intervention on a client's repertoire of available skills.

The former is pride of discipline and scholarship and the latter is the effects of such discipline and scholarship in rendering appropriate services in an effort to obtain desirable effects.

Thus, it would be a fundamental clinical responsibility for clinicians to be able to explicitly state which philosophical views and theoretical perspectives establish a rationale for rendering clinical services in particular ways. This responsibility is a measure of pride in a clinician's competency and appreciation of disciplined scholarship. It is a measure of pride in the training institutions that foster the importance and relevance of philosophical views and theoretical perspectives as the disciplined way in which a viable clinical rationale may be derived; thus, it is such perspectives that ultimately make things practical (Muma, 1991). It is a measure of pride for a profession that claims to be grounded on scholarship. Furthermore, it would be a great achievement to realize that clinical endeavors grounded on relevant philosophical views and theoretical perspectives actually result in desirable effects on client repertoires.

SUMMARY

From the field of cognitive socialization, the basic premise of this book is to address the state of clinical affairs from the twofold perspective of appropriateness. One perspective is to have clinical views, principles, and practices in accordance with what is most supportable by the contemporary scholarly literature. This in turn means deriving clinical issues and endeavors in accordance with the philosophical views and theoretical perspectives pertaining to CCCE in the scholarly cognitive socialization literature. The second is that these clinical policies and endeavors should be directly relevant to an individual's available repertoire of skills.

By adhering to this principle, the clinical fields would attain some measure of justification for being scholarly and disciplined. Unfortunately, a survey of training programs in speech-language pathology and audiology yielded some evidence that scholarship and discipline may be at risk. The survey indicated that philosophical views and theoretical perspectives are typically ignored or given only passing consideration. Furthermore, the 1983 ASHA conference on training standards recognized this potential threat to the scholarly base of the clinical fields by recommending that training programs review course work to assure a strong theoretical orientation.

Against this concern for increased scholarship and discipline, there is ample concern and evidence that the clinical fields have become too reliant on authoritarianism, anarchy, elitism, dogma, hearsay, and hype. One form of such evidence is the use of atheoretical and exclusionary definitions. Such definitions beget hype, authoritarianism, and dogma.

Based on the cognitive socialization literature, appropriate clinical services are envisioned in terms of assessment and intervention: clinical assessment (a descriptive approach) and clinical intervention (a facilitative approach).

It is hoped that clinicians, like scholars, will find this volume provocative and that technicians will find it sufficiently informative in their effort to become clinicians.

By grounding the clinical model on the relevant contemporary philosophical views and theoretical perspectives, the clinical fields in general and individual clinicians in particular would be positioned for two great clinical achievements: (a) rendering appropriate services that reflect the substantive base of the CCCE literatures and obtaining desirable changes in client repertoires of skill.

2

PHILOSOPHICAL VIEWS AND THEORETICAL PERSPECTIVES

Philosophical views and theoretical perspectives provide the substantive base of the clinical fields. They provide perspectives whereby issues and concepts may be predicted, explained, and understood, thereby establishing a rationale for rendering appropriate clinical services. Thus, continuity counts toward making things practical. Accordingly, it is incumbent on every clinician to know precisely which philosophical views and theoretical perspectives underlie the clinical services rendered.

Clinical services that are not predicated on accepted philosophical views and theoretical perspectives reflect nothing more than authoritarianism, dogma, hype, hearsay, elitism, and misused eclecticism. For example, reinforcement and generalization are behavioristic notions that are no longer recognized as viable accounts of language acquisition according to such major scholars as Bruner, Cazden, Chomsky, Mandler, K. Nelson, Searle, and so on. Such services reduce down to technicianship rather than clinicianship.

Needless to say, it is necessary to establish the philosophical views and theoretical perspectives of cognitive socialization so that a clinical model can be offered. By doing so, the clinical model would attain some measure of continuity with the substantive issues in cognitive socialization.

This chapter has three sections: relevant philosophical views, relevant theoretical perspectives, and clinical implications. Several views and perspectives are considered. The emphasis is on those views within the field of cognitive socialization that are compatible with each other.

PHILOSOPHICAL VIEWS

Overviews of the following philosophical views are provided: innatism, interactionism, rationalism, empiricism, positivism, functionalism, mentalism, constructionism, social mediation, experiential realism, and experiential cognition. Most of these views are inherently compatible with each other and they are evidenced in the cognitive socialization literature.

Innatism is the view that individuals are endowed with the characteristics of their species. The extent to which language is a unique human capacity is the extent to which it is innately available. However, the literature over the past decade, especially K. Nelson (1996), has shown that both cognition and language are acquired in a "social nexus" (Bruner, 1981, 1990; Mandler, 1979; Rogoff, 1990; Wertsch, 1991) with biological factors operating as constraints. Thus, language acquisition is evidently the product of the interplay between biological constraints and interaction with one's environment.

Interactionism is the view that one's environment plays a significant role in acquiring various capacities. In language acquisition, there is no doubt that interaction with one's environment is a major factor simply because an individual learns the language in which that person is reared.

Rationalism is the view that it is necessary to have a perspective that is rationally sound. It relies on coherence. Interestingly, formal logic was the traditional benchmark of rationality.

About the turn of the century, Russell (1905) invoked formal logic to define a definite referent, whereas Frege (1892/1952) relied on context to ascertain sense. Until recently, formal logic dominated the study of cognition and language. However, in the past decade it has become clear that cognition relies much more on fuzzy concepts that make sense in particular contexts than on formal discrete concepts. In communication, it has become evident that slippage in "mutual manifestness" (Sperber & Wilson, 1986) is an essential mechanism for negotiated meaning. With these developments, rationalism has taken a decisive turn away from reliance on formal logic to an abiding interest in coherence in actual social commerce.

Furthermore, the distinction between brute and institutional facts (Lakoff, 1987) has shown that traditional logic was much too myopic by only considering brute facts. *Brute facts* are those that have been formally defined; for example, dictionary definitions, laws, regulations, measurements, plant and animal classifications, the periodic table, and so on. In contrast, *institutional facts* are those that individuals come to know by virtue of participation in various institutions; for example, family, social groups, professional groups, recreational groups, educational and training institutions, culture, and so on. Far and away, most of what one knows of the world is institutional knowledge. Thus, it behooves rationalists to address coherence of these institutions. Needless to say, the clinical fields have relied on brute rather than institutional facts, but it is the latter that comprises most of what individuals know and do.

Empiricism is the view that data are needed to substantiate or verify issues. Much traditional research is a formal pursuit of data for substantiation or verification. Data without a rationale is brute empiricism. Both rational and empirical evidence are needed to substantiate or verify issues; furthermore, rational evidence should have priority over empirical evidence because data are meaningless when they are not predicated by rationale. Therefore, data must have continuity with the relevant underlying philosophical views and theoretical perspectives.

Positivism is the view that natural phenonema and things constitute the nature of the world that needs explanation. Behaviorism (dealing with observables), empiricism (counting instances of behavior as presumed evidence of acquisition), and probability theory (placing single instances in the context of a population or sample; e.g., comparing an individual's performance to a norm) are traditional ways in which natural phenonema have been studied. Accordingly, behaviorism, empiricism, and psychometric normative approaches have been regarded as traditional positivist perspectives.

Functionalism is the view that function has priority over form or structure. The functional views of language over the past decade have stressed the point that in both cognition (K. Nelson, 1996) and communication (Sperber & Wilson, 1986) function has priority over form. In cognition, several new developments evidence a functionalistic perspective: "basic level concepts" (Anglin, 1977), "prototypic concepts" (Rosch, 1973), functional attributes (K. Nelson, 1974), progress from procedural knowledge to semantic knowledge (Mandler, 1983), representational redescription beyond modularity (Karmiloff-Smith, 1992), paradigmatic or narrative "possible worlds" (Bruner, 1986), and event knowledge becoming narrative in a situated mind (K. Nelson, 1996). In communication, functionalism is evident as well. Both intent and content are the crucial aspects of language and communication, whereas words, sentences, pragmatic devices, and gestures are forms for conveying meaning in the realization of communicative intent.

Mentalism is the view that mental events underlie human thought and action including communication. Said differently, it is necessary to understand the mind as a crucial account of cognition, language, and action. Explanations of these domains are ultimately cognitive.

This view often bifurcates into the dualistic notions of brain and mind. Scholars who study brain mechanisms should ultimately be interested in the mind. However, some of these individuals ignore the mind under the rationalization of "never mind the mind" simply because they believe that everything will ultimately be explained by understanding the brain. This view is known as *monism*, which suffers from a lack of coherence (Searle, 1992), and even dualism (mind–brain) lacks coherence.

Constructionism is the view that an individual actively constructs possible worlds or situated minds by virtue of living in the world. Early constructions are evidently derived from embodiment (Lakoff, 1987), whereby schemas may be established. Such schemas are rudimentary notions of one's situated place in scripts and formats and they constitute early versions of event representations (K. Nelson, 1996) or procedural knowledge (Mandler, 1983). The essence of constructionism is that an individual from infancy throughout adulthood is an active learner in constructing possible worlds or a situated mind.

Social mediation is the neo-Vygotskian view that cognition is inherently social and cultural in nature. The implication is that cognition and language are not entities unto themselves; rather, they are products of a socially and culturally situated mind.

Both *experiential realism* and *experiential cognition* are constructionistic views. Both hold that the central source of meaning and learning is experience predicated by intent. Experiential realism (Lakoff, 1987) deals with the preconceptual infant, whereas experiential cognition (K. Nelson, 1996) deals with the preschool child in establishing a situated mind. Several issues are crucial for establishing an adult situated mind: The learning process is continuous rather than stagelike; "context is all" (Bruner, 1981, p. 172); variation rather than repetition provides the means for discrepancy learning; experience embraces biological maturation, psychological processing, emotional state, social commerce, and cultural context; and finally the irreducible nucleus is intent. Needless to say, experiential cognition has become the most elegant and comprehensive account of cognitive and language acquisition to date.

THEORETICAL PERSPECTIVES

In the interest of continuity, it behooves us to consider some of the theoretical perspectives that have continuity with the preceding philosophical views. Accordingly, the following theoretical perspectives are considered: bootstrapping theory, cohesion theory, discrepancy learning theory, old/new information theory, informativeness theory, shared meaning of event knowledge theory, speech act theory, and relevance theory.

Bootstrapping theory is the perspective that learning may be facilitated by varying the contexts in which behavior occurs. Needless to say, this theory is about context. Several different kinds of bootstrapping theories have been offered to deal with different aspects of language acquisition. Prosodic bootstrapping (Bruner, 1975a, 1975b, 1981; Gleitman & Wanner, 1982), semantic bootstrapping (Pinker, 1984), and syntactic bootstrapping (Gleitman, 1994) have been posited to appreciate different kinds of contexts (K. Nelson, 1985, 1986) that apparently facilitate language acquisition.

Syntactic bootstrapping, for example, is a mapping process, in which a child not only uses knowledge of an event to discern meaning (K. Nelson, 1986) but narrows down the hypothesis testing arena by virtue of appreciating the basic predicate–argument structure entailed in syntax. Thus, syntactic bootstrapping is oriented on predication (verb and entailed arguments). Gleitman (1994) regarded syntactic bootstrapping as sentence-to-world mapping. She indicated:

> Such an approach can succeed because, if the syntactic structures are truly correlated with the meanings, the range of structures will be informative for deducing which word goes with which concept. . . . The difference between semantic bootstrapping and syntactic bootstrapping, then, is that the former procedure deduces the structures from the word meanings that are antecedently acquired from the observation of events, while the latter procedure deduces the word meanings from the semantically relevant syntactic structures associated with a verb in input utterances. (p. 197)

The 10 language intervention techniques (Muma, 1971a) such as expansion or expatiation coupled with the parallel talk strategy (Muma, 1978b) constitute bootstrapping strategies derived from the language acquisition literature.

Cohesion theory is not a formally espoused theory. Yet, the syntactic and pragmatic literatures allude to the importance of coherence. Apparently, once an individual achieves repertoires of skill at a rudimentary level a threshold is reached whereby both grammatical and pragmatic learning are propelled forward by virtue of an available smooth-running or coherent system. Said differently, partial learning is characteristic of language acquisition; it has to be partial learning simply because of the diversity and complexity of contexts. However, once an individual achieves a repertoire of partial skills that evidently fall into place, the available systems and processes take on a new coherent understanding, thereby affording the acquisition processes the capability of moving forward much more rapidly and with fluidity. Thus, cohesion itself has emerged as a viable account of some aspects of language acquisition.

Discrepancy learning theory is the perspective that variation from what was previously known constitutes a potent stimulus in eliciting and maintaining attention (Kagan, 1970; Kagan & Lewis, 1965). There is a great deal of research that substantiates discrepancy learning from infancy (3 months old) throughout adulthood. Needless to say, variations of known information constitute an important learning principle.

Old/new information theory and *informativeness theory* are the perspectives that in both thought and language new information is placed into the context of known information as a way of incorporating new information. Informativeness is the unexpected or unknown information that becomes available in relation to what is expected or known; that is, something is informative if it is not already known or expected. Thus, for an intention to become recognized, it is necessary for an utterance to contain a proposition in which given and new information are in particular relations. For example, the utterance "I like Coke" would be informative if the listener's knowledge of the world (implicit knowledge) included an awareness of old information ("I" and "Coke") with respect to the new or explicit information ("like"). Such issues of awareness constitute the given or old information in relation to new information. What is informative, however, is the knowledge expressed in the relations between these issues of awareness. That is, this statement conveys that "someone likes Coke," which is presumably something new that the listener had not known before.

The importance of informativeness theory is that it establishes the significance of the relations between what is coded in a message (explicit content, proposition) and what is known about the world (implicit content, presupposition, possible worlds, situated mind) for a message to work as intended—recognition of intent. Thus, messages in a code matrix (Muma, 1975a) are coded to make intentions recognizable (Grice, 1975; Sperber & Wilson, 1986). This means that explicit content is carefully measured with respect to implicit content or presupposition for the recognition of intent. This also means that words, grammatical structures, and pragmatic devices are, in effect, subordinate to their roles in achieving recognition of communicative intent.

Another implication is that informativeness theory is essentially a theory about the cognitive basis of language. Still another major implication is that informativeness entails a negotiation process as to what is informative between the participants in the communication process.

What is crucially important for this theory is that context defines what is old (known) and what is new (unknown). Furthermore, such contexts are both internal and external. Thus, an individual needs to be in a position to appreciate the perspective of the listener in order to produce appropriate messages and play the communication game (Muma, 1975a). With these dynamics, it is obvious that the traditional clinical programs that are a priori in nature (normative tests that impose systems and intervention programs that are preestablished) are of marginal value.

Informativeness theory is the perspective that operating under the felicity conditions, communication is an attempt to inform. The felicity conditions are a set of assumptions whereby information operates. These conditions are to be truthful, informative, relevant, and unambiguous. Intentional violations of these conditions result in deceit. Should such deceit be discovered, credibility is lost.

Shared meaning of event knowledge theory is the perspective that individuals who are learning and using language are operating from knowledge of events. Early on, such knowledge is scriptlike, whereby the infant and toddler come to know which routines constitute their world or situated place. Such knowledge is not about objects or entities per se, but about what happens and who the participants are in these events. Furthermore, this knowledge is acquired with the calibrated participation of a caregiver (Bruner, 1981) and is therefore a shared enterprise. The shared dimension underscores the social and cultural nature of learning.

Script learning for events launches cognitive, emotional, social, and language acquisition, and there are two crucial aspects of such learning. First, it is not the repetitiveness of the scripts that make them potent; rather, it is their variations (discrepancy). Furthermore, the child is usually the source of many variations; children will often fuss when variations are made by others but they are entertained by their own variations. Subsequently, they will permit and enjoy variations by others. Second, participation in shared events is intentional. The central issue in the cognitive socialization literature is intent. Needless to say, elicited or structured responses in clinical intervention are not intentional and of questionable value. It behooves clinicians who are interested in this literature to render clinical services (both assessment and intervention) that deal with spontaneous communication simply because it is intentional.

Speech act theory is the perspective that language should be viewed from a broader orientation than merely utterances. This theory posits four basic issues of communication: intent, proposition (explicit content in relation to implicit content), message or locution (code matrix: utterance, gesture, facial pattern, etc.), and effects of the message on the listener (perlocution). Speech act theory was first posited by Grice in 1967, but it was not published until 1975 and appeared in subsequent renditions (Austin, 1962; Clark & Clark, 1977; Grice, 1975; Searle, 1969). *Relevance theory* is a more elegant rendition and derivation of speech act theory. What may be relevant to one individual in thought and communication may not be relevant to another. Furthermore, context is a significant aspect of relevance.

Both speech act theory and relevance theory are inherently cognitive and social in nature. Both rely on basic cognitive capacities, notably categorization, representation, inference, problem solving, and intent. In doing so, both theories strive to account for the unique human capacity for language in terms of general cognition rather than a unique language module. Both theories view cognition as a social venture. Speech act theory addresses the effects of a message on a listener. Relevance theory holds that in order for communicative intent to become recognizable, it is necessary for the participants to establish mutually manifest perspectives of the topic–comment relations in a message. Furthermore, both recognize that when communication fails, which is often, the participants have options for negotiating messages (Muma, 1975a).

With speech act theory and relevance theory, the study of language acquisition and use shifted to a broader perspective than word, grammar, and pragmatic domains. Over the past two decades it has become evident that language should be considered from the following perspectives: cognition, codification, communication, and expression. Indeed, it would be desirable to also incorporate a biological dimension (K. Nelson, 1996). Needless to say, the clinical fields should adopt such a broad perspective and that perspective should have continuity with the cognitive socialization literature with its attendant philosophical views and theoretical perspectives.

CLINICAL IMPLICATIONS

Together, the principles issuing from the previously mentioned philosophical views and theoretical perspectives offer a rationale for deriving appropriate clinical principles and practices. It is necessary to place them into a coherent perspective. One way of doing this is to consider a model for the cognitive-social bases of language which appears in Table 2.1.

This model is a revised rendition of earlier ones (Muma, 1978b, 1986a). The revisions reflect the developments that have occurred in the recent cognitive socialization literature. This model is discussed throughout the book, especially in chapter 4. Therefore, rather than giving a full discussion of the model here, it is useful to give a number of clinical implications of this model, which follow.

The first major clinical implication is that these philosophical views and theoretical perspectives, and this model of the cognitive-social bases of language place the modality perspective (expressive and receptive language) in a rather subordinate or marginal perspective. That is, the modality view of language merely deals with marginal aspects, effectively missing the central or core issues (Muma, 1978b).

Unfortunately, the clinical fields have effectively elevated the modality view by virtue of organizing assessment and intervention principles and

TABLE 2.1
A Model for the Cognitive-Social Bases of Language

Level 1:	*General cognitive base*: Categorization, representation, inference, and problem solving that result in "possible worlds" or a social-culturally experienced "situated mind."
Level 2:	*Substantive functions of grammar and pragmatics*: Content (explicit content in the negotiable context of implicit content) and communicative intent.
Level 3:	*Cognitive processes underlying messages*: Production (planning and execution) and comprehension (construction and utilization).
Level 4:	*Metacognitive and metalinguistic capacities*: Reflective abilities that allow an individual to recollect and play with thought and language.

practices around the notions of expressive and receptive language. Indeed, even policies for obtaining certification in speech-language pathology are officially predicated on a modality model. By taking this modality perspective, the clinical fields have effectively shunted themselves off to marginal issues.

The second major clinical implication is that the clinical fields have had a much too narrow view of language (i.e., words, semantics, syntax, phonology, and pragmatics). Furthermore, these dimensions were typically considered separate entities. In contrast, the cognitive socialization literature deals with a much more expansive and integrated perspective. The CCCE domains are inextricably related to the others. Furthermore, the expression domain in this context pertains to Brown's (1977) use of the term, which pertains to the emotional aspect of language acquisition and use.

The third major clinical implication is that the normal language acquisition literature provides many substantive issues that are applicable for rendering appropriate clinical services. The traditional behavioristic view is that individuals with language impairments had failed the normal language acquisition process and therefore the normal acquisition literature was not needed. This was merely a false argument. It is what Bruner (1978) regarded as *corrosive dogma*. In contrast, the compelling evidence is that the children themselves have indeed largely succeeded in language acquisition; only relatively small aspects of their language are impaired; much more is the product of the normal acquisition process. It would take a myopic view to ignore these achievements and hold that an individual with a language impairment had failed the normal acquisition process.

The fourth major clinical implication is that a central issue of the cognitive socialization literature is context. Context pertains both to internal context (possible worlds, situated mind) and to perceived external context (event, social, emotional, cultural). In instances of language use and acquisition, context is importantly construed as the interrelations between explicit content and implicit content toward the recognition of communicative intent.

The fifth major clinical implication is that individual capacities are the focus rather than group performances or norms. The reason that individual capacities are important is because individual differences are large in early language acquisition with normal children. That is why Brown (1973a, 1973b) cautioned that rate indices such as age should not be used to gauge language acquisition; rather, acquisition sequences should be used.

Deviations of about 6 months are expected in normal language acquisition for very young normal children. Clinical populations are even more varied. It is exceedingly difficult, if not impossible, to find two individuals in the same clinical category that have precisely the same difficulties. Thus, it is ironic that the clinical populations are characteristically heterogeneous; yet, the clinical fields are bent toward dealing with these groups with services that are grounded on the homogeneity assumption, specifically normative tests, a priori intervention procedures, and a priori attribution criteria (80–100% correct performance).

Curiously, attempts (Leonard, 1987; Rice & Wexler, 1996) to empirically define specific language impairment (SLI) have been vested on the normative assumption (homogeneity). The clinical fields need to focus more solidly on the heterogeneous nature of clinical populations. If the clinical fields do not do so, heterogeneity will haunt them to the core.

The sixth major clinical implication is the acknowledgment of partial learning. It is a foregone conclusion that if language acquisition is contextual in nature, partial learning would be symptomatic. This has to be so simply because it is virtually impossible for an individual to encounter or realize the full contextual significance of any aspect of language from a single instance. Accordingly, children have developmental sequences that are relatively stable (Brown, 1973a, 1973b).

The seventh major clinical implication is that language acquisition typically occurs in spurts of learning. This also implicates contextual learning. What is provocative about spurts of learning is that there is very little information about when a spurt will occur, how long it will last, and what will be learned during the spurt. Needless to say, prognosis is more of an act of wishful, even illusionary, thinking than a disciplined venture. The widespread use of developmental checklists and profiles do more to uphold this illusion than appropriately address the prognosis issue.

The eighth major clinical implication is that with heterogeneous clinical populations, contextual learning, partial learning, and spurts of learning embedded in event knowledge and social-cultural influences, it is incumbent on the clinical fields to rely on principles and practices that are consistent with facilitation rather than teaching or instruction (Muma, 1978b). The instructional or teaching model is one in which content, sequencing, pacing, and reinforcement are tacitly determined by the teacher or clinician. Traditional clinical models have employed reinforcement schedules and a priori intervention agendas in managing children. In contrast, facilitation models recognize that the learning process is essentially the province of the learner. Consequently, the learner's performance defines the content, sequencing, pacing, and intent within bona fide social, emotional, and cultural contexts. It is important for clinicians to be sufficiently trained to be able to ascertain which aspects of language acquisition an individual is ready to learn and which contexts are likely to induce such learning.

The ninth major clinical implication is that the notion of specific language impairment lacks viability when construed as a normative premise but is viable when construed as a predicate premise. Following Pinker's (1984) notion of low phonetic substance, Leonard (1987, 1989) attempted to substantiate the notion of specific language impairment in accordance with the normative premise. He studied children who were language impaired to ascertain if they evidenced difficulties with a common denominator (normative premise), specifically low phonetic substance. Some had such difficulties and some did not; within the individuals, some of the difficulties evidenced low phonetic substance problems and some did not. Therefore, Leonard concluded that the notion of specific language impairment was not a viable notion. However, his conclusion was premature and myopic. If this notion is construed as a predicate meaning *to specify* rather than a categorical (normative) perspective meaning *specific*, the notion of specific language impairment provides a viable perspective. That is, it is desirable to specify the particular impairments and their contexts for each individual.

Rice and Wexler (1996) invoked the normative premise in their study of tense marking and reference marking. Although their study was eloquent in design and rather successful in showing that individuals with SLI evidenced tense marking difficulties, the obvious omissions were the grammatical repertoires of accomplishments and the kinds of other errors that these children evidenced. The moral of the normative premise is that it confines issues only to those of specific interest while ignoring relevant ones. However, SLI as a predicate, relieved of the normative premise, opens up the notion of SLI to full disclosure.

The 10th major clinical implication is to rely on attribution criteria that are relative and contextual rather than absolute and acontextual. In the course of specifying particular verbal behaviors, the question arises as to what criteria are needed to attribute such skills to a child. The Piagetian criteria are somewhat attractive for clinical use (Muma, 1986a, 1991; K. E. Nelson, 1981, 1989, 1991; Prutting, 1979). These criteria are preparation, attainment, and consolidation. *Preparation* pertains to a behavior that is infrequent, context bound, and difficult to elicit. *Attainment* pertains to a behavior that is relatively frequent, not context bound, and relatively easy to elicit. *Consolidation* pertains to a behavior evidenced in variation with other co-occuring behaviors. For example, the definite article would be regarded as consolidated when it is used with varied co-occurring structures: the hat, the boy, the blue shirt, the cow, and so on.

Some studies have used single instances of grammatical skills for attribution. Bruner (1986) indicated that this is a mistake; sometimes we believe that single instances reveal a skill but that is unlikely. He said, "We have extraordinary faith in one-shot instantiation" (p. 51). Other studies relied on three instances (Watkins & Rice, 1991) or three varied instances (Bloom, Rispoli, Gartner, & Hafitz, 1989). Either way, one instance or three varied instances seem to be useful ways of describing estimated grammatical repertoires. One or a few instances may not actually evidence attainment, but rather pending acquisition.

The 11th major clinical implication is that clinicians can obtain viable leverage for facilitating language acquisition by addressing the following four assessment issues: available repertoire, progress in acquisition sequences, available strategies of learning, and active loci of learning.

The 12th major clinical implication is that communicative intent is the single most important issue for language. Intent has emerged as the single most important issue in the cognitive socialization literature over the past two decades. Bruner (1986) regarded intent as the irreducible nucleus of narrative. Searle (1992) indicated that consciousness is the central issue of cognition and language. They are in accord because intent is a specific instance of consciousness.

Needless to say, the clinical fields that deal with cognition and language should render assessment and intervention services that are predicated on intent. This means that it is desirable to have descriptive evidence derived from representative spontaneous (intentional) language samples as the prima facie evidence and intervention should be in actual social commerce. Over the past two decades, we have rendered highly successful (desired effects) clinical services predicated on descriptive evidence and focused on communicative intent.

The way in which we have made a concerted effort to deal with communicative intent is the use of communicative payoff (Muma, 1981c). When an individual initiates a communicative effort, by whatever means (gesture, line of regard, linguistic, pragmatic), the clinician is vigilant for these efforts and stays on the individual's topic. Typically, this concerted effort results in the individual talking more and trying new things. It has been effective not only with children but with adults with traumatic brain injury, dementia, and aphasia.

The 13th major clinical implication is that because language acquisition is a socially shared enterprise, it is incumbent on clinicians to exploit this context by utilizing parents in language intervention. Early on, parents—especially mothers—play a significant role by virtue of being tuned to what their children can do and raising the ante in contexts that apparently warrant doing so (Bruner, 1981). Needless to say, parents become active partners in clinical services rendered from infancy through the early school years. Parents want to participate in these activities. Over the past two decades, we have established a three-stage model for parent participation in language intervention. This model is discussed in chapter 8.

The 14th major clinical implication is that once an individual becomes socially active with peers, or has the potential for doing so, peer modeling becomes a viable aspect of intervention. There is a large literature on peer modeling that substantiates the view that peers can be potent intervention agents. Over the past two decades or so, we have used peer modeling and have obtained impressive results in doing so.

Because the clinical populations are heterogeneous, it is relatively easy to find reciprocal models within a group of three or four children. One child could have difficulties with the pronominal system (object forms in subject positions; anaphora: loaded, competing, vacant) yet this child may have good articulation. Another child may have a good pronominal system but have difficulties with articulation. These two children would offer good opportunities for reciprocal peer modeling, especially when coupled with the parallel talk intervention strategy.

The 15th major clinical implication is that many of the children seen clinically are socially and experientially impoverished. In order to launch peer modeling, it is necessary to socialize the children. Accordingly, clinicians typically have a socializing goal whereby they give brief comments to the children as to the activities of others. The children thus become oriented to the roles and activities of each other and then peer modeling becomes useful. It is in such contexts that the neo-Vygotskian principle of appropriaton becomes available (Rogoff, 1990).

Because many of these children have a rather impoverished experiential base and because varied experiences constitute an essential substantive base for learning, it behooves clinicians to have goals to expand the experiential base for each child. Parents are asked to bring in notes of some new experiences each time they bring their child to therapy. The experiences need only be slight variations of what the child is already doing.

In early cognitive and language acquisition, regular events with their attendant episodes comprise possible worlds in which procedural knowledge (Mandler, 1983; K. Nelson, 1996) eventually shifts to mimesis (re-enactment or imitation) and then to semantic knowledge toward establishing narrative for the situated mind. Actual objects (animate or not) offer much more opportunity for learning than pictorials or words. Actual objects afford the learner opportunities to act on the objects in an effort to establish function-based schemas that can subsequently become augmented by perceptual information. Indeed, the embodiment activities in infancy may provide preconceptual awareness (Lakoff, 1987).

The 16th major clinical implication is that a viable intervention role for the clinician is to provide a parallel talk strategy (Muma, 1978b). Once intervention goals have been established, clinicians become vigilant during ongoing events for opportunities to provide selected comments to the children. Clinicians may derive their comments from available peer models or from the nature of events in actual social commerce, typically play. A discussion of the nature of the parallel talk strategy appears in chapter 8.

The 17th major clinical implication is that metacognitive and metalinguistic activities offer potent means of cognitive and language acquisition, especially when an individual has obtained a basic repertoire of skills. Any time an individual spontaneously engages in such activities it behooves clinicians to appreciate their significance and to exploit them.

Perhaps a brief discussion of the value of multiple goals is in order. That is, each child typically has the following kinds of clinical goals:

1. *Communicative payoff:* Stay on the topic when a child initiates a topic thereby being appropriately responsive to communicative intent.
2. *Socialization:* Comment to the child about the roles and activities of other children and, reciprocally, comment to other children about the roles and activities of the child. This socializes the child and establishes opportunities for peer modeling.
3. *Language goals:* These are the goals pertaining to particular aspects of language (i.e., speech, syntax, pragmatics).

The traditional clinical view is that a child can only deal with one aspect of language at a time. Consequently, it was held that a child should have only one goal at a time. However, that thinking is patently false simply because it would take an individual an inordinate amount of time to learn language that way. Furthermore, it means that a child would have to bypass various learning opportunities that became available but were not pertinent to a particular goal.

Table 2.2 summarizes all of these major clinical implications. The basic message is that continuity with philosophical views and theoretical perspectives not only provides a rationale for rendering appropriate clinical services, but by doing so these views and perspectives define what is practical (Muma, 1991).

TABLE 2.2
A Summary of the Major Clinical Implications

1. Not a modality perspective
2. Core of language: CCCE
3. Normal language acquisition principles: applicable
4. Context is essential
5. Individual differences or heterogeneity
6. Partial learning
7. Spurts of learning: when, duration, content
8. Facilitation
9. Predicate premise: to specify
10. Attribution criteria
11. Viable leverage: available repertoire, acquisition sequences, available learning strategies, active loci of learning
12. Communicative intent: communicative payoff
13. Parental participation
14. Peer modeling
15. Socialization and expanded experiential base: events, episodes, objects
16. Parallel talk strategy
17. Metacognition and metalinguistic events

More is said throughout the book about various aspects of the model for the cognitive-social bases of language. At this juncture it is useful to give the model as a means of appreciating its continuity with the underlying philosophical views and theoretical perspectives. Thus, the model with the attendant major clinical implications substantiates the proposition that philosophical views and theoretical perspectives make clinical endeavors practical.

These major clinical implications are not only promising, but they have been used over the past two decades. Many clinicians are already well on track in utilizing many, if not most, of these principles. Many clinicians, however, may not have these perspectives. With these and other new developments issuing from the cognitive socialization literature, it is incumbent on clinicians to continually upgrade their knowledge and practices with the goal of rendering appropriate clinical services.

SUMMARY

Philosophical views and theoretical perspectives provide the substantive base for the clinical fields. They provide coherent prediction, explanation, and understanding of various issues. That is precisely what the clinical fields need in order to establish a rationale for rendering appropriate clinical services and to make legitimate claims for a scholarly disciplined profession.

Accordingly, several philosophical views and theoretical perspectives within cognitive socialization were given. A model predicated on this literature was offered that deals with the cognitive-social bases of language. With these views and perspectives, several major clinical implications were raised.

3

A CLINICAL MODEL: COGNITIVE SOCIALIZATION

The previous chapter identified some clinical principles issuing from some philosophical views and theoretical perspectives in cognitive socialization, and these views and perspectives offered a useful model for appreciating the cognitive-social bases of language. The purpose of this chapter is to expound on some of those issues toward establishing a clinical model for assessment and for intervention.

Before dealing with the clinical model, it is necessary to provide further substantiation of the language core, give some basic thoughts about the delimitation of this core toward a valid definition of language impairment, and too examine briefly what is meant by three basic kinds of language impairments. With these issues in place, the clinical model may be appropriately appreciated.

LANGUAGE CORE: FURTHER SUBSTANTIATION

Cognitive socialization is much more than cognition on the one hand and socialization on the other (K. Nelson, 1996). With respect to language, cognitive socialization pertains to biological, psychological, emotional, social, and cultural influences in acquisition and use. In a sense, these issues are inherently cognitive and they constitute the cognitive-social bases of language. Socialization pertains to social, emotional, and cultural influences that are inextricably related to cognition. In a crucial sense, cognitive socialization underscores the cognitive and communicative functions of language. The formal grammatical and pragmatic mechanisms of a language are subsumed by their functions. With these perspectives, it should become abundantly clear that the primary tenets of cognitive socialization are that cognitive, social, emotional, and cultural influences have priority over structure. Said differently, form, or structure, is in the service of function—the functionalistic message over the past few decades.

The basic cognitive functions of language are variously known as abstraction (Ninio, 1988), mental representation (Mandler, 1988, 1990), representational redescription (Karmiloff-Smith, 1992), and mediation (K. Nelson, 1996) with the cumulative product being a theory of the world (Palermo, 1982), possible worlds (Bruner, 1981, 1986), or situated mind (K. Nelson, 1996).

The basic social or communicative functions of language are content and intent (Clark & Clark, 1977; Grice, 1975; K. Nelson, 1985, 1986; Sperber & Wilson, 1986), which become negotiable manifestations of narrative (Bruner, 1986; K. Nelson, 1996). Moreover, content is in the service of intent because the purpose of content is to make intentions recognizable (Grice, 1975; Sperber & Wilson, 1986).

Content has two fundamental dimensions: implicit and explicit. These operate within the cooperative principles (truthful, informative, relevant, unambiguous; Grice, 1967) and felicity conditions (ability, desire, future action, reason; Austin, 1962; Searle, 1969, 1975). Implicit content is presupposition (possible worlds, situated mind) and implicature (particular known information that is coded in relation to new information so intent could be recognized). Explicit content is a proposition entailed in a message and a message may be a composite of linguistic, pragmatic, and paralinguistic codes in a code matrix (Muma, 1975a). Thus, a message may be expressed by action, affect, or language (Bloom et al., 1988).

Inasmuch as the clinical fields are oriented on a modality perspective of language, perhaps it is necessary to pause briefly to comment on that perspective. The modality perspective stresses differences between the expressive (speaking, writing, gesture) and receptive (listening, reading) language modes. There are differences between modalities, but such differences are relatively minor in comparison to the core issues of language: CCCE.

An examination of the contemporary literatures on the philosophies and theories of language for support of the modality view would come up empty. It is true that the Osgood model of information processing (Osgood, 1957) provided theoretical justification for the Illinois Test of Psycholinguistic Abilities (Kirk, McCarthy, & Kirk, 1968). That model was a modality view. However, the literature on information processing has long since abandoned the modality view and offers perspectives on the core of language (Tallal, 1990). Another way of appreciating that the contemporary literature has long since dashed the modality view is to try to find instances in which major scholars such as Bates, Bever, Bloom, Brown, Bruner, Cazden, Clark, Pinker, Mandler, Maratsos, K. Nelson, Searle, Snow, Sperber, Wilson, and many others address it. It is virtually impossible to find instances of modality differences in the works of the major scholars; rather, as discussed in the following, these scholars have provided a literature that is focused on the CCCE aspects of language. Yet, the clinical fields have held tenaciously to the modality view.

A speaker has to make decisions about what should be coded in a message, how it should be coded (linguistically, pragmatically, paralinguistically, gesturally, emotionally) and what information may reside in implicature for a particular intention to be recognized. For example, a person may say, "I want a Coke" to convey the intent of wanting a Coke. Usually, it would be unnecessary to explain what a Coke is because it would be presumed that the listener knows that information. If the listener did not know that information, the utterance would not work as intended. Thus, some information is explicitly coded, whereas other relevant information is presumed or implicated. A measured balance between implicit and explicit content presumably operates to make intentions recognizable.

If a speaker superimposed a frown or an intonational contour indicating that really a Coke was not wanted, the linguistic message would be overridden by paralinguistic devices. Thus, communication is not effected merely by what is said but also by the code matrix of how it was said.

Given these issues, an appropriate clinical model may be derived from philosophical views and theoretical perspectives issuing from the contemporary cognitive socialization literature. The literature over the past few decades has provided several rich and promising views and perspectives. As a group, the various functionalistic perspectives are especially promising. In this regard, I consider the following particularly promising: experiential realism (Lakoff, 1987), informativeness (Clark & Clark, 1977; Greenfield, 1980), rare-event theory (K. E. Nelson, 1981, 1991), intentionality-based theory of expression (Bloom & Beckwith, 1986; Bloom et al., 1988), representation (Mandler, 1983, 1990), representational redescription (Karmiloff-Smith, 1992), speech acts (Austin, 1962; Bruner, 1981, 1986; Clark & Clark, 1977; Grice, 1975; Searle, 1969, 1975), relevance theory (Sperber & Wilson, 1986), social mediation (Bruner, 1981, 1990; K. Nelson, 1996; Rogoff, 1990; Vygotsky, 1962; Wertsch, 1991), shared meaning for event knowledge (K. Nelson, 1985, 1986), and experiential cognition toward obtaining a situated mind and narrative (K. Nelson, 1996).

These views are promising because they are derived from recognized philosophical views and theoretical perspectives and they have been well enunciated and partially substantiated. Furthermore, Perera (1994) indicated that such perspectives have been prominent influences in the study of child language since the early 1970s. In contrast, neither the modality view nor reinforcement have survived as offering viable accounts of language acquisition.

Fortunately, although there are many varied views and perspectives within cognitive socialization, they are also relatively compatible with each other so it is possible to draw on one and incorporate others into a coherent clinical model. These views are compatible because they define intentionality as the central or nuclear issue for language acquisition and/or use. They are compatible because they provide unified accounts of cognitive, linguistic, social or communicative, and expressive aspects of language. They are compatible because they hold that structure is in the service of function.

Perhaps speech act theory and relevance theory are more fully developed and substantiated than several of the others. They offer much potential for deriving a rationale for a clinical model. Therefore, they are taken as the centerpieces for the clinical model here. The other compatible models mentioned previously are also incorporated. To underscore their compatibilities with speech act theory and relevance theory, two quotes convey a common theme:

> A theory of semantic development must deal with three problems: the communicative context within which meaning is expressed and learned; the child's cognitive system, which interprets and intends meaning; and development—cognitive, linguistic, social—which changes the parameters of the system throughout the period." (K. Nelson, 1985, p. 7)

> We offer a theory of language development which integrates the social interaction, cognitive, and linguistic theories." (Bloom et al., 1988, p. 103)

In the latter quote, it appears that the content–form–use model of Bloom and Lahey (1978) has been replaced by the CCCE model simply because the latter provides a more encompassing perspective that has continuity with several other cognitive socialization perspectives.

What is very impressive is the extent to which Brown's (1956) comment that language acquisition is "a process of cognitive socialization" (p. 247) has not only held up, but has become the central underlying premise for much of the literature. This means that the cognitive and social functions of language have priority and that the linguistic (semantic–syntactic–phonological–prosodic) forms and mechanisms, extending to pragmatic mechanisms, are subsumed. Furthermore, Brown (1977a) extended his considerations of cognitive socialization to include "expression of affection" (p. 4). Lock (1978) reaffirmed the importance of affect(expression) in accounts of language acquisition, saying "the great chasm to be bridged in both speculations on the evolution of language and those on its development is that between affective and referential communication" (p. 8). Bloom and

Beckwith (1988, 1989) picked up the baton of addressing the role of affect in language acquisition.

Most of the major scholars share the view that the core of language is CCCE. There are some deviations from this perspective, to be sure, but the undeniable perspective is essentially the same. Clark and Clark (1977) dealt with cognitive, linguistic, and pragmatic domains. Grice (1975) dealt with cognitive, linguistic, and pragmatic issues. Sperber and Wilson (1986) addressed cognition, codification (by implication), and communication. Bruner (1981, 1986) considered cognitive, linguistic, and communicative-social aspects. K. Nelson (1985, 1986, 1996) addressed cognitive, linguistic, and social issues. The list goes on but there is no need to do so simply because the cognitive socialization perspective with expression is richly evident in these scholarly perspectives and much of the language acquisition literature in general.

In the clinical fields, some individuals have departed from the modality view by focusing on the core issues. Prutting and Kirchner (1983) addressed cognitive, linguistic, and pragmatic or social domains. Leonard (1982, 1983, 1987) and Fey and Leonard (1983) viewed language in regard to cognitive, linguistic, and pragmatic issues. Muma (1978b, 1981a, 1986a) addressed cognitive, linguistic, and communicative aspects of language. Thus, both the scholarly literature in language acquisition and some of the clinical literature view language in terms of CCCE systems and processes.

Table 3.1 shows some particular perspectives by individuals in the language acquisition literature and in the clinical literature; these perspectives are remarkably similar in terms of the core issues of language. Herein lies the virtue of addressing CCCE as a unified model.

These are comprehensive cognitive socialization perspectives. It is not fortuitous that comprehensive models of language evidence a common perspective. In short, the contemporary cognitive socialization literature simply reflects the nature of human social commerce or narrative (Bruner, 1986, 1990; K. Nelson, 1985, 1986, 1996).

Perhaps it is useful here to underscore the compatibility of these cognitive socialization perspectives in another way. Their compatibility is not only in the range of issues addressed (namely CCCE), but also the centrality of communicative intent. That is precisely why speech act and relevance theory are so attractive. Similarly, the intentionality model advocated by Bloom and Beckwith (1986) and Bloom et al. (1988) provides a unified view of cognition, language, and affect. The neo-Vygotskian perspectives (Rogoff, 1990; Wertsch, 1991) convey the social–cultural influences on cognition and languages. K. Nelson's (1985, 1986) theory of making sense for shared meaning also has a similar unified view of language acquisition and intentionality. The clinical implication of intent (Bruner, 1986, 1990; Searle, 1992) is that it gives priority for representative natural spontaneous behavior over performance on contrived tasks such as normative tests and a priori intervention activities.

TABLE 3.1

Cognitive Socialization

1. Bloom and Lahey (1978) model
   Content: Meaning or semantic domain
   Form: Words and grammar; lexicon, semantic-syntactic, phonological domains
   Use: Pragmatic domain
2. Bloom and Beckwith (1986) and Bloom et al. (1988) model: Intent from expression to language
   Cognitive domain
   Linguistic domain
   Social domain (action, affective, linguistic expression)
   Expression
3. Clark and Clark (1977) model: Speech acts
   Cognitive domain
   Linguistic domain
   Pragmatic domain
4. Grice (1975) model: Intent recognizable
   Cognitive domain
   Linguistic domain
   Communicative domain
5. Sperber and Wilson (1986) model: Mutual manifestness
   Cognitive domain
   Codification domain
   Communicative domain
6. Bruner (1981, 1986) model: Narrative
   Cognitive domain
   Linguistic domain
   Communicative-social domain
7. K. Nelson (1985, 1986, 1996) model: Situated mind
   Cognitive domain
   Linguistic domain
   Social domain
   Cultural domain

Clinical Perspectives

8. Prutting (1979, 1982) model
   Cognitive domain
   Linguistic domain
   Social-communicative domain
9. Leonard (1982, 1983, 1987), Fey (1986), Fey and Leonard (1983) model
   Cognitive domain
   Linguistic domain
   Pragmatic domain
10. Muma (1978b, 1986a) model
    Cognitive domain
    Linguistic domain
    Pragmatic domain

DELIMITATION

Speech act theory seems to offer a useful perspective for deriving an appropriate clinical rationale for four reasons. First, it is comprehensive. It entails not only semantics, syntax, prosody, and phonology, but it is very much oriented on the cognitive bases of language (intent, explicit and implicit content) and pragmatics. Second, it reflects cognitive socialization and is therefore compatible with a model of CCCE. Third, it offers an opportunity to incorporate other complementary views and perspectives, notably K. Nelson's (1996) comprehensive perspective on the emergence of the situated mind and the neo-Vygotskian perspectives of the social origins of the mind. Fourth, it defines intent as the central issue of communication.

It is necessary to indicate the range of issues in speech act theory in order to delimit the potential problem spaces that could be specified in describing a specific language impairment and the scope of issues that should be considered in intervention. Figure 3.1 shows the range of issues is speech act theory.

With the developments concerning the role of affect, especially in early language acquisition, it is appropriate to extend the issues in speech act theory to affect from the onset. Expressed affect is both propositional and intentional; moreover, it can override a linguistic message in much the same way that paralinguistic devices can.

Given this array of domains, it makes sense that an appropriate account of specific language impairment may entail any aspect or combination of aspects for these domains. The point is that it behooves clinicians to ascertain what an individual can do—one's repertoire—with these domains, what progress the

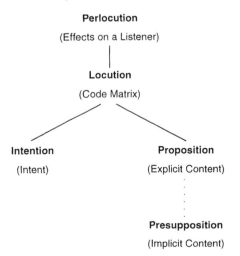

FIG. 3.1. Aspects of speech acts functioning in social commerce.

individual has made in acquisition sequences or phases, which available language learning strategies an individual may be using, and which particular loci of learning may be active at any particular time. To address these issues, it is necessary to obtain representative language samples from varied contexts to obtain descriptive evidence of what an individual can do. Furthermore, the heterogeneity issue that is so richly evident in clinical populations can be appropriately addressed by descriptions of what each individual can do with particular aspects of speech acts in actual social commerce.

Needless to say, it may be necessary "to describe an individual's command of various cognitive–linguistic–communicative systems and processes—to the extent possible—then exploit such behavior" (Muma, 1978b, p. 7). Some shortcuts are justifiable but others are not. Each shortcut carries risks; some shortcuts are excessive, resulting in detrimental practices. It is necessary to ascertain the extent to which some shortcuts may be too risky. For example, the shortcuts afforded by normative tests and developmental profiles may be questionable because they may have excessive risks. Muma (1986a) summarized 10 risks in using developmental profiles. I (Muma, 1986a, 1991) have advocated descriptive procedures issuing from the cognitive socialization literature because they provide standardized assessments and because most psychometric tests used in the clinical fields have excessive risks as evidenced by their lack of construct validity.

The criteria as to whether risks may be excessive may be at hand. That is, the criteria for acceptable evidence could also be used to define acceptable risks. In short, data that are supportable by the contemporary cognitive socialization literature and are relevant to a particular child constitute evidence. Notice that these criteria rule out a priori tests, developmental profiles, checklists, and inventories. Implicitly, relevant data should retain needed contextual information. Moreover, other functionalistic perspectives, especially shared meaning for event knowledge (K. Nelson, 1985, 1986, 1996), rare-event learning (K. E. Nelson, 1981, 1991), social origins of cognition (Rogoff, 1990; Wertsch, 1991), and informativeness (Greenfield, 1980) focus on how language functions under various contextual influences in actual social commerce.

Another implicit issue is relativity (Kagan, 1967); that is, it is necessary to establish patterns of behavior before inferences may be made about presumed skills (Muma, 1978b, 1986a). Single or a few instances merely provide speculative information that needs further substantiation to draw inferences about presumed skills. Notice that normative tests, developmental profiles, and checklists do not address this issue.

Still another implicit issue is ecological validity. This is an issue that was eloquently addressed by Bronfenbrenner (1974, 1977, 1979), Karmiloff-Smith (1984, 1992), and Rogoff (1990) among others. I (Muma, 1978b, 1986b) have attempted to champion this message in the clinical fields. The issue is simple; yet, it may have been usurped by a reliance on a priori normative tests. The issue is that which is ecologically real is relevant to what an individual can do. In contrast, that which is ecologically irrelevant is of questionable value because of the requisite inferential leap required to draw conclusions about what an individual can do in social commerce. "The dichotomy between laboratory versus ecologically natural tasks is an over-simplification that neglects to focus on the effects of particular contexts and particular goals on problem-solving behavior" (Karmiloff-Smith, 1984, p. 45).

For example, Donaldson (1978) showed that some infants who did not evidence object permanence on formal tests, specifically the Uzgiris and Hunt (1975) scale, actually evidenced object permanence on "human sense" inquiries in their homes. The later evidence was ecologically valid.

Advocates of normative tests have been blind to this issue. For example, McCauley and Swisher (1984a) claimed to do a review of language tests for preschool children but did not raise the issue of ecological validity. Salvia and Ysseldyke (1988) skirted this issue. Darley (1979) missed it. Bronfenbrenner (1974) put this issue cogently when he indicated that the literature on child development—let us add the clinical fields—had children perform tasks that they had never done before and would never do again in their lives; yet, conclusions were drawn about their lives. The results may be regarded as ecologically invalid. Does this ring a bell in the clinical fields for such a priori tests as the Peabody Picture Vocabulary Test–revised (PPVT-R), Test of Language Development (TOLD), Clinical Evaluation of Language Function–revised (CELF-R), Developmental Sentence Scores (DSS), and others, or are the clinical fields deaf to such issues?

The widely used normative tests fall short in providing needed evidence. They fall short for five basic reasons:

1. The heterogeneity issue.
2. A priori normative categories of questionable relevance.
3. Lack of construct validity.
4. Lack of necessary and sufficient evidence.
5. Lack of objectivity.

These issues are discussed in chapter 7 and in Appendix B.

One area for shortcutting with reasonable risks is language sampling. It is necessary to obtain representative language samples in order to make inferences about presumed capacities. Such samples should be from large and varied contexts to sample repertoires of what individuals can do. However, some shortcuts are available in using representative language samples to ascertain what individuals can do.

Muma et al. (see Appendix D) have shown that the prevailing language sample sizes of 50 or 100 utterances in the clinical fields have excessively large error rates, on the order of 40% to 55% when compared to sample sizes of 400 utterances. It is necessary to have language samples of 200 to 300 utterances to be within the sampling error range of 15% for 400-utterance samples. Gavin and Giles (1996) found that it was necessary to have language samples over 175 utterances for most quantitative measures. With such samples, it is possible to identify some speculative information about an individual's available repertoire, where an individual may be in acquisition sequences, which language learning strategies the individual may be using, and which loci of learning are active for the individual (Muma, 1986a). However, further substantiation is needed to meet the criteria of relativity.

Another shortcut with reasonable risks is to restrain the areas of inquiry. Different assessment procedures for pregrammatical children and grammatical children may be used. These are discussed in chapter 7. Briefly, the areas of assessment for pregrammatical children include categorization and cognitive precursors, intent, content (semantic sequence, semantic categories, semantic combinations), affect, symbolic play, formats and routines or scripts, and, of course, hearing. The areas of assessment for grammatical children include evidence of the situated mind or possible worlds, vertical and horizontal correlates, available repertoires for grammatical systems, phonological systems, pragmatic systems, acquisition sequences, learning strategies, active loci of learning, and hearing. Even here, these areas of inquiry may be selectively addressed depending on the apparent needs of each client. The objective is to provide descriptive evidence of what an individual can do. Thus, assessment is a process for delimiting or specifying the nature of a problem, which gives credence to the notion of a specific language impairment.

TOWARD A DEFINITION OF LANGUAGE IMPAIRMENT

Prutting and Kirchner (1983, 1987) and Fey and Leonard (1983) provided interesting perspectives on different kinds of language impairments. The former was derived from a speech act perspective and empirical evidence yielded the latter. Interestingly enough, both yielded somewhat similar results. They both found three basic kinds of language impairments that were remarkably similar. Prutting and Kirchner (1983) identified one group of individuals that "lack sensitivity to the various dimensions of the social context" (p. 58). A second group evidenced a cognitive limitation manifest as "a delay in onset, rate, and sequence of language acquisition" (p. 58). This cognitive limitation may be manifest as a restricted lexical repertoire and limited pragmatic skills. The third group had more specific pragmatic problems.

Fey and Leonard (1983) described the following three kinds of language impairments. One pattern of impairment was that of a general unresponsiveness in social commerce: "These children may be regarded as having general pragmatic impairments since their unwillingness or inability to engage in conversations has a profound influence on all areas of language use" (Fey & Leonard, 1983, p. 77). The second group was described as being "responsive but nonassertive" (Fey & Leonard, 1983, p. 77). They evidenced "selective pragmatic deficits that often seem to reflect the severity of their impairments in the comprehension and production of syntax" (Fey & Leonard, 1983, p. 77). These children evidenced 'back channel' comments, few requests for clarification, difficulties in expressing alternative forms to convey the same meaning of misunderstood messages, few requests for action or information, limited lexical and linguistic options, and possible difficulties with anaphoric reference. The third group had limited syntax skills for specific forms. Fey (1986) converted these findings into a matrix on assertiveness and responsiveness.

In general, both studies indicated that language impairments pertain to CCCE. The point is that these views of language impairment reflect a common perspective compatible with the cognitive socialization literature.

Also, it is interesting to note that the types of language problems that Prutting and Kirchner (1983, 1987) and Fey and Leonard (1983) found reflect the inherent perspective of speech acts. Thus, the underlying CCCE model for cognitive socialization in general and speech act theory in particular is applicable for identifying specific language impairments.

An obvious issue arises from these studies. It is the extent to which the inherent model may have determined the outcome. Going in, the CCCE model was known to the researchers and coming out it was evidenced. The model should have influenced the outcome because it reflected the available literature. However, another major domain had not been addressed when these studies were conducted. It is expression (Bloom & Beckwith, 1986; Bloom et al., 1988). Furthermore, the developments in speech acts, especially the importance of intentionality, and pragmatic theory, especially shared meaning (K. Nelson, 1985, 1986, 1996) offer other understandings of the nature of language impairments that were not yet available when the Prutting and Kirchner (1983, 1987) and Fey and Leonard (1983) studies were done. These developments were not reflected in the matrix of pragmatic skills by Fey (1986).

Thus, speech act theory provided a useful perspective for identifying different kinds of language impairment and, therefore, for defining language impairment. However, speech act theory was insufficiently comprehensive. Subsequent developments showed that affect or the expressive function of language should also be considered. The moral of the story is that any theoretical perspective is vulnerable to new developments. For example, the full clinical implications of experiential realism and experiential cognition for establishing a situated mind are before us. Thus, speech act theory coupled with relevant new developments is useful for delimiting the potential problem spaces of language impairment. It behooves the definition of language impairment to be sufficiently open-ended so that "to specify" remains a viable perspective for detailing the unique problems an individual may have. In doing so, this approach to defining specific language impairment provides the substantive arena for specifying but leaves the details to be filled in in accordance with each individual's problems. This perspective more adequately deals with the heterogeneous nature of clinical populations than the normative notion of specific language impairment.

TWO CLINICAL MODELS

Given the unity of perspectives that verifies the principle of cognitive socialization in general and speech act theory in particular, a substantive base has emerged for establishing two clinical models, one for assessment and one for intervention. Given the cognitive socialization literature, the rationales for these models are straightforward. In clinical assessment, descriptive procedures are appropriate. Such procedures should be predicated on representative samples from actual social commerce because such samples offer viable opportunities to ascertain what individuals can do. Descriptive assessment deals with the major substantive domains of speech acts in an attempt to address the seven basic clinical assessment issues (Muma, 1983b): complaint, problem–no problem, nature of a problem, individual differences, intervention implications, prognosis, and accountability or efficacy.

Descriptive assessment relies on representative samples of spontaneous speech obtained in varied contexts and attribution criteria. Spontaneous speech samples are needed because they are intentional and presumably provide evidence of actual productive grammatical, pragmatic, and phonological systems. Varied sampling conditions are needed because they offer various opportunities to observe an individual's repertoire of available skills. Table 3.2 outlines a clinical assessment model that addresses these issues.

In clinical intervention, the best that can be done is to ascertain what an individual can do in actual social commerce, then exploit what the individual is doing by varying contexts toward expanded repertoires and replacing earlier skills with subsequent skills in accordance with acquisition sequences and active loci of learning. This is in accord with the observations by Bates (1979) that the two basic principles of language acquisition are expansion and replacement. Such exploitation was called a *facilitation* strategy (Muma, 1978b, 1986a) because it attempted to facilitate what an individual was actively striving to do. The substantive domains of exploitation and facilitation are available repertoires, progress in acquisition sequences, available

TABLE 3.2
A Clinical Assessment Model for Descriptive Assessment

Descriptive Assessment:
Providing Evidence of What an Individual
Can Do in Actual Social Commerce

Representative language samples: 200 to 300 utterances, spontaneous speech, varied contexts
Substantive domains: Function has priority over structure
  Cognition
  Codification
  Communication
  Expression
Basic clinical assessment issues:
  Complaint
  Problem—no problem
  Nature of a problem
  Individual differences
  Intervention implications
  Prognosis
  Accountability and efficacy
Attribution criteria:
  Preparation
  Attainment
  Consolidation

---

available strategies of learning, and active loci of learning that may be identified in descriptive assessment.

Thus, issues of content, sequencing, pacing, and intentionality are essentially within the province of the language learner by virtue of evidence of actual skills in representative samples. It is necessary to identify what an individual can do so that appropriate decisions can be made to facilitate learning.

This means that the substantive base for appropriate language intervention is a rationale derived from what an individual can do and principles of language acquisition issuing from the cognitive socialization literature. Empirical evidence initially provides speculation of the degree to which a relation may exist between what is warranted by the rationale and subsequent changes in performance. Subsequently, empirical evidence may substantiate and verify a rationale. Unfortunately, however, this relation is indirect, which has an inherent limitation that prevents making much ado about presumed changes.

The bottom line is that the most that can be done to justify doing intervention a particular way is a rationale predicated on what an individual can do and principles of language acquisition issuing from the cognitive socialization literature in general (philosophical views) and contemporary theories such as speech act theory, relevance theory, social origins theory or situated mind theory in particular.

Pertinent empirical evidence, although enticing for accounts of efficacy, is at best speculative simply because the research design literature is clear that mere pre–post data are insufficient to account for change and that within-subjects designs that have been widely used in attempts to deal with accountability or efficacy may be inappropriate (Ventry & Schiavetti, 1986). Table 3.3 outlines a clinical intervention model for establishing an appropriate *rationale* to facilitate acquisition.

Needless to say, this clinical model was derived from the philosophical views and theoretical perspectives of cognitive socialization. Accordingly, it reflects the philosophical views of constructionism, functionalism, experiential realism, experiential cognition, and so on, and the theoretical perspectives of speech acts, relevance, representational redescription, informativeness, possible worlds, social origins, situated mind, and so on. In doing so, it offers a coherent clinical rationale. It is such coherence that comprises the substantive base of the field.

CODE OF CONDUCT

It is assumed that clinicians will abide by the ASHA Code of Ethics and the policies of P.L. 94-142 that call for appropriate services, it may be well to establish a code of conduct also. Ashley and Krych (1995) have had a

TABLE 3.3
A Clinical Intervention Model for Establishing an
Appropriate Rationale to Facilitate Language Acquisition

Rationale: Exploiting What an Individual
Can Do in Actual Social Commerce

Principles
  Expand
  Replace
  Begin with what the client can do
  Sheer talking time
  Intent and communicative payoff
  New forms with old functions, new functions with old forms
  Negotiable
  Event related: social commerce
Intervention agents
  Parents
  Peers and siblings
  Others
Intervention activities
  Parallel talk
  10 techniques: Expand and vary repertoire
Alternative strategies
  Metalinguistic activities

Centre for Neuro Skills

Mark Ashley, **CEO**, Bakersfield, California
Dave Krych, **CEO**, Irving, Texas

Code of Conduct

Environmental Validity

Environmental validity refers to ecological validity. The environment sets the stage for learning. It provides a set of expectations and opportunities that are useful for intervention. Intervention at CNS strives to emulate real-world settings thereby achieving ecologically valid services for the clients. By doing so, the traditional problem of a lack of carryover becomes a moot issue.

Rhythm of Living

Individuals have a rhythm of living wherein particular activities occur at particular times and in particular ways. These are routines of daily living. Behaviors and social expectations issue from these routines. The rhythms of the work week usually differ from those of the weekend. CNS strives to re-establish these rhythms and to encourage them to be productive and adaptive, thereby leading to happy and productive lives for the clients.

Clients Don't Plateau

The progress that has been seen with many, indeed most, clients with traumatic brain injury, makes it abundantly clear that some degree of recovery and learning is expected for all clients. These clients typically have different rates and sometimes different ways or manners of learning. Usually when a client "plateaus," it is the result of limited service delivery rather than client limitations. Consequently, it is incumbent on all clinicians to be continually vigilant and introspective about their services to a client so that if a client should reach a limit it is a true limit rather than a perceived limit in the eyes of the clinician.

Why?

"Why" is the most important clinical question for a clinician. A clinician must know why particular services are rendered in particular ways. The best way to address this issue is to have a solid grounding on the scholarly literature relevant to the services rendered. This means that it behooves clinicians to keep abreast of new developments in order to provide viable clinical services. Such services are grounded on knowledge of the underlying philosophical views and theoretical perspectives with the attendant literature. Such an awareness provides a clinical **rationale** for addressing **"WHY"** particular services are rendered in particular ways. In this way, clinicians are recognizing their responsibilities to each client to render the most appropriate services.

Bias for Action

Clinicians should view themselves as facilitators in rendering appropriate services to clients. In this way, clinicians become active participants in the clinical process. As a facilitator, clinicians are continuously taking what **action** is deemed most appropriate at any particular time. Thus, the facilitator function is one of positive, flexible, and constructive action.

Clients as Peers

With the facilitator approach, clients are regarded as partners in the clinical endeavor. Implicit in this perspective is the notion that a client deserves dignity and respect.

FIG. 3.2. Code of conduct, Centre for Neuro Skills, Bakersfield, California, and Irving, Texas. Reprinted with permission from the Centre for Neuro Skills.

long-standing Code of Conduct for the Centre for Neuro Skills. Because it is attractive and effective as evidenced by the clinical results of many years, it is reproduced as Fig. 3.2.

SUMMARY

In accordance with the cognitive socialization literature, clinical services should become focused on the core issues of language, specifically CCCE. By doing so, the clinical fields would become released from the relatively peripheral modality perspective of language and enter into the more mundane and ecologically appropriate arena of the situated mind.

This new orientation carries with it the obligation to be grounded on philosophical views and theoretical perspectives within the field of cognitive socialization. Several views and perspectives within this field are compatible, so it is appropriate to adopt a particular perspective and other perspectives can be incorporated to establish a unified perspective. Speech act theory provides a useful perspective for incorporating other perspectives.

By adopting a speech act perspective, a frame of reference becomes available for specifying the nature of language impairments. This perspective affords a way of defining specific language impairment as an open-ended perspective that appropriately addresses the heterogeneous nature of clinical populations. In so doing, the traditional normative notion of specific language impairment is overcome.

Two clinical models were offered: clinical assessment and clinical intervention. These were derived from the principles issuing from the cognitive socialization literature. The clinical assessment model addresses the seven basic clinical assessment issues. The clinical intervention model establishes a rationale for carrying out clinical assessment certain ways.

In addition to the ASHA Code of Ethics, a code of conduct was deemed appropriate to reaffirm the principles issuing from the cognitive socialization literature.

4

COGNITION

Over the past few decades, several major advances have occurred in the study of cognition. Some of the impetuses for these advances are apparent:

1. Brown's views of cognitive socialization, especially in language acquisition.
2. Bruner's notion of going beyond the information given.
3. Werner and Kaplan's perspectives on symbolization.
4. Austin and Grice's speech acts theories; Sperber and Wilson's relevance theory: centrality of intent.
5. Bloom's theory of expression.
6. Mandler's accounts of representation.
7. Karmiloff-Smith's perspectives on representational redescription.
8. Rosch's perspectives on natural categories.
9. Kagan's discrepancy learning theory.
10. Chomsky's views of generative capacities.
11. Fodor's notion of modularity.
12. Searle's importance of consciousness.
13. Bruner's notion of possible worlds.
14. Vygotsky's notion of the social origins of the mind.
15. K. Nelson's notion of situated mind.

There are also others. Interestingly, the centrality of intent (Bruner, 1986) or more generally, consciousness (Searle, 1992), in understanding human affairs are unifying constructs in the contemporary appreciation of cognition, especially cognitive socialization.

Taking these into account, two other great developments have taken place that are of utmost importance. Indeed, these developments constitute thresholds for redefining psychology in general and cognition (and language) in particular. These developments are:

1. The distinctions between science and human affairs (narrative), or what Bruner (1986) also called two modes of thought and two castles.
2. The views of experiential (biological, cognitive, emotional, social, cultural) cognition toward obtaining a situated mind (K. Nelson, 1996).

Needless to say, these are discussed in the following and in other parts of this volume. One very important point about both is that they have passed the test of coherence (Searle, 1992). This is important to note from the onset because some other theoretical notions about cognition have fallen short on coherence, notably behaviorism (reinforcement) and connectionism.

With these developments, the traditional notions of cognition seem to have slipped from center stage: "Descartes *might* have been right in thinking that there were separate mental phenomena; it just turned out *as a matter of fact* that he was wrong" (Searle, 1992, p. 36). That is, sensation, discrimination, perception, categorization, memory, and thinking as various parts of the "cognitive elephant" (to borrow from the parable of the blind man and the elephant) seem to have run their course. In a sense, there is a great deal known about cognition from the perspectives of topology and taxonomics. The cognitive elephant has been distinguished essentially from the cognitive rat!

It now appears that the work before us is to appreciate not only what has been learned topologically but, more crucially, what the cognitive elephant can do and does—biologically, mentally, emotionally, socially, and culturally. What has become abundantly clear is that these domains are in dynamic relation with each other and what is crucial for each is how they function in various contexts. For example, the tired and poorly conceived notions of digit recall forward and backward or recall of number of commands as presumed indices of memory become nakedly exposed by simply asking: So what? What is the interpretative significance of such data?

Although the distinctions between short- and long-term memory, episodic and semantic memory, working and static memory, and declarative and nondeclarative memory have each advanced an appreciation of memory, it is when issues of accessibility for information in particular contexts (Bruner, 1964; Mandler, 1983) are addressed that major advancements emerge in understanding memory and how it functions. More specifically, the manner in which working memory has been operationally studied (Just & Carpenter,

1992) is a long inferential way from how working memory operates in actual social commerce. Thus, the cognitive-domain approach, although easier to study in a formal way, seems to have yielded psychologically, sociologically, and ecologically barren outcomes in understanding possible worlds or situated minds.

More recent developments, such as those just mentioned, bring new, more viable perspectives oriented on the functions of domains in context. The newer perspectives bring us closer to the cognitive enterprise of actual social commerce and they bring different—and so far more productive and promising (Bruner, 1990; K. Nelson, 1996)—theoretical perspectives requiring adjustments in traditional thinking about thought (cognition). The new cognitive perspective is eloquently stated as follows: "The primary cognitive task of the human child is to make sense of his or her situated place in the world in order to take a skillful part in its activities" (K. Nelson, 1996, p. 5).

Inasmuch as cognitive socialization is a relatively new field, it may be useful to begin with some general comments about the contributions of three major scholars: Freud, Piaget, and Vygotsky. This discussion is followed by a series of general topics in cognition beginning with memory, discrepancy learning, and brute and institutional facts. These topics are followed by discussions of:

1. Representation.
2. Cognitive modularity.
3. Representational redescription.
4. Process, level, phase, stage, and strategy.
5. Top-down and bottom-up processing.
6. Left–right processing or two modes of thought.
7. Modality processing.
8. Experiential cognition.
9. Science and human affairs.

These topics culminate in a model for the cognitive-social bases of language, which is an extension and modification of an earlier model (Muma, 1986a). This model appears in chapter 2 as the product of philosophical views and theoretical perspectives. As promised, we have returned to the model and do so again.

THE TITANS

Bruner (1986) indicated that Freud, Piaget, and Vygotsky are three titans of cognitive psychology. With such accorded status, it is incumbent on us to make some very brief comments about their views, especially concerning the relations between cognition and language. Indeed, these comments are derived from Bruner (1986).

Freud's theory was one of reform and liberation: "Man frees himself from the shackles of his own history" (Bruner, 1986, p. 139). From the presumption of the archaeological premise, an individual would use language to talk through various issues. This enabled one to face up to the past in order to become liberated and thereby deal effectively with the present and future. Bruner (1986) indicated that this view has a hydraulic feature because the instincts are pressing for release; as people release themselves from the past, they become more aware and free to deal with the present and future.

Piaget's theory was based on stages. However, the structural nature of the Piagetian perspective is "insufficiently human" (Bruner, 1986, p. 147). A person becomes freed from the past by virtue of progressing through stages. For Piaget, language reflects thought but does not determine it. The constructionistic aspect of Piagetian theory is attractive because children construct possible worlds and use such constructions to deal with present experience as well as for contemplation of the past, the future, and the plausible. In so doing, children become released from reliance on direct stimulation and increasingly reliant on representation.

Mandler (1983, 1990) found the Piagetian account of the sensorimotor stage wanting. Piaget held that in early infancy the sensory modalities were unconnected; thus, the integration of modalities was considered a feat in sensorimotor achievement. Indeed, some clinical assessment and intervention approaches, even for individuals beyond infancy, are based on the notion that the sensory modalities are unconnected (e.g., auditory learning, visual learning, and motor learning). Mandler (1983, 1990) provided evidence that the modalities are connected in early infancy, and that causality, object permanence, and some symbolic skills are also evidenced in early infancy.

K. Nelson (1996) also felt that Piagetian theory was too restrictive. It focused on object learning as the essence of categorization and symbolization. However, object learning is only one aspect of knowledge of the world. Rather, it behooves scholars of cognition to understand the dynamics of acquiring a situated mind from embodiment (Lakoff, 1987), to shared event knowledge (K. Nelson, 1986), to mimesis, then narrative and possibly poetics and theory (K. Nelson, 1996). This shifts the study of cognition to a consideration of biological, mental, emotional, social, and cultural influences and it moves the arena of study away from ecologically invalid tasks to performance in actual social commerce.

In contrast to Piaget, Mandler (1983) was more persuaded that the acquisition of cognitive capacities occurs in a continuous or progressive manner rather than in stages. More specifically, she showed that procedural knowledge, which was deemed the province of the sensorimotor Piagetian stage, was actually evidenced throughout life. Similarly, topological awareness was maintained throughout life with Euclidean awareness becoming a discretionary complement. Mandler also expressed concern about the vagueness of symbolization in the Piagetian accounts of cognitive acquisition.

The implication of the sensorimotor stage was that an individual's actions on the world provide the essential means of knowing. Such actions would afford individuals opportunities to discern schemas from available routines or scripts and thence discover object permanence, means–ends, causality, and enablement. Subsequently, individuals would become symbolically oriented and thereby freed of a reliance on direct stimulation. Although Piaget's notion of freedom from direct stimulation was a major contribution, his reliance on stages was not so impressive. For example, dynamic systems theory (Karmiloff-Smith, 1984, 1992, 1994) details three phases, rather than stages, of cognitive processing that enable individuals to become progressively freed from direct stimulation.

Vygotsky's perspective draws on an interaction between predispositional and environmental influences, especially social and cultural influences. In reference to Vygotsky's views, Bruner (1986) said, "the mind grows neither naturally nor unassisted" (p. 141). Vygotsky's theory is one of cognitive socialization in which language plays a crucial role as, "a *social* support system for leading the child through the famous zone of proximal development" (Bruner, 1986, p. 142). "For Vygotsky, language was an agent for altering the powers of thought—giving thought new means for explicating the world. In turn, language became the repository for new thoughts once achieved" (Bruner, 1986, p. 143). "Vygotsky turns the cultural past into the generative present by which we reach toward the future: growth is reaching" (Bruner, 1986, p. 145).

The views of Freud, Piaget, and Vygotsky have been major influences in traditional cognitive psychology. Developments in recent years, especially by Bruner and K. Nelson, have reaffirmed and expanded the Vygotskian perspective and cast doubt on some aspects of the Freudian and Piagetian perspectives. Neo-Vygotskians such as Hagstrom, Rogoff, and Wertsch are currently advancing the social origins theory. The result has been a concerted interest in the emerging situated mind. Furthermore, this interest encompasses biological, cognitive, linguistic, emotional, social, and cultural influences.

MEMORY

Memory has been an old wart in traditional psychology. The traditional view was that memory was simplistic. It was the notion that there is a single memory and it has a fixed capacity that presumably could be estimated by forward or backward recall of digits or memory for commands. Such views were too simplistic and these estimates were excessively crude (Blankenship, 1938; Jenkins, 1974).

The simplistic notion of a single memory gave way to the view of two basic kinds of memory: short- and long-term (Atkinson & Shiffrin, 1968; Craik & Lockhart, 1972; Crowder, 1982) with the former providing a mental buffer whereby information is purged of modality and converted into the coin-of-the-realm of mental processing. Such information is stored in a recoverable way, thereby providing access to useful information.

Bruner (1964) indicated that the most important function of memory is retrieval of information in a usable form: "The most important thing about memory is not storage of past experience, but rather the retrieval of what is relevant in some usable form. . . . The end product of such a system of coding and processing is what we may speak of as a representation" (p. 2). Language may facilitate memory in both ways—getting information in and getting it out in a usable form (Carmichael, Hogan, & Walter, 1932; K. Nelson, 1996).

Memory became viewed from other perspectives, namely primacy and recency effects and iconic and symbolic memory. Primacy and recency effects were evidenced for information that has little or no inherent structure. That is, faced with the task of remembering information that either lacked inherent structure or had indiscernible structure, primacy and recency effects typically occurred. *Primacy effects* were those aspects of information that were recovered by virtue of rehearsal strategies. They were regarded as primacy effects because the rehearsal strategies were evidently successful in placing the information in primary memory and recovering it in a usable form. *Recency effects* reflected the short-term store of information that was necessarily dumped from mental processing before it could be lost because short-term storage either loses information in a fashion similar to a screening function—only potentially relevant information is allowed to pass—or the information is passed on to long-term storage in a converted, reduced, and usable form. Thus, primacy and recency effects are not kinds of memory, but they provide evidence that memory is very much related to the inherent structure of the information. Furthermore, inherent structure is a psychological enterprise rather than determined externally (G. Miller, 1956; Simon, 1974), although external influences may exist.

The distinctions between iconic and symbolic memory (Glucksberg, 1966) were reflected in what was subsequently regarded as episodic and semantic memories (Tulving, 1972), respectively. However, the distinction between procedural and declarative knowledge is not the same as that between episodic and semantic memory (Mandler, 1983). Iconic (or ikonic) and episodic memories are forms of imagery that have a relatively small capacity and short-term life before the information begins to fade away. The notion of iconic memory is that it affords an individual a snapshot of information.

However, the notion of episodic memory is more attractive than the notion of iconic memory because episodic memory affords an individual the capability of recouping an entire episode (participants, agents, objects, sequences, location, time). Except for snapshot or flashbulb memory that occurs under conditions of heightened stress (Brown & Kulik, 1977), information in episodic memory fades away over relatively brief periods, thereby raising the potential of mental representations in semantic memory replacing more faithful information of episodic memory. When this happens, which is the prevailing experience, individuals believe they are dealing with modality-specific information but, in fact, they are dealing with mental events that are the products of inference rather than modality-specific input (Loftus, 1975). Mandler (1983) expressed it this way: "Much of what we think we have seen, we have only inferred" (p. 454).

In contrast to episodic memory, semantic memory has a large capacity by virtue of the available representational or categorization architecture. Thus, semantic memory provides useful information over extended periods of time—months and years. Furthermore, if particular aspects of memory become lost, the active nature of mental processing may fill in the gaps so that the available information retains coherence.

Baddeley (1994) indicated that semantic memory is "assumed to result from the accumulation of many episodes" (p. 354). This account is strikingly similar to:

1. Anglin (1977) and Rosch's (1973, 1978) views of natural categories.
2. Lakoff's (1987) views of experienced-based knowledge of the world.
3. K. Nelson's (1973a, 1974) notion of prototypic learning in concept formation.
4. K. Nelson's (1996) views of experiential cognition whereby event knowledge becomes semantic knowledge toward attaining narrative and beyond.

It is true that each perspective has its own spin on it, but what is strikingly shared by all is the role of experience in the eventual representation of possible worlds or the situated mind.

According to Baddeley (1994), episodic memory entails differentiating one experience from another, thus providing access to particular information for a particular episode. Episodic memory provides "more or less accurate access to the residue of a single experience" (Baddeley, 1994, p. 354). However, it should be acknowledged that accuracy in this context means psychological accuracy, which is the product of a perceptual system with output, at least, that is governed by what is already known (Garner, 1966). In contrast, semantic memory is a more generic product of "abstracting what the various instances have in common" (Baddeley, 1994, p. 354). This is precisely what prototype theory is about (K. Nelson, 1973a, 1974).

Relatively recent developments point to multiple memory systems (Squire, 1994). With the distinctions between short- and long-term memory and between episodic and semantic memory, other major distinctions were soon to follow: explicit (conscious, intentional) and implicit (nonconscious, unintentional) memory and their respective parallels declarative and nondeclarative memory. Schacter and Tulving (1994) indicated that these are not memory systems but different kinds of expressions of memory. Thus, it appears that memory is of two basic kinds, further understood as different kinds of expressions of memory. Figure 4.1 and Table 4.1 provide two different perspectives on the ways in which memory may be understood.

Squire (1994) indicated that declarative memory is "fast, accessible to conscious recollection, and flexible, i.e. available to multiple response systems. Nondeclarative memory is nonconscious and less flexible, i.e., it provides limited access to response systems not involved in the original learning" (p. 214). Declarative memory may be evidenced by recall and recognition. It is called declarative because it is consciously available and because an individual can declare its content. Declarative memory "refers to a biologically meaningful category of memory dependent on a specific brain system, nondeclarative memory embraces several kinds of memory and depends on multiple brain systems" (Squire, 1994, pp. 204–205).

In contrast, nondeclarative memory (Schacter, 1992) is evidenced in various kinds of skill knowledge rather than recollection. This distinction be-

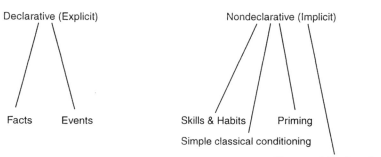

FIG. 4.1. Classification of memory. Declarative (explicit) memory refers to conscious recollections of facts and events. Nondeclarative (implicit) memory refers to a heterogeneous collection of abilities whereby experience alters behavior nonconsciously without providing access to any memory content. From "Declarative and Nondeclarative Memory: Multiple Brain Systems Supporting Learning and Memory," by L. Squire, 1994, in D. Schacter & E. Tulving (Eds.), *Memory Systems 1994*, p. 205, Cambridge, MA: MIT Press. Copyright © 1994 by MIT Press. Reprinted with permission.

TABLE 4.1
Major Systems of Human Learning and Memory

System	Other Terms	Subsystems	Retrieval
Procedural (cognitive skills)	Nondeclarative	Motor skills Simple conditioning Simple associative learning	Implicit
Perceptual representation (PRS)	Nondeclarative	Visual word form Auditory word form Structural description	Implicit
Semantic	Generic Factual Knowledge	Spatial Relational	Implicit
Primary	Working	Visual Auditory	Explicit
Episodic	Personal Autobiographical Event memory		Explicit

Note. From *Memory Systems 1994* (p. 26), by D. Schacter & E. Tulving (Eds.), 1994, Cambridge, MA: MIT Press. Copyright © 1994 by MIT Press. Reprinted with permission.

comes useful in understanding the mental behavior of individuals with amnesia. Interestingly, these individuals evidence great difficulty with declarative memory but their nondeclarative memory remains essentially intact.

The notion of "priming" memory has received much attention, contributing to the distinctions between processes and systems. The traditional notion of priming was that preexisting representations were activated. However, the contemporary literature indicates that priming has a facilitation effect whereby priming may lead to new more useful perception. As for the processes versus systems issue, Squire (1994) indicated, "when the discussion is broadened to include skill learning, habit learning, and conditioning, a brain-systems view of multiple memories is more consistent with the biological and psychological facts than a processing view" (p. 215). However, he also indicated that it is not clear that the processing and systems notions are mutually exclusive. The systems perspective is attractive because:

> Organisms have available to them multiple ways of benefiting from experience and acquiring knowledge. In most situations, more than one memory system will be engaged. These memory systems have different operating characteristics, acquire different kinds of knowledge, and depend on different brain structures and connections for their operation." (Squire, 1994, p. 224)

Schacter and Tulving (1994) discussed five major systems of human learning and memory. It should be emphasized that this perspective is one that views memory from a broader perspective than the traditional notions of storage and retrieval. In doing so, it approaches the perspective of ACT

(Anderson, 1983). That is to say, the various approaches that have traditionally compartmentalized the brain functions in terms of sensation, discrimination, perception, and memory have incorporated these functions into accounts of various cognitive systems.

According to Schacter and Tulving (1994), the five major systems for learning and memory are procedural, perceptual representation (PRS), semantic, primary, and episodic. They are listed in Table 4.1.

"Procedural memory is characterized by gradual, incremental learning and appears to be especially well-suited for picking up and dealing with invariances in the environment over time (Sherry & Schacter, 1987)" (Schacter & Tulving, 1994, p. 26). Procedural memory deals with behavioral skills and procedures that can be acquired by virtue of action rather than conceptualization. The other four mental systems are cognitive in nature. Except for primary or working memory, the other kinds of memory are long-term systems. Working memory is a temporary holding and processing system with an output that is in the coin-of-the-realm of mental processing and manipulation. The PRS deals with word and object recognition via visual and auditory means. It may be the basis of priming and it is a presemantic system.

Semantic memory deals with the acquisition of factual information about the world. It is the representational essence of one's theory of the world, possible worlds, or situated mind. It is a prototypic summary of experience. In contrast, episodic memory pertains to the conscious recollection of experienced events. Such memory has a short life span before details begin to fade away and become lost or become translated into semantic memory.

Clark and Clark (1977) used the notion of working memory in accounts of verbal production and comprehension, but Baddeley (1994) advanced the notion of working memory: " 'Working memory' may be defined as the system for the temporary maintenance and manipulation of information, necessary for the performance of such complex cognitive activities as comprehension, learning and reasoning" (p. 351).

This definition addresses perception by virtue of dealing with "the temporary maintenance and manipulation of information" and it appreciates the potential for intermodality integration.

"While a working memory system that coordinates information from a number of sources is likely to aid perceptual organization of the world, it would not necessarily benefit from experience" (Schacter & Tulving, 1994, p. 352). Such a perspective seemingly resolves one issue while raising another. It resolves the notion that mental processing of information, at a perceptual level, may be initially modality specific but becomes purged of modality information as the information becomes converted into the coin-of-the-realm of mental processing. That is, the act of bringing together information from a number of sources implicates a modality purge whereby the information is manipulated to conform to the coin-of-the-realm of mental processing.

This definition also raises the problem that although manipulation may occur, this mental activity does "not necessarily benefit from experience." This appears to be a non sequitur simply because the act of mental manipulation—indeed perception (Garner, 1966)—entails an experientially derived knowledge of the world or possible worlds. That is, in order for new information to be manipulated in accordance with the available cognitive system, it is necessary for the system to have already processed relevant information. Therefore, the uptake of new information implicates an executive function for transforming new information into the coin-of-the-realm of mental processing.

However, in accordance with the modularity perspective, top-down influences may occur only on modular output, which raises a knotty problem as to whether working memory is relegated to dealing only with raw input or somehow plays a role in the interface between modular output and top-down influences in order to achieve manipulation of information. Baddeley (1994) stopped short of saying that working memory yields concepts; rather, he indicated that such memory "is likely to aid perceptual organization of the world" (p. 352).

With the various perspectives on memory, one principle has emerged: Memory is not an entity per se; rather it is an enabling faculty that provides access to previously known information. Furthermore, as Bruner (1964) indicated many years ago, this faculty yields information in a usable form. To reiterate, Hudson and Fivush (1990) made the following comment about memory: "Memory is no longer considered as a separate and distinct cognitive process that can be isolated from other cognitive processes; rather, remembering is viewed as a cognitive activity embedded in larger social and cognitive tasks" (p. 1).

There seems to be a disconnection between the clinical fields' understanding of memory and mental processes for encoding and decoding messages. In the clinical fields, efforts to deal with memory are still in regard to memory for digits forward or backward or for number of commands. Such notions were shown to be invalid many decades ago (Blankenship, 1938) and reiterated (as if reiteration was necessary) more recently (Jenkins, 1974). Yet, undaunted, the clinical fields continue to use such antiquated practices.

DISCREPANCY LEARNING

Kagan (1968, 1969, 1970, 1971) posited a theory of attention and learning that has come to be known as *discrepancy learning*. This theory has emerged in explicit (K. E. Nelson, 1981, 1989, 1991) and implicit (Bruner, 1981; K. Nelson, 1985, 1986, 1996) accounts of cognitive socialization, especially regarding script theory. Originally, there were three stages to discrepancy learning theory: all-or-none, discrepancy, and density. The theory posited that if a schema or concept is not available, a young child responds to all-or-none changes in the state of a stimulus. Thus, very young babies become preoccupied with "peek-a-boo." Mother is present, then absent, then present again in a "peek-a-boo" sequence. This is a relatively brief period of eliciting and maintaining attention.

The more substantial aspect of this theory is discrepancy learning, the nature of learning that lasts throughout one's life. A discrepant stimulus is one that is slightly different from what an individual already knows in his or her repertoire of possible worlds. Thus, discrepancy is a psychological notion rather than an external notion. What may be discrepant for one individual may not be so for another.

Much research has been done on discrepancy learning (Kagan & Lewis, 1965; Lewis, 1970; McCall & Kagan, 1969). This literature was summarized earlier (Muma, 1978b). Much of this research was done at Harvard University. I had the privilege of observing some of these studies in action and carrying out similar studies with inner-city infants and preschool children living in poverty. The work was under the supervision of Phil Zelazo, then at Harvard University.

Both overt and covert measures were made of 3-month-old infants attending to discrepant stimuli. The overt measures included smiling, eye tracking, pointing, body orientation, and fretting. Smiling was particularly sensitive to information processing (Kagan, 1971; Sroufe & Waters, 1976). The covert measures included skin galvanic responses, respiration rate, and cardiac rate. Cardiac rate was very sensitive to discrepancy. Cardiac deceleration indexed an orienting response, whereas acceleration indexed hypothesis testing in which infants presumably reconciled discrepancies between what they knew and what they perceived. The thrust of this research is that variations of what is already known are potent in eliciting and maintaining attention.

This research raises major questions about the presumed value of repetition and drill. Such activities may actually interfere with learning. In addition, if an individual carries out such activities for an extended period and reaches 80% to 100% correct performance, another problem may occur. It is what might be called *overlearning*, when an individual concludes that what is learned is all there is to be learned, with the learning process essentially shutting down. Mandler (1983) also expressed concern that overlearning may yield different results than learning to mastery.

To what extent does the educational system wage an overlearning campaign with children? They are told to get 100% correct throughout their education, and the teachers are often the sole judges of what is right or acceptable: "If the teacher wishes to close down the process of wondering by flat declaration of fixed factuality, he or she can do so" (Bruner, 1986, p. 127).

K. E. Nelson (1981, 1989, 1991) drew on discrepancy learning for his theory of rare-event learning. Discrepancy learning is richly evident in the accounts by K. Nelson and Bruner dealing with scripts, formats, and shared meaning for events. Discrepancy learning is a basic assumption in the acquisition theory concerning intentionality by Bloom et al. (1988), who wrote, "Children will acquire words and language structures as the contents of their mental states become increasingly *discrepant* from the data of perception" (p. 106).

To give some indication of the potency of discrepancy learning and why it is desirable to deal with partial learning rather than overlearning, it may be useful to appreciate how these issues are addressed in *Sesame Street*. *Sesame Street* programs have a common theme. For example, "This program is brought to you by the number 'four.' " Then, the notion of "fourness" is exemplified in many varied ways. It is the variations that elicit and maintain the attention of the children. Also, the number of instances of "four" are many more than a child could possibly derive. Thus, children come away knowing that some instances of "four" were picked up, but also knowing that out in the world there are many other instances that are yet to be discerned. This induces children to become active learners rather than satisfied learners deceived by overlearning.

Another way in which discrepancy is incorporated in *Sesame Street* is that a topic is presented for a few minutes then it is dropped, only to be resumed a few minutes latter. During the interim, children are actively considering what might be going on and on returning to the topic, they are frequently surprised to find that developments occurred that they had not anticipated. This leaves them open to new developments in actual events in their own world. When the program returns to more instances of "four," the usual format is to incorporate some of the previously presented examples with some new ones added. This is discrepancy learning: It heightens attention and learning.

Another issue that was discussed in chapter 1 should be reiterated here: That the field of learning disabilities remains atheoretical (Cruickshank, 1972). The field of learning disabilities lacks construct validity simply because it is not derived from any recognized theory of learning. Discrepancy learning theory is one of several recognized theories that could be useful in defining a learning disability. Other worthy candidates are representation theory (Mandler, 1983), theory of dynamic systems (Karmiloff-Smith, 1992), and experiential cognition in forming the situated mind (K. Nelson, 1996).

Other issues in cognition that warrant implementation in the clinical fields include cognitive tempo, rule versus nonrule governed learning, iconic versus symbolic thinking, analytic versus synthetic thinking, technology of reckoning, perceptual salience, categorization, inferencing, and informativeness. Informativeness is summarized in the following and discussed in chapter 2; the others are addressed in the Muma Assessment Program (MAP; Muma & Muma, 1979).

BRUTE AND INSTITUTIONAL FACTS

Developments in the philosophy of cognition and language (Lakoff, 1987) have raised some fundamental questions about the traditional cognition literature. Traditionally, it was held that concepts should be defined objectively in order to obtain necessary and sufficient evidence. Such concepts or categories were considered neutral or free from bias. It was the role of science to discover the necessary and sufficient attributes of categories in order to ascertain which categories are which and to discern the nature of these categories. This is what Kaplan (1964) regarded as the "realist" approach. This whole endeavor reflects a Kantian philosophy and it is modeled strikingly on the so-called "hard" sciences; it parallels the thinking behind the periodic table in physics and Linnaeus' taxonomy in biology. In a sense, the necessary and sufficient criteria were efforts to discover natural categories or the periodic table of the mind.

Information about concepts or categories issuing from this perspective resulted in *brute facts* (Lakoff, 1987). Such facts, like norms, are context free. Brute facts are those that are formally defined; for example, dictionary meanings, laws and regulations, rituals, standard measures, and the like. Dictionaries provide necessary and sufficient meanings of words. However, most word meanings are neither acquired nor used by turning to dictionaries. Most word meanings are acquired as a function of experience in the world and such experiences become named.

Perhaps it should be recalled that McNeill (1966) indicated that language acquisition was experientially based rather than instructionally based. Bruner (1981) used the phrase *initial dubbing ceremony* to refer to the words provided to children and their immediate uptake in word learning. More recently, this process has been called word capture or fast mapping (Crais, 1992; Dickinson, 1984; Dollaghan, 1987; Heibeck & Markman, 1987; Rice, Buhr, & Nemeth, 1990). It has also been called "spontaneous" in contrast to "scientific" word learning (Vygotsky, 1962). In dubbing, capture, fast mapping, or spontaneous learning, words are given to what a child already knows to some extent; thus, such words have spontaneous meaning and not necessarily adult meaning. Such meaning is essentially vested in context and therefore it is not the same as that for brute facts. Thus, there are two basic kinds of word meanings: context-free, brute facts, and context-sensitive, experiential, or institutional facts.

Experiential realism contends that brute facts comprise a relatively peripheral aspect of psychological meaning and that experiential meaning is the essence of natural thinking and social commerce. Such meaning is based on institutional facts. *Institutional facts* are those that are mutually manifest (Sperber & Wilson, 1986). For example, two individuals usually do not need to define the necessary and sufficient parameters of "apple" to talk about apples. By virtue of presupposition, it is presumed that both individuals have spontaneous experiences that are sufficiently comparable to have mutually manifest appreciations of what apples are. Such appreciations are widely shared or institutional; therefore, conventional words may be used to index them in a functional matrix of given and new information. Should the need arise for new information about apples or a particular apple, appropriate words may be invoked.

Thus, the distinction between brute facts and institutional facts raises the distinction between traditional physics- and biology-based notions of cognition in general and categorization in particular and function- or experiential-based notions. This distinction is about the science of science and the science of human affairs. It is also about the difference between realist and instrumental approaches (Kaplan, 1964).

REPRESENTATION

Mandler (1983) provided a comprehensive review of the literature on representation. The following is a summary of issues that she raised. She began with the distinction between representation as knowledge and the way it is organized as contrasted with representation as a symbolic perspective. The focus of her work was the former (knowledge and organization).

The two fundamentally distinct kinds of representational knowledge are procedural and declarative. They are both attractive in accounting for representation but for different reasons. *Procedural representations* derive from knowledge of familiar scenes and events; they establish expectations and reference for appreciating variations. Furthermore, the hierarchical organization of procedural knowledge issuing from scripts not only allows for different levels of representation but provides building blocks of cognition. "Nelson and Gruendel (1981) suggest that generalized event representations are the building blocks of cognition; the formation of superordinate classes may be due in large part to a generalization across the things that go into particular slots in scripts and other schemata" (Mandler, 1983, p. 467).

Procedural representation deals with spatial and temporal information. Space schemata pertain to location and orientation, whereas event representation deals with the additional temporal, causal, or enabling dimensions. Schemata are constructions that themselves are motivated by top-down considerations of what was previously known. Direct experience affords opportunities to establish basic level schemata that become organized in a hierarchical way. The hierarchical organization itself provides a means of deducing superordinate realizations. With such realizations, declarative representation becomes progressively available. Thus, relations among schemata (either procedural or declarative) provide an individual the means to go beyond the information given (Bruner, 1973) and realize novel notions not only from direct experience but about the past, the future, and the plausible.

Such capacities become available because they have a hierarchical organization; they are open-ended by virtue of both top-down and bottom-up processing, and they are active and dynamic in nature. Although early cognition is somewhat data driven or stimulus bound and context bound, it becomes progressively released from direct stimulation and is both data driven (bottom-up) and concept driven (top-down) depending on the available repertoire and intended applications. Thus, early routines evolve into varied experiences providing a launching pad for learning. What is important is that declarative knowledge is initially derived from procedural knowledge but takes on its own potentials of going beyond the information given. With such capacities, "it is possible to turn one kind of knowledge into the other . . . children gradually become able to access knowledge beyond the demands of the immediate (procedural) context" (Mandler, 1983, p. 424).

Early on, when infants rely on procedural knowledge, perceptions and actions are context bound and thinking lacks symbolization. It is cognition of dependency and responsiveness to stimulation. Lacking symbolic cognition, the infant is unable "to query memory or to solve problems without recourse to action—in short, to think" (Mandler, 1983, p. 425). Said another way, the infant does not have the cognitive capacity to reflect on what he or she knows for applications of what to do.

Perhaps it is useful to turn to Fig. 4.2 to portray these and other related developments in the acquisition of representational capacities. Figure 4.2 is provided not only as a summary of these issues, but also as a call for a theoretical model in this arena. It should be noted that Mandler (1983), Karmiloff-Smith (1992), and K. Nelson (1985, 1986, 1996) have already picked up the baton so it is a belated call. It is nevertheless a valid call simply because this arena is on the threshold of redefining viable accounts of cognition as experiential cognition.

Symbolic capacities are very powerful in going beyond the information given. Mandler (1983) summarized the Piagetian view of symbols:

The symbol must be completely internalized; the symbol must be a mentally evoked image (or an intentionally chosen object used to stand for a class of objects or events); the symbol must be able to be used retrospectively for purposes of recall and prospectively for purposes of anticipating the future. (p. 426)

Procedural knowledge	Declarative knowledge
Context bound - - - - - - - - - - - - - -	Context free
Stimulus bound - - - - - - - - - - - - - -	Symbolic
Experiential - - - - - - - - - - - - - - -	Inferential
Topological - - - - - - - - - - - - - - -	Euclidean
Basic schemata - - - - - - - - - -	Superordinate awareness
Schema - - - - - - - - - - - - - - - -	Categories

FIG. 4.2. Implications of the distinction between procedural knowledge and declarative knowledge.

Perhaps we should add that symbolic representation as a conceptual capacity is richly invested in the constructionistic notions of inference and plausibility. Perception, for example, is not a passive event as was traditionally held; rather, "Perception is a constructive process and not merely a passive registration of stimulation" (Mandler, 1983, p. 430). "Perception of even the simplest stimuli is saturated with knowledge" (Mandler, 1983, p. 453). Inference plays a subtle and often decisive role in perception: "The economy of this sort of top-down, or conceptually driven, processing (Bobrow & Norman, 1975) means that much of what we think we have actually seen, we have only inferred" (Mandler, 1983, p. 454).

Mandler (1983) also referred to language as "a symbol system used to refer to other knowledge" (p. 431). Symbolic capacities relieve individuals from context-bound cognition and afford increased flexibility in accessing what is known and what can be done mentally. It constitutes a qualitative shift (not stage) in which "the onset of the ability need not be abrupt or even general across the entire system" (Mandler, 1983, p. 433). Such flexibility yields cognitive capacities that have multiple accesses to what one knows and conscious reflective abilities. Behaviorally, individuals self-monitor and self-correct what they say and do. Introspection is at hand.

In addressing various issues of representation, Mandler (1983) frequently referred to Piagetian accounts of cognitive acquisition. She was careful to acknowledge and appreciate various contributions of Piagetian theory, but she showed that the representational perspective raises major questions about Piagetian theory, especially concerning the acquisition of symbolic capacities and stages of learning. Regarding the later, perhaps the following comment will suffice:

The way in which knowledge is acquired remains functionally invariant throughout life. The principles of assimilation and accommodation together with the universal tendency to organize incoming information can be seen in all aspects of learning and development regardless of the age at which it is taking place. (Mandler, 1983, p. 476)

This carries a major substantive message for the clinical fields about the reliance on age as a metric for learning. Thus, there are both psychometric (Carrow-Woolfolk, 1985; Lawrence, 1992; Salvia & Ysseldyke, 1988) and substantive reasons for not relying on age as an assessment reference. Similarly, major questions have arisen about the validity of stages. Indeed, it is to Brown's (1978, 1988) credit that he, himself, was concerned about whether the five early stages, especially Stages III, IV, and V, of language acquisition were valid and that the relationships between age and mean length of utterance (MLU) over 4.5 may be an invalid index of language ability simply because individuals learn to shorten as well as lengthen sentences with increased verbal capacities.

COGNITIVE MODULARITY

Fodor (1983) raised a provocative issue about cognition that is closely related to Chomsky's (1980) notion of language as a unique cognitive capacity (Maratsos, 1989). It is the prospect that the brain may be organized and function in a modular fashion.

This issue is intuitively attractive (what Bever, 1992, termed "pretheoretically satisfying"). Intuitive support for this prospect exists in the following ways: primary sensory functions are evidently localized to particular areas of the cortex; the primary motor functions are similarly localized; language is localized in the left hemisphere whereas music is apparently localized in the right; children seemingly evidence spurts of language acquisition for words, grammar, and phonology differently; and in dementia, aphasia, and traumatic brain damage selected aspects of language seem to be affected. Thus, there are various issues that seem to make intuitive sense for modularity. Moreover, the modularity perspective seems to rely to some extent on cortical localization. To that extent, the modularity view seems to be another rendition of localization.

The reliance on cortical localization may, however, be a conceptual trap for cognitive modularity. The underlying premise is that if the primary sensory cortex and motor cortex are localized, therefore presumably modular, then it is likely that the whole cortex is organized similarly and therefore functions similarly. The conceptual trap has three dimensions. It pertains to the following:

1. Functions of the secondary sensory and premotor cortical tracts (Geschwind, 1965a, 1965b).

2. Functions of subcortical and interhemispheric cortical connections (Geschwind, 1965a, 1965b).

3. The extent to which language operates on shared cognition (Anderson, 1983; Bever, 1992; Karmiloff-Smith, 1992; Lakoff, 1987).

In the latter, information is in the coin-of-the-realm of mental processing. Thus, the modularity view would be difficult to hold for cognition in general and language in particular.

The extent to which cortical localization is evidenced is the extent to which modularity may be supported, but there is a glitch: The secondary sensory cortex and premotor cortex have abundant cortical connections with other parts of the cortex, connections to the opposite hemisphere, and subcortical connections. That is, secondary cortical connections could hardly be regarded as localized. The modularity perspective would be strapped to discern the functions of these connections as modular. Rather, it appears that the primary systems seem to be way-stations for provisionally processing information (coming in or going out) while the essential neurofunctions seem to be linked up—rather than modular—to functions in an integrative fashion. Fundamentally, why are the sensory systems interconnected if not for integration? Baddeley (1994) indicated that the function of the central executive system is "to coordinate information from separate subsystems" (p. 361).

Furthermore, there may be a subtle artifact in some of the research on brain localization of language. Technological advances now make it possible to localize brain functions for semantic, lexical, syntactic, and phonological capacities (see Tulving, 1995, Plates 1–27). Unfortunately, the timing is bad for this research for two reasons. First, it is necessary not to be too quick to take evidence of localization as evidence of modularity; that is, localization itself is not the same as modularity. As enticing as the localization evidence may be, it is also necessary to account for the richly evident connections within the brain, between hemispheres, and subcortically in order to tie down the significance of localization. Second, to isolate semantic, lexical, syntactic, and phonological processing as localized cortical capacities flies in the face of major advances in language over the past few decades. This strategy has a circularity that feeds itself whereby components of language (semantic, syntax, phonological, prosodic) may be cortically localized; but, unfortunately, the language literature has moved away from such compartmentalization just when the physiological studies want to preserve such distinctions as part of the localization and modularity perspectives. It is also plausible that such localization research merely finds the cognitive bin for mental processing of induced processing of a priori and externally contrived tasks rather than substantive bins of language itself. Just like the fancy factor analytic analyses are confined to what is put into them, so too may these kinds of localization studies be limited by themselves. It is when localization yields a perspective on intentional language used in actual social commerce that it may offer plausible accounts of relevant mental capacities. Even then, such localization needs to be tied down to interconnections to other parts of the brain.

Moreover, the sensory and motor systems share a function with cognition that is putatively against modularity—specifically *dynamism*: "Dynamic processes are in continual interaction with the experienced world, yielding ever-changing models of reality" (K. Nelson, 1996, p. 6). Cognition is inherently dynamic (Black, 1995) in nature. A fundamental principle of the brain in general is that it is dynamic in nature. The principle of dynamism (Muma, 1983b, 1986a) is that the more a system is used, the more it can be used; and conversely, when a system is not functioning it is vulnerable to loss of function.

Dynamism should be distinguished from the principles of elasticity, adaptability, and creativity or productivity. *Elasticity* is the notion that faced with a disruption or loss of a function, the brain is capable of recovering, to some extent, by virtue of compensation (Locke, 1994) and even restructuring or actual neurophysiological remodeling (Black, 1995; Chalupa, 1995). The brain has specialized potentials to function *adaptively* (Gallistel, 1995) in a physiological sense and in a behavioral sense. In language, for example, it is a given that individuals can shift or adapt to a new utterance to convey intended meanings of an utterance that did not work as intended and adaptability can be construed as a person's ability to share social commerce by switching between speaking and listening, switching between modalities of language (speaking, listening, reading, writing, gesturing), utilizing different aspects of the code matrix, and playing the communication game (Muma, 1975a) to realize communicative intent. Moreover, adaptability is crucial to effective problem solving (Karmiloff-Smith, 1992; K. Nelson, 1996).

Creativity or *productivity* is the cognitive ability to go beyond the information given (Bruner, 1973; Karmiloff-Smith, 1992; K. Nelson, 1996) and thereby generate novel utterances or comprehend them in particular contexts. For example, virtually all utterances in adult speech and progressively more in child speech are novel. Needless to say, it is difficult to know when and which early semantic functions and relations are productive. Greenfield and Smith (1976) appreciated the complexity of attributing productivity for early semantic skills after acknowledging the problem of not knowing which semantic skills may have been available before the skills that they studied. They commented further:

> A second problem is that frequency of occurrence, one aspect of productivity, is very much affected by situational structure, and some semantic functions are used only in relatively rare situations. Thus, measured productivity is a function of the context and, therefore, does not directly measure children's linguistic abilities. (p. 68)

There is plenty of behavioral evidence for dynamism. The motoric system is dynamic. Athletes train to their peak performances but know that to maintain such performances, and to extend them even further, it is necessary to continue training. If training should cease, a loss of skill is likely to ensue. The comment, "I'm at the peak of my game" is tacit recognition that such skills are inherently dynamic in nature. For individuals with cerebral palsy, it is necessary to establish a physical therapy and bracing program in order to maintain and hopefully extend motor function; otherwise, the dynamic nature of the system works against the individual, resulting in contracture and eventually atrophy.

The visual system is dynamic. When an individual has a muscle imbalance for the ocular muscles, a patch is placed over the "good" eye for brief periods, thereby forcing the "poor" eye to function. If this intervention is not done during a certain window of opportunity, a child could become functionally blind in the poor eye simply because that eye had not been used.

Apparently, the cognitive system is generally dynamic. When individuals strive to remember particular information, they reach a point whereby the more they remember the more they can remember—within limits, of course. Casual observation suggests that dynamism may be operating in language acquisition. That is, sheer talking time may be a significant issue in language acquisition and, by implication, language intervention. It is no surprise that those individuals that talk a great deal are also those that are more advanced in language acquisition. Similarly, those that are more active socially are also those that are socially more adept. Thus, the behavioral evidence of the dynamic nature of the central nervous system is apparent as well.

The clinical implications of dynamism seem to be redistribution or remodeling, reorganization, and compensation. That is, if a cognitive insult occurs, a cognitive function is not necessarily lost. The brain has recourse for redistributing or remodeling functions both locally (Chalupa, 1995) and hemispherically and even to establish compensatory functions (Locke, 1994). Such capacities, although speculative, are surely a threat to the notion of encapsulation in particular and modularity in general. Furthermore, it is likely that the more a system has been used, the more neural resource allocations (Locke, 1994) may be available for recovery.

Aside from the localization issue, the modularity perspective raises a fundamental notion about the architecture of cognition. Should cognitive modularity hold, it would mean that particular cognitive skills develop, function, and may be disrupted relatively independent of others, thereby providing a viable account of selective development and loss of cognitive functions. This would mean that there is a plurality of various cognitive functions such as different kinds of memory (Schacter & Tulving, 1994).

Cognitive neuroscientists, as they trace out the functional circuitry of the brain, should be prepared to identify adaptive specializations as the most likely functional units they will find. At the circuit level, special-purpose circuitry is to be expected everywhere in the brain, just as it is routinely expected in the analysis of sensory and motor function. At the cellular level, the only processes likely to be universal are the elementary computational processes for manipulating neural signals in accord with the laws of arithmetic and logic and for storing and retrieving the values of variables. (Gallistel, 1995, p. 1266)

Thus, physiologically speaking, it appears that modularity is upon us.

On the other hand, it may be that the modularity view is merely a convenient cognitive account lacking psychological validity. That is, if modularity does not hold, there would be reason to account for language and thinking in terms of general or shared cognitive capacities such as dynamism. In this view, language would share basic capacities of general cognition (Anderson, 1983; Bever, 1992; Karmiloff-Smith, 1992; Lakoff, 1987; Mandler, 1983; K. Nelson, 1996) rather than being unique (Chomsky, 1980; Fodor, 1983). Needless to say, three especially difficult issues for modularity are symbolization, representation or coin-of-the-realm of mental processing, and intent.

It may be that there are general principles of cognition that are manifest in different ways (Anderson, 1983; Karmiloff-Smith, 1992) or at different levels of cognitive architecture (Bever, 1992) that appear to be modular but lack sufficient validity for such an interpretation. For example, the notion of perceptual priming is a general capacity that is applicable across perceptual modalities. Baddeley (1994) indicated that perceptual priming is the operation of a single system "apparently extending across modalities and across processing levels" (p. 355). Yet, Baddeley held that a single system view of memory is inappropriate; he indicated that to assume that the "underlying process as a single system seems unnecessary and potentially rather misleading" (p. 355). Karmiloff-Smith (1984, 1992, 1994) identified three phases of information processing that were not modality specific and were shared with language and general cognition.

Bever (1992) conceded that modularity may pertain to the primary sensory and motor systems, but he was dubious about the possibilities for cognitive modularity:

> I pointed out that modular separation of capacities rooted in sensory or motor systems is not controversial. The modularization of cognitive skills such as language is controversial just because their neurological roots are difficult to determine. Furthermore, insofar as such skills assume the interaction of distinct kinds of levels of representation, impenetrability between levels occurs by definition. This follows from the fact that each level has its own internal computational language that is immiscible with that of other levels. Hence, experimental investigation may show modular-like segregation of levels of representation, results that would follow from their informational opacity, not necessarily from architectural segregation. (p. 206)

Bever (1992) then indicated that learning an abstract system such as language entails a general cognitive capacity, namely *abduction* (the antecedent of Piaget's notions of assimilation and accommodation): "The abduction of grammar in particular calls on general learning mechanisms not unique to language" (p. 207).

Abduction is the process (neither induction nor deduction) through which internally generated hypotheses interact with data as a person arrives at a correct abstract structure.... there are two contrasting forms of the interaction of data and internalized abstract hypotheses: In one method, new data can be used to refine an existing hypothesis; in the other, the data can be used to choose between competing alternative hypotheses. (Bever, 1992, p. 197)

Regarding language as seated in the left hemisphere (a potential issue for modularity), Bever (1992) raised another prospect, which is that the left hemisphere may be closely linked to language not because of cognitive capacities unique to language but instead because of general cognitive capacities: "Rather, the specific differences between the hemispheres reflects the logical distinction between relational and unary processing" (p. 193). Relational processing deals with the relations between entities, whereas unary processing "involves direct processing of a single representation" (p. 191). Thus, the fundamental difference between the hemispheres may not be particular mental capacities devoted to unique performance capacities such as language, but what Bever termed *raw computational power*. Similarly, the modular expectations for learning a lexicon (words) and for syntax as uniquely different are likely misdirected because the former deals with the basic cognitive capabilities of relating words to concepts, whereas the latter pertains to computational knowledge for rule acquisition. Moreover, in lexical learning, "Object recognition cannot inform word recognition" (Bever, 1992, p. 184). Also, "Language is better handled by the left hemisphere because of what language is, but the unique *cause* of what language is lies elsewhere" (p. 193).

The localization contention for modularity has a downside. Consider Geschwind's (1965a, 1965b) evidence about the localization of the primary sensory functions. In vision, for example, the primary visual cortex is localized in the occipital cortex, which by itself is a good candidate for modularity, especially because this cortex is isolated from the rest of the central nervous system by virtue of having only connections to the secondary visual cortex (Geschwind, 1965a, 1965b). Thus, it is not only functionally encapsulated but structurally encapsulated as well. The downside arises when considerations are made for the secondary visual cortex and subsequent connections within and between hemispheres and subcortically. In short, beyond primary sensory cortex the notions of localization and encapsulation (structurally and functionally) crumble for lack of validity. Herein lies a weighty problem for claims of modularity of language. In its defense, selective survival of different aspects of language after traumatic brain injury, dementia, or cerebral vascular insult and spurts of learning for selected aspects of language in early acquisition are weighty issues for modularity.

The notion of encapsulated function is basic to the notion of modularity. Such functions take raw input, vision for example, and convert it into the coin-of-the-realm of mental processing, thereby making the output of the visual module a mental message freed of modality and available for representational manipulation or representational redescription in general cognition. This means that the encapsulated nature of cognitive modules may be free from top-down or central influences. Thus, sensory detection, discrimination, and perception would presumably be good candidates for modularity. Unfortunately, however, research on signal detection, discrimination, and perception reveals a top-down influence. For example, Garner (1966) showed that in order to perceive something it is necessary to know; that is, conceptual knowledge determines what may be perceived (Mandler, 1983).

Advocates of modularity are not bothered by this apparent paradox. They maintain that top-down influences are made on modular output rather than directly on modular function.

Another issue that may be problematic for modularity is, interestingly enough, localization. Inasmuch as language relies on general cognition (i.e., categorization, inference, etc.) and decisions about what should be explicit in relation to what should be implicit for a message to work as intended, advocates of modularity of language are strapped with the very messy problem of attempting to deal with an encapsulated process that is already in the coin-of-the-realm of mental processing rather than dealing with raw input. In effect, advocates of modularity take a very peculiar stance. On the one hand, their position rests crucially on the notion of encapsulated cognition so in striving for continuity of argument they hold that language is modular—a Chomskian notion of a mental organ for language. However, it is necessary to be myopic for such a stance simply because language draws from possible world knowledge in order to know what to say or comprehend (Clark & Clark, 1977). By drawing from such knowledge, language could hardly be encapsulated. Thus, the encapsulation notion that is central to modularity becomes incoherent in accounting for language:

> The increasing acceptance of the modularity of mind has the effect of shunting language off into its own impenetrable modules, while the central processor (where all the interesting activity takes place) carries on in terms of manipulating symbolic representations in its own innately specified Language of Thought (Fodor, 1983). (K. Nelson, 1996, p. 4)

TABLE 4.2
Pros and Cons of the Modularity View of Language

Pros

Raw input (screen information, convert to usable form)
Encapsulation (primary sensory and motor cortex)
Localization (lexical, semantic, phonological processing)
Uneven acquisition of syntax, prosody, phonology, and pragmatics
Selective cortical effects of trauma and disease

Cons

Coin-of-the-realm (language does not operate on raw input; rather, it operates on the coin-of-the-realm of mental processing)
Nonencapsulated (richly interconnected: cortical, hemispheric, and subcortical)
Nonlocalization (general cognitive capacities: possible worlds, categorization, inference)
Dynamism (remodeling, redistribution, compensation)
Messages (intentionality)

Furthermore, the issuance of a message may or may not be linguistic, pragmatic, or gestural. This circumstance invites more complexity than it solves, and modularity is unattractive in accounting for such complexity. These issues are listed in Table 4.2.

Furthermore, Gropen, Pinker, Hollander, and Goldberg (1994) raised another issue that has a bearing on the language modularity notion. Gropen et al. indicated that the presumed similarity between noun inflectional acquisition and verb inflectional acquisition attested by Bowerman (1990) was not viable. From the Gropen et al. perspective, inflection learning for verbs is qualitatively different from that of inflectional acquisition in noun phrases. Such differences may implicate different modules. Thus, the module saga means that it would be necessary to invoke new modules for every qualitatively different aspect of acquisition. Needless to say, such a perspective would eventually prove unparsimonious in much the same way that learnability theory became unwieldy and unduly selective (Snow & Tomasello, 1989).

REPRESENTATIONAL REDESCRIPTION

Karmiloff-Smith (1984, 1992, 1994) proposed and substantiated the dynamic systems theory of cognition that occurs beyond modularity. That is, after information becomes representational or in the coin-of-the-realm of mental processing, it is available for various cognitive applications, such as long-term storage (Schacter & Tulving, 1994), manipulation for thinking and problem solving (Karmiloff-Smith, 1984), expression of relational meaning (implicit information placed in a useful relation to explicit information to make intentions recognizable) in communication (Clark & Clark, 1977; Sperber & Wilson, 1986), and various creative endeavors of going beyond the information given (Bruner, 1973) or representational redescription (Karmiloff-Smith, 1992), thereby yielding reflection, insight, wonder, conjecture, plausibility, metacognition, and art forms. From this perspective, the traditional views of cognition, namely detection, discrimination, perception, memory, thinking, and abstraction not only seem unnecessarily clumsy but detrimental to an adequate appreciation of cognition. That is precisely why the *architecture of cognition theory* (ACT; Anderson, 1983) and experiential cognition (K. Nelson, 1996) are so attractive.

Dynamic systems theory of cognition, also known as the representational redescription (RR) model, has three reiterative phases: procedural, metaprocedural, and conceptual. What is so attractive about RR is that it accounts for developmental changes across various cognitive systems whereby available representations "become progressively more manipulable and flexible, for the emergence of conscious access to knowledge, and for children's theory building" (Karmiloff-Smith, 1992, p. 17). Needless to say, psychological theory building pertains to one's theory of the world, possible worlds, or situated mind. Furthermore, "Whatever their age and whatever the domain, children pass through three recurrent phases in the way in which progress takes place both macrodevelopmentally and microdevelopmentally" (Karmiloff-Smith, 1992, p. 42).

The *procedural phase* (Phase 1) is a data-driven phase in which an individual is responsive largely to external stimulation. Thus, this adaptation to external stimuli means that the environment is largely in control of the behavior. This orientation is success oriented because it is "aimed at narrowing the distance between present state and goal state. Once the distance is zero, the child has attained procedural success" (Karmiloff-Smith, 1984, p. 42). This endeavor uses both positive and negative feedback to solve a problem. Interestingly, it can be successful with only positive feedback.

Although the cognitive end products of Phase 1 are representations, they have a major limitation, which is a lack of integration with other representations. These representations are merely compiled and are rather independent of each other. Thus, their uses yield seemingly competent behaviors, but such behaviors lack essential coherence with other potential behaviors that will eventually become integrated into a full-fledged system capable of rendering a productive skill. With this limitation, it is necessary for an individual to "recompute afresh for each part of a problem" (Karmiloff-Smith, 1984, p. 43). Eventually, such mental activity becomes clumsy and awkward simply because the system becomes excessively burdened with new input and limited storage capacity.

The *metaprocedural phase* (Phase 2) offers a solution to this mental burden. The solution is mental organization achieved by rewriting or redescribing Phase 1 representations into a coherent scheme: "Metaprocedural processes rewrite in explicit form the implicit information in the procedural representations in order to operate on them" (Karmiloff-Smith, 1994, p. 84). Two important implications of this mental organization are integration and a definition of usable information. Integration is very powerful because representations may be integrated within a domain and across domains. With this achievement, systems not only become coherent within but also between other systems including intermodality integration. With this available capability, modality processing becomes purged very early in information processing (Clark & Clark, 1977) with the bulk of information processing occurring on a representational level.

Mental organization defines what information (and what form of mental representation) is most usable to the system. Thus, a top-down governor is in place that, initially at least, dictates what information is usable. This means that the child is now more reliant on mental organization than environmental stimulation. Phase 2 is "an internally driven phase during which the child no longer focuses on the external data. Rather, system-internal dynamics take over such that internal representations become the focus of change" (Karmiloff-Smith, 1992, p. 19).

Interestingly enough, during this phase, a child is likely to have such a rigid theory-in-action (Karmiloff-Smith, 1984) that useful environmental feedback may be ignored, thereby yielding errant behavior, whereas previous behavior was successful but lacking cognitive integration. For example, it is well known that early on (Phase 1) children evidence a vocabulary stage wherein they would use appropriately inflected utterances (ate/eat, man/men) but subsequently (Phase 2) they would say ated/eated and mans/mens and then (Phase 3) they would say ate/eat and man/men. This curvilinear function for behavior is thus accounted for as three phases of cognitive acquisition. What is important about this curvilinear function is that deterioration occurs "at the behavioral level, not at the representational level" (Karmiloff-Smith, 1992, p. 20).

The *conceptual phase* (Phase 3) entails a balance between internal (top-down) and external control (data driven, bottom-up). A coherent and consolidated mental reorganization arises, affording the child a flexible and creative system that "can take environmental feedback into account without the overall organization being jeopardized" (Karmiloff-Smith, 1984, p. 44). What is achieved by Phase 3 is a cognitive system that is richly coherent and consolidated, capable of going beyond the information given in conscious and even unconscious ways. For example, Muma and Zwycewicz-Emory (1979) showed that responses to various kinds of linguistic contexts became progressively differentiated, integrated, and consolidated. Such representationally based capacities for human cognition are species specific: "The pervasiveness of representational redescription in human cognition is

. . . what makes human cognition specifically human" (Karmiloff-Smith, 1992, p. 192).

Karmiloff-Smith (1984, 1992, 1994) raised some very provocative issues not only regarding RR theory but research procedures that have provided substantiation for RR theory. She made a subtle but potentially very important observation about what research procedures have to offer. Specifically, she indicated that the guiding observations to substantiate her research was not so much the endpoint of performance (product) but the ways in which an individual went about addressing problem-solving tasks (process): "Minute details of children's ongoing behavior were recorded rather than the scores of the number of steps to solve a problem. Qualitative analyses were, in general, favored over quantitative ones" (Karmiloff-Smith, 1984, p. 45).

I can attest to the validity of this perspective of research. Recently, I asked a normal adult to do an object-sorting task based on the theory of natural categories (Rosch, 1973, 1978) in which five competing categories containing three focal and three peripheral items were to be sorted. The final sort was as expected. Each category was evidenced with its respective focal and peripheral exemplars. However, what was revealing in observing minute details of the ongoing behaviors was the fact that the focal items were sorted first (from a pile of randomly presented items) followed by the peripheral items. Furthermore, the participant verbalized about the peripheral items with such comments as "I don't know what I'll do with this one. I guess I'll put it here."

Another instance occurred with a child who responded to a series of cards containing three pictures on each card. The child was supposed to select two of the three items on each card. Instead, the child merely choose the first and third pictures throughout the task. Consequently, there was no opportunity to discern a pattern of choices for the variables on this task. I suggested to the research group that we should bring the child back for another chance to perform on the task, thereby allowing him to be selective. Strangely enough, the students in the research group took my suggestion as an indictment of my research ethics. They were indoctrinated by the psychometric fallacy that once a test is given, no matter what the performance, the data are precious. Yet, common sense indicates that this circumstance warrants another effort. Said differently, it would be ethically irresponsible to allow these data to be taken as evidence of his abilities; yet, this is the tacit implication of the one-shot live-or-die psychometric performance.

The theory of representational redescription raises some interesting notions concerning the child as a linguist, a physicist, a mathematician, a psychologist, and a notator. The child as a linguist refers not just to a child's abilities to learn words, grammar, and pragmatic devices, but to reflect on the nature of these abilities. It is this metalinguistic capacity that is uniquely human and that affords an individual the abilities to "go beyond the information given," to borrow a phrase from Bruner (1973). As a physicist, a child organizes data into a coherent understanding and holds such perspectives as reliable accounts or theories of the world.

> Children are not just problem-solvers. They rapidly become problem generators, and move from successful data-driven actions to theory-mediated actions that are often not influenced by environmental feedback. If ever children are empiricists, it is only very briefly as they first approach a new microdomain. Then, data are all-important. But subsequently children exploit the information that they have already stored in their internal representations. Children constantly develop theories, and they simplify and unify incoming data to make them conform to their theories. (Karmiloff-Smith, 1992, p. 88)

The child as a mathematician begins with the low end—the environmentally relevant end of the numeral community. After all, the infant is an N of one who is very much oriented on another one—his or her mother—and subsequently to a few. Thus, the infant's notion of numerosity is biased toward one or a few in an unlimited domain. What is putatively useful is not only sensitivity to "number relevant inputs" (Karmiloff-Smith, 1992, p. 114) but when these inputs become too numerous they can be reduced to a manageable size.

The child as a psychologist entails the development of a theory of the mind. A theory of the mind, like other theories, relies on inference, posits coherence for causal relations between mental states (thinking, feeling) and actions, attains an increasing awareness of the distinction between theoretical predictions and evidence (hypothesis testing), and has an explicit or conscious awareness of the limits of explanatory potentials (Karmiloff-Smith, 1992, p. 138). Furthermore, a theory of the mind is unique in that it recognizes the computational capacities for propositionality (plausibility) and for filling in when information is needed (inference). With these capacities, an individual can posit new thoughts and ideas that may be cast into language.

A child as a notator is one who not only has thoughts and ideas but intends to leave a trace of them. Karmiloff-Smith (1992) put it this way:

> There is something about the architecture of the human mind that enables children and adults also to produce external notations, that is to use cultural tools for leaving an intentional trace of their communicative and cognitive acts. Humans have a "print-out facility" (Wilks, 1982) for creating notations of various kinds. (p. 139)

Drawings by cavemen, Egyptian pyraminds, epitaphs, badges and uniforms, signatures, art forms, books, newspapers, and television are cultural devices for leaving a trace. Indeed, most cultural devices have such potentials.

Without much extension, each message—whether an utterance or a gesture—has an intentional trace to another. They are realized in a communal form for communication. From this perspective, children strive to acquire and use communal devices in the code matrix (i.e., grammatical, pragmatic, gestural, etc.).

These analogies of a child are interesting and provocative, but they have the implication that the learner is a miniature adult with the further implication that the learning process is linear in nature and a learner only needs to learn more to become an adult. However, there is plenty of evidence that in both cognitive and language acquisition such learning is often curvilinear if not qualitatively different from that of adult learning and performance (Bowerman, 1976; Gleitman, 1994; Rogoff, 1990; White, 1965). "Analogies abound in contemporary developmental writing to the child as scientist, linguist, philosopher, or psychologist, or . . . epistomologist. The view here denies all these analogies and insists that the child's mind differs qualitatively from that of these adult models" (K. Nelson, 1996, p. 9).

PROCESS, LEVEL, PHASE, STAGE, STRATEGY

There seem to be some disconnections between the clinical fields and the scholarly fields in cognition and language with regard to such basic terms as process, level, phase, stage, and strategy. The result is terminological confusion (Gallagher, 1991).

Turning to the dictionary, *process* can mean "a system of operations in the production of something" (*American Heritage Dictionary: New College Edition*). In this sense, process may have an acquisition connotation. This is precisely the way in which Prutting (1979) used the term to discuss various developmental sequences reported in the literature on language acquisition.

Another scholarly use of the term *process* is for the mental processes employed in coding or decoding messages in the realization of communicative intent. Thus, Clark and Clark (1977) detailed planning and execution processes in encoding messages and construction and utilization processes in decoding messages. Such processes provide the functional architecture of mental processing for speech acts (Sperber & Wilson, 1986).

In the clinical fields, process has been used in these ways, but it has also unfortunately been misused. For example, Semel and Wiig (1980) used the word *process* to refer to comprehension in contrast to production (Muma, 1984b). Others have used it to refer to language modalities (N. Nelson, 1989).

Fischer (1980) used the term *level* to refer to increasing complexity within a skill:

> The levels specify skills of gradually increasing complexity, with a skill at one level built directly on the skills from the preceding level. Each level is characterized by a reasonably well defined type of structure that indicates the

kinds of behaviors that a person (child or adult) can control at that level. (p. 479)

For example, at the motor level, a referential point may become a communicative point by virtue of taking on the added feature of eye contact to address the point to an intended participant (Bates, 1979; Bruner, 1981; Ninio & Bruner, 1978). At the word or lexical level, a communicative point, a referential display, and other forms of performatives become replaced by conventional words or vocables (Ferguson, 1978) or phonetically consistent forms (PCFs; Dore, 1975).

The replacement of one kind of behavior with another may implicate a qualitative change. When true qualitative changes occur, the individual cannot return to an earlier stage. This is what Gleitman (1981) characterized as metamorphosis or "tadpole-to-frog" changes. However, some changes may occur in which it would be difficult to attribute qualitative change. For example, the progressive attainment of representational abilities does not seem to be stagelike. Mandler (1983) indicated that the acquisition of representational abilities is progressive rather than stagelike, writing, "The way in which knowledge is acquired remains functionally invariant throughout life" (p. 476).

Karmiloff-Smith (1984) provided the following distinctions among stage, phase, and level.

> I wish to stress a distinction that I make in this paper between "stage," "phase," and "level." These terms are frequently used interchangeably (and thus atheoretically) in the developmental literature. A "stage" designates a stretch of time that is characterized by a qualitative change with respect to both the preceding and following stages. In other words, once a child has reached . . . stage 3, she does not return to stage 1. For the term "stage" to have any theoretical depth, it must, in my view, cover more than one particular domain of development and explain children's approach to problems *across* a variety of domains. . . .
>
> Another theoretical approach to behavior *across* domains is to invoke changes which, unlike stages, are considered to be *recurrent*. For this type of change, . . . I use the term "phase," with the hypothesis that children (and adults, for that matter) attack any new problem by going through the same three phases, both within the various parts of particular domains and across different domains. The phase concept is focused on underlying similarity of process, whereas the stage concept usually refers to similarity of structure. . . .
>
> Moreover, the recurrent-phase concept can be extended to the analysis of microdevelopmental change, whereas the stage concept cannot . . . while stages are loosely age-related, phases clearly are not.
>
> The term "level" will be used to designate qualitative changes *within* a specific domain, rather than across domains. Like stages, and unlike phases, levels are not recurrent. . . . The word "phases," then, refers to *general processes*

by which children interact with new issues and problems in different domains. By contrast, the word "levels" accounts for specific changes within a particular domain. Much of the developmental literature refers to "stages" where, . . . "levels" would be more appropriate. (pp. 40–42)

Flavell (1971, 1982) and Kessen (1962) provided additional discussions about the distinctions among structures, stages, and sequences. Qualitative changes may denote levels and they may culminate in a new stage. Thus, this example raises the distinction between level and stage. Expanded repertoires of performatives would be within a level; in word acquisition, expanded repertoires of conventional and nonconventional words would be within a level; furthermore, expanded referents for old words would be within a level.

In the clinical fields, such distinctions are usually not made, resulting in careless uses of terms (Gallagher, 1991). Sometimes two terms are even used interchangeably. Worse yet, *level* is often used clinically in a vague and obscure way: "We need to deal with children at their level." To say that a clinician is dealing with children at their level without establishing their repertoires is merely making an oblique comment open to virtually any interpretation. In phonology, for example, it is necessary to identify an individual's repertoire of phonological skills ranging from the phonetic inventory to homonymy to simplification processes to phonological avoidance. However, such comments have traditionally ignored an individual's repertoire of skills and relied on such notions as MLU, age, or grade levels linked to a psychometric test or measure. These notions of level are inadequate estimates of any particular cognitive or language domain. To say merely that a clinician is operating at a child's level without ascertaining relevant repertoires of skills is playing loose with a client and raising the prospect of misrepresenting the child, the clinician's competences, and the profession. To this extent, clinicians may be duped by their own claims.

As just mentioned, the notion of stage means that there is a qualitative shift. Bowerman (1976) and others have discussed stages of language acquisition. Bloom (1970, 1973) discussed a prelinguistic stage followed by the indicative stage (a period of acquiring basic semantic functions and relations) and then the grammatical stage. Brown (1973b), Schlesinger (1977), Greenfield and Smith (1976), and others have detailed various stages of language acquisition. Berman (1988) discussed three steps (stages) in language acquisition: pregrammatical (rote and formulaic utterances), structure bound (interim and end-state rule learning), and discourse oriented (refinements of use and scripting).

Piaget proposed stages of cognitive development. The significance of the sensorimotor stage is that an individual becomes freed from reliance on direct stimulation while becoming increasingly reliant on representation. Evidence of freedom from direct stimulation issues from evidence on object permanence, anticipation, deferred imitation, and symbolic play. However, Mandler (1983) showed that such freedom is a continuous process throughout life rather than the result of qualitative shifts indicative of stage changes.

Early complex hierarchical categorization and problem solving are largely confined to learning from the use of actual objects (physical or social) rather than from information in drawings or pictures. This raises the Piagetian notion of cognitive distancing. *Cognitive distancing* refers to the ease of cognitive processing for different kinds of stimuli. Information about actual objects is easier to process by virtue of varied actions (procedural knowledge) toward the objects than information about the same objects in pictures (primed conceptual knowledge). There is no opportunity to act on the objects in pictures; therefore, pictures only provide iconic information. Yet, pictorials provide more direct information than words (another form of primed conceptual knowledge). Words are dependent on the available stored information for the concepts underlying words. In short, the cognitive distancing hypothesis (Sigel, 1971; Sigel & Cocking, 1977) indicates that objects are psychologically easier to process than pictorials which are easier to process than words.

Cognitive distancing has direct clinical implications (Muma, 1978b, 1983b, 1986a). For example, Burger and Muma (1980) showed that individuals with aphasia with word-finding difficulties did significantly poorer categorizing objects according to peripheral exemplars than other individuals with aphasia and matched-age participants. The cognitive distancing aspect was incorporated in the study by having the participants categorize objects and then pictures of the same objects. There was an overall better performance for objects than pictures for the two aphasic groups and the matched-age group.

The Piagetian perspective placed much emphasis on object construction (psychological objects that were primarily physical objects but could extend to social objects), space, time, and causality. Such constructions were thought to be accomplished essentially as entities relatively freed of the social-cultural context in which the learner functions. The contemporary literature, however, views such perspectives as too narrow in which crucial social-cultural dimensions have been overlooked, notably social-cultural influences and intent. K. Nelson (1996) summarized such limitations of the Piagetian approach and she contrasted the Piagetian approach with the cognitive socialization approach that incorporates social-cultural considerations in cognitive and language acquisition:

> From the present perspective, knowledge of the physical, object world is embedded within knowledge of the social-cultural world of the human child, and it is the latter than enables and guides the former. . . . Actions of others, and interactions with important others, are as central—perhaps more central—to the child's knowledge schemas as the child's individual actions on objects.

. . . The infant's knowledge-constructing activity takes place within a social world. (pp. 5–7)

The notion of strategy is that there are alternative means of reaching a goal or of acquisition. For example, K. Nelson (1973b) showed that some children are referential learners and some are expressive learners. Dore (1974) showed that some children are message learners and some are code learners. Bloom, Hood, and Lightbown (1974) showed that some children are imitators and some are nonimitators. Bloom, Lightbown, and Hood (1975) found that some children are pronominal learners, whereas others are nominal learners. Locke (1979) found that some children used homonymy whereas others did not. Some children learn the object noun phrase before the subject noun phrase whereas others, the minority, do the opposite (Brown, 1973b). Thus, the cognitive socialization literature has identified several language learning strategies (Bates, Bretherton, & Snyder, 1988).

It should be stressed that the strategies of language learning that have been identified in the cognitive socialization literature are not the same as the strategies discussed in the clinical fields by those who advocate whole language, school language, and language in the classroom. For example, Buttrill, Nizawa, Biemer, Takahashi, and Hearn (1989) claimed to deal with a strategies-based model for language-learning-disabled adolescents. Unfortunately, it was very difficult to discern what they meant by the notion of strategies. In another example, L. Miller (1989) indicated that:

> Some common strategies used by successful learners are verbal mediation, rehearsal, paraphrasing, visual imagery, construction of concept networks and bridges, and the building of systematic retrieval strategies (Lasky, 1985). Language specialists have incorporated many of these strategies in their intervention programs (Tattershall, 1987; Wallach & Miller, 1988; Wiig & Semel, 1980). Though the research literature documenting the success of strategy-based language intervention is relatively sparse to date, those who use strategy-based programs report substantial progress among their students in terms of improved grades, fewer dropouts, and higher attendance rates in school (Bashir, 1987). (p. 161)

The extent to which this quote represents the clinical fields is the extent to which the clinical fields are disconnected with the scholarly literature on alternative strategies in language acquisition. Moreover, this quote is embarrassing for another reason. It contains a non sequitur that undermines itself, specifically the claims about "successful learners," acknowledged limitations in the literature concerning the success of strategy-based intervention, and "substantial progress." The obvious questions are where is the evidence that validates such claims and are the data significant? Without such evidence, these comments are merely dogma and hype—the signature of the clinical fields—rather than scholarly evidence.

It should be pointed out that the literature on alternative language learning strategies constitutes a heavy blow to the validity of developmental profiles and other psychometric normative tests. Such profiles and tests are based on the assumption of homogeneity and the assumption that a norm indexes a single unitary increment of acquisition. Alternative strategies of learning, on the other hand, provide evidence that heterogeneity is the issue rather than homogeneity.

Still another example of messy issues is the use of the word *process* by Semel and Wiig (1980). I (Muma, 1984b) showed that this and some other terms used by Semel and Wiig (1980) were bastardized in comparison to the two well-recognized uses of the term in the cognitive socialization literature. On the one hand, as indicated earlier, *process* may refer to acquisition processes or sequences (Prutting, 1979) and, on the other hand, it could refer to mental processes in comprehension (construction and utilization processes) and in production (planning and execution processes) as detailed by Clark and Clark (1977). Yet, strangely, Semel and Wiig (1980) used *process* to refer to comprehension. And, Tallal (1991) used the word to refer to different task processing demands; she then turned to a discussion of expressive and receptive processes. It appears that Tallal's use of the term *process* compares to Karmiloff-Smith's (1984, 1992) notion of phase.

In summary, the stage theories posit qualitative shifts from one stage to the next. Level refers to increased repertoires or complexity within a skill. Phase pertains to recurrent cognitive skills both within and between domains. Strategy refers to alternative means of achieving an end.

TOP-DOWN AND BOTTOM-UP PROCESSING

Information processing may proceed from the top down or the bottom up. *Top-down processing* is governed by what is known as possible worlds; this knowledge constitutes the substantive base for initiating and directing thought. This is what Anderson (1980) called *goal-directed processing* and what Norman (1968) called *conceptually driven processing*. In contrast, *bottom-up processing* begins with data, presumably raw data, that will ultimately be transformed to be compatible with existing representational information (Mandler, 1983, 1990). Such transformed data become the coin-of-the-realm of mental processing, thereby eventually becoming available for mental manipulation resulting in novel and creative cognitive endeavors.

To reiterate, the modularity (Fodor, 1983) view is that modular functioning is only bottom-up. Karmiloff-Smith (1992) summarized the modularity view as follows:

> The modules are deemed to be hard-wired . . . , of fixed neural architecture, domain specific, fast, autonomous, mandatory, automatic, stimulus driven, giving rise to shallow outputs, and insensitive to central cognitive goals.
>
> A further characteristic of modules is that they are informationally encapsulated (or, as Pylyshyn [1980] put it, "cognitively impenetrable"). Other parts of the mind can neither influence nor have access to the internal workings of a module, only to its outputs. . . . In other words, what the mind knows and believes cannot affect the workings of a module. (p. 3)

Thus, the modularity view does not deny top-down processing, it relegates such processing to the outputs of modules and beyond.

At first glance, it would seem that the Piagetian notions of assimilation and accommodation may have parity with the notions of top-down and bottom-up processing. In *assimilation*, new information is readily incorporated into existing representation because it is compatible with existing possible worlds. Such information verifies and extends existing knowledge. Thus, assimilation is governed by the existing substantive base. In *accommodation*, new information alters existing knowledge; such information is sufficiently different to cause the previous organization of information to change. The intrusion of new information in the system with the resulting change in the system itself smacks with the notion of bottom-up processing. However, there is more to the notions of top-down and bottom-up processing that nullifies a direct comparison to the Piagetian notions of assimilation and accommodation.

Anderson (1980) indicated that data-driven or bottom-up processing is "automatic, less capacity-limited, possibly parallel, invoked directly by stimulus input" (p. 126). In contrast, goal-directed or top-down processing "requires conscious control, has severe capacity limitations, is possibly serial, and is invoked in response to internal goals" (p. 126). These characteristics are not the same as the Piagetian notions of assimilation and accommodation. Thus, top-down and bottom-up processing are different than assimilation and accommodation.

LEFT–RIGHT PROCESSING OR TWO BASIC MODES OF THOUGHT

It is widely believed that the cerebral hemispheres operate somewhat differently. For right-handed people, the left hemisphere presumably serves a logical function, whereas the right hemisphere presumably serves an artful function. Thus, scientists may be functioning more with the left hemisphere than artists. There is also an intuitive gender difference. Men are generally thought to be more serious and logical than women, who tend to be more playful and artistic. Does this mean that there are hemispheric differences between the sexes? Furthermore, the cortical hemispheres typically evidence a left dominance for language but when "volumetric symmetry of the perisylvan areas occur" the two hemispheres apparently do not dance well together, resulting in various cortical difficulties such as language impairment (Locke, 1994, p. 609). Could this be relevant to the early finding that stutterers have a much higher incidence of ambidexterity than the normal population (VanRiper, 1954)?

In addition to hemispheric differences, consider the distinction between two basic modes of thought, scientific or paradigmatic and humanistic or narrative (Bruner, 1986). The *scientific mode* is one that relies on the "heartlessness of logic" (Bruner, 1986, p. 18) and strives to establish how things fit into categories. *Causality* is the irreducible mental category for this mode. This mode seeks to establish logical relations and presumes control of issues.

The *humanistic* or *narrative mode* is a "concern for the human condition" (Bruner, 1986, p. 14). The human condition may be manifest simultaneously in action or in consciousness. Action entails at least intent, agent, and a goal, plus a presumed means for achieving the goal. Consciousness entails knowing, thinking, and feeling. In this mode, knowledge of the real world is implicit. The humanistic or narrative mode "deals with the vicissitudes of human intentions" (Bruner, 1986, p. 16). Thus, the irreducible mental category for the scientific mode is *causality*, but it is *intent* for the narrative mode.

What is putative about both modes of thought is that they "trade on presupposition" (Bruner, 1986, p. 28). Thus, the two basic modes of thinking are fundamentally different yet they share the same underlying mental process. Furthermore, Bruner did not strive to attribute one mode to one cerebral hemisphere and the other mode to the other hemisphere. He was more interested in functions of the brain than topology. Further discussion of the two modes of thought appears in Appendix B.

MODALITY PROCESSING

Traditional clinical views have made much of modality differences. Clinicians held that there are crucial differences between the expressive and receptive language modalities or comprehension and production. Strangely, Paul (1995) attributed this view to Chapman et al. (1992) and J. Miller (1981). Furthermore, differences between speaking and writing and between listening and reading were regarded as important issues in clinical assessment and intervention of language. Indeed, many of the language tests and intervention programs have been based on presumed differences between language modalities. Another traditional modality view has been the so-called notions of auditory, visual, and tactile stimulation or processing. In short, the modality perspective has three faces:

1. Expressive and receptive modalities.
2. Speaking, writing, gesturing, reading, and listening.
3. Tactile, auditory, and visual stimulation or processing.

There are differences between language modalities, but I (Muma, 1978b, 1986a) held that such differences are relatively peripheral in comparison to the core issues of language. This topic was discussed in chapter 2.

The traditional modality views may be excessively peripheral to the core issues of language. Rather than modalities, it could be argued that the extent to which the clinical fields address the core issues of CCCE is the extent to which these fields are compatible with the cognitive socialization literature and therefore render appropriate services. On the other hand, the extent to which the peripheral aspects of language are evidenced in the clinical fields at the expense of the core issues would define the clinical fields as marginally valid.

The notion of auditory processing in the clinical fields is an instance of a commitment to a modality view. Proponents of auditory processing in the clinical fields have largely ignored the relevant literature on information processing and steadfastly held to their beliefs by virtue of rather simplistic reasoning. They reason that if children hear a sentence they are doing auditory processing, whereas if they see a sentence they are doing visual processing. They believe, intuitively, that this is not only patently true but essentially true.

However, the information-processing literature (Clark & Clark, 1977; Leonard, 1987, 1989; Rees, 1973, 1981; Tallal, 1990) has raised serious questions about the significance of auditory processing. In a comprehensive review of the literature pertaining to encoding and decoding messages, Clark and Clark (1977) showed that auditory information is purged very early in information processing with the bulk of mental processing devoted to inference and problem solving focused on the proposition of a message in the realization of communicative intent (Sperber & Wilson, 1986).

Infants have a tendency to finger, touch, and mouth objects in their environment as an early means of learning. Scholars in cognitive development have appreciated the significance of these activities in dealing with sensorimotor acquisition (Piaget, 1952, 1964), enactive processing (Bruner, 1964; Mandler, 1983), and embodiment (Lakoff, 1987). The traditional modality account has been to view such activities as tactile in nature. However, the modality or tactile account misses the crucial nature of such activities, especially manipulation. The sensorimotor, enactive processing, and embodiment perspectives all recognize that the crucial notion of going beyond the information given or beyond tactile stimulation is an infant's ability to act on objects as a means of embodying knowledge. For example, an infant fingers, touches, and mouths a ball or block as a means of learning what to do with it. To merely say that the infant receives tactile stimulation from these acts greatly underestimates what is transpiring. The significance of learning by virtue of embodiment and enactment is that such activities constitute an individual's functional knowledge not only of objects in the environment but notions of agency in relation to these objects. An appreciation of these perspectives leads to an understanding that functional or dynamic attributes precede static attributes in object knowledge acquisition (K. Nelson, 1974).

There is, however, reason to posit a brief or transitory modality perspective for learning in general and speech acquisition. Baddeley (1994) described the phonological loop as a mental process that is tailored to function in learning in general and speech acquisition in particular. This loop has two components:

> A brief speech-based store that holds a memory trace, which fades within approximately two seconds, coupled with an articulatory control process . . . which resembles subvocal rehearsal, is capable of maintaining the material in the phonological store by a recycling process, and . . . feed information into the store by a process of subvocalization . . . auditory spoken information gains automatic and obligatory access to the store. (pp. 356–357)

This sounds remarkably similar to the account provided by Clark and Clark (1977). Gathercole and Baddeley (1990) showed that individuals with specific language impairment evidenced marked impairment for repeating material such as nonwords of varying length, which is also a good predictor of vocabulary acquisition (Gathercole & Baddeley, 1989).

Baddeley (1994) described another candidate for modality processing—the visuospatial sketchpad. This is also a brief storage mechanism for registering visuospatial information and refreshing it by rehearsal. This sketchpad has two types of components—pattern-based and spatial—that evidently function somewhat independently.

Anderson (1983) indicated that cognition has three basic kinds of mental representations: temporal, spatial, and abstract. This is what he called "the tri-code theory of knowledge representation . . . a temporal string, which encodes the order of a set of items; a spatial image, which encodes spatial configuration; and an abstract proposition, which encodes meaning" (p. 45). Table 4.3 shows the properties of these kinds of representations.

"The basic assumption is that representations can be defined in terms of the processes that operate on them rather than the notation that expresses them" (Anderson, 1983, p. 46). It is important to note that Baddeley (1994) was considering memory processes as an entity, whereas the Anderson (1983) ACT theory of cognition is a general theory of cognition that no longer carries the traditional distinction of memory as a separate cognitive domain (Fivush & Hudson, 1990). Both raised the prospect of modality processing

TABLE 4.3
The Properties of the Three Kinds of Representations

Process	Temporal String	Spatial Image	Abstract Proposition
Encoding process	Preserves temporal sequence	Preserves configural information	Preserves semantic relations
Storage process	All or none of phrase units	All or none of image units	All or none of propositions
Retrieval process	All or none of phrase units	All or none of image units	All or none of propositions
Match process			
Degree of match	End-anchored at the beginning	Function of distance and configurations	Function of set overlap
Salient properties	Ordering of any two elements, next element	Distance, direction, and overlap	Degree of connectivity
Execution: Construction of new structures	Combination of objects into linear strings, insertion	Synthesis of existing images rotation	Insertion of objects into relational slots, filling in of missing slots

Note. From *The Architecture of Cognition* (p. 47), by J. Anderson, 1983, Cambridge, MA: Harvard University Press. Copyright © 1983 by Harvard University Press. Reprinted with permission.

to some extent—as a transitory process. Inasmuch as considerations of sensation, discrimination, perception, and memory entail central or executive governing processes such as representation and inferencing, modality distinctiveness in appreciating cognition seems to be less useful than how the modalities function in relation to each other to provide the learner with a functional rather than a modality perspective of the world.

As the result of a comprehensive program of research on auditory processing, Tallal (1990) concluded that information processing was not modality specific, and therefore, the problems that individuals evidence with language are not modality specific. Tallal (1990) said, "These deficits are neither specific to speech stimuli nor confined to the auditory modality" (p. 616). Tallal added, "The deficit in rapid temporal analysis and production is not specific to linguistic information per se, or to the auditory modality" (p. 617). This is a heavy blow to the credibility of the traditional modality view.

The clinical fields have various tests and intervention activities that claim to deal with auditory processing and modality differences but the relevant literature indicates that information processing in language—although briefly modality specific for auditory and spatial information—is essentially committed to representation (initially functionally invested in embodiment and procedural or event knowledge) and inference, which are modality free. Thus, much of what goes on in the clinical arena that presumably deals with modality differences may be not only of limited value, but it may also miss the crucial functional achievements that are taking place. Rather than amplify possible modality processing, it behooves the clinical fields to attend to the mental processing that is evidenced by various tasks that are deemed to be modality processes. The tasks for cognitive tempo, analytic and synthetic processing, rule and nonrule governing learning and flexibility of learning, and symbolic (functional) and iconic thinking all use picture selection as a way of establishing patterns of performance for attributing each respective mental capacity. Strangely, the clinical fields look at these tasks as if they were visual processing tasks, whereas the cognitive psychology literature, from which these tasks were taken, regards these tasks as providing evidence of different kinds of mental processes.

Taking the visual processing perspective effectively puts blinders on the clinical fields whereby the modality perspective overrules a mental processing perspective. In doing so, the clinical fields have effectively dismissed or overlooked potentially useful information for understanding various cognitive aspects of these tasks. One solution for this dilemma for the clinical fields is to attend more appropriately to the cognitive literature simply because the modality view and the all-purpose memory view are merely convenient ploys that effectively miss important substantive issues in cognition. Another solution is to appreciate various models of the cognitive bases of language because they put the modality view into perspective with other mental processes. Both solutions are compatible.

As for cognitive models, the representation model by Mandler (1983) puts procedural and symbolic knowledge into perspective. This model coupled with that of Karmiloff-Smith (1992) puts the modularity model into perspective with the more crucial central mental processes. K. Nelson's (1996) experiential cognition model is a much more comprehensive model that unifies input cognition (modality, procedural, script) with central cognition (coin-of-the-realm of mental processing) toward obtaining a biological, psychological, verbal, emotional, social, and cultural situated mind. Cognitive models that are more specific to language include those by Clark and Clark (1977), Sperber and Wilson (1986), and Muma (1986a), which are predicated on speech act theory.

EXPERIENTIAL COGNITION

As indicated earlier experiential cognition (K. Nelson, 1985, 1986, 1996) offers a major new perspective on cognition in general and language in particular. This development offers such a fundamental change in understanding these substantive areas that it has been used throughout the entire book. Rather than reiterate the various issues here, only some basic principles are mentioned. It is anticipated that interested readers have already grasped the importance of this development and will see further implications in the rest of the book.

The general cognitive capacity has been historically regarded as intelligence or, psychometrically, as simply IQ. These constructs have essentially lost their values by virtue of becoming popularized. In the contemporary cognitive socialization literature other renditions of intelligence have emerged. They are the notions of possible worlds or situated minds. What is putatively attractive about possible worlds and several other sister notions is that they are about active dynamic cognitive capacities that are the products of both biological faculties and experience (K. Nelson, 1996). Alternative perspectives to possible worlds include theory of the world (Palermo, 1971, 1982), Whole-Earth Catalogue (Mandler, 1983), world model (K. Nelson, 1996), and situated mind (K. Nelson, 1996). These perspectives are attractive because they ascribe the role of experience in acquiring cognitive and language capacities. Thus, they depart substantially from the traditional perspectives in which cognition and language were thought to be stand-alone products of sensation. Furthermore, they are dynamic in nature simply because experience is ongoing social–cultural experience. Inasmuch as experience is socially and culturally biased, one's possible worlds are inherently shaped accordingly. Such perspectives do not deny biological influences; rather, they bring to the front the notion that cognition is very much the product of social and cultural influences. "Human minds are equipped to construct complicated 'mental models' that represent the temporary as well as enduring complexities of our social and cultural world" (K. Nelson, 1996, p. 12). "The primary cognitive task of the human child is to make sense of his or her situated place in the world in order to take a skillful part in its activities" (K. Nelson, 1996, p. 5). Mandler (1979) indicated that "Cognitive growth occurs mainly in a social nexus" (p. 375). These quotes and the attendant literature underscore and substantiate Brown's (1956) earlier observation that language acquisition is "a process of cognitive socialization" (p. 247).

K. Nelson (1996) envisioned the cognitive acquisition process as two tiered somewhat similar to that described by Macken (1987) and Mandler (1983): "Cognitive change involves movement from the procedural to the computationally accessible (where procedures may be recombined or broken apart) and then to the consciously accessible (where the knower can consciously reflect on and manipulate procedures)" (K. Nelson, 1996, p. 14).

Moreover, coherence apparently is a driving and unifying acquisition force. That is why the traditional interest in negative evidence as a means of delimiting rule acquisition toward the prevention of rogue languages may have been a wrong turn. Cohesion may be perceived as a unifying force for codification both grammatically and pragmatically that makes social–cultural

dynamics fluid. Apparently cohesion is such a powerful and pervasive dimension that it was until recently overlooked or simply missed. In any case,
the acquisition of both cognition and language benefits greatly by positive
instances once an individual has achieved a basic repertoire that enables
the learner to appreciate coherence: "In this view cognition is a self-organ-
izing system that is success driven" (K. Nelson, 1996, p. 14).

TWO MODES OF THOUGHT

Bruner (1986) discussed two basic modes of thought (which were also known
as two castles). They are the paradigmatic (the castle of science) and
narrative (the castle of human affairs). *Science* strives to categorize the world
toward understanding causality. In contrast, *narrative* is oriented on intent
and context toward the realization of intent.

Science is said to be neutral or objective whereas, human affairs is said
to be humanistic or subjective. The former is said to be scientific but the
latter is experiential. The former is context free, whereas the latter is context
sensitive. Finally, the former is said to be nonintentional, whereas the latter
is intentional. Anthropologists have raised similar distinctions, specifically
the *emic* (experiential) and *etic* (experimental) approaches; these assessment distinctions have been raised in speech-language pathology (Bloom &
Lahey, 1978). These distinctions between the scientific mode of thought and
the narrative mode appear in Table 4.4.

The domain of science is not the same as the domain of human affairs;
therefore, each should have its own set of principles and methodologies.
Even the cardinal principle of objectivity for the sciences has been challenged both conceptually and empirically. Conceptually, Lakoff (1987)
showed that objectivity is a myth simply because there is no access to a
"God's-eye view of reality" (p. 164). Whatever is done in the name of science
and neutrality or objectivity is the product of human endeavors. In this
sense, science and objectivity are ultimately subjective.

TABLE 4.4
The Distinctions Between the Scientific
Mode and Narrative Mode of Thought

Scientific Mode	Narrative Mode
Brute facts	Institutional facts
Neutral, objective	Experiential, subjective
Context free	Context sensitive
Nonintentional	Intentional
Realist	Instrumental

Empirically, Quine (1978) held that even the hard sciences are fundamentally subjective. He indicated that in physics, for example, about 99% of the effort is conceptualizing and 1% is observation (see Bruner, 1986). The importance of the subjective enterprise in science, hard or behavioral, is discipline. The extent to which the subjective aspects of science are disciplined is the extent to which subjectivity plays a useful function.

With these differences between the scientific and narrative modes of thought there has been a concern that principles of so-called objective science may have been superimposed on the humanities, resulting in a disservice to understanding some aspects of the humanities. For instance, when performance on a standardized test is compared to that of spontaneous social commerce, the results may be in conflict. The obvious question when such conflicts occur is which results should be believed? The traditional view has been to accept the standardized normative test results as the preferred evidence simply because such results were presumably objective and provided necessary and sufficient evidence. However, it may be more appropriate to accept evidence issuing from actual social commerce simply because such evidence is more relevant to an individual's repertoire of skills and the product of the contexts in which the individual functions. Coupled with various concerns about the lack of construct validity for various normative tests, the latter course may be more appropriate. Indeed, Donaldson (1978) provided compelling evidence that the latter is indeed a better choice, assuming, of course, that the evidence was obtained in a disciplined manner. Appendix B provides further discussion of the distinctions between science and human affairs.

COGNITIVE-SOCIAL BASES OF LANGUAGE

Recall that chapter 2 gave a model for the cognitive-social bases of language and many clinical implications were discussed. It is necessary to return to this model here for further discussion.

Before addressing details of the cognitive-social bases of language, it is necessary to make some general comments. First, it should be abundantly clear that the notion of intelligence is not synonymous with the cognitive-social bases of language. Various efforts to show a correlation between intelligence testing and language acquisition are superficial to the substantive question of the cognitive-social bases of language.

Second, the relations between language and thought are not isomorphic (Sinclair, 1969). Isomorphism was the basic premise concerning linguistic determinism, which held that language determines thought, verbal mediation studies in the 1950s and 1960s notwithstanding. If there was a direct or isomorphic relation between thought and language, it would be necessary to memorize literally millions of sentences and the appropriate contexts of their use. That is, isomorphism (direct one-to-one correspondence between thought and language) would be such a violent and ruthless threat to generative capacities that it would be their utter downfall. Thankfully, isomorphism does not hold simply because it is possible and pervasively true that many different messages can convey essentially the same thoughts toward the recognition of communicative intent. For example, if the sentence "I like Coke" does not work as intended, the encoder has recourse to other messages that may work such as "Give me a Coke" or "Would you please give me a Coke?"

However, K. Nelson (1996) revived linguistic determinism not so much from the perspective of isomorphism but from the perspective that one's social–cultural context plays a major role in shaping what is thought and said. We are prone to think and talk about things that are socially and culturally relevant. This reflects the neo-Vygotskian perspective (Rogoff, 1990; Wertsch, 1991).

Third, all four CCCE domains are inherently cognitive. As indicated in chapter 2, dualists take a myopic view of cognition by asserting a distinction between mind and brain whereby the mind may be dismissed, leaving the study of the brain as the only important domain of study. Such thinking effectively dodges the mind as a crucial domain of study (Bruner, 1990; K. Nelson, 1996; Searle, 1992), which is central to an appropriate understanding of cognition. Fourth, the mental processes for language are not unique but processes in general cognition: intent, representation, and inference. "Language, for all its peculiarities, uses conceptual properties from nonlinguistic systems in central aspects of its semantics and structure (Jackendoff, 1983)" (Maratsos, 1989, p. 110). Fifth, language use is essentially that of calling on explicit content in relation to implicit content to make intentions recognizable. The mental decisions and processes used to carry out this task are crucially cognitive. Sixth, the actual realization of messages in social contexts means that for the substantive relations of informativeness to work as intended it is frequently necessary to negotiate appropriate messages. Thus, language learning and use occurs in cognitive socialization or in a social nexus (Mandler, 1979; K. Nelson, 1996; Rogoff, 1990).

Given the inherent CCCE model in the contemporary cognitive socialization literature and its application to the identification of language impairments, it is useful to reiterate the four main levels of the cognitive-social bases of language model and discuss them further. These levels are general cognitive base, substantive functions of grammar and pragmatics, cognitive processes underlying messages, and metacognitive and metalinguistic capacities.

General Cognitive Base

In order for a child to have a reason to communicate—indeed think—it is necessary to know something about the world. With this knowledge, individuals become motivated to name objects (social, physical, abstract) and agents in their world and to predicate perceived relations. In this sense, basic cognitive development is an antecedent to language acquisition. Subsequently, language itself plays an important role in mediating cognitive development (K. Nelson, 1996). Thus, cognition and language are inextricably related with each deriving acquisition from the other: "Cognitive development is not separable from language" (K. Nelson, 1996, p. 4).

The general cognitive base in this model includes fundamental cognitive capacities of categorization and inferencing extending to symbolic play and representational redescription in problem solving and thinking. Categorization is the content and structure of abstraction or mental representation. Abstraction is mental representation of previous experience. Mental representation is organized in such a way that needed information can be readily recovered or recalled for use in thinking or language. This general abstract repository of information about previous experience provides a theory of the world (Palermo, 1971, 1982), possible worlds (Bruner, 1981, 1986), or situated mind (K. Nelson, 1996) from which known or given information is used to deal with new information.

Mandler (1983, 1990) studied mental representation extensively. Karmiloff-Smith (1984, 1992) has a provocative theory in this arena called *representational redescription*. Flavell (1985) summarized the literature on mental representation. The Mandler model indicates that mental representation has two basic functions—knowledge, especially script knowledge early on—and symbolization. Early on, knowledge is organized according to one's knowledge of events. Such knowledge is about routines, formats, and scripts (Bruner, 1981; K. Nelson, 1981b, 1985, 1986). Subsequently, this knowledge becomes expanded and redescribed representationally, thereby yielding a flexible, coherent, and creative cognitive system. Moreover, this symbolic system converges on the meanings shared by others (K. Nelson, 1985, 1986, 1996; Rogoff, 1990) resulting in a socialized cognitive system for thinking and language.

Deregowski (1977) described these two functions of mental representation (knowledge and symbolization) in the following way: "One refers to the artifacts created by the child which are intended to represent the external world, the other to the internal schema or frames of reference which the child uses in his interaction with the external world" (p. 219).

The Piagetian sensorimotor period is regarded as a time when the infant lacks representation or symbolization; therefore, infants in this stage presumably lack the cognitive abilities for symbolic activity, namely thinking and imagining. According to Mandler (1983), "It is a most unproustian life, not thought, only lived" (p. 424). At the end of the sensorimotor period, mental representation begins to emerge thereby freeing infants from direct stimulation. "Sensorimotor knowledge . . . is subsymbolic knowledge; it is knowing how to recognize something or use a motor skill, but it does not require explicitly knowing *that* something is the case" (Mandler, 1990, p. 236). However, Mandler (1983, 1990) showed that infants early in the sensorimotor stage may be capable of some symbolic behavior. As Mandler (1990) indicated, the former accords well with knowledge of events and script theory (knowing how), whereas the latter accords well with categorization (knowing that).

Turning to space perception, Mandler (1983) credited Piaget as follows, "Piaget emphasizes that the representation of space is a construction, not a simple reflection of perception" (p. 443). Indeed, one's concepts govern perception (Garner, 1966). This, of course, has a major implication for the clinical fields wherein it has been erroneously believed that visual and even auditory processing drive the conceptual system. Here the clinical fields interests in visual and auditory processing have been apparently disconnected from the scholarly literature.

Mandler (1983) indicated that an individual shifts from an orientation about self (egocentric) that is subjective to an orientation about nonself (allocentric). Acredelo (1978) indicated that this shift is facilitated by an infant's increased mobility.

In mental processing, stimulation does not work alone; it is necessary to convert input information into a usable form or the coin-of-the-realm. Thus, it could be said that input is actively calibrated to the system. Evidently, short-term memory provides the interim buffer for converting input into the coin-of-the-realm.

The notion of a situated mind (K. Nelson, 1996) is the most eloquent cognitive-social perspective to date. It is eloquent because it breaks away from the traditional cognitive model and addresses the contributions of biological, cognitive, verbal, emotional, social, and cultural influences in both acquiring and using thought and language. It is eloquent because it defines the situated mind in regard to intent and context and because it provides an acquisition sequence that is ecologically valid. This sequence proceeds from early shared event knowledge for making sense of one situated place to mimesis (various forms of imitation and re-enactment), which is not merely imitation of behaviors but carries the sociocultural weights of identification, turn taking, and intention. Mimesis is followed by semantic knowledge (categorization, representation) toward establishing narrative or the storied mind grounded in the social–cultural events of one situated place. Then an individual acquires a theoretical perspective that affords an individual cognitive capacities for going beyond the situated mind to speculation, inference, imagination, plausibility, and reflection (metacognition and metalinguistics). It is eloquent because it provides a continuum rather than a stagelike perspective. Thus, early capacities continue to be available.

Inference is an essential function of action, perceiving, knowing, and thinking. In action, inference is needed to solve the problems concerning intent, agent, appropriate action, object or goal, and means of achievement. The action of eating a cookie entails wanting food (intent), someone (agent), eating (action), a cookie (object), and chewing (means). The act of communicating entails a desire to communicate (intent), speaker (agent), utterance (action), explicit information in the context of implicit information (object), and conventional and even unconventional codes including the code matrix (means). Table 4.5 illustrates these parallels. These issues entail inference and problem solution operating on knowledge of the world or possible worlds.

Such rudimentary problem-solving skills, based on inference, are evidenced with toddlers (Rocissano & Yatchmink, 1983). Problem solving is the fundamental cognitive skill in perception (Garner, 1966) in general and in speech perception and comprehension (Clark & Clark, 1977). It is also central to knowing, understanding, thinking, and creativity. For these endeavors, possible worlds provide the abstract substantive base for identifying and resolving cognitive discord.

To reiterate, Karmiloff-Smith and Inhelder (1974–1975) studied inferential and problem-solving skills of children from 4 to 9 years old. The title of their article was "If You Want to Get Ahead, Get a Theory." This title conveyed their findings that as children develop more sophisticated theories about what to do in problem-solving tasks they become increasingly more adept in solving the problems facing them. Yet, behaviorally, they take a circuitous route in doing so because they evidence a curvilinear function whereby their theories are initially useful but subsequently become bothersome until the children are able to appreciate the conditional limitations of their theories (Karmiloff-Smith, 1984, 1992).

One kind of task presented to the children was a beam-balancing task. Children were given a variety of beams that required a variety of solutions. Children from 4 to 6 years old relied on proprioceptive information—data-driven solutions. They tended to begin with a group of several different

TABLE 4.5
Parallels Between Action (Eating a Cookie)
and Communication (Requesting a Cookie)

	Intent	Agent	Action	Object	Means
Action	Want	Someone	Eat	Cookie	Chew
Communication	Desire	Speaker	Utterance	Explicit/implicit information	Conventions

actions but progressively narrowed down the potential actions to those that were shown, by trial and error, to work. They usually used length of the beam (geometric center theory) for their solutions. This worked for simple beams but not for some of the other beams.

Beyond their eventual solution, the manner in which they approached the task was most revealing. Simply put, early on, they attempted to solve each task as an independent event wherein each solution was recomputed anew. Children between 6 and 7 years old generated theories and were resolute in the applications of their theories even to the extent of having more errors than the younger children. This is a top-down approach to the solution of a task that Karmiloff-Smith (1984) regarded as a "theory-in-action." By about 8 years of age, children considered plausibility (inference in abeyance) of a solution before actually attempting a particular solution. Furthermore, plausibility was not solely committed to either data-driven or theory-driven solutions. Rather, the theoretical applications were open, flexible, and thereby amenable to environmental influences. Thus, measured and inferentially based solutions became available and used.

Moreover, there is reason to make provision for affect in problem solving. This was attempted many years ago in the theory of cognitive dissonance (Festinger, 1957). Even so, it is well known that emotional states may override cognitive considerations (Bruner, 1986). Also in language acquisition, a so-called neutral affective state has been identified as a predictor of spurts of word learning (Bloom, 1990, 1991; Bloom & Beckwith, 1989; Bloom et al., 1988).

Although abstraction provides, by definition, a representational rendition of previous experiences that may be prototypic (K. Nelson, 1974; Rosch, 1973, 1978; Rosch & Mervis, 1975), there is much information that is lacking. The cognitive mechanisms for coping with the lack of necessary information are inference in thinking and implicature (Clark & Clark, 1977; Sperber & Wilson, 1986) in communication. Said another way, for abstraction to have utility in thinking and language, various aspects need to be filled in to deal effectively with particular instantiations. This is the function of inference.

Bruner, Goodnow, and Austin (1956) indicated the importance of categorization or abstraction as follows: "Virtually all cognitive activity involves and is dependent on the process of categorizing" (p. 246). Bowerman (1976) commented, "The grouping of discriminatively different stimuli into categories on the basis of shared features is an adaptive way of dealing with what would otherwise be an overwhelming array of unique experiences" (p. 106). Mervis and Pani (1980) put it this way:

> Categorization allows a person to make the unfamiliar familiar. And because a person is able to generalize about an object or event based on knowledge of its category, he is able to know more about that object or event than just what he can ascertain by looking at it. (p. 496)

This comment implicates the relatively minor role of visual or auditory processing in categorization and thinking. Indeed, in contrast to the clinical fields that try to make much of modality differences, the cognition and the language literatures are one with respect to the point that modalities—either visual or auditory—play relatively minor roles in information processing.

Returning to categorization, abstraction provides a way of reducing the complexities of reality to a manageable size (Tyler, 1969). Information recovered for use in problem solving needs fulfillment in accord with what is at hand; it is inference that achieves such fulfillment. Thus, problem solving entails the use of inference. Furthermore, such inferencing is not highly formal in the sense of formal logic. Rather, there is slippage (Sperber & Wilson, 1986) that affords thinking and communication the capacity for flexibility. The ultimate test of its validity is the degree to which it works as intended in social commerce, which may be another turn on the importance of problem solving with inference and affect grounded on the situated mind.

In cognitive psychology, there are several different ways in which general cognitive skills have been assessed. Of course, the traditional notion of intelligence is based on a *g* factor or general cognitive capacity notion. Presumably, then, various intelligence tests would be good candidates for assessing general cognitive skills (i.e., Stanford–Binet Test, Wechsler Intelligence Test Battery, Leiter Intelligence Test, etc.). An astute clinician should be aware that there are some major questions about the validity of these tests. First, the kinds of cognitive skills addressed by these tests are somewhat peripheral to the basic skills used in everyday cognition. For example, memory for digits forward and backward is rather trivial information. Second, the kinds of cognitive skills tapped by these tests merely reflect a compilation of relatively easily packaged skills rather than a set of skills that substantiate recognized theories of cognition. For example, the notions of enjoyment of learning, exploration, inference, problem solving, categorization, and metacognition would be high on a list of important cognitive skills, but such notions are merely peripheral to intelligence test performance. Third, these skills are relative, not absolute. Under certain conditions certain cognitive skills have relatively more value than other skills; yet, no provision has been made for relativity and conditionality. It is to Wechsler's (1975) credit that he criticized intelligence tests from this perspective. Fourth, intelligence tests—and achievement tests for that matter—are level of performance measures. However, the field of cognition over the past few decades has shifted away from level of performance measures to cognitive style and mental processes that have ecological validity. The reason that cognitive style is so important is that it is better to have a handle on how an individual obtained a score than the score itself (Karmiloff-Smith, 1984, 1992). Therefore, a great deal of research has been devoted to memory, cognitive tempo, rule versus nonrule governed learning, analytic versus synthetic processing, perceptual salience, categorization, problem solving, and so on. These are issues the clinical fields have yet to address in a significant way. The bottom line is that intelligence tests, and their estimates, lack a great deal in dealing with cognition.

Regarding categorization or concept formation, major developments have occurred over the past two decades. The theory of natural categories (Anglin, 1977; Heider, 1971; Rosch, 1973, 1978; Rosch & Mervis, 1975) has been an especially potent force in understanding categorization. It is based on the distinction between focal and peripheral exemplars. *Focal exemplars* are those that are good examples of a category. For example, apple, orange, and banana are good exemplars of fruitness. In contrast, *peripheral exemplars* are questionable. For example, nut and rhubarb might be questionable exemplars of fruitness. The distinction is not a scientific distinction, but one for social commerce. Therefore, these are institutional facts rather than brute facts. Presumably, the categorization of focal exemplars indexes rudimentary prototypic awareness, whereas the incorporation of peripheral exemplars with focal exemplars means that an individual's categories extend to or overlap with other categories. Thus, it might be said that focal exemplars provides evidence of prototypic knowledge, whereas the inclusion of peripheral exemplars provides evidence of extended knowledge. Extended knowledge is very important because it means that things can be categorized differently for different purposes; for example, learned equivalence or learned distinctiveness (Dollard & Miller, 1950).

Another view of theories of categorization are those concerning schemas (Mandler, 1983, 1990). Schemas derive from knowledge of events. Such knowledge entails who or what is doing something in relation to something else. Thus, schemas are not encapsulated categories but packages of knowledge about events. Eventually, schemas become abstracted into knowledge of the world.

Unfortunately, the clinical fields are generally unaware of this literature or have made some limited interpretations and uses of it. For example, the Boehm test (Boehm, 1969, 1986) and Bracken test (Bracken, 1986) are commonly used in the clinical fields to assess concept development. Yet, these are some in a long list of tests lacking construct validity in the clinical fields. Strangely, neither the Boehm nor Bracken tests make any claims about theories of concept development or categorization and certainly no claims are made about prototypical or extended knowledge. Yet, these are fundamental issues in assessing concept development. For example, Burger and Muma (1980) showed that the distinctions between prototypic and extended knowledge and also cognitive distancing are significant issues in word recall in aphasia.

Piagetian theory, especially regarding the sensorimotor skills, has been prominent in attempts to deal with general cognitive skills. Early evidence was disquieting in regard to presumed cognitive precursors, but subsequent studies and adjustments for methodological problems pertaining to the Uzgiris and Hunt (1975) scales have yielded a literature that supports the notion of cognitive precursors for such sensorimotor skills as object permanence, causality, alternative means, and symbolic play (Bates, 1979).

Symbolic Play

Symbolic play provides a means of learning about the nature of the world without having to abide by the consequences of the real world. Sylva, Bruner, and Genova (1976) indicated that play is an opportunity to elaborate and explore alternative means for achieving a desired goal. Yet, this arena is freed of accountability and responsibility as the test of reality. Thus, the simulations provided by play seem to constitute an important arena for learning.

Garvey (1977) described the simulation function of play in the following way, when a behavioral system is "temporarily uncoupled from its usual relations to other systems, but still operates normally in respect to its own internal dynamics, it is functioning in the simulative mode" (p. 6). It is not easy to define play simply because play is about everyday experience. Thus, the content of play is the content of daily experience. What is characteristic of play is that the experiences of play are intentionally set aside as such. They are temporarily uncoupled and buffered from the normal consequences of events. From this perspective, "objects are the prime currency of social exchanges for the toddler" (Garvey, 1977, p. 51). Garvey (1977) gave the following characteristics of play:

1. Pleasurable, enjoyable, positively valued.
2. No extrinsic goals; intrinsic motivation.
3. Spontaneous, voluntary with "little redeeming scientific value."
4. Active engagement.
5. Not play and play: contrast. (pp. 4–5)

Piaget (1952, 1964) identified three levels of play:

1. Sensorimotor play (birth–2 years): Repeating and varying motions to master control and experimenting with touch, sight, sound, and causality.
2. Symbolic or representational play (2–6 years): Play with symbols, pretending.
3. Games with rules (over 6): Social concepts; objective thought.

Garvey, however, indicated that social play occurs from the beginning with mother–infant exchanges.

A child's play varies according to age, gender, familiar and unfamiliar participants, and whether speaking is needed or not. There are four basic states (Garvey, 1977) for children: play, nonplay, social, and nonsocial. Various combinations of these states result in varied behaviors.

Because the development of the smile somewhat parallels that of play, it is useful to review briefly the development of smiles. Sroufe and Waters (1976) reviewed the literature on the development of smiling and laughter. There are two basic kinds of smiles: endogenous and exogenous. The *endogenous smile* is faint, fleeting, and internally triggered, often during sleep. The *exogenous smile* appears at about 3 weeks of age as children respond to discrepancies between what they know of the world and new experiences (Kagan, 1970; Kagan & Lewis, 1965).

To reiterate, what happens in discrepancy learning is two steps, the orienting response and the hypothesis testing response. During the orienting response, a child orients to a discrepancy; that is, the child ceases other activity and focuses on what for him or her is a newly discovered discrepant stimulus. During the orienting response, cardiac rate decelerates and the child enters a brief period of neutral affect. Then, the hypothesis testing response occurs wherein the child's cardiac rate accelerates and a smile grows often turning into laughter. The key notion for discrepancy learning is variation of previously known information. It is important that such variations be slight or discrepant rather than large or novel.

Another perspective pertains to whether a child will smile or laugh as an indication of learning or cry and move away from an event. The tension–relaxation theory (Garvey, 1977) holds that when individuals are under threat they will become sober, maybe cry, and move away from the threat; however, in a nonthreatening situation, individuals will smile, laugh, approach, and reach for an object.

It should be recognized that smiles are very powerful social devices. Infants learn that when they smile to familiar faces, they often benefit from social encounters. Smiles invite parents to pick them up and love them. Even as adults, smiles invite social interaction.

A rather striking observation of infant play is the presence of motion. Parents offer infants opportunities to observe motion or to cause motion—mobiles in the crib. Later, various toys involve motion such as a pounding bench, blowing bubbles, trucks and cars, dolls, blocks, and pull–push toys. Then, in childhood, action toys extend to the toys on the fairgrounds and eventually cars, boats, guns, and so on. Children frequently use eye gaze to entice participation of others in their activities. Play with motion has social roots (infant–parent interaction) but social play with peers begins at about 3 years of age. Rough and tumble play is mostly with boys; younger children or new acquaintances tend to watch rough and tumble play rather than participate.

Garvey (1977) indicated that play with objects has some special aspects: "Objects are the prime currency of social exchanges for the toddler" (p. 51). Objects are usually offered as overtures for friendship. Interestingly enough, gender differences in toy choices may reflect parental decisions rather than preferences of children.

Garvey (1977) provided a developmental sequence for playing with toys:

- 9 months: Mouthing, waving, banging, inspecting.
- 12 months: Investigating before acting on objects.
- 15 months: Investigating before acting, according appropriate functions for different objects.
- 21 months: Find items that go together.
- 24 months: Carries out schematic relations between objects.
- 30 to 36 months: Elaborate relations between several toys.

McCune-Nicolich (1975, 1977, 1981b) provided a developmental sequence for symbolic play; the following is an abridged version:

- *Functions*: A child will play differently with different toys.
- *Autosymbolic*: A child pretends to do things toward himself or herself.
- *Others*: A child may adopt the behavior of others or he or she may address pretend behavior toward others.
- *Alternative means*: A child may have several actions toward one toy or he or she may have one action toward several toys.
- *Substitute objects*: A child substitutes one object for another such as a block of wood stands for a gun.

Children also play with language. Much of the early play with language is nonsocial. Before 2 years of age, nonconventional sound making occurs for sheer enjoyment. By age 2, children have enough command of words to intentionally play with sounds, make funny talk, and perform casual chants. Somewhere between ages 2 and 3, they engage in systematic play with language that Garvey (1977) called "private linguistic excursions" (p. 65). Then they engage in social play with language. Such play includes spontaneous rhyming and word play (rhymes, diminutives, intonation variations), fantasy and nonsense play (nonsense words, scatological overtones, "insulting" play), and speech act and discourse play (intentional violations of the cooperative principle).

As a child's knowledge of the world expands, play becomes more elaborate. Children tend to play less with regard to the properties of objects and more according to plans and ideas. "When overt make-believe play decreases, it may be that make-believe continues but goes underground to become private fantasy or daydreaming" (Garvey, 1977, p. 80). Pretending could be regarded as "a voluntary transformation of the Here and Now, the You and Me, and the This or That" (Garvey, 1977, p. 82). The child is the engineer or director of pretending. The enactment is the action, mode, or representation that constitutes the event of pretending. Roles and plans provide a coherent arena for enactment; they are frequently varied and elaborated in the course of enactment and readily available objects are usually incorporated.

Play with rules entails social negotiation. The participants have to accept and adhere to the particular set of rules. Infractions carry specific penalties and sanctions. Most peer games are cooperative ventures until about 7 or 8 years of age when competitive games appear. Many social games test limits of one's abilities or the tolerance of others. Many such games intentionally violate rules and social limits.

Ritual play is controlled, usually rhythmic with a controlled tempo. The features of ritual play are that it has a characteristic style, the transitions from ritual play to nonritual play are easily identified, and such play can be interrupted for procedural corrections.

Thus, play offers children opportunities to learn about their world without risking some of the consequences. Furthermore, play is constrained by what a child knows about the physical, social, and cultural worlds.

There may be parallels between the acquisition of language and the acquisition of symbolic play; that is, it is reasonable to expect that individuals with specific language impairments may also evidence impaired acquisition of symbolic play. Rescorla and Goossens (1992) found that toddlers with specific language impairment did not differ from toddlers with normal language development with respect to the amount of engagement with toys or in functional conventional play.

> However, the children with SLI-E displayed less decentered play (use of play schemes with a doll or another person), less well-developed sequential play, and fewer occurrences of symbolic play transformations (use of a neutral object or an absent object to carry out pretending). The provision of structure in the form of thematically related toy sets, instructions, and modelling did not reduce the discrepancy between demonstrated play behaviors of toddlers with SLI-E and their normally developing peers. (p. 285)

In addition to the possible relation between the acquisition of language and symbolic play, it is reasonable to expect that individuals who are language impaired or who are "late bloomers" in language acquisition may rely more on gestures for communication than normal language learners. Thal and Tobias (1992) and Thal, Tobias, and Morrison (1991) found that late talkers used significantly more communicative gestures and a greater variety of communicative functions than did a matched group of normal language learners. A 1-year follow-up study indicated that these findings reflected the late bloomers; the truly impaired individuals did not differ from normals in the use of gestures, type of gestures, or number of different functions of gestures. Thus, late bloomers evidently used gestures to compensate for their lack of oral expression.

Substantive Functions of Grammar and Pragmatics

In addition to the general cognitive base composed of possible worlds with its attendant aspects, there are cognitive aspects that comprise the substantive functional base of language. These are intent, explicit content (proposition), and implicit content (presupposition, implicature, felicity conditions). Explicit content in relation to implicit content conveys new information in the context of old so that communicative intent may be recognized.

It should be stressed that speech act theory is basically about these cognitive issues; that is, speech act theory is about intent, explicit content (proposition), implicit content (presupposition, implicature, felicity conditions), utterance (locution), and effects of utterances on listeners (Austin, 1962; Clark & Clark, 1977; Grice, 1975; Searle, 1969, 1975; Sperber & Wilson, 1986). Thus, speech act theory is attractive.

Intent and content comprise the functional base of communication. Intent has emerged as the irreducible nucleus of social cognition for both language and thinking. In language, Grice (1967) and Sperber and Wilson (1986) defined intent as the essence of communication because the purpose of communication is to make intentions recognizable. In the narrative mode of thinking, Bruner (1986) said, "Narrative deals with the vicissitudes of human intentions" (p. 16). He indicated that causality is the irreducible mental category for the scientific mode of thinking, but intentionality is the fundamental mental category for the humanistic mode. He and others have discussed the centrality of intention for language (Bloom & Beckwith, 1986; Bloom et al., 1988; Bruner, 1981, 1986; Cazden, 1977; Halliday, 1975; K. Nelson, 1985, 1986, 1991, 1996; Ninio & Snow, 1988; Searle, 1992).

Because the clinical fields have a heritage of instruction or teaching, the notion of intent playing a central role in language acquisition is somewhat foreign, possibly even repugnant. Indeed, the literature on the centrality of intent has been clearly evident since Grice's original enunciation in the mid-1960s. Yet, until recently, it has been difficult to find evidence of its importance in the clinical fields. Chapman (1981) gave a summary of taxonomies for intent. Even the whole language fad has missed the centrality of intent. Except for some passing comments, where does Fey (1986) appreciate the significance of communicative intent? Strangely, the various pragmatic accounts of language in the clinical fields have missed the centrality of communicative intent. Fortunately, however, Abbeduto and Benson (1992), Muma (1986a, 1991), Wetherby (1991), and Wetherby and Prizant (1990) drew clinical implications about the centrality of communicative intent.

Intent is very important simply because what is done with language is for the purpose of making intent recognizable. Furthermore, there is reason to be concerned that elicited behavior is not the same as, or even a good estimate of, spontaneous intentional behavior (Fujiki & Brinton, 1987; Prutting, Gallagher, & Mulac, 1975). Slobin and Welch (1971) showed that elicited behavior was not a good estimate of what children could do spontaneously. In phonological assessment, there is the concern that a child's performance on formal tests may not be representative of what he or she can do in spontaneous speech.

Needless to say, it behooves clinicians to rely on spontaneous speech as the source of prima facie evidence of what children can do. When there are differences between spontaneous speech and test performance, it is apparent that reliance should be placed on spontaneous speech.

Explicit content refers to the meaning of a message within the context of implicit content. This is the semantic aspect of a message. A speaker strives to encode a message that is informative. In order to make a message achieve informativeness, it is necessary to make various decisions about what is intended, what the speaker knows and perceives about a topic or event, the speaker's perspective as contrasted to that of others, and options available in language such as word or lexical choice, grammatical alternatives, and pragmatic alternatives to make intents recognizable. Furthermore, if a message does not work as intended, the encoder needs to be able to ascertain the nature of the problem and make whatever adjustments are needed to play the communication game (Muma, 1975a) to achieve the message of best fit in making intentions recognizable.

Explicit content is the proposition of a message. Propositions are made up of basic cognitive notions, some of which are encoded in relation to each other, thereby establishing relational meaning. Other relevant information remains as implicit content, which is implicated by explicit content in a particular communicative context.

There are many ways of portraying semantic or propositional meaning in language. Bloom (1970, 1973), Bowerman (1973), Brown (1973b), Schlesinger (1971), and others have delineated various early semantic categories. These delineations were remarkably similar. They fell into two basic categories: semantic functions and semantic relations.

Perhaps the delineations by Greenfield and Smith (1976) are especially useful for the clinical fields because acquisition sequences were identified. The main sequence is performative, indicative, volition, agent, action, object, dative, locative, and modification. Within action, another sequence was identified: protolocative, intransitive, transitive, and state.

A *performative* is a prenaming act that indexes a referent but is not a name or label. The following are prenaming acts: communicative point, referential display, and specific noises that index particular referents such as a barking noise to index a dog. A communicative point is when someone points to an intended referent then turns to the other participant to address the point (Ninio & Bruner, 1978). A referential display is when a child holds up the referent in front of the intended audience; sometimes a referent is actually imposed on the intended audience by virtue of pushing the referent in the face of the audience.

Indicative means to indicate and naming or labeling are the means by which an indicative is usually achieved. Naming of objects may be by non-conventional or conventional means. It is very common for young children to have a small set of nonconventional words. Such words have been called vocables (Ferguson, 1977, 1978) and PCFs (Dore, 1975). Such forms eventually drop out of one's vocabulary to be replaced by conventional forms. This loss of nonconventional forms has been called *word mortality* (Bloom, 1973). Conventional words are those that are shared by others in a mutual language. For example, apple is a conventional term shared by others who speak English.

Volition is expressed by a superimposed intonational contour that carries certain meanings. For example, the question intonation contour contrasts with the declarative contour. The former ends with a rising intonation, whereas the latter ends with a falling intonation. Research has shown that the difference between rising and falling intonation contours of parental speech toward their children denotes the difference between presumed or known information and new information (Bruner, 1981). Performatives, indicatives, and volition comprise the category of semantic functions.

The remaining semantic categories deal with semantic relations. Such categories deal with meaning in relation to other categories. An agent is the instigator of an action and action can be characterized in different ways (Bowerman, 1976; Greenfield & Smith, 1976). Early action may be evidenced as protolocatives whereby a child may say a locative such as "up" but mean an action such as "pick me up." This is followed by intransitive action (action without an object) and then transitive action (action with an object). These are followed with "state" verbs such as "feel," "appear," "be," etc.

An object is the recipient of an action. Object, and sometimes agent, are further distinguished according to animateness and inanimateness (Greenfield & Smith, 1976; Schlesinger, 1974). *Dative* is the indirect object and *locative* is the identification of location. Finally, *modification* includes modulations of meaning achieved by the inflectional system, such as variations in singular or plural, tense, noun–verb concordance, noun phrase modifications such as adjectives and relative clauses, and verb phrase modifications, known as adverbials.

The semantic period of language acquisition is a very short period. It begins with the first words and ends when a child can produce a variety of basic subject–verb–object (SVO) relations (Bloom, 1973). Others concur (Brown, 1973b; Schlesinger, 1971). Greenfield and Smith (1976) agreed and they added another indicator of the end of the semantic period: varied use of datives. Semantic relations are subsumed within grammatical relations. Therefore, it would be rather peculiar to conduct a semantic analysis when grammatical skills are evident.

A semantic analysis for emergent relational meaning should include the following:

1. Ascertain the progress a child has made in acquisition sequences.
2. Ascertain the range of available semantic category types.
3. Ascertain the various combinations of semantic relations available to a child.

Such information would be useful when assessing children who are pregrammatical (not yet evidencing varied SVO constructions). It may be necessary to expand their repertoires of available skills as a means of getting them ready for more advanced skills.

Explicit content is only the tip of the iceberg in which words are only meaningful in relation to presumed or implied relevant information. This means that semantic relations are only meaningful in relation to what an individual knows in possible worlds. Thus, to say "apples" not only draws on what apples may mean in a dictionary sense but also draws on one's previous experience with apples to extract virtual meanings from possible worlds. Thus, for the sentence "I like apples" to work as intended, it is necessary to draw on the presupposition that possible worlds knowledge affords the individual to whom this utterance is addressed. It is presumed that this individual has had sufficient experience with apples that permits this utterance to work as intended. Thus, explicit content is reliant on implicit content in making communicative intents recognizable.

Cognitive Processes Underlying Messages

Clark and Clark (1977) provided a comprehensive review of the literature regarding the nature of encoding and decoding processes in language. As might be expected, these mental processes operate on possible worlds knowledge and employ problem solving and inference for planning and execution of intended propositions, encoding messages, and constructing and utilizing propositions for decoding messages in the recognition of communicative intent. Sperber and Wilson (1986) offered a compatible view of mental processes in language. Interestingly, both dealt with speech act theory (Grice, 1967). Both also indicated that very little initial information processing entails modality processes such as auditory processing. Such information is purged early in mental processing with the bulk of the work dealing with possible worlds, problem solving, inference, and intent.

This means that the clinical fields' notions about the importance of so-called auditory processing is misplaced, resulting in attention to relatively peripheral aspects of language and ignoring the core issues. Indeed, even within the clinical fields, serious questions have been raised about the validity of auditory processing in a viable account of language (Leonard, 1989; Rees, 1973, 1981; Tallal, 1990).

Metacognitive and Metalinguistic Capacities

Metacognitive and metalinguistic skills constitute other areas of the cognitive-social bases of language. Metalinguistic skills are the abilities to reflect on the nature of language (Cazden, 1975; Karmiloff-Smith, 1992; Kretschmer, 1984; vanKleek, 1984; Winner, 1979; Winner, Engel, & Gardner, 1980). Reflection may be in the form of questions or comments about language itself or it may take the form of intentional violations of language for entertainment while exploring the nature of language. The following are examples of metalinguistic activities: "What does 'suspense' mean?" "Don't use such big words." "I saw a red leaf, a yellow leaf, a stripped leaf, a poka dotted leaf (giggling)." Some of these utterances were made to intentionally violate rules of modification and thereby entertain this child's peers. In order to intentionally violate rules, it is necessary for an individual to not only know a rule but the range of applications for it. Such spontaneous activities by children provide useful metalinguistic activities wherein peer feedback about the nature of rules and their ranges becomes useful in acquisition.

In summary, the cognitive-social bases of language from the perspective of speech act theory deal with general cognitive skills, notably possible worlds, the substantive functions of grammar and pragmatics (intent, explicit content within the context of implicit content), cognitive processes underlying messages, and metacognitive and metalinguistic skills. Thus, the cognitive-social bases of language define language and communication as cognitive enterprises.

The purpose of communication is to be appropriately informative in particular communicative contexts so communicative intent can be recognized. What is crucial about informativeness is that conscious decisions are made about what is explicit and what is implicit in a message of best fit in an attempt to make communicative intent recognizable.

SUMMARY

Freud, Piaget, and Vygotsky had very different perspectives about the role of language in child development. Freud held that individuals were burdened by their past and that language provided a mechanism for talking through the problems of the past, thereby freeing oneself from this burden. Thus, language provides a liberating force for happiness. Piaget employed the notion of stages of acquisition. As an individual passes from one stage to another, qualitative changes occur whereby issues of the past no longer pertain. For Piaget, language was of little consequence. Vygotsky held that culture is the overriding influence for cognitive development and language is the primary means of culturalization. Vygotsky did not deny biological or maturational issues; he emphasized experiential learning shaped greatly by cultural influences.

Developments in cognition over the past few decades seem to have shifted away from the traditional domains per se (i.e., sensation, discrimination, perception, concept formation, and thinking). The shift reflects an interest in how the various aspects of cognition function in various contexts rather than ascertaining the nature of each domain itself. This shift seems to be directed at not just ascertaining what cognition is in a taxonomic sense but how it functions in the applications of possible worlds for thinking and functions for communication in actual social commerce.

Development in the study of memory reflects this kind of shift. The traditional notion of a single fixed memory that could be assessed by memory for digits or for commands has long since been dashed. The distinction between short-term and long-term memories has become redefined as episodic and semantic memories and became further elaborated with respect to declarative and nondeclarative manifestations of memory.

Discrepancy learning theory, a well-known and substantiated theory in cognition, has received increased attention in accounts of language acquisition. K. E. Nelson's (1981, 1991) theory of rare-event learning in language acquisition is grounded on discrepancy learning. The intentionality theory advocated by Bloom and Beckwith (1986) and Bloom et al. (1988) is based, to some extent, on discrepancy learning. K. Nelson (1985, 1986) drew on discrepancy learning as a viable account of language acquisition within the theory of shared meaning. The significance of discrepancy learning is that deviations from what an individual knows are significant in eliciting and maintaining attention, thereby providing the substantive base for learning. Variation is crucial for learning.

The distinction between brute and institutional facts also reflects the shift away from the traditional acontextual laboratory studies of cognition in which only brute facts are studied either directly or in analogies. The interest has become more ecologically valid (to borrow from Bronfenbrenner, 1977, 1979), whereby it is desirable to appreciate what an individual learns from social, emotional, and cultural institutions.

Cognition studied from the perspective of the acquisition of representational knowledge is an example of the ecologically oriented approach. This literature has established how procedural knowledge not only leads to declarative knowledge but sustains its own capacities.

In recent years, there has been a great deal of interest in the notion of cognitive modularity. There are some provocative issues favoring modularity, but there are also some basic issues that give pause to such prospects.

Beyond the question of modularity, there is a great deal of interest in what transpires with higher mental functions to afford individual possible worlds. In this arena the theory of referential redescription has much to offer not only about categorization but the phases that individuals pass through to achieve adult capacities.

Because the clinical fields have been so careless in the use of terminology, especially regarding cognition, the notions of process, level, phase, stage, and strategy were discussed. These considerations permitted discussions of top-down and bottom-up cognitive processing, left–right processing, and two modes of thought.

The clinical fields have tenaciously held on to the traditional notions of modality difference (expressive vs. receptive; auditory vs. visual processing). These perspectives were shown to be peripheral to the more substantive CCCE domains issuing from the cognitive socialization literature. Accordingly, it would be desirable for the clinical fields to be more firmly aligned to the substantive issues in CCCE with their attendant philosophical and theoretical perspectives.

I contend that speech act theory provides a more reasonable appreciation for the mapping question, especially in view of other compatible views such as representational theory (Karmiloff-Smith, 1992; Mandler, 1983), situated mind (K. Nelson, 1996), social origins of the mind (Rogoff, 1990; Wertsch, 1991), and the distinction between science and human affairs (Bruner, 1986). Therefore, I have established a model of the cognitive basis of language (Muma, 1986a) that was further enunciated here (see chap. 2).

Language was seen as a cognitive domain extending to linguistic and communicative domains resulting in the CCCE model. This model was amplified whereby the cognitive bases of language were delineated in terms of:

1. General cognition (inference, possible worlds).
2. Substantive functions of grammar and pragmatics (intent, implicit content, explicit content).
3. Cognitive processes underlying messages.
4. Metacognitive and metalinguistic capacities.

Furthermore, informativeness is useful in appreciating communication as a cognitive endeavor.

5

CODIFICATION:
MESSAGE OF BEST FIT

The basic reason messages are coded is to make communicative intentions recognizable (Grice, 1975; Sperber & Wilson, 1986). This means that codification is not limited to linguistic messages but extends to a code matrix (Muma, 1975a) whereby linguistic, prosodic, pragmatic, gestural, and other coding devices may be used to convey communicative intent. Codification itself is a structural product of underlying mental capacities whereby decisions are made regarding what and how a message should be coded in the context of what is known or expected. Because codification occurs for the purpose of making communicative intent recognizable and in a social currency—such as language conventions—it is necessary to appreciate that not just any message should be coded in a particular context; a message needs to be a message of best fit for the competing parameters (Muma, 1975a). Brown (1973b) likened the process of coding a message of best fit in the coin-of-the-realm of social commerce to working a jigsaw puzzle: "A sentence well adapted to its function is, like a piece in a jigsaw puzzle, just the right size and shape to fit the opening left for it by local conditions and community understandings" (p. 68). That is to say, in order for a message to work as intended, it is necessary for an individual to have sufficient knowledge of the world, language, and audience to make appropriate decisions about the informative nature of a message in a particular context. In so doing, there are many risks of producing messages that may not fit encoder–decoder expectations, thereby creating an unintended communicative outcome. Thus, both participants may become active in negotiating appropriate messages. The communicative challenge, then, is to code messages of best fit for the communicative demands of particular contexts in order to recognize communicative intents.

TRADITIONAL NOTIONS

The traditional notions of dealing with language and grammar were seriously flawed. They were a priori in nature and essentially structuralistic (i.e., barren of function and sociocultural aspects of communication), thereby missing the dynamic and negotiable nature of communication. Notice that the traditional structuralistic views missed communicative intent and functional relations both within and between utterances and between codes, and the traditional notions were essentially acontextual. In short, the traditional notions focused on language rather than communication and on structure rather than function. The a priori nature of the structuralistic approaches created a strange twist that essentially missed the essence of a message of best fit.

Traditional views of grammar were structuralistic in regard to the notions of parts of speech and sentence taxonomies. The parts of speech notion was that parts of sentences could be categorized a priori (i.e., noun, verb, adjective, adverb, helping verb, pronoun, etc.). However, the development of function-based theories of language acquisition and grammar raised serious questions about a priori views such as the so-called parts of speech and sentence taxonomies. It is to Chomsky's (1957) everlasting credit that he successfully challenged these traditional notions as atheoretical and apsychological.

Most contemporary functional views and perspectives of language are both theoretical and psychosocial. Furthermore, they posit that structure is in the service of function in becoming informative in efforts to recognize communicative intent in particular contexts.

The main problem with the traditional parts of speech notion is that words may function differently from one linguistic context to another. For example, the word *fishing* is a verb in Sentence 1 but it is a nominal in Sentence 2.

1. He is *fishing*.
2. *Fishing* is fun.

This is not an isolated example or an exception to the rule; rather, it is a pervasive principle of language that words function differently in different intentional, referential, relational, and social contexts. Accordingly, the traditional notion of parts of speech carries with it considerable difficulties because it does not deal adequately with how words function.

Similarly, the traditional sentence taxonomies are also lacking. Traditionally, sentences were characterized as simple, compound–complex, and elaborated (Templin, 1957). These are very crude categories. These taxonomies are not specific to the kinds of grammatical skills entailed by the sentences characterized in one way or another, and they do not convey information on how sentences function as a message of best fit in making intentions recognizable. Unfortunately, such taxonomies were atheoretical in appreciating grammar and the products of grammar—utterances: semantic–syntactic, prosodic, phonological manifestations of informativeness.

Another way that sentences have been characterized is in regard to their general intentions: declarative, interrogative, exclamatory, and imperative (Templin, 1957). Chapman (1981) provided a summary of some other taxonomies for intentions. Such views are much better than the structuralistic notions given earlier; yet they are also lacking because they say nothing about how particular lexical, grammatical, and pragmatic machineries are brought to bear in the service of achieving a message of best fit in the realization of intents in actual social commerce.

The traditional notions of one- and two-word early utterances are similarly vacuous; it is necessary to identify the particular semantic function(s) or relation(s) for these utterances in order to appreciate how they function. To merely report that an individual is using only one- and two-word utterances is not saying much.

More recently, however, there has been an interest in direct mapping of word meaning from possible world knowledge that may circumvent a semantic buffer (K. Nelson, 1985, 1986, 1996; Ninio, 1988). That is, drawing directly on procedural knowledge rather than semantic knowledge, young learners are capable of rendering useful messages that are restricted to those routines, formats, or scripts available to them. Eventually scripts vary, thereby extending procedural knowledge that ultimately becomes semantic knowledge. Two important outcomes of this process are the freeing of the individual from direct stimulation and increased mental, linguistic, and pragmatic potentials for greater flexibility in the productive use of these capacities.

In the clinical fields, various traditional taxonomies have been used, even to claim assessment of grammatical abilities. For example, the Brigance (1978) test claims to measure a child's verbal abilities with regard to sentences of increasing word length. Unfortunately, a two-word sentence such as "he runs" was regarded as less difficult than a three-word sentence such as "the boy runs." Yet, the acquisition literature indicates that pronominals are more difficult to learn for nominal learners (Bloom et al., 1975) than simple determiner plus noun constructions such as "the boy." To make matters worse, this test also has two-word elliptical sentences that were regarded as simpler than unmodified three-word sentences. For example, a sentence like "he can" was considered simpler than a sentence like "he can run." Obviously, there are serious questions about the validity of the Brigance test (Brigance, 1978) and other similar tests.

These issues extend to the Developmental Sentence Scores (DSS; Lee, 1974; Lee & Canter, 1971; Lee, Koenigsknecht, & Mulhern, 1975), which also has some serious conceptual and measurement problems. This procedure strives to credit an individual for grammatical skills by giving quantitative weights for various grammatical categories (noun, pronoun, auxiliary, verb, etc.) evidenced in 50-utterance language samples. The problems with the conceptualization of DSS include the following:

1. Assignment of quantitative values for grammatical categories without considering how the words function grammatically.
2. Lack of appreciation of theoretical models for underlying hierarchies in sentence construction (Johnson, 1965, 1966; Yngve, 1960).
3. Reliance on 50-utterance language samples that have been shown to have excessively high error rates.
4. Reliance on form as evidence of grammatical capacities, which is precisely the opposite of what the functional message has been over the past three decades.

Regarding the last problem, it is more appropriate to assume a functionalistic perspective whereby form is in the service of function. By doing so, the question of grammatical capacities is not merely which grammatical forms have been evidenced in language samples, but how various forms function in various grammatical and pragmatic contexts. This perspective converts the issues of grammatical and pragmatic capacities evidenced in language samples to evidence of the following:

1. Evidence of available grammatical and pragmatic repertories.
2. Evidence of progress in acquisition sequences.
3. Evidence of available strategies of learning.
4. Evidence of active loci of learning.

The clinical fields have been remiss in addressing these issues relying instead on the rationalization that the DSS is justified by virtue of normative assessment. Thus, DSS is just an instance of brute empiricism.

PRODUCTIVITY AND SYSTEMS

It is one thing for an individual to produce grammatical constructions but quite another to be given credit for productive knowledge and use of grammatical systems. "While the need to establish productivity has been expressed in recent work, little has been done to develop a methodology" (Ingram, 1989a, p. 333). Raw frequencies and percentages are insufficient criteria to attribute language acquisition. The problem with raw frequencies is that early on children may have excessive use of formulaic, frozen, or ossified forms. Such forms may not be decomposable; therefore, the children may not appreciate the latent grammar that may be entailed by such utterances. It would thus be inappropriate to attribute verbal capacities merely because children had many instances of a particular grammatical structure. Grammatical structures need to be decomposable and evidence lexical and co-occuring variations in order to entertain the notion of attainment. Mere frequency counts are simply insufficient.

For example, a frequency count does little to distinguish the grammatical capacities between the following two children.

Child A: He run. He run. He run fast. He run there.
Child B: He run. He ran. He goes.

For Child A, four instances of "run" or "he run" are evidenced. For Child B, one instance of "run" or "he run" is evidenced. However, Child B evidences more advanced acquisition by virtue of changing "run" to "ran" to "goes."

Another problem evidenced in the clinical fields is the misuse of percentages. Basically, the clinical fields have a penchant for misusing percentage in such a way that behaviors are inflated and disproportionately so with various comparisons such as with pre- and postintervention data. Inflation occurs when the frequencies of behaviors are much less than 100. Disproportionate inflation occurs when the frequencies are both much less than 100 and they are not from the same base of instances of behavior. The result is that data are obtained without much evidence. For example, Child A evidenced four instances of "he run," two of which have adverbs. It would be fallacious to say that 50% of these constructions evidence adverbs, yet this kind of thinking is evidenced clinically. Unfortunately, these flaws are easily found in clinical journals and clinical services.

In a systems approach, it is necessary to identify the array of alternatives available for codification; that is, if one message does not work as intended, does an individual have alternative codes that could still make a particular communicative intent recognizable? When an individual has a variety of ways of coding the subject of a sentence, options are available for coding subjects. The issue becomes which code is likely to work as intended. If it should be necessary to play the communication game (Muma, 1975a), the issue becomes which alternative should be used to replace the initial code in order to sustain the same communicative intent. A speaker who has several options for coding in the subject nominal system, for example, could say any of the following in reference to Bill: Billy, the boy, that boy, my boy, he, somebody, the boy in the red hat, and so forth. Suppose the speaker actually said, "He works hard," but a listener did not get the intended message, so the listener said, "Who works hard?" Now, the speaker can draw on knowledge of available alternatives in the subject nominal system to revise the initial code in response to the listener enquiry. The point is that a systems approach addresses the issue of a repertoire or array of available codes for any particular grammatical system.

The issue of an array of grammatical and pragmatic constructions and devices, respectively, raises again the issue of the value of single instances of behavior. It is inappropriate to use single instances of behavior to attribute grammatical or pragmatic skills; nonetheless, single instances raise the prospect that such skills may be available to an individual by virtue of evidencing a possible scope or repertoire of skills. Thus, single instances may be useful in appreciating the array of skills available to an individual. However, such considerations are only speculative; they await further substantiation. It is precarious to attribute a grammatical skill from single instances; rather, patterns of performance may be more justifiable.

The notion of productivity is very closely related to a systems approach. Productivity can be attributed if a child cannot only produce many instances of a grammatical construction but can vary the instances in different contexts. Variation is important for two reasons. First, variation is evidence that a construction is not ossified. Rather, variation provides evidence that a construction is decomposable and therefore productive. Second, variation provides evidence that the constructions are indeed generated or produced. Bloom et al. (1989) indicated that grammatical constructions must evidence at least three variations before it can be attributed to a child. Notice that the clinical fields have been silent about this issue. "If certain categories are attributed some criterial number of times, then the category is considered to have psychological reality for the child" (Bloom et al., 1988, p. 103).

Another way to attribute grammatical learning may be the use of the Piagetian criteria of preparation, attainment, and consolidation (Muma, 1983b, 1986a; K. E. Nelson, 1981, 1991; Prutting, 1979). These are discussed in the following. For the present purpose, it is only useful to say that these criteria are relative rather than absolute.

MEAN LENGTH OF UTTERANCE (MLU)

Sentence length is a measure which continues to show increase in normal children until maturity. The use of the measure has been criticized by some writers, and a few substitute measures have been suggested, but none seems to have superseded the mean length of sentence for a reliable, easily determined, objective, quantitative, and easily understood measure of linguistic maturity. (McCarthy, 1954, pp. 550–551)

MLU was a language acquisition index defined and empirically supported by Brown (1973b). An MLU of about 1.0 is not very useful simply because one-word utterances are readily evident. There is no need to calculate MLU for single-word utterances. Furthermore, a child at the one-morpheme level typically also has a set of highly rehearsed formulaic utterances that offer viable entries into grammar when they become decomposable. Such potentials are not reflected by MLU.

"The MLU measures provide an index of syntactic complexity in the child's speech at least up to Stage V (MLU in morphemes = 4.0, Brown, 1973)" (Miller & Chapman, 1981a, p. 22). Once MLU reaches 4.0 or 4.5, it loses value as an acquisition index and becomes a performance index (Bloom, 1970; Brown, 1973a, 1973b; Cazden, 1968; Cowan, Weber, Hoddinott, & Klein, 1967; Shriner, 1969). The reason that MLUs lose value as acquisition indices is because children obtain grammatical repertoires that afford various options for constructing a message of best fit in the realization of communicative intents. Some options shorten or pronominalize messages, whereas others lengthen messages. For example, "he swims" is shorter but grammatically more advanced for nominal learners as contrasted to pronominal learners (Bloom et al., 1975) than "the boy swims." Also, "he eats" and "he will" are shorter and more complex than "he eats jellybeans" and "he will sing," respectively. Accordingly, utterance length over 4.0 or 4.5 is no longer useful because it fails to be a valid index of learning but may instead be a performance index.

In contrast, MLUs of approximately 2.0 have been shown to be useful in appreciating the shift between the pronominal and nominal strategies of language acquisition (Bloom, 1978). Thus, MLUs within the range of 1.0 to 4.0 (possibly 4.5) evidently are useful indices. Even so, there is the perplexing problem of large variances for MLUs (Lahey, 1994). Such variances undermine the precision of measurement for MLUs as indices of Brown's five stages.

Miller and Chapman (1981a, 1981b) provided MLU norms with standard deviations. It is tempting to compare MLUs obtained in language assessment with these norms. However, such comparisons are risky for several reasons. First, Brown (1973b) cautioned that relatively large variations in performance are to be expected in language samples once MLU exceeds 4.0. This is because in one situation children may use relatively short utterances, whereas in other situations they may use relatively long utterances—even intentionally long, to borrow from Furth (1984)—to "celebrate" what they can do. Miller and Chapman (1981a) commented, "MLU is to be used only as a general indicator of structural development, and it can only be reliably interpreted when it falls between 1.01 and 4.49" (p. 25). Even so, it was not very reliable for Klee and Fitzgerald (1985). Gavin and Giles (1996) found that MLU only became a reliable index when the sample size exceeded 175 utterances. Second, Miller and Chapman (1981a, 1981b) reported that they deviated from Brown's procedures for calculating MLUs. Referring to how their procedures departed from those by Brown (1973b), they said, "They differ from his in using only 50, rather than 100, utterances and in failing to omit the first pages of the transcript" (p. 22). Third, inasmuch as the participants used in the Miller and Chapman norms were not randomly selected, there is the question as to whether their norms should be generalized to others. Fourth, the Miller and Chapman norms were not generated from systematically varied sampling conditions within parent–child interactions and across other situations. Yet, there is the prospect that situational variations may be significant for MLUs over 4.5, as well as those under 4.5. Fifth, there is some concern about the manner in which Miller and Chapman calculated their MLUs. Conant (1987) reported, "It should be noted that in the Miller and Chapman analyses, both age and MLU were first categorized . . . and midpoints rather than raw values were used" (p. 170). The use of midpoints may have created an artifact greatly reducing or eliminating the overall variance, thereby creating the illusion that the normative increments are clean and neat. This is merely a calulation device to dress up the data. Sixth, perhaps it should be noted that the correlations between MLU and age are not very robust across studies (Conant, 1987; Klee & Fitzgerald, 1985; Miller & Chapman, 1981b) possibly because of restricted ranges in sampling, sampling error, or large variances (Cole, Mills, & Dale, 1989). Moreover, Brown (1973b) cautioned that rate of learning is notoriously varied because of spurts of learning, whereas sequence is highly stable. The implication is that rate of learning indices such as age may be inappropriate.

Further, Miller and Chapman (1981a, 1981b) did not provide reliability indices for transcription, segmentation, or morphemic analyses used to calculate MLUs. Because the findings by Klee and Fitzgerald (1985) were different from the Miller and Chapman (1981b) norms, there is concern that either or both may be unreliable.

Finally, the contemporary cognitive socialization research has indicated that formulaic utterances are rather prevalent in the early speech of some children. Such utterances constitute a direct threat to the value of MLU calculations. If such utterances are prevalent, MLU calculations based on such utterances could be misleading. On the other hand, if such utterances are excluded from MLU calculations (which is the usual practice) another limitation of the MLU emerges: Grammatical estimates of what an individual can do are restricted only to constructions outside of such utterances. This is paradoxical because individuals typically use available formulaic utterances as a format for learning. To cleave off such utterances as a convenient quantitative ploy does more to reveal our earnestness for quantification than to appreciate the functional significance of what is transpiring in language acquisition.

With these issues, it is difficult to know what value should be placed on the Miller and Chapman (1981b) MLU norms. Said differently, to ignore such substantive concerns about the Miller and Chapman MLU norms is to blindly believe in brute empiricism. Blind adherence to norms with questionable substantive aspects means that one believes that norms provide necessary and sufficient information regardless of other substantive issues that seriously threaten their validity.

Following Brown (1973b), MLU measures have been used as criteria to attribute stages of early language acquisition. However, Brown (1978, 1988) was reluctant to hold that these stages are psychologically valid. He admonished that the stages were hypothetical and in need of substantiation. Nevertheless, the clinical fields took Brown's five early stages of language acquisition at face validity and basically canonized them. The clinical fields acted as if the stages were indeed psychologically real and the MLU index was valid, even beyond Brown's intended range without regard to Brown's admonishment to substantiate them.

BASIC GRAMMATICAL SKILLS

Bates and MacWhinney (1987) indicated that in Italian and English, "the 'basic' or pragmatically-neutral word order is Subject-Verb-Object (SVO)" (p. 160). Sinclair and Bronckart (1972) raised the question as to whether SVO is a linguistic universal. Bloom (1973) described basic grammatical relations in English as SVO constructions or two-word reductions of SVO: "Thus, in addition to sentences in which conceptual relations between persons, objects, and events were coded by the BASIC GRAMMATICAL RELATIONS subject-object, verb-object, subject-verb" (p. 23). Such two-word utterances are reduced renditions of SVO that gave rise to Bloom's (1970) notion of reduction, criticized because it presumably lacked transformational credibility. However, it was never offered as a transformation in a grammatical sense; rather, it was an account of reduced surface SVO manifestations attributed to limited mental capacity. Bloom showed that across many two-word utterances, reduced versions of SVO were evidenced presumably due to restricted mental processing capacities.

There are two rather striking observations of such utterances. First, reduced versions of SVO in two-word utterances implicate an information-processing constraint. A child may have insufficient mental processing capacities to adequately deal with all of SVO. The so-called two-person sentence (Greenfield & Smith, 1976) may provide an interim solution for overcoming such limitations. Second, reduced SVO constructions are relevant to informativeness in accounts of language acquisition because what is generally omitted is given, known, or presupposed information, whereas what is generally coded is new, unknown, or unexpected information. Thus even early on, grammatical mechanisms seem to operate in the service of informativeness. Limber (1976) made a similar observation in regard to babbling behaviors of infants in the crib as they verbalized to the intentional movement of mobiles.

Evidently, early two- and three-word utterances are informational, first as indicatives (persons, places, things) and subsequently as predications (actions, states) and other relations (possessives, location, time, causality). Bloom (1973) indicated that early two-word utterances provide evidence of basic grammatical relations. Such two- and three-word utterances conveyed "inherently relational meaning" (p. 23). Relational meaning was distinguished from functional meaning in much the same way that Gopnik (1981, 1984) and Gopnik and Meltzoff (1984, 1986) distinguished the two. Schlesinger (1971) and Brown (1973b) made similar distinctions. Bloom (1973) held that these two categories reflected linguistic and cognitive functions of the utterances: "The important distinction for the child's learning language is more likely between LINGUISTIC categories—categories that are dependent on semantic and syntactic specification of relationships—on the one hand, and COGNITIVE categories on the other hand" (p. 31).

This distinction was useful to Gopnik (1981) in accounting for the nature of early cognitive utterances as contrasted with early communicative utterances. Gopnik separated nonnominal expressions from nominal expressions. A high percentage of early one-word utterances are nominals, whereas the remainder of the utterances express mostly semantic functions such as "all gone," "bye bye," and "no." Therefore, the distinction by Gopnik (1981) between nonnominal and nominal expressions for early one-word utterances corresponds somewhat with the distinctions made by Bloom (1973), Brown (1973b), and Schlesinger (1971) between utterances that expressed semantic functions and semantic relations.

Gopnik (1981) indicated that nonnominal expressions do not refer to specific types of objects, relations between objects, or particular actions or types of actions. Moreover, they do not appear to be social, conversational, or expressive devices. They seem to have "a certain egocentric quality," especially early on. They seem to be used "to mark relationships between themselves and objects, or between themselves, their actions, and objects" (p. 101). Thus, they seem to denote problem solving and other cognitive activities such as categorization and inferencing.

Gopnik (1981) stated further, "The expressions did not seem to encode actions or intentions as such: instead, the expressions were used when the child predicted that a certain consequence would ensue if he acted in a particular way, or if other actions occurred" (p. 102). "The concepts encoded by these expressions seem to be both egocentric and abstract" (p. 103). Such comments seem to be about cognitive achievements of reference.

Even as two-word expressions appear, nonnominal expressions persist. The second word in two-word expressions usually identifies the intended referent. Gopnik (1981) held that such expressions "play an important role in the cognitive development of 1–2-year-olds" (p. 103). She held that such expressions may assist a child in problem solving. She indicated that the importance of these expressions is not that they name referents but referential relations. Thus, such comments may be used to spontaneously encode newly realized relations in event knowledge. Even as one-word utterances, many utterances have inherent combinatorial meaning (Greenfield & Smith, 1976) whereby the event or context of use defines the intended relation (McCune-Nicolich, 1981a). K. Nelson (1996) provided a more comprehensive and eloquent perspective of the ways in which words may be deduced from procedural knowledge of events with their attendant highly rehearsed utterances.

In summary, the traditional notions of parts of speech and sentence types are tangential to how they function in actual social commerce. Function-based information is more appropriate. In regard to grammatical systems, basic grammatical relations in English center on SVO or the transitive system. Indeed, the verb is crucial for appreciating relational meaning (Gleitman, 1994; Gropen et al., 1994). Thus, what may be coded is that which is informative and early utterances evidently have two basic functions: cognitive or communicative.

MODULATIONS OF MEANING

Brown (1973b) detailed five stages of early language acquisition. With various developments in the literature and because these stages were only hypothetical and insufficiently substantiated, he urged caution in regarding them as true stages (Brown, 1978, 1988). Issues concerning cognition and affect in early word acquisition coupled with a child's understanding of objects, events, and relations in regard to what may be informative have raised many issues about Brown's Stage I. As Bloom (1973) indicated, "In short, children using single-word utterances know little if anything about sentences, but they have begun to know considerably more about the world of objects, events, and relations" (p. 31). This underscores Bruner's (1981) and K. Nelson's (1985, 1986, 1996) theme that early language acquisition is lodged or formatted in pragmatics whereby a child learns how to conduct social commerce, even in rudimentary ways, which in turn provides a scaffold for acquiring semantic, syntactic, prosodic, and phonological capacities. Moreover, this perspective accords well with those of the neo-Vygotskians.

Bloom (1990, 1991), Bloom and Beckwith (1988, 1989), and Bloom et al. (1988) showed that the expressions of affect are the predominant early means of expression that eventually become supplanted by words for expressing desires and beliefs. For example, early on a baby learns that a cry will bring mother for soothing and comforting; subsequently, the baby replaces the cry with words such as "mommy" to realize the same functions. Such perspectives were not addressed or reflected by Stage I (Brown, 1973a, 1973b).

Bruner (1981, 1986, 1990) and K. Nelson (1985, 1986, 1996) provided major developments—especially in regard to the centrality of intent, the roles of formats and scripts, and event knowledge—that redefine the importance of the semantic notions of Stage I. In short, such semantic categories may have to be reconsidered in relation to issues of possible worlds and event knowledge in the early situated mind.

Stage II (modulation of meanings) has held to some extent. Rice and Wexler (1996) invoked the optional infinitive (OI) model as one that more adequately accounts for the acquisition of those modulations of meaning that deal with tense marking (-s, -ed, BE, DO) and may be related by virtue of reference marking (a, the). Part of their motivation was theoretical and part was because the acquisition of some modulations of meaning extend beyond Stage II, indeed beyond Stage V.

The sentence types in Brown's Stage III have a structural orientation. More recent developments have redressed these perspectives as different kinds of intentions (Halliday, 1975; K. Nelson, 1985, 1991).

Brown also pointed out that Stages III, IV, and V are only hypothetical and they are in need of further substantiation and clarification. Brown (1978) said, "Stages III, IV, and V can only be characterized in a hypothetical way at the present. Roger Brown and many others are still trying to settle the sequences of constructions involving sentence modalities, sentence embedding, and sentence coordinating" (p. 189). Brown (1988) reaffirmed his position:

> The detailed analyses of presumptive Stages III, IV, and V did not yield up to Brown, then, any strong generalizations comparable to those of the early stages, and he could see no value in publishing the possibly quite idiosyncratic details available in the unpublished grammars. (p. 398)

It is so refreshing to see a true scholar at work. Here Brown is criticizing his own work, rather than hyping, and he is open to any worthy contributions, rather than capricious claims by pretenderers. The clinical fields have a worthy model of scholarship.

A major limitation of Brown's five stages is that they are basically structural. Developments in the cognitive socialization literature have stressed function, especially the centrality of intent. The essence of grammatical relations is relational and shared meanings within a message that is plausible from a possible worlds perspective and manifest for the purpose of recognizing communicative intent in particular contexts. Thus, the nature of language and language acquisition is much more functional than structural.

TABLE 5.1
The 14 English Morphemes for Modulating Meaning

Morpheme	Example
Progressive (-ing)	He go*ing*.
Locative (in)	Ball *in* box.
Locative (on)	Ball *on* truck.
Regular plural (-s)	Doggie*s* run.
Irregular past	*Ate* cookie.
Possessive ('s)	Mommy*'s* cookie.
Uncontractible copula	There he *is*.
Articles	*The* doggy ate *a* bone.
Regular past (-ed)	He open*ed* the door.
Regular third person (-s)	She run*s*.
Irregular third person	He do*es* it.
Uncontractible auxiliary	He *be* going.
Contractible copula	He*'s* big.
Contractible auxiliary	She*'s* sleeping.

Note. From *A First Language: The Early Stages*, by R. Brown, 1973b, Cambridge, MA: Harvard University Press. Copyright © 1973 by Harvard University Press. Adapted with permission.

Even so, Stage II has held up rather well. It deals with modulations of meaning. This is achieved primarily by the inflectional systems, noun and verb. The 14 morphemes (Brown, 1973b) that comprise Stage II include the following: plurality, tense marking, noun–verb concordance, possessive, un-contractible and contractible forms, locatives, and articles. They appear in Table 5.1.

The present progressive has two disjointed aspects: *be* and *-ing*. The tense marker is attached to the *be* to form *is/was*, whereas the *-ing* is attached to the verb to form constructions such as *working*. An example of the present progressive is: She *is* work*ing*. In acquisition, the *-ing* appears before the *be*. The acquisition sequence is the following:

I walk.

I walk*ing*.

I (*be*) walk*ing*.

I *am* walk*ing*.

The present progressive only pertains to action verbs in contrast to state verbs (Bloom, Lifter, & Hafitz, 1980). Thus, a child not only has to learn this mechanism but also draw appropriate semantic distinctions between verb types.

Marking of the regular plural conveys the perceptual distinction between singular and plural. Brown (1973b), Cazden (1968), deVilliers and deVilliers

(1978), Kuczaj (1982), and Palermo and Eberhart (1968) identified three stages in the acquisition of plural, possessive, and tense marking. Children begin with the *vocabulary stage*, in which words are learned holistically (Carey, 1982). Words are not yet decomposable. Decomposition occurs when children realize that words have a stem and possible inflectional (indeed, even derivational) markers. During this stage, children will say "boys," "man," and "men." The second stage is called *overgeneralization*. This is when certain inflectional rules are discerned but they are generalized to irregular forms as well as regular forms. The result is that the following are produced: "boys," "mans," and "mens." The third stage is *appropriate generalization*. This is when children learn to use the regular rules for regular forms but not for irregular forms. They then say "boys," "man," and "men." This shows a rather circuitous route in the acquisition of the inflectional system. It appears children had a skill, lost it, then regained it. However, this is not the case. What happened is that vocabulary became decomposed into various components and rules were learned that selectively apply to certain components. Karmiloff-Smith (1984, 1992) explained these events as three phases (procedural, metaprocedural, and conceptual) in which an individual obtains progressively flexible representational capacities although the surface manifestations have a curvilinear function. A similar event occurs in phonological acquisition. It is not uncommon for mothers to notice these events and incorrectly think that their children are losing language.

The irregular past is relatively common in English. Inasmuch as early word learning is rote learning as opposed to rule-governed, irregular past tense marking is early simply because of the high frequency of irregular verbs. However, such early learning does not necessarily mean that they can decompose words and make the distinction about past tense marking. It takes a relatively long time, possibly several years, to fully realize which verbs are regular and which are irregular and which semantic subtleties distinguish one verb from another (Gropen et al., 1994).

There is a somewhat confusing picture about the emergence of possessive markers. Part of the problem is that possessiveness can be marked in different ways (*-s* as in "Bob's hat," pronominal as in "his hat," and prepositional as in "the hat of his"). Bowerman (1973) and Cazden (1968) found possessives relatively early in acquisition. Brown (1973b) put possessive markers in the middle of the 14 morphemes. Greenfield and Smith (1976) showed that they occurred somewhat late.

The uncontractible copula means that the BE verb in certain contexts cannot be contracted to the preceding noun phrase (e.g., Here he *is*. There he *is*.). In contrast, there are other contexts in which the BE verb can be contracted (e.g., He's happy. He's a cowboy.).

It would be useful to consider the different kinds of BE verbs and the auxiliary *be* in English. Table 5.2 illustrates these distinctions.

TABLE 5.2
Distinctions Between the BE Verbs and the Auxiliary *Be* in English

Auxiliary *be* + -*ing*	I *am* walk*ing*.
Copular BE + NP	I *am* a student.
Noncopular BE + Adj	I *am* big.
Noncopular BE + Adv-pl	I *am* here.

The definite article (the) and indefinite articles (a, some, etc.) are part of a larger determiner system that also takes several years to become fully acquired. These particular articles are especially important because they function to mark the distinction between given and new information (Maratsos, 1976). Emslie and Stevenson (1981) reviewed research on the acquisition of definite and indefinite articles and found that they are different in regard to nominative (indefinite articles) and identifying (definite articles) functions. There are adverbial counterparts to these distinctions pertaining to naming and specifying, respectively. Nominative is a naming function, whereas identifying is a specifying function and nominative appears before specifying in acquisition.

Although Brown (1973b) and Maratsos (1976) showed that by 3 or 4 years of age most children distinguished between definite and indefinite articles, Warden (1976) found that this may hold for naming tasks, but it was not so for describing tasks: "Warden concluded that children under 5 fail to take into account their audience's knowledge of a referent (their referring expressions are predominantly definite), that there is referential language only from 9 onwards" (Emslie & Stevenson, 1981, p. 315).

This raises another issue in the acquisition of articles: egocentrism. The definite article is usually used to denote the distinctions between known and unknown information. For example, Sentence 1 identifies a particular cat, whereas Sentence 2 employs the definite article because this particular cat is now known (established as a topic).

1. My cat is named Shadow.
2. I feed *the* cat once a day.

It is conceivable that under certain conditions the definite article can be used deictically (to distinguish speaker–listener perspectives). Egocentrically oriented individuals may use definite articles excessively because they assume that what they know or do not know pertains to others as well.

Another part of the determiner system is evidenced before articles. The demonstrative, or at least the protodemonstrative /um/, appears very early in conjunction with the early communicative point (Bruner, 1981). Ramer (1976) reported the early use of the demonstrative pronominal "that one" as explicit deixis with other two-word utterances.

The regular past is the use of -ed to mark past tense. It may appear as an overgeneralized form of irregular verbs resulting in the following: "goed," "wented," and "hitted." These eventually become sorted out in relation to which verbals have regular tense markings and which have irregular tense markings. Overgeneralization rarely occurs with modals, yet modals carry tense markers also.

The third person singular is a device in English to indicate concordance or agreement between the plurality of the third person grammatical case of subject noun phrases and its verb. This is shown in the following:

Third person singular:	*He* works hard.
Third person plural:	*They* work hard.
First person singular:	*I* work hard.

The full acquisition of the third person singular marker may be protracted. Indeed, full acquisition of the 14 morphemes may be protracted.

In accordance with Labov (1970), Brown (1973b) discussed the distinction between "contractible" and "uncontractible" for the *be* in the auxiliary and the BE as a copula. Table 5.3 illustrates these distinctions.

Again in accordance with Labov (1970), Brown (1973b) gave a "contractibility" principle: "Wherever SE can contract, child English can delete (whether is, are, or am) and vice versa; wherever SE cannot contract child English cannot delete and vice versa" (p. 67; SE refers to Standard English).

Taking the contractibility issue further, it could be viewed from the perspective of productivity. That is, instances of contracted forms should initially be regarded as vocabulary (nondecomposable) rather than gram-

TABLE 5.3
Distinctions Between the Contractible and
Uncontractible Auxiliary *Be* and BE Copula

Contractible
Aux *be*
I'*m* going.
He'*s* going.
Copula BE
I'*m* a cowboy.
He'*s* a cowboy.

Uncontractible
Aux *be*
I *be* going.
He *be* going.
Copula BE
Here I *am*.
There it *is*.

TABLE 5.4
Examples of Uncontracted and Contracted Auxiliary Forms

Auxiliary	Uncontracted	Contracted
Modal	I will swim.	I'll swim.
Be	I am eating.	I'm eating.
Have	I have eaten.	I've eaten.

matically productive. However, when both contracted and uncontracted instances for contractible constructions become observed, the child should be credited for this option. Table 5.4 illustrates uncontracted and contracted forms for contractible auxiliaries.

It is not unreasonable to think of the acquisition of the 14 morphemes during the modulations of meaning stage as grammatical tinkering within the basic SVO grammatical relations as a way of figuring out the coherence of the grammatical system in achieving a message of best fit for communication. For example, it is not unusual to observe children tinkering with their utterances in the course of actual social commerce. Once some degree of tinkering within sentences has been achieved, children then may turn to different kinds of intentions (Searle, 1969, 1975, 1977) such as the differences between representatives, directives, commissives, expressives, and declaratives. This notion of tinkering with grammatical constructions was motivated by the observations that young children spontaneously hold communication in abeyance while they tinker.

CENTRALITY OF VERBS

The focus of possible tinkering within SVO is surely the verb with its attendant structures. Following Chomsky (1965) and Harris (1965), it may be useful to consider the basic verbals (verb with attendant structures) of English. Table 5.5 provides this information.

It is conceivable that at some point of language acquisition children strive to discern the nature of various kinds of verbals. Moreover, it is likely that such considerations include not only structural considerations such as those already mentioned, but semantic distinctions within verb classes (Bowerman, 1982; Gleitman, 1994; Gropen et al., 1994) or propositional potential. Maratsos (1988b) posited that although the verb is the focus of grammatical learning, it is not the verb per se but its propositionality—predication—that is the focus of learning: "Children necessarily analyze along the dimension of predication" (p. 137).

Gleitman's (1994) syntactic bootstrapping proposal relies to a large extent on verb acquisition with the attendant structures. She indicated that verb

TABLE 5.5
The Basic Verbals of English

I *am here.*	aux. BE Adv-pl
I *am a student.*	aux. BE NP
I *am happy.*	aux. BE adjective
I *work.*	aux. VI
I *ate a cookie.*	aux. VT NP
I *have a cookie.*	aux. Vh NP
I *seem happy.*	aux. Vs adjective
I *became happy/a student.*	aux. Vb adjective/NP

use across situations constitutes a way in which various interpretations can be sorted out and the prospective meanings (propositional potential) with the greatest utility become the essential meanings. Furthermore, co-occurring structures help to narrow down prospective meanings. This is what she regarded as "linguistically sanctioned" (p. 184). Thus, both situational awareness and linguistic context are useful for appreciating the meaning of verbs. These sources of information are coupled with assistance provided by mothers who may be tuned to what their children can do (repertoire) and what is useful to perceive (salient) and to say (relevant). Thus, mothers become active partners whereby they carry out an "attentional conspiracy" (Gleitman, 1994, p. 183) in the best interests of their children (Bruner, 1981). These mechanisms not only set the stage for assisting language acquisition but do so in a way in which the child is provided narrowly focused yet flexible opportunities to learn language.

As Gleitman (1994) indicated, there is a cost for operating in such a narrowly focused way. It is that a child may errantly dismiss certain information that would eventually be useful for developing a full-fledged system. This by itself may not be a serious problem as long as a child remains open and flexible. It simply means that the learning process must be open, flexible, and capable of recovering from wrong turns.

What is so attractive about learning grammar from the perspective of verbs is that verbs are not only central to clausal (propositional) frameworks but such frameworks themselves offer a means of narrowly focusing learning.

> Each verb is associated with several of these structures. Each such structure narrows down the choice of interpretations for the verb. Thus these limited parameters of structural variation, operating jointly, can predict the possible meanings of an individual verb quite closely. (Gleitman, 1994, p. 198)

Thus, situational and linguistic input coupled with the attentional conspiracy offer potent potentials for language acquisition. Furthermore, a child may have the potential of vertical or horizontal learning of the verbal systems. In language intervention, the parallel talk strategy (Muma, 1978b, 1983b, 1986a) is the clinician's means of establishing an attentional conspiracy.

Another point should be made regarding informativeness. It is that the predicate system is that which is most informative. This means that children tend to invest their learning in those aspects of grammar that are most informative. This issue is amplified by the observation that the object noun phrase (most informative) is typically learned before the subject noun phrase (given information) and the former is usually elaborated before the latter (Brown, 1973b). This means that grammatical learning is not merely a semantic endeavor but also a propositional one.

VERTICAL AND HORIZONTAL LEARNING

The notions of vertical and horizontal learning are not new in the language acquisition literature. Fodor (1983) credited Gall for the basic notion of vertical and horizontal mental processing. McNeill (1970) discussed horizontal and vertical learning for the lexicon. Lexical horizontal learning is basically compiling new words with fragmented or partial meanings; vertical learning is when words enter the lexicon with rich meanings, by virtue of appropriate previous experience, but the underlying semantic structure may not yet be available to integrate words with each other into a coherent lexicon. McNeill's perspective is somewhat complementary to Vygotsky's (1962) notions of spontaneous and scientific word learning. Jakobson (1960) also discussed vertical and horizontal learning. Wanner (1988) considered vertical and horizontal parsing as different means of language acquisition.

Bates and MacWhinney (1987) used the notions of vertical and horizontal relations in language acquisition. Drawing on a deSaussurian perspective, they indicated that there are three basic kinds of correlations to be deduced in language acquisition:

1. Direct vertical correlations between forms and functions.
2. Horizontal correlations between forms.
3. Horizontal correlations between functions.

Vertical correlations pertain to the awareness of not only what forms appear in verbal constructions but also how they function in a coherent relational message of information in the realization of communicative intent. An extension of this notion is the realization that given that a particular word works or functions a certain way, a child comes to realize that other words may also function in similar ways. The addition of other words that operate or function similarly is evidence of vertical correlates. For example, the word *carry* functions transitively (it takes an object) in the sentence "He carried the box." As a child comes to realize that other words can also function transitively, vertical learning for the transitive system transpires.

Horizontal correlates for forms is the realization of privileges of occurrence of various forms in particular linguistic contexts. Harris (1965) gave a comprehensive account of the role of form–form correlates or co-occurrence in linguistic context in language learning. Bates and MacWhinney (1987) regarded this as positional patterning. According to Bates and MacWhinney (1979, 1987), the early formulaic expressions or ossified forms provide relatively fixed form–form relations. As these eventually become decomposed, a learner is afforded opportunities to discern form–function correlates. For example, "Daddy go" may be an ossified form that is originally unaltered and the child comes to know its meaning as a function of the contexts of use. Because "daddy" may also be used referentially to indicate a particular person, the co-occurrence of "go" offers the child an opportunity to discern daddy as agent and go as action, thereby affording the child the eventual realization of agent–action semantic relations and ultimately the realization of its grammatical relations (subject–action).

Horizontal correlates for functions pertain to the permissible combinations of semantic relations. This is what Bates and MacWhinney (1987) called *semantic connectedness*. A child may arrive at horizontal correlates for functions in two basic ways, via horizontal correlates for forms as mentioned earlier or via awareness of the meaning of events (K. Nelson, 1985, 1986). That is, sheer knowledge of the world (Palermo, 1982), possible worlds (Bruner, 1981, 1986), or situated mind (K. Nelson, 1996) as it is applied to an event provides a child with potential semantic relations.

Given these potential correlates for learning language, it is not surprising that alternative language learning strategies have been identified (Bates et al., 1988). It is also evident that partial learning takes place (Muma, 1978b). Bates and MacWhinney (1987) made the following comments that recognize partial learning of grammatical systems:

> The child does not consider **all** possible correlations between **all** items in **all** sentences in acquiring an accurate set of form–form correlations. . . . The child appears to be guided by two principles in deciding what to correlate with what. One principle is that of semantic connectedness. The other is positional patterning. Together, these two principles tightly delimit the scope of the co-occurrence patterns that the learner considers. (p. 166)

Macken (1987) indicated that both grammatical and phonological rule learning evidently take place in two tiers somewhat comparable to the Bates and MacWhinney (1987) perspective. Macken held that early learning seems to be based on a stochastic model (distributional learning) concerning frequency of occurrence, whereas subsequent learning deals with inferring algorithms for rule abstraction.

Bates and MacWhinney (1987) indicated that the mappings that drive the system are the vertical correlates. With this account, they credited their views of functionalism (Bates & MacWhinney, 1979, 1987) as being compatible with Maratsos' (1982) notions of correlational learning. These accounts are also compatible with the emerging notions of bootstrapping (Gleitman, 1994; Pinker, 1984) and of coherence (Berman, 1988; Braine, 1988; Schlesinger, 1988).

Crystal (1987) had a theory of language acquisition called the *bucket theory*, which posited that increased demands in one aspect of language may result in decreased performance in another. This is what Masterson and Kamhi (1992) termed *trade-off*. This also has a compatibility ring with the resource allocation view (Locke, 1994). Presumably, such trade-offs occur when a child's verbal system is limited and operating at capacity. Masterson and Kamhi (1992) indicated that Camarata and Schwartz (1985) and Prelock and Panagos (1981) found trade-offs between syntactic, semantic, and phonological aspects of utterances, whereas Kamhi, Catts, and Davis (1984) did not. There are two disturbing issues in these kinds of studies that should be raised, specifically what justifications warrant the selections of the dependent variables used and their measurement metrics. These studies do not provide such information; they merely assert that particular variables were used and measured in particular ways.

Nevertheless, the bucket theory is interesting. The previously mentioned studies sought to find trade-offs between semantic, syntactic, and phonological domains. Surely, this inquiry could be extended to the cognitive-social domains and to the pragmatic domain. For example, Berko's (1958) famous study indicated that inflectional markers were influenced by phonological contexts. Menyuk and Looney (1972a, 1972b) showed trade-offs in different aspects of language. Within syntax, the notion of co-occurring systems (Bloom, 1970, 1973; Bloom & Lahey, 1978; Brown, 1973b; Brown & Bellugi, 1964; Brown, Cazden, & Bellugi-Klima, 1969; Harris, 1965; Muma, 1973b) may provide evidence of such trade-offs.

AVAILABLE REPERTOIRE

Strangely enough, clinicians in the field are virtually oblivious to the notion of available repertoire. This is strange simply because if a clinician wants to know what an individual can do with language it is necessary to have some evidence of what the individual actually does as an estimate of available repertoires. Prima facie evidence for estimating grammatical capacities issues from representative language samples. The fact that most clinicians may not know the gravity of such samples for estimating what an individual

TABLE 5.6
Kinds of Evidence Derived From Representative Language
Samples for Estimating Available Grammatical Repertoire

Estimating Available Grammatical Repertoire
1. Grammatical structure variations.
He *goes*. He *wented*. He *went*.
2. Lexical variation within structures.
He *went*. He *walked*. He *ran*.
He went. *She* went. *They* went.
3. Variations of co-occurring structures.
He went. He went *home*. He went *away*.

can do may be an indirect indictment about the level of reliance on, or indoctrination of, psychometric testing in the clinical fields.

Representative language samples provide evidence of available repertoires by virtue of:

1. The range of grammatical skills evidenced—different kinds of structures and functions.
2. Levels of productivity of the skills, especially as evidenced by lexical variation within structures.
3. The variety of co-occurring structures (Harris, 1965; Muma, 1973b).

Such evidence is useful in not only appreciating the range and productivity of grammatical and pragmatic skills but in appreciating an individual's potential for overcoming communicative obstacles when a message does not work as intended. Table 5.6 illustrates these issues.

In the first example the goal for intervention would be to follow the acquisition sequence for this inflectional marker. In the second example, the intervention goal would be to vary lexical targets within a selected domain. This is done by using the *parallel talk strategy* (Muma, 1981c, 1983b) in spontaneous play and by using the *10 techniques* (Muma, 1981c, 1983b). In the third example, the parallel talk strategy and 10 techniques are also used, but the targets are different.

There is no test or formal assessment procedure with sufficient potential for addressing these issues. Simply put, it is essential that clinicians obtain and analyze representative language samples to appreciate an individual's repertoire of available skills.

ACQUISITION SEQUENCE

Brown (1973a, 1973b) showed that sequence is a crucial index of language acquisition. Indeed, the cognitive socialization literature over the past few decades has identified many acquisition sequences. Thus, comments about an individual's presumed language skills should be about how a particular person has progressed in reference to various acquisition sequences.

For example, functionally, the acquisition sequence for negation is: non-existence, rejection, and denial (Bloom, 1970, 1973). Structurally, negation has the following sequence: marked external to a sentence (I go, *no*), marked internally but not integrated into the auxiliary (I *no* go), and finally marked internally and integrated into the auxiliary (I wo*n't* go; Klima & Bellugi-Klima, 1969). Summaries of various acquisition sequences are available (Bloom & Lahey, 1978; Muma, 1978b, 1981c, 1986a; Prutting, 1979).

Turning to clinical practices and behaviorism, it is common to find instances in which claims are made about an individual's presumed language acquisition skills according to either the number of instances of a grammatical structure in a baseline or percentages of so-called correct and incorrect performances. However, little, if any, attention is given to language acquisition sequences or variation either within or between constructions. Indeed, such clinical practices are based on the premise that it is unnecessary to attend to acquisition sequences because percentage of correct performance may suffice. Thus, frequency or percentage has effectively replaced sequence, contexts, and variations within and between constructions in accounts of language acquisition in the clinical fields.

For example, Fey (1986) indicated that "the *quantity* of responses produced by the child may not be nearly as important as the *quality* (i.e., the use of a target form in a relevant and meaningful social context)" (p. 116). Then he indicated that he was not familiar with any descriptive approaches that provided such information so he concluded that clinicians should take baseline data based on the number of instances of a relevant behavior. This is a strange myopic stance. However, Bloom and Lahey (1978), Harris (1965), and Muma (1973b, 1978b) described the use of varied co-occurring structures as a means of substantiating the linguistic contexts in which an individual has achieved a productive capacity. Following Brown (1973b), several scholars such as Bloom et al. (1989) and Ingram (1989a) discussed lexical variation within grammatical constructions as qualitative evidence of productive capacity.

Moreover, most of the studies that relied merely on frequency counts have questionable criteria for learning and failed to address appropriately form–function relations. Yet, many of these studies claim to provide evidence for language intervention and presumed efficacy. Such views and perspectives are of questionable value if the scholarly cognitive socialization literature is to be considered. In a word, the clinical fields' reliance on frequencies and percentages at the cost of not considering available repertoires, progress in acquisition sequences, alternative learning strategies, and evidence of active loci of learning may have been a disservice to the clients and the clinical fields.

ACQUISITION STRATEGIES

Another of the most important contributions of the language acquisition
literature is the identification of alternative strategies of learning. Bloom et
al. (1974) found that some learners are imitators and some are not. Bloom
et al. (1975) showed that some individuals learn the nominal system initially
as simple nominals such as proper nouns and simple determiners (the, a,
that, etc.) plus nouns. Other individuals begin learning the nominal system
in regard to pronominals (definite and indefinite). Bloom (1978) indicated
that when children reach MLU of about 2.0 the respective nominal and
pronominal strategies integrate. Thus, there is evidence for nominal and pronominal strategies in early learning. Moreover, most children learn and
elaborate object nominals before subject nominals (Brown, 1973b), but some
children strive to learn subject nominals first. In a related matter, Vihman,
Ferguson, and Elbert (1987) distinguished very young children who had
relatively clear phonology from others who had phonology that was not
very clear. The former group typically developed a pronominal learning
strategy. Cromer (1974) showed that some children preferred to learn adjectival constructions in object nominals, whereas other children had a
preference to do so with subject nominal constructions.

K. Nelson (1973b) found that some learners followed a referential strategy,
whereas other learners followed an expressive strategy. Referential learners
seem to be oriented on the principle that one word has many referents and
one referent has many words. Expressive learners seem to be oriented on
the principle that new forms come in with old functions and new functions
come in with old forms (Slobin, 1970; Werner & Kaplan, 1963). Ramer (1976)
found two strategies: rapid and slow. Rapid learners reached the syntactic
criterion in 4.5 months, whereas slow learners took 6.5 months. Peters (1983)
indicated that some learners follow an analytic strategy whereas others
follow a Gestalt strategy. Dore (1974) identified code learners and message
learners. The code-oriented learner used language "primarily to declare
things about her environment" (p. 350), whereas the message-oriented child
strived "mainly to manipulate other people" (p. 350). The code-oriented child
used more words and these words were to label, repeat, and practice. The
message-oriented child used fewer words but seemed to control a larger
repertoire of prosodic features (intonation patterns). Perhaps code-oriented
children are focused primarily on the SVO (or at least verbs with their
attendant structures), whereas message-oriented children are focused primarily on the prosodic envelope. Vihman (1981) and Locke (1979) indicated
that some children strive to learn phonemic contrasts to overcome homonymy but other children may actually seek homonymy. Regarding the
latter, Vihman (1981) said:

> They may resort to such processes in order to merge two or more adult words
> in a single sound pattern. In short, instead of demonstrating a desire to achieve

efficiency in performance, the child's goal in such cases almost seems to be the production of a maximum number of lexical items with a minimum repertoire of sound shapes. (p. 241)

Similarly, Ferguson (1978) and Menn (1979) showed an inverse relation between phonetic accuracy and vocabulary growth. Some children tend to acquire vocabulary slowly but produce their words accurately. In contrast, other children tend to acquire vocabulary relatively fast but they have a high rate of articulation errors. Schwartz and Leonard (1982) showed that some children tended to learn and use words that were within their phonological capacities but they tended to avoid words with phonological characteristics outside of their phonological repertoire.

Bates et al. (1988) summarized several language learning strategies. For example, Bretherton, McNew, Snyder, and Bates (1983) found that some toddlers followed an analytic strategy, whereas others followed a holistic strategy in language acquisition. Chapman and Kohn (1978) raised the prospect of different comprehension strategies. This reminds me of the studies by Bever (1970), Huttenlocher (1974), McNeill (1970), and Muma, Adams-Perry, and Gallagher (1974), which showed that young children have an initial preference for a syntactic strategy in comprehension then shift to a semantic strategy. It is also possible that differences in apparent learning strategies may reflect different functions of language in different events (Strohner & Nelson, 1974).

In general, some strategies seem to be true strategies but others may be transitional devices. Surely further research will provide fuller accounts of the nature of alternative language learning strategies. Nevertheless, the evidence for alternative language acquisition strategies is a heavy blow against normative tests and behavioristic attempts to deal with efficacy. This evidence shows that there may be different yellow brick roads for language acquisition to the kingdom of effective social commerce.

With respect to the cognitive socialization literature, the clinical fields have different, even strange, perspectives about language acquisition strategies. For example, L. Miller (1989) and Buttrill et al. (1989) regarded verbal mediation, rehearsal, paraphrasing, visual imagery, concept networks and bridging, and retrieval strategies as language acquisition strategies. Here again, the clinical fields evidence substantive disconnections with the scholarly fields that deal with language acquisition.

ACTIVE LOCI OF LEARNING

Given the complexities of cognition, language, communication, and expression, there are many options for learning. Indeed, it is not unusual for a child to be learning several aspects of language at the same time either within a system or between systems. Also, apparently children are constrained by limited mental capacities and limited knowledge that comprise their readiness to learn. Furthermore, it is desirable for children to avail themselves of opportunities in regard to knowledge of events (K. Nelson, 1985, 1986, 1996) and relevant contacts with their language in the realization of communicative intents. Given the complexities of language and communication, and given an individual's readiness to learn and available opportunities to do so, it is reasonable to assume that at any given moment evidence of active learning may be at hand.

Thus, it behooves clinicians to obtain evidence of active loci of learning. The best source of such evidence is language used in actual social commerce because spontaneous speech is constructed to make intentions recognizable. Assuming a representative sample, evidence of active loci of learning should be available. Furthermore, continuous sampling should yield additional evidence of active loci of learning as an individual proceeds to learn.

Active loci of learning (Muma, 1983a, 1983b, 1986a) means evidence of active learning for particular aspects of language. Fortunately, the cognitive socialization literature has provided good evidence of active loci of learning. Coupled with appropriate attribution criteria of preparation, attainment, and consolidation (Muma, 1986a; K. E. Nelson, 1981; Prutting, 1979), the notion of active loci of learning provides an impressive way of doing language assessment. It is impressive simply because such procedures cannot be beat by psychometric normative tests that are sometimes touted as offering the best means of assessment.

For example, a child said, "I like soup. I like big soup." On the surface, it appears that this child is actively striving to learn how to modify inanimate nouns functioning in object noun phrases. Thus, such utterances may reveal an active locus of learning. However, it is necessary to regard such information as speculative until it is confirmed by substantiation. The best way to substantiate loci of learning is to compare such utterances with a representative language sample to ascertain to what extent this particular skill may be available; for example, preparation (few instances, context bound, difficult to elicit), attainment (many instances, not context bound, easy to elicit), or consolidation (co-occurrence with varied constructions). The clinical fields have not yet seriously broached such considerations.

The following are some examples of the ways in which active loci of learning may be ascertained. Folger and Chapman (1978) and Scherer and Olswang (1984) found that children tend to spontaneously imitate adult utterances that are expansions of their own (child's) speech. However, Bloom et al. (1974) revealed an interesting principle about spontaneous imitation that holds great promise for identifying active loci of learning. It is that spontaneous imitations are selective. Moreover, selectivity is not merely a response to parental expansions of their own utterances, which was the interpretation of Fey (1986). Rather, children typically do not imitate what they know and they do not imitate what they do not know. What they spontaneously imitate is what they are striving to learn. For example, an individual who was striving to learn possessiveness would imitate the following utterances: "my hat," "my shoes," "our car," "their cookies," and so on. Yet, he or she would not imitate the counterparts that do not mark possessiveness (i.e., "a hat," "that shoe," "a dog," etc.). Needless to say, an astute clinician would mark spontaneous imitations and compare them to the entire language sample to ascertain new active loci of learning and their linguistic contexts.

Similarly, spontaneous rehearsals should have the same potential for discovering active loci of learning. It makes sense that if spontaneous imitations are selectively utilized for active learning, then spontaneous rehearsals should have the same potentials. Said differently, a child may "celebrate learning" (Furth, 1984) by demonstrating a new achievement. Thus, a child who may have just discerned how to make some *wh* questions may celebrate this achievement by intentionally producing a series of *wh* questions just for the sake of doing so.

Weir (1962) made an interesting observation concerning build-ups. It was that children occasionally build up utterances whereby a series of utterances are made in which subsequent utterances are built from preceding ones. For example, a real child made the following utterances in succession:

Security base: I walk by myself.

New structures: I *can* walk by myself *when get home*.

Rehearsal: I can walk by my ____ (unintelligible)____.

New structure and glossing: I *could* **do it**.

Built-up utterance: I could walk *all* by myself ____ (unintelligible)____ *at* home.

A spontaneous rehearsal was the third utterance. What is impressive is that it occurred after the child was relatively successful in incorporating two new loci of learning. Then, the child proceeded to go further but he chose to gloss the predicate in order to incorporate another new locus (tense marking of the modal).

Interestingly, children seem to have some options for dealing with excessive complexity. Their options seem to be the following:

Option A: Quit.

Option B: Simplify by reducing the number of new loci.

Option C: Simplify by pronominalization (assuming that this capability is available).

Option D: Simplify mental processing capacity by glossing (a form of pronominalization).

Option E: Farm out some complexity by engaging in a two-person sentence.

Option F: Stay within a circumscribed arena of grammatical and pragmatic devices that are "known" or available.

Option F would not result in new learning. It might be useful as a transitory strategy so that an individual may obtain increased command of what he or she can do, but it would eventually be necessary to venture into new territory of language acquisition.

Menyuk (1964) described a dampened oscillatory function for error reduction that may reflect periods of "playing it safe" and confining what is produced to what an individual feels secure in doing followed by a period of "risk taking" in which errors increase because the individual is venturing into new territory.

Muma (1986a) described another kind of evidence of active loci of learning, which was called *buttressing*. It is evidenced when a child who has had difficulty with the pronominal forms begins to resolve the problem. Such children had been using object forms of pronouns in the subject position. For example, these children would say "me here," "them go," and "him eat." Interestingly, these children seldom went directly to the counterparts "I here," "they go," and "he eat." Rather, they typically buttressed by using an old form as a double marker with a new form. For example, they would typically say "Daddy, he here." Thus, "Daddy" was an old form that was used to buttress a new form "he." Behaviors of this sort evidence active loci of learning.

Bloom (1978) made a similar observation. She pointed to the presence of redundant forms as evidence of a shift in pronominal and nominal encoding: "Such utterances seemed to represent the children's attempt to learn the alternative forms of pronominal and nominal encoding in making the transition from one form of reference to the other" (p. 234). Bloom's comment pertained to the recognition of pronominal and nominal strategies of grammatical learning that evidently merge into an integrated encoding potential once a child reaches MLU of about 2.0: "Even though the children started out with either one or the other linguistic system, there was a significant shift with development as both systems of reference were gradually integrated for all of the children" (p. 234). The systems were pronominal and nominal.

Muma (1983a, 1986a) summarized several kinds of evidence issuing from the cognitive socialization literature that can be used by astute clinicians to ascertain active loci of learning. Self-corrections, mentioned in chapter 8, constitute another kind of evidence of active loci of learning. There are no formal tests that have this capability. Again, as with acquisition sequences, strategies of learning, and appropriate criteria of learning, the clinical fields have yet to grasp the significance of active loci of learning as evidence of language assessment, intervention, and efficacy.

CODE MATRIX

It is one thing to code a message linguistically (semantic, syntactic, prosodic, phonological) but quite another to understand that in the pragmatic arena linguistic codes may be affirmed, emphasized, and subverted. Thus, a person may say, "I liked the movie," but facial and body gestures may be used to support, emphasize, or even negate a linguistic assertion. In this context, it would be necessary to appreciate indirect messages. This means that a linguistic code provides only one of several other potential codes in a code matrix that may be used to make communicative intents recognizable. It is the communicative context in which shared meaning is negotiated that ultimately defines which aspects of a code matrix (Muma, 1975b, 1986a) should be relevant in making intentions recognizable. This is one reason pragmatic views and perspectives have become so important.

PHONOLOGY

I have some very brief comments about phonology. First, the scholarly field of phonology has evidenced a shift from phoneme-based approaches to syllabic approaches (Daniloff, 1984; Daniloff & Hammarberg, 1973; Ferguson & Farwell, 1975; Ferguson & Garnica, 1975; Stoel-Gammon & Cooper, 1984; Waterson, 1984). This shift has provided descriptive evidence about phonological processes used by a child (Ingram, 1976, 1989b; Vihman & Greenlee, 1987), phonetic inventory (Ingram, 1976), homonymy (Locke, 1979; Priestly, 1980; Vihman, 1981), and phonological avoidance (Schwartz & Leonard, 1982). Second, this literature has shown a close relation between phonological acquisition and word acquisition. Third, it is apparent that essentially the same kind of rule acquisition occurs in phonology and syntax (Macken, 1987). Early on, rule learning appears to be stochastic or probabilistic, whereas rule learning eventually becomes algebraic or abstract. Furthermore, there is reason to believe that such rules are not unique to language but reflect the general architecture of cognition (Anderson, 1983; Karmiloff-Smith, 1984, 1992; Newell, 1992). The point of these brief comments is that the field of phonology relies on descriptive evidence rather than formal tests. By doing so, this field is more firmly aligned with the cognitive socialization literature than the efforts in the clinical fields to deal with syntax and even pragmatics, which strives to be descriptive but has lost sight of context and intent.

SUMMARY

The traditional notions of parts of speech and the crude notion of sentence types were found to be atheoretical and apsychological. In learning codification, evidently children strive to learn relational meanings for SVO, then they tinker within SVO to modulate meanings, then they strive to learn how to code different kinds of basic intentions, and this is followed by modification and elaboration. Knowledge of events and verbal systems plays a central role in learning grammatical systems.

Brown (1973a, 1973b) recommended that language acquisition be indexed by sequence rather than rate of learning. This and approximately eight other reasons indicate that MLU is of questionable value as an index of language acquisition. For example, MLUs over 4.5 index language performance rather than acquisition.

The basic grammatical skills in English are entailed in SVO relations. As individuals obtain basic command of SVO, they then apparently turn to tinkering with modulations of meaning. The center of this enterprise is verb acquisition with the attendant constructions and functions. Interestingly, learning the grammatical systems, especially predication, may proceed vertically or horizontally. Furthermore, acquisition is very much a function of available repertoire and readiness to learn. Readiness to learn is a function of available repertoire, progress in acquisition sequences, available learning strategies, active loci of learning, and available opportunities.

Traditionally, raw frequencies and percentages have been used to attribute verbal skills to children in language acquisition. Both of these have flaws. Rather, it is necessary to consider different ways in which language learning should be attributed. The Piagetian notions of preparation, attainment, and consolidation have much to offer. Alternatively, at least three varied instances of grammatical constructions may be used for attribution and single instances may be considered as indexing the possible range of available skills.

A linguistic code is only one of several other potential codes that may convey an intended message. Finally, the phonology literature is leading the way in appreciating many of these issues.

6

COMMUNICATION AND EXPRESSION

PRAGMATICS

Pragmatics deals with language use in context. In contrast to language used intrapersonally for thinking, pragmatics deals with language used interpersonally for communication. Moreover, expression (affect) may be superimposed on language to alter a message. Bruner summarized the importance of pragmatics by saying "Everything is use" (Bruner, 1986, p. 87) and "Context is all" (Bruner, 1981, p. 172).

Before dealing with some substantive issues in pragmatics, perhaps a brief historical perspective is in order. The pragmatic perspective is directly traceable to Frege (1892/1952) because he indicated that indexical expressions made sense in their contexts of use. Thus, Frege indicated the importance of context in language use for making sense. Indeed, Wittgenstein (1953), who has often been credited for being the father of pragmatics, apparently derived much from Frege.

Frege's views were largely quieted by Russell's (1905) views of reference. In contrast to Frege, Russell relied on formal logic to define a referent. Russell's views dominated the theory of reference for about 50 years, until Strawson (1950) revived Frege's views, which constituted the central theme for what became known as pragmatics.

Both Strawson (1950) and Donnellan (1981) regarded presupposition as an implicit assumption for Frege's notion of sense. *Presupposition* is knowledge of the world that is relevant to a particular message. It is a necessary aspect of reference as defined from the Frege notion of sense because it frees meaning from a strictly logical or Russellian view, but, more importantly, presupposition places meaning for messages in a larger arena, namely theory of the world, possible worlds, or situated mind. In so doing, language becomes a cognitive endeavor operating on general cognitive principles rather than unique capacities.

The general cognitive principles entailed in presupposition are twofold: categorization or representation and inference employed in problem solving (Karmiloff-Smith, 1984, 1992). That is, in order for an individual to know what to code in a message it is necessary to have knowledge of the world as representational knowledge. It is also necessary for an individual to make decisions about what should be explicitly coded in the context of what is implicitly known. These cognitive matters are biological, psychological, emotional, sociological, and even cultural, which themselves are loosely logical (Sperber & Wilson, 1986) yet communicate effectively by virtue of mutual manifestness. This perspective dethrones the Russellian perspective.

Subsequently, both the sense and logical notions were regarded as inadequate (Kripke, 1972). Kripke held that the Frege notion of sense relied on a priori categories of truth and was too restrictive (proper names, singular definite descriptions). He also held that Russell's requirements for formal logic were ruefully and regularly violated in popular reference. Kripke proposed the *cluster concept theory of names* for designated reference. In this theory, an individual has a cluster of available terms that may be used but the contexts of use determine what terms are most useful. This is remarkably similar to Brown's (1958a) notion of utility for word use.

Speech act theory could be regarded as a product of Frege's notion of sense. This theory was posited by Grice in the 1967 William James Lecture at Harvard University but it was not published in the original version; a revised rendition was published in 1975. Meanwhile, Austin (1962) posited his rendition; and, Searle (1969, 1975, 1977) contributed his perspectives. Clark and Clark (1977) provided a substantiated perspective of speech act theory. This work was the most fully enunciated and substantiated account of speech act theory. Sperber and Wilson's (1986) relevance theory provided further developments of the Gricean perspective in which the cognitive basis of language was more formally elaborated and the centrality of intent was advanced. Thus, pragmatic theory has obtained increased credibility as evidenced by the contributions of speech act theory.

Brown's (1956) comment that language acquisition is "a process of cognitive socialization" (p. 247) has attained fuller meaning as evidenced by various functionalistic perspectives of language in general and speech act theory in particular. Furthermore, the informativeness perspective and the more recent perspectives concerning social origins of the mind (Rogoff, 1990; Wertsch, 1991)—making sense or shared meaning for events (K. Nelson, 1985, 1986) culminating in the situated mind (K. Nelson, 1996)—are not only compatible with cognitive socialization and speech acts but also contribute to their advancement.

The importance of speech acts and pragmatic perspectives is that they hold four fundamental assumptions that have become increasingly important in accounting for language acquisition and use. First, they are broad based. The issues entailed in these perspectives extend from the underlying cognitive base to semantic, syntactic, prosodic, phonological, and pragmatic systems and processes. Indeed, affect is also considered (Bloom, 1991; Bloom & Beckwith, 1989). Second, they are derived from the functionalistic view that structure is in the service of function. Third, they recognize the importance of dealing with language in context. To reiterate, "Context is all" (Bruner, 1981, p. 172). Furthermore, context can be construed in different ways:

1. Internal–external contexts.
2. Intentional, referential, relational, and social and shared contexts.

Indeed, K. Nelson's (1985) notions of contexts are even more elaborate, issuing from three main themes: subjective (individual cognitive capacities), shared (social influences), and objective (cultural influences). Fourth, and most important, they establish the centrality of communicative intent. Specifically, Grice (1967) held that the purpose of communication is to make intentions recognizable. Referring to Grice, Sperber and Wilson (1986) commented, "as long as there is some way of recognizing the communicator's intentions, then communication is possible" (p. 25).

THE PRAGMATIC ARENA

Pragmatics has several dimensions. Table 6.1 lists some prominent dimensions of pragmatics.

TABLE 6.1
Various Pragmatic Activities

Greetings, openings, initiating turns
Topic invitation
Topic development
Topic sharing and back channel behavior
Attending to decoder feedback, contingent queries
Turn maintenance
Deictic reference
Anaphora
Topicalization
Indirect messages
Preclosing
Closing

In order to conduct social commerce, it is necessary for participants to engage in a variety of activities for the purpose of recognizing communicative intents. Communication begins with an opening that is initially a greeting such as "Hi." Within discourse, topic openings or changes occur as well. Some individuals are rather restrained and tend to initiate topics infrequently, whereas other individuals are more outgoing and initiate topics frequently. Sometimes an invitation is used to initiate a topic (Garvey, 1977). For example, a person said, "I heard that you cut yourself yesterday." The other person cannot just say "Yes," because this kind of statement (or question) invites the person to talk about the incident rather than merely acknowledge it.

It is fairly common for a few topics to be mentioned briefly, then topic development may occur, whereby one individual elaborates on a particular topic. Such elaboration may be shared between the participants. Thus, topic development may be by one person or between others. When topic development is between participants, it is usually called *topic sharing*. Some individuals may decline participation by the use of back channel comments (Fey & Leonard, 1983), whereby an opening is extended to a person but the individual merely throws the topic back by saying as little as possible. For example, one person may say, "Did you like the movie?" The other person may merely respond by saying, "Yes." With this response, the responsibility for talking is thrown back to first person.

Young children have what is known as a "talk to" attitude, whereby they tell someone something but they often fail to attend to the feedback of their listeners (Bloom, 1973). This kind of communication is egocentric rather than social. As individuals become cognitively able to consider the perspective of others and to attend to listener feedback, they use feedback to appropriately adjust their messages thereby achieving better communication. The use of listener feedback to adjust messages begins to be evidenced as early as 2 years of age and is not fully developed until about adolescence (Flavell, 1968; Gallagher, 1977, 1981; Gallagher & Darnton, 1978; Garvey, 1975, 1977, 1979).

It is rather common for preschool children to retain their talking turns while they are thinking of something to say. For example, these children will frequently use filled pauses such as "um," "and," and "and then" at the end of utterances and even in the middle of utterances. Harry Caray, the television announcer for the Chicago Cubs, frequently uses very long pauses in the middle of sentences as he tries to think of what to say.

Deictic reference is a pragmatic skill that indicates different perspectives between a speaker and listener. For example, the following words distinguish between speaker and listener perspectives: this–that, these–those, and mine–yours.

Pronominalization with its function of anaphoric reference offers unique ways of codification. Pronouns and proverbs may be used to refer to previously designated referents. For example, reference to "John" can be pronominalized in the sentence "John caught a fish." The new sentence would be "*He* caught a fish."

The function of the pronominal system is to maintain a previously identified referent. This is known as *anaphoric reference*. Thus, the pronouns in the following sentences maintain their respective referents:

John caught a fish.

He knew *it* was a bass.

It had to be 14" long to keep.

It was only 11" so *he* had to throw *it* back.

Soon, *he* caught another bass that was big enough to keep.

Adult speakers of English know that the three instances of "he" refer to John. Thus, "he" maintained reference. Furthermore, "it" was used to maintain reference also. Notice that the relative clause seems to be related in some way to anaphoric reference.

This example provides evidence of two important issues in anaphoric reference. First, the example provides evidence of *anaphoric loading*; that is, reference to John and the bass were maintained over several instances of referencing. An overlooked issue in the clinical fields is the extent to which an individual can deal adequately with anaphoric loading; that is, how many instances of anaphoric loading can an individual handle before losing track of the intended referent? It has been speculated that some language-impaired individuals (Fey & Leonard, 1983; Prutting & Kirchner, 1983), hearing-impaired individuals, and retarded individuals may evidence trouble with anaphoric reference. It may very well be that part of this trouble is with the degree of anaphoric loading.

Second, the example has two referents that were pronominalized. This raises another major issue, which is *competing anaphora*. It is possible and likely that an individual can more adequately handle an anaphoric referent that is not in competition for mental processing space with other anaphoric referents than when it may be in competition. In this example, "John" is in competition with "a bass" for anaphoric reference processing space. Thus, the clinical problems with pronouns may be with anaphoric loading or competition.

A third problem that may occur with anaphoric reference is the *vacant anaphoric reference*. This occurs when an individual uses pronouns without establishing the intended referent. This would be evidenced in this example by replacing "John" with "he" from the onset. Again, individuals with poor pragmatic skills may use vacant anaphora.

Topicalization is when something is made into a topic when it typically functions as a comment in topic–comment relations. There are some grammatical devices for topicalization (there transformation, passive transformation, and possibly the particle shift). The there transformation may be illustrated by changing the following sentence:

The horse is *there*.
There is the horse.

The passive transformation is illustrated as follows:

The dog chased *the cat*.
The cat was chased by the dog.

The particle shift is illustrated as follows:

He took *out* the garbage.
He took the garbage *out*.

Another pragmatic issue is *indirect messages*. In order for indirect messages to work as intended, it is necessary for the decoder to be signaled in some way that the intended message is indirect. For example, the person that said, "I liked the movie" but frowned actually signaled an indirect message of disliking the movie.

Preclosing behaviors are used to convey to the encoder that the speaker is about to give up his or her speaking turn or that he or she is about to terminate communication. These are done by the use of eye contact, posture changes, looking at a watch, or simply announcing "It's late. I have to go." Then, the participants negotiate closings, such as "Just a minute."

Needless to say, it behooves clinicians to attend to these various pragmatic issues. Sometimes individuals may be awkward in the use of these various pragmatic domains. When this occurs, a language problem may be evidenced. As indicated earlier, Prutting and Kirchner (1983, 1987) identified three kinds of language problems. One group of individuals lacked sensitivity to the social context. This problem is evidenced by a lack of sensitivity to the rules of social interaction. For example, a child may not acknowledge the partnership of interaction and lack responsiveness to topics initiated by others. The second group evidenced cognitive deficits resulting in limited lexical and grammatical skills, difficulties establishing and maintaining topics, and problems establishing and maintaining referents. The third group was insufficiently constrained by conversational and social rules of conduct. Consequently, they evidenced some peculiar communicative behaviors.

Interestingly, Fey (1986) and Fey and Leonard (1983) also identified three groups of language-impaired individuals who were somewhat similar to the three groups identified by Prutting and Kirchner (1983, 1987). One group was "generally unresponsive in all types of social interaction relative to same-age NL children" (Fey & Leonard, 1983, p. 77; NL referred to normal language). They were regarded as having a general pragmatic impairment that was manifest as an unwillingness or inability to engage in conversation. The second group was more responsive than the first. They were responsive but nonassertive. They evidenced selective pragmatic impairment and they relied on back channel behaviors to relieve them of the conversational load. For example, they were likely to respond to a conversational or topic opening by others with a brief comment that threw the topic back to the individual who opened it.

Topic opened: "That is a pretty bird."
Back channel comment: "Yep."

These individuals make few requests for clarification to play the communication game (Muma, 1975a). They evidence relatively few lexical or structural revisions in response to clarification requests by others. They may have difficulties with anaphoric reference and perhaps deictic reference. These individuals may benefit from the 10 techniques (Muma, 1971a). The third group evidenced a "lack of the specific linguistic forms required to produce certain speech acts" (Fey & Leonard, 1983, p. 78). It is unclear whether this problem is one of competence (not knowing how to be selectively explicit) or performance (knowing but not wanting to use the appropriate knowledge).

On the one hand, it is desirable to have these three kinds of language impairments identified. On the other hand, it may be more useful to keep an open mind and refrain from categorizing individuals with language impairment in these ways. The former is simply another rendition of the normative mentality, whereas the latter is needed to preserve the heterogeneous nature of individuals with language impairment. The former is vulnerable to making the client conform to the clinical delivery system, whereas the latter offers an opportunity for clinicians to appreciate what each client can do in actual social commerce. The former underwrites an instructional or teaching intervention approach, whereas the latter provides the substantive base for facilitation.

Because there are many different parameters in the pragmatic arena and because individual differences are prominent clinically, it behooves clinicians not to be myopic and look only for the pragmatic problems mentioned here. Rather, it is desirable to describe how an individual functions in these various domains. Functionality itself can be a valid index of a problem. Said differently, if the way an individual functions with the various pragmatic parameters draws attention to itself, it is likely to be a problem.

EXPRESSION: AFFECT

In addition to various pragmatic dimensions, affect can play a decisive role in making intent recognizable. Lock (1978) indicated that "The great chasm to be bridged in both speculations on the evolution of language and those on its development is that between affective and referential communication" (p. 8).

Brown (1977) considered Ferguson's three basic functions of the "baby talk" register by parents:

> "Simplifying" (as in replacing difficult consonants with easy ones or eliminating inflections or replacing pronouns with proper names); "clarifying" (as in speaking slowly, clearly and with many repetitions); and "expressive" (as in the use of hypocoristic affixes, "cute" euphemisms and "nursery tone"). I suggest that these three . . . collapse into two "components" in a co-occurrence analysis. (p. 4)

Simplifying and clarifying functions are essentially alike and therefore could be collapsed into one, whereas expression "has as its chief motive the expression of affection with the capturing of the addressee's attention as a secondary goal" (Brown, 1977, p. 4). Parents seem to be intuitively aware that an affective base supports language acquisition.

As for the child's part, until relatively recently the role of affect in language learning has been largely ignored. Bloom (1990, 1991) and her colleagues (Bloom & Beckwith, 1986, 1988, 1989; Bloom et al., 1988) have addressed the role of affect in language acquisition. Bloom et al. (1988) indicated that tool use should not be the central theme in a theory of language development; rather, they held that language is acquired to express the contents of states of mind and to interpret the speech of others to ascertain their state of mind. The notions of content and state of mind for Bloom et al. (1988) are comparable to content and intent in speech act theory (Grice, 1975; Sperber & Wilson, 1986).

Bloom et al. (1988) indicated that a young child has two communication systems available: the expressive or affective system and a language system. Because the affective system is available prior to the language system, Bloom et al. (1988) were interested in the question of how the emergence of words may be related to communication with affect. They held that this inquiry is based on a theoretical model of intentional states (Brentano, 1966; Dennett, 1978; Searle, 1983). The two main intentional states are about beliefs and desires; furthermore, they dealt with attitudes and contents. Again, the parallels to speech acts are intent and content.

In infancy, Bloom et al. (1988) indicated that content is constrained to here and now perception but eventually mental representation emerges, thereby freeing the child from reliance on direct stimulation and extending cognitive awareness to past, future, and plausible events.

Bloom et al. (1988) recognized that intention has been considered, either implicitly or explicitly, in different cognitive socialization accounts. For example, Bruner (1975a, 1975b, 1981) held that mothers attributed intentions to their children; in this sense, intention meant purpose, desire, or goal of a child. This is what Gleitman (1994) regarded as "the attentional conspiracy" (p. 183). What is important about mothers attributing intentions to their children based on the children's communicative efforts is that mothers operate to fulfill these intentions, thereby giving them validity and establishing them as the central issue or nucleus of communication. In this way, children learn that their intentions become recognized and presumably will increase verbal capacities to make intentions more explicit, thus becoming more adept in making their intentions recognizable. This is why Muma (1981c) stressed the importance of communicative payoff in language intervention.

Bloom et al. (1988) indicated that another perspective for intentions is "directedness," which means "repeated or sustained actions that incorporate other persons toward a goal in a communication event" (p. 101). This perspective stresses the purpose or goals of communication and has the potential of inflating the instrumental or tool notion of language use to a central role. A major problem with the so-called tool use perspective of language is that it only deals with the instrumental notion of language but there are several other uses. Halliday (1975) identified seven early intentions, only one of which was instrumental. Using the Bloom et al. (1988) perspective of desires and beliefs, the instrumental function is only one kind of desire.

Intentionality offers the perspective of recognizing active mental processing in actual social commerce. Indeed, speech act theory, informativeness theory, shared meaning for events theory, social origins of the mind, and situated mind are attractive because they also recognize active mental processing in actual social commerce. Bloom et al., (1988) indicated that in relying on an intentional state, a theory of language development integrates social interaction, cognitive, and linguistic theories. Furthermore, they indicated that the use of intentionality theory in accounting for language acquisition has three basic assumptions (Bloom et al., 1988, p. 103):

> What individuals think about in their conscious states of mind underlies their actions . . . which in turn determines their development. . . . Children endeavor to express what they are thinking about, and to interpret the speech of others so as to discover what others are thinking about. . . . Children actively engage in acquiring words and constructing the grammar of a language in that endeavor. (p. 103)

In addition to intentionality, Bloom et al. (1988) recognized three modes of expression: action, language, and affect. They devised a model for attributing mental states to words and affect. The model deals with a child's attitude (desire or belief) and presumed content. A desire is "an intention to make some change in the world; that is, a desire matches the way the world ought to be according to the child (see Searle, 1983)" (Bloom et al., 1988, p. 105). A belief "marks reality as it is from the child's point of view; that is, a belief matches the world as the child sees or imagines it to be" (Bloom et al., 1988, p. 105).

They had three assumptions about changes in the content of mental states that drive language acquisition. First, as discrepancy learning transpires, children will learn more words and more language mechanisms. That is, new information expands what one knows of the world, theory of the world, possible worlds, or situated mind, leading to increased awareness of and a need for new words and more effective use of language. Second, "the more complex the contents of mental states become, the more the child will need to know of the language for both expressing and interpreting the expressions of others" (Bloom et al., 1988, p. 106). Third, different intentional states have different modes of expression: "Qualitative differences in the contents of mental states—as opposed to changes in discrepancy and complexity—will underlie the difference between expression through words and expression through an affect display" (Bloom et al., 1988, p. 107). Table 6.2 shows the Bloom et al. (1988) model for attributing mental states to word and affect communication.

This model closely resembles speech act theory but it does not address proposition in relation to presupposition. However, the informativeness relation is implicit in the Bloom et al. (1988) model. What is essential about this model, namely attitude and content, is also essential to speech acts, namely intent and content (implicit and explicit). What this model advances over speech acts is the complementary relations of expression for affect and language and even for action.

TABLE 6.2
A Model for Attributing Mental States to
Word and Affective Communication

Attitude:	Desire (seeks change)
	Belief (marks reality)
Content:	Proposition (predicate-argument)

Note. From "Expression Through Affect and Words in the Transition From Infancy to Language," by L. Bloom, R. Beckwith, J. Capatides, and J. Hafitz, 1988, in P. Baltes, D. Featherman, and R. Lerner (Eds.), *Life-Span Development and Behavior*, Vol. 8, pp. 99–127. Copyright © 1988 by Lawrence Erlbaum Associates. Adapted with permission.

The Bloom et al. (1988) study showed some qualitative differences between affect and language expressions:

> The frequency of affect displays, and propositions attributed to them, did not increase appreciably over time, while the frequency of words and propositions attributed to words increased substantially. We interpret this stability in affect expression as an indication that the children were already able to express how they felt about the contents of mental states—through facial expression, body posture, and affective vocalization—before words appeared. Words, in contrast, were acquired in order to express what those contents were. Thus, words did not replace affect, but emerged as a new system for expressing aspects of the contents of mental states—with names of persons, objects, and actions primarily—while affect continued to express the children's feelings about those contents. (p. 123)

Their study gave some other interesting information about vocabulary spurts of learning. First, periods of neutral affect seemed to precipitate spurts of word learning. Second, "Affective expression was already in place and was the far more frequent form of expression at the time that first words appeared" (Bloom et al., 1988, p. 123). Then, 85% of the expressions were affective. Third, when spurts of word learning occurred, 43% of the expressions were affective: "This shift reflected the approximately eightfold increase in both the number of words and the numbers of propositions attributed to words" (Bloom et al., 1988, p. 120). "Thus, while affective expression was developmentally prior to language, it was surpassed by the expressive power of words by the time of the vocabulary spurt" (Bloom et al., 1988, p. 124).

MAKING SENSE: SHARED MEANING

Much has been made about speech act theory and the centrality of communicative intent. K. Nelson's (1985) theory of making sense: shared meaning is not only compatible with speech act theory but it is based on some of the same underlying assumptions and principles, especially the centrality of communicative intent.

K. Nelson took as a starting point the early scripts, routines, and formats that are ubiquitous in mother–child interactions. These routines comprise a subculture in which a parent and child know most referents, roles, relations, and actions. Furthermore, these participants know their roles and intentionally take part in these roles. This is what K. Nelson (1985) called the "idiosyncratic two-person game" that "gradually evolves into a multicontexted conventional plurifunctional system of relationships" (p. xi).

K. Nelson (1985) indicated that any theory of word or language acquisition must deal with the communicative context, and development of cognitive, linguistic, social, and cultural systems. She indicated that the outcome of learning—the adult system—should not determine the ways in which acquisition may be studied simply because the acquisition process is likely to be different than adult capacities for using language. Furthermore, K. Nelson (1985) indicated that because language acquisition takes place in the course of actual social commerce, it is appropriate to derive an account of this process in a "use-based model of meaning" (p. 8) rather than an a priori perspective in which an individual presumably strives to discover the criterial features of concepts. Thus, in accord with experiential realism (Lakoff, 1987), the language learning process is viewed as a subjective enterprise that eventually becomes conventionalized by virtue of the parent–child subcultures expanding and elaborating to converge on increasingly mutual perspectives of others and culture.

K. Nelson (1985) discussed two basic kinds of meaning: conventional meaning and subjective meaning. *Conventional meaning* is that given in dictionaries and the repository of meanings afforded by a culture, whereas *subjective meaning* is that used in particular contexts for the recognition of particular communicative intents. Thus, meaning can be seen structurally as a priori notions in conventional meaning and functionally as a posteriori notions intended in particular contexts. K. Nelson cited deSaussure (1915) for this distinction: *langue* (meaning independent of a speaker) and *parole* (language functioning in social commerce). They are comparable to the distinctions made by Lakoff (1987) between brute and institutional facts, respectively and parole corresponds somewhat with the Vygotskian principles of social origins and appropriation (Rogoff, 1990; Wertsch, 1991).

K. Nelson (1985) posited that the internal meaning system emerges from experiences in contexts. Such contexts are multidimensional, including affective, referential, relational, and social relations. The meaning system is initially motivated by intentions resulting in a subjective understanding of oneself in relationship to others in their routines: "Central to the development of the meaning system is the event representation (or script), which generalizes from experience of events to provide an interpretation of context" (K. Nelson, 1985, p. 9).

The conceptual system is another level derived from event representation; the conceptual system is "an organized base of general knowledge relatively unconstrained by specific spatial-temporal context" (K. Nelson, 1985, p. 9). The semantic system is yet another level that deals with semantic relations and word meanings in the realization of messages. Table 6.3 outlines these systems.

This view indicates that subjective meaning is an individual's perspective pertaining to his or her understanding of relevant events in particular in-

TABLE 6.3
The Cognitive or Meaning System

Langue: A priori meaning, structure, "objective," conventional.
Parole: A posteriori meaning, social commerce, functional, subjective, pragmatic.
Conventional meaning: Dictionary meaning; cultural meaning.
Subjective meaning: Event representation or schemas, scripts.
Conceptual system: General knowledge, possible worlds, situated mind.
Semantic system: Semantic relations, word meaning in messages.

---

stances and the perspectives issuing from his or her possible worlds. In contrast, K. Nelson cited Popper's (1972) notion of objective knowledge or what might be called objective meaning that is invested in one's culture. K. Nelson indicated that the subjective meaning system (individual) is apparently organized differently from the objective meaning system (culture) simply because they are the products of different contexts of language use. She cited Putnam (1975) regarding the distinction between individual and cultural meaning systems and the failings of traditional philosophy to sustain this distinction:

> Ignoring the division of linguistic labor is ignoring the social dimensions of cognition; ignoring what we have called the **indexicality** of most words is ignoring the contribution of the environment. Traditional philosophy of language, like much traditional philosophy, leaves out people and the world; a better philosophy and a better science of language must encompass both. (p. 271)

Here we see that Putnam's notion of indexicality corresponds with Frege's (1892/1952) notion of indexical expression for making sense.

As K. Nelson (1985) and Bruner (1981) indicated, language learning takes place in language use in actual social commerce. Children are not removed from social commerce and given special instruction for language acquisition; indeed, the behaviorists have shown that such instruction is superficial because they have repeatedly complained that it results in failures to generalize. Thus, the behaviorists themselves have provided information that discredits reinforcement theory as a viable account of language acquisition. What is crucial for language acquisition is active participation in language use in actual social commerce. Such active use entails the recognition of communicative intents in appropriate contexts.

From these perspectives, K. Nelson (1985) extended the notion of the meaning or cognitive system. She discussed three types of meaning: subjective meaning (individual: possible worlds, situated mind), shared meaning (mutual manifestnes—Sperber & Wilson, 1986—within a given context), and objective meaning (cultural repository). These were regarded as individual, social, and cultural meanings, respectively.

In the meaning triangle, a word is thought to provide access to an underlying concept that in turn refers to a referent. Thus, there is an indirect relation between a word and its referent. Lyons (1977) was concerned that the meaning triangle was inadequate because it relied on underlying concepts to discern word meaning when it is possible—indeed likely—that many concepts are acquired by understanding the words as they are situated in events. Furthermore, the meaning triangle did not adequately address issues relevant to social or shared meaning and cultural meaning.

Turning to the more generic issues, K. Nelson (1985) indicated that subjective meaning, shared meaning, and objective meaning seem to have counterparts in regard to reference, denotation, and sense, respectively. *Reference* refers to the relations of words to the world; *denotation* refers to the relations of words to concepts; and *sense* refers to the relations of words to words. Referring to the latter two, K. Nelson (1985) said:

> It is important to note here that denotation in this discussion refers to the applicability of a term and not to its actual reference in an utterance, while sense refers to the relations of a word (lexeme) to other words in the vocabulary and not to, say, a concept. . . . It nonetheless seems intuitively obvious that in development reference precedes denotation, which precedes sense relationships. . . . Note that denotation is not the same as reference; it determines **possible** referents or uses of the term. Sense, in contrast, is defined in terms of all of those relations that can hold between words themselves. . . . Referential meaning then relates terms to context-specific individuals whether they are present, past, or even imaginary. . . . Denotation specifies the possible referents. In this sense it is equivalent to a concept. (pp. 14–16)

Developmentally, "The meaning system develops from reference (context) to denotation (concept) to sense (culture)" (p. 17). Table 6.4 shows these distinctions.

TABLE 6.4
The Meaning System Revised

Subjective meaning:	Individual
Shared meaning:	Social context
Objective meaning:	Cultural
Reference:	Words to possible worlds
Denotation:	Words to concepts
Sense:	Words to words
Developmentally:	Reference (context), denotation (concept), sense (culture).

K. Nelson (1985) used deSaussure's (1915) distinction between syntagmatic and paradigmatic relations to discuss similarities and differences between physical and social reality. *Syntagmatic* relations are structural and relational whereby components enter into a larger structural relation. For example, the words "Mommy" and "go" would be syntagmatic in an expression "Mommy go." *Paradigmatic* relations are categorical and functional whereby items within a category can replace other items and function comparably. For example, the words "the boy" can replace "he" and function comparably in the sentence "He ran."

She used this distinction to comment that the study of cognition and language seems to reflect a paradigmatic tradition. For example the study of concept development has traditionally been that of discovering the physical categories of the world and their constituent features or attributes that are presumably necessary and sufficient to define a category. K. Nelson (1985) and others, notably Bruner (1986) and Lakoff (1987), were concerned that the study of cognitive socialization had been invested in a paradigmatic tradition (e.g., acontextual, categorical or normative, elicited). However, the essential aspects of social cognition are syntagmatic: contextual, relational, and intentional. For example, in categorization, the traditional notions have been to identify brute facts and their attendant features—a paradigmatic enterprise. However, Mandler (1983, 1990) and others have advanced the view that schema acquisition, rather than traditional category formation, is inherently functional and relational and it constitutes the essential entry into concept acquisition.

As discussed previously, Bruner (1986) made similar comments regarding science and social affairs or between the paradigmatic world and the narrative world. He regarded these two contrastive perspectives as two different modes of thought and two different fields of study: the sciences and the humanities. He said that they both trade on presupposition and are illusionary. Paradigmatic thinking and science strive to discover the categories of nature and their relations. This view is intolerant of variance, context independent, and relies on logic. The irreducible mental category of this mode of thinking and of science is causality.

In contrast, the syntagmatic mode of thinking and the humanities deal with the "vicissitudes of human intentions" (Bruner, 1986, p. 16). Variance is inherent in human endeavors because of varied contexts and the vicissitudes of human intentions. The irreducible mental category for the syntagmatic or humanities view is intent. "Discourse is governed by the communicative intentions of speakers" (Bruner, 1986, p. 81). Two other quotes from Bruner (1986) underscore the importance of intent: "Meaning is not 'what' but 'what for' " (p. 157) and, "We construct many realities, and do so from differing intentions . . . meaning . . . is an enterprise that reflects human intentionality" (p. 158). Furthermore, the interpersonal (pragmatic) functions precede ideational (mathetic) functions in acquisition, which is a Vygotskian message.

COMMUNICATIVE CONTEXT

To reiterate again, "Context is all" (Bruner, 1981, p. 172). For K. Nelson (1985) and Bruner (1981, 1986), and indeed Frege, the role of context is essential for understanding meaning, including intentional context. As Bates (1979) urged, early on, language use is very much context bound; then, it eventually becomes decontextualized, and finally recontextualized in accordance with one's culture. Because meaning becomes extended across new contexts, K. Nelson (1985) held that rather than decontextualization, it may be more appropriate to regard this learning process as *transcontexted*. Beginning with embodiment and scripts that provide event knowledge, infants launch their careers toward situated minds.

K. Nelson (1985) provided a detailed account of contexts. She held that contexts are comprised of multiple layers of different kinds of contexts. Table 6.5 lists the different kinds of contexts she addressed.

The *objective context* is the complex array of issues in the physical situation. These issues include physical context, cultural context, social context, activity context, agenda context, affective context, communicative act context, action context, and specific linguistic context.

Physical context refers to the immediate context of objects, actions, and relations. The larger physical context is the geographical setting with its

TABLE 6.5
Different Kinds of Communicative Contexts

Objective Context
  Physical context: Immediate context, "referential," security base: objects, actions, relationships.
  Cultural context: Cultural values and customs.
  Social context: Actual social contexts encountered and in which a child participates.
  Activity context: Actual activities in which one participates.
  Agenda context: Intents, purposes, goals for activities.
  Affective context: Expressive or emotional state.
  Communicative act context: Sensitivity to the type of speech act.
  Action context: Associated gestures that carry presumed meaning.
  Specific linguistic context: Relational meanings within utterances including cohesion and topical relations between utterances including anaphora.
Subjective Context
  Cognitive context: "Possible worlds": Physical and social; categorical and schematic.
  Schemas: Spatial, temporal, or causal relations for an experience.
  Event representations: "An ordered sequence of actions appropriate to a particular spatial-temporal context, organized around a goal" (K. Nelson, 1985, p. 40).

attendant architecture. The immediate physical context is the places where a child's activities occur. As physical places become familiar, they constitute security bases for living in the world and transacting social commerce.

Although early names are for familiar objects in the physical context, the "general understanding of object relations does not appear to be affected by familiarity" (K. Nelson, 1985, p. 27). However, young children are affected by familiarity of places in which they conduct social commerce. "Thus, unlike objects, places represent specific contexts, and a strange place can be disruptive to talk as well as action" (K. Nelson, 1985, p. 28).

Cultural context is the culture in which an individual is raised and lives. Individuals are subject to particular cultural values and customs. Cultural symbols (e.g., food and dress preferences) and language practices may vary considerably from one culture to another.

Social context is the social structure within cultures, which varies also. For example, the family structure, sibling ages and gender, presence of other relatives, parental education, economic status, perceived roles of oneself and others, and personalities all impinge on the social context. Moreover, individuals take part in social contexts in different ways depending on who the other participants are.

Activity context is the activities or episodes that occur within the general framework of the physical, social, and cultural contexts. Child-oriented activities in our culture include caretaking routines such as bathing, eating, dressing, playing games, and reading. Adult-oriented activities include shopping, working, traveling in cars, meeting with friends and strangers, and general family business in the community. Important parameters in activities include centrality of a child, goal, means, result, number of participants, roles, and locution. Activities may range from highly predictable to highly varied in terms of a child's behavior and a child's activity level in one context may vary greatly from that of another.

Agenda context is the intent, purpose, or goal of activities or episodes. Within any given activity, children may switch goals. For example, a problem-solving activity may shift to a game of silliness or entertainment. Children can easily shift from one agenda to another and back again. This flexibility means that children become capable of interpreting the same utterance different ways. Also, it is common to have a child's agenda at variance with their parents' agenda, which could lead to misunderstandings and conflicts.

Affective context deals with the emotional context. "While models of language acquisition built explicitly on assumptions of positive and negative reinforcement are no longer acceptable, the possible influence of the affective context on the child's interpretation of meaning cannot be discounted" (K. Nelson, 1985, p. 33). Bloom (1990, 1991a, 1991b) and her colleagues conducted a series of studies on the effects of the expressive or affective state in language acquisition. One of the more interesting outcomes of these studies is that early preverbal expression is largely affective, eventually becoming affective and symbolic. Another interesting outcome is that neutral affect may precipitate spurts of word learning.

Communicative act context refers to the kinds of speech acts that are directed toward a child or that the child uses. That is, this context refers to the sensitivity to whether utterances are declarative, expressive, interrogative, exclamatory, directive, or informative. Indeed, this notion of context also extends to the sensitivity for indirect speech.

Action context is the gestural and action complex that accompanies an utterance. It is these gestures and actions that provide useful information for interpreting the meaning of utterances. Bretherton et al. (1981) and Bretherton et al. (1983) found that reliance on gestures decreases as children obtain increased command of their language. However, this is for early language acquisition because it is well known that adult language is embedded in a code matrix (Muma, 1975a) whereby gestures may override a linguistic message.

Specific linguistic context includes the coherence of relational meanings within utterances and it extends to topical meanings between utterances and anaphoric meanings for retained referents. Thus, words in relation to other words both within sentences and between sentences comprise linguistic contexts.

The *subjective context* is the affective and substantive (both conscious or *phenic* and unconscious or *cryptic*) knowledge of the world. The affective state may facilitate or inhibit understanding. Both the affective and substantive knowledge of the world comprise the cognitive context, schemas, and event representation.

Cognitive context deals with both physical and social reality. Thus, the personal and social worlds are different from the physical worlds. This is a message that has been advanced by Bruner (1986) and Lakoff (1987). To reiterate, the physical world or the world of "hard" sciences strives to figure out the natural categories of the world and to understand cause-and-effect relations. This world is intolerant of variance and individual differences. In contrast, the personal and social worlds are characterized by variance and individual differences that are governed by intents. They are qualitatively different. Yet, as Bruner (1986) indicated, both of these worlds trade on presupposition and are illusionary.

Both K. Nelson (1985) and Bruner (1986) expressed concern that the traditional study of psychology reflected an imposition of the principles of the physical world on the personal or social worlds, resulting in literatures that have missed the essential issues that are contextual and intentional.

Schemas specify "essential elements in spatial, temporal, or causal relations to one another as well as elements that may be optional" (K. Nelson,

1985, p. 38). The source of information for schemas is experience, either direct action or perceptual. Schemas are composites of various relevant experiences. They are abstractions of experiences; therefore, they do not have a direct or isomorphic relation to the real world. Because they are abstractions, they represent knowledge rather than reflecting a priori categories of the world. Thus, schemas are subjective and biased rather than objective and neutral.

An individual's knowledge of the world constitutes, therefore, a theory of the world (Palermo, 1971, 1982), possible worlds (Bruner, 1986), or situated mind (K. Nelson, 1996). Within communication theory, especially speech act theory (Clark & Clark, 1977; Grice, 1975; Sperber & Wilson, 1986), such knowledge is known as presupposition. The explicit content (proposition) of a message is carefully measured in reference to what is known (presupposition) in order to make intentions recognizable.

Event representations have special functions in communication. They are called scripts (K. Nelson, 1978, 1981b; Schank & Abelson, 1977). A *script* is "a general event representation derived from and applied to social contexts" (K. Nelson, 1985, p. 40). The regularity of routines provides a familiar context, or microculture, from which discrepancies of information can be appreciated. Eventually, these routines become increasingly varied, providing a means for expanding to encompass more of the social-cultural world and actual social commerce in the realization of communicative intents.

Weak scripts prescribe the objects, roles, and component events that may be expected in a situation but not the precise sequence because varied sequence may occur. Strong scripts, however, provide sequences because causal relations are essential. Scripts are initially unanalyzed whole representations. Eventually, they become varied and extended toward a larger social-cultural community.

What I find especially intriguing about scripts is that children not only know them in some detail but they stake a claim to them such that they are disturbed if someone else varies or violates them; yet they are truly entertained by their own intentional variations. After they have introduced variations, they will also allow others to do so.

COOPERATIVE PRINCIPLE AND FELICITY CONDITIONS

The cooperative principle has four major dimensions. This principle refers to the implicit assumptions that communication will be informative, truthful, relevant, and clear.

According to Searle (1969), felicity conditions are those that must be fulfilled in order for intentions of messages to be appropriately recognized.

There are four basic felicity conditions: the propositional content rule, the preparatory rule, the sincerity rule, and the essential rule. The *propositional content rule* is that the content of a message must be legitimate—in accord with possible worlds. The *preparatory rule* is essentially informativeness; that is, the speaker assumes that the message is informative in the realization of an intention. The *sincerity rule* is that the intent is genuine. The *essential rule* is that whichever speech act is performed is essentially logical and therefore deducible.

SPEECH ACT TYPES

According to Searle (1969, 1975, 1977), there are five major kinds of speech acts in adult speech: representatives, directives, commissives, expressives, and declaratives. Wells (1981) summarized these speech acts as shown in Table 6.6.

The notion of "getting the point" (Schank, Collins, Davis, Johnson, Lytinen, & Reiser, 1982) is another way of appreciating different kinds of speech acts. Schank et al. (1982) said:

> It is quite possible for someone to understand exactly what a speaker said, but not understand why it was said, or why it was said to him in particular. Alternatively, a decoder may think he knows why something was said to him, but he may be incorrect. In such cases, we usually say he has "missed the point," and the speaker may find a response he receives to be incoherent. (p. 255)

Such fallibility is common in everyday communication. Table 6.7 shows the different kinds of communicative points discussed by Schank et al. (1982).

Schank et al. (1982) indicated that the essence of communication is to figure out the point of communication. This is the essence of speech act theory (Grice, 1975; Sperber & Wilson, 1986) and informativeness (Clark & Clark, 1977). Schank et al. (1982) indicated that the search for the point guides communicative processing and directs inference. The encoder makes certain decisions about the nature of a message in order for the decoder to make

TABLE 6.6
The Five Major Kinds of Speech Acts and Their Functional Relations

Speech Act	Direction of Fit	Psychological State	Example
Representatives	Words match world	Belief	I thought we won.
Directives	Worlds match words	Want	I want a sucker.
Commissives	Worlds match words	Commitment	I will play.
Expressives	Words match affect	Expression	Ouch!
Declaratives	Words create state	State	You are under arrest.

TABLE 6.7
Kinds of Communicative Points

Affect	Positive, negative, neutral
Empathetic	Understand feelings of others
Need	Express need for possible help
Explanation	Explain or account
Prescription	Govern, direct, constrain
Argumentation	Establish logical and/or empirical evidence
Interest	Attention

Note. From "What's the Point?" by R. Schank et al., 1982, *Cognitive Science, 6.* Copyright ©
1982 by Ablex Publishing Corporation. Reprinted with permission.

certain inferences about a message's content to discern the point, purpose, or intent of communication. In this sense, the goal of communication is to discern the point, purpose, or intent of communication. Furthermore, explicit content or proposition of a message is used in relation to implicit content or presupposition (possible worlds, theory of the world, situated mind).

Proposition or explicit content is the social or shared meaning of a message. It is that which is coded in relation to the presuppositional or implicit content of a message. For example, the sentence "The boy ate a hamburger" presumably has a shared proposition in which an animate agent acts on an inanimate object. In order for this proposition to work in making an intent recognizable, it is necessary for it to be placed in relation to presuppositional knowledge about the world. That is, it is assumed, or presumed, that both the encoder and decoder know that a hamburger exists and that it is edible by the boy. What is informative is that this particular boy ate a hamburger and such information is presumed to be needed to make particular intentions recognizable.

The processing models by Clark and Clark (1977) and Sperber and Wilson (1986) have provided detailed accounts of cognitive processing in communication. The bottom lines are that the mental processing entailed in both encoding and decoding messages are grounded on:

1. The results of categorization variously known as representation, presupposition, possible worlds, theory of the world, theory of mind, and situated mind.
2. Inferencing and problem solving.
3. The recognition of intent.

These mental processes are not modality specific; indeed, modality information is purged very early in mental processing (Clark & Clark, 1977).

In contrast to these models, which have been well enunciated and substantiated, the clinical fields evidently have missed the substantive point by their reliance on such mundane notions as modality differences (auditory and visual processing; expressive and receptive language). There are modality differences, to be sure, but they are relatively peripheral in comparison to the well-substantiated mental processing skills in the cognitive socialization literature.

Returning to the Clark and Clark (1977) model, the cognitive processes for production are planning and execution of intended propositions. Critical aspects of planning are the decisions made about what content should be explicit and what should be implicit to be appropriately informative for making intentions recognizable. Contexts are vital for deciding what information should be implicit and explicit. Available contexts pertain to both internal contexts of what a person may be thinking about and intentions to communicate and external contexts of mutually shared meaning in event knowledge, as well as the speaker's perspective of the listener. With all of these considerations, the speaker strives to issue a message of best fit (Muma, 1975a) or a piece of the communication puzzle that has the greatest utility (Brown, 1958a). Ninio and Snow (1988) regarded the decisions for coding some information, but not other information, toward the recognition of communicative intents as the application of selection rules.

In comprehension, the cognitive task is initially to convert an acoustic message into usable cognitive currency, then the acoustic information is purged (Clark & Clark, 1977). The bulk of the cognitive activity is committed to constructing a plausible proposition for the intended message and utilizing this potential proposition as a source of information in the context of what an individual knows (Clark & Clark, 1977). The enterprise of resolving the nature of new information with that which is known entails basic problem solving and inference oriented on the recognition of communicative intent (Grice, 1975; Sperber & Wilson, 1986) within the cooperative principle (Clark & Clark, 1977) and felicity conditions (Searle, 1969, 1975, 1977).

INFORMATIVENESS: NEGOTIATED MEANING

In accordance with speech act theory, *informativeness* is conveying appropriate information to make intentions recognizable. There appear to be two tiers of decisions in becoming informative. The first tier is the decisions pertaining to what could remain in presupposition or implicature (implicit content, presumed mutual knowledge) as contrasted to what should be coded in a message (explicit content). The second tier deals with the decisions about lexical, grammatical, and pragmatic—indeed nonlinguistic—mechanisms and devices that should be used to appropriately convey the desired relations between given and new information in explicit content to make intentions recognizable (Clark & Clark, 1977). Table 6.8 portrays these two tiers of decisions in becoming informative.

TABLE 6.8
Two Tiers of Decisions in Becoming Informative

Tier I:	What information should be implicit and what should be explicit to make intent recognizable?
Tier II:	How should explicit information be coded to make intent recognizable?

These decisions pertain to several issues including an individual's knowledge of the world or possible worlds, knowledge of language and options in the code matrix, perception of an event or topic, perception of the decoder, affective state, and intent to communicate.

What is important about informativeness is that it is a socially shared and negotiable enterprise. Decisions at both tiers are not just psychological but social and even cultural, often requiring negotiation. The resulting message is presumed to be a message of best fit (Muma, 1975a) in making intentions recognizable. Given the complexities of this arena, messages frequently fail to be messages of best fit. When this happens, the participants have additional decisions about whether they want to participate in the communication process and what should be negotiated to achieve more appropriate messages. Needless to say, cognitive socialization is active, dynamic, and negotiable in actual social commerce.

MESSAGE OF BEST FIT

Brown (1973b) recognized the cognitive-social nature of language use: "A sentence well adapted to its function is, like a piece in a jigsaw puzzle, just the right size and shape to fit the opening for it by local conditions and community understandings" (p. 68). Notice that Brown's comment is about how messages function; this reflects the functionalistic views that have developed in recent years. "The size and shape to fit an opening" in social commerce pertains not only to the explicit content (proposition), but also to the implicit content (presupposition and implicature) in one's situated mind. The volition "to fit" accords well with an intention. Indeed, it accords well with the goal of making intentions recognizable.

I (Muma, 1975a) drew from Brown's jigsaw puzzle analogy to deal with the notion of a message of best fit for achieving communication. The encoder strives to take into account intent, possible worlds, emotional state, knowledge of the event and topic, and perspective of the listener. Then a presumed message of best fit may be issued for the purpose of making intentions recognizable. If the message does not work as intended, it would be necessary to negotiate a better message if the desired communication is to succeed. The negotiation of a better message is what I have called playing the communication game.

NARRATIVE

The message of best fit not only entails the previously mentioned issues for dealing with propositions in the realization of communicative intent but there is a larger communicative arena, namely narrative. There are the story lines of thought and of communication, narrative thought, and narrative language (Britton & Pellegrini, 1990). Indeed, there are narratives of social affiliations, cultures, sports, hobbies and recreational endeavors, movies and the arts, professional groups, armed forces, political groups, and so on. "Collections of narratives pull people together and push them apart" (Britton & Pellegrini, 1990, p. 223). "Narratives collect into recognizable bodies because recognizable social groups control them, not vice versa" (Britton & Pellegrini, 1990, p. 224). Could it be that the journals and conventions in the clinical fields are under the grip of a positivist narrative (behaviorism, reductionism, empiricism, probability) so that other recognized views and perspectives are withheld? Could it be that the clinical fields may be prone to issue glib notions about theoretical perspectives, validity, cognition, language, emotion, pragmatics, efficacy, attribution, and so on because their narratives are less penetrating and are shared by those less interested in the attendant scholarly literature?

For example, in the clinical fields an oft quoted narrative of oblique significance is "We should deal with the child at his level." This engenders a responsibility of a provider toward a child in rendering clinical services of a particular kind—"at his level." The level notion is sufficiently vague that it can be interpreted many different ways, thereby having many different clinical services and clinicians unified by this single narrative—motto.

There are a number of story lines in the clinical fields that warrant scrutiny. The story lines in the clinical fields need scrutiny simply because they are too often glib stories rather than substantive stories. The signature of these glib stories is silence about crucial aspects of a narrative. If not by glib statements, another way to remain silent about crucial issues is to provide examples, thereby leaving the onus for discerning the essence of an example to the reader. Throughout this book, especially in chapters 7 and 8 and the appendices, a number of narratives in the clinical fields are brought to task.

Silence for crucial aspects of story lines seems to be a ploy in the clinical fields but crucial issues need a hearing to aspire to a disciplined understanding. Take the notion of narrative itself and consider how it has been addressed in the cognitive socialization literature in contrast to the clinical fields. At the risk of being glib, the following is a summary of the issues raised by K. Nelson (1996) in her review of the narrative literature. She began with the acknowledgment that narrative has had glib treatment: "It is quite clear from recent writing that for most authors 'narrative' is one of those Humpty Dumpty words that may mean whatever one wishes it to" (p. 185). With this, it is useful to summarize the crucial issues of narrative in accordance with K. Nelson's considerations.

An early notion of narrative was that it was an account of a sequenced event over time (Labov & Waletzky, 1967). A dictionary account of narrative was too narrow and circular: "a story or description of actual or fictional events" (*American Heritage Dictionary: New College Edition*). McCabe and Peterson (1991) indicated that narrative is not only a story line but it can be real or imaginary. This perspective brings in the mind as a virtual source of narrative. Gee (1991) held that the central notion of narrative is thematic structure rather than temporal order.

In the literary fields, narrative encompasses "*characters* in *action* with intentions or *goals* in *settings* using particular *means*" (K. Nelson, 1996, pp. 187–188). These issues are placed against a background of the *canonical event* (Bruner, 1986; K. Nelson, 1996). A canonical event is a known script or perspective of what is likely to happen in a given context with particular participants. In contrast, the narrative provides a twist on what is expected or known. In this sense, narrative provides new information in the context of old—a rendition of informativeness theory. It is the deviation from what is known in the context of what is known that makes a narrative interesting—discrepancy learning theory. Furthermore, it is the nature of the participants in a narrative that places the story line into recognizable consciousness and in so doing establishes meaning as those participants conduct their affairs in particular contexts. "Gee (1991) stakes the claim that space, not time, is basic to narrative, and it follows that theme, not plot, is central. . . . Narrative structure has two dimensions: temporality (its syntax), theme or meaning (its semantics)" (K. Nelson, 1996, p. 189).

Notice the differences in the narratives of jazz contrasted with the drumming of "adolescent" music and the droning of hymns. Adolescence seeks affiliation and the music is that of deep-note cycles of affiliation with superimposed squeaky and raspy notes of separation from parental narrative—yet such music is culturally sanctioned. In contrast, hymns drone, not seeking enlightment of the unpredicted but rather confirmation of the known toward deeper knowing. Similarly, the staying power of the classics and the old standards is likely to be seen in new voices in the context of old or a revival of the old against the narratives of modern culture.

Taking the stance of the situated mind (K. Nelson, 1996), narratives are of different forms in different contexts. Furthermore, narratives are qualitatively different over development. Early on, embodiment (Lakoff, 1987) and event knowledge (K. Nelson, 1985, 1986, 1996) provide frames of reference for knowing what is happening and for deciding how to express intentions. Subsequently, procedural knowledge becomes semantic knowledge or representational knowledge (Mandler, 1983) affording an individual the ability to reconstruct virtual worlds as a means of thinking, communicating, and acting. All of this transpires in accordance with biological constraints, cognition, emotion, socialization, and culturalization. The result is what has come to be known as possible worlds (Bruner, 1986, 1990) or the situated mind (K. Nelson, 1996).

The narratives of the sciences and of the humanities have experienced a major shift in recent years (Bruner, 1986) that has profound implications for the clinical fields. Previously, the sciences and the humanities were regarded as two castles (Bruner, 1986) and one was defended against an onslaught by the other. Science held that it was in pursuit of objective truth, which was outside of the purview of the humanities. In contrast, the humanities held that subjectivity was the essence of art—indeed all human affairs.

Bruner (1986) indicated that the narrative of the sciences is to categorize the world and to account for causality in its many guises. Thus, the irreducible nuclei of science are categorization and causality. In contrast, the narrative of human affairs is that of the realization of intention in contexts. The irreducible nuclei of human affairs are thus intent and contexts. However, the sciences are the product of human affairs by virtue of striving to intentionally account for various aspects of the world and indeed the universe. Furthermore, the great scholars of both the sciences and the humanities acknowledge that both endeavors are crucially subjective. This motivated Bruner (1986) to not only acknowledge these two castles but also to indicate that they are ultimately one because they both trade in the narrative of illusion and intentionality. For instance, there would be no science without intent. From this perspective, Bruner's notion of narrative is the whole of human affairs. Furthermore, narrative is motivated by intentionally being grounded in context. Indeed, the situated mind (K. Nelson, 1996) is derived from biological constraints, cognition, emotion, socialization, and culturalization in the realization of intent or consciousness (Searle, 1992).

There are major clinical implications of Bruner's human affairs perspective of narration. Hoshmand and Polkinghorne (1992) acknowledged this shift in perspective for psychology. Appendix B discusses the clinical implications of this shift for the clinical fields. In short, the clinical fields may want to shift reliance on normative tests (human category) to descriptive evidence predicated on the available cognitive socialization literature and on what an individual can do in actual social commerce. This shift is warranted both by the procedures in the available cognitive socialization literature thereby providing a standardized assessment and by the central point that clinical populations are heterogeneous.

SOCIALIZATION

Pragmatics, communication, and expression are fundamentally cognitive and social in nature. That is why the field of cognitive socialization provides the substantive base for the clinical fields, and that is why the discussion of defining language impairment included a social imperative and the notion of "specifying" as a predicate is critical for the notion of specific language impairment (SLI).

Another way of appreciating the importance of socialization is the widely acknowledged fact that many language-impaired individuals are also socially inept. Experienced clinicians know that many language-impaired individuals are on the periphery of available social groups, loners, or more oriented toward adults than their peers. Indeed, for many years, we conducted language intervention in 15-minute units, one of which was just for socialization.

Gallagher (1991) provided a comprehensive perspective on social dynamics of language-impaired children. She indicated that there is a much higher incidence of social-interactional problems with language-impaired individuals than others (Aram, Ekelman, & Nation, 1984). Gallagher (1991) indicated that the following communicative skills relate to peer acceptance and that language-impaired individuals may lack such skills:

- Initiate conversation successfully.
- Adjust messages.
- Ask appropriate questions.
- Contribute to ongoing topics.
- Make intentions recognizable.
- Address all participants.
- Generally positive.

Because the cognitive socialization literature has shown that both cognitive (Mandler, 1983; K. Nelson, 1996) and language development (Bruner, 1981; K. Nelson, 1985, 1986, 1996; Ninio & Snow, 1988) are socioculturally based, and because individuals with language problems also evidence social difficulties, it is necessary to have a social dimension to language intervention. This is precisely why peer modeling has been so beneficial in language intervention over the past two decades.

SUMMARY

Communication and expression are best appreciated from a pragmatic perspective. Modern pragmatics is traceable to Frege's notion of making sense in communicative context. The pragmatic arena extends across many issues in playing the communication game including openings; topic initiation, development, and maintenance; topic sharing; attending to listener feedback; topicalization; anaphora; deictic reference; preclosings; and closings. In addition to the various grammatical and pragmatic mechanisms for making communicative intents recognizable, expression or affect also plays a significant role.

K. Nelson's (1985) theory of making sense, also derived from Frege's notion of making sense, provides an elegant appreciation of cognitive socialization in language acquisition. As so many cognitive socialization theories, this theory posits the centrality of communicative intent. K. Nelson's (1986) theory of shared meaning in event knowledge and her theory of the situated mind (K. Nelson, 1996) provide elegant renditions of the centrality of communicative intent in biological, psychological, emotional, social, and cultural contexts. K. Nelson's theories are very much in accord with Mandler (1979), who commented that "cognitive growth occurs mainly in a social nexus" (p. 375).

Furthermore, K. Nelson (1985) provided the most fully enunciated account of different kinds of contextual influences in language acquisition. Such influences center on two basic kinds of contexts: subjective and objective.

With these views and perspectives, speech act theory has emerged as the most fully enunciated (Sperber & Wilson, 1986) and substantiated (Clark & Clark, 1977) perspective that is compatible with these various perspectives by virtue of the common denominator of the centrality of communicative intent. In a sense, speech act theory provides a viable unifying theory for cognitive socialization in general and language acquisition in particular.

Informativeness, another unifying perspective that is compatible with speech act theory, is very attractive not just because of the centrality of communicative intent but because it addresses the relational perspective between implicit and explicit content of messages in making communicative intent recognizable and because it recognizes the social-affective negotiation of messages in playing the communication game.

A message of best fit (Muma, 1975a) provides a useful appreciation of the complexity of becoming informative on the one hand and recognizing communicative intent on the other. Such messages are not just linguistic but embedded in a code matrix.

Narrative thought and narrative language are new dynamic appreciations of thought and communication. Narratives in the clinical fields sometimes do not match up well to those in various scholarly fields ranging from the importance of philosophical views and theoretical perspectives to various substantive areas in CCCE. Indeed, the notion of narrative itself in the clinical fields seems to lack the substantive appreciation evidenced in the scholarly literature. For example, the clinical fields have not yet grasped the significance of narrative as the essence of human affairs (Bruner, 1986) nor narrative thought as a constituent of the situated mind (K. Nelson, 1996).

With these perspectives, the literature in recent decades has not only attended to pragmatic issues but in so doing has elevated the importance of the social aspects of language acquisition. Here again Prutting (1982) was a front-runner in the clinical fields. Gallagher (1991) and Hagstrom (1994) have been two of the foremost clinical scholars to appreciate the social dynamics of language acquisition and the social implications for under-standing language impairment and rendering appropriate intervention.

7

Clinical Assessment: Description

Prutting, Epstein, Beckman, Dias, and Gao (1989) made a cogent comment about clinical assessment. They said, "An assessment well done is a treatment half begun" (p. 12). This comment goes directly to the heart of the notion of appropriateness because an assessment that has construct validity (Messick, 1980) as evidenced by continuity with the available cognitive socialization literature with its attendant theoretical perspectives and relevance to an individual's repertoire of skills is indeed an assessment well done and intervention half begun.

In an attempt to offer assessment that is well done, over the past two decades, I (Muma, 1973a, 1973b, 1978a, 1978b, 1981a, 1981b, 1981c, 1983a, 1983b, 1984b, 1985, 1986a, 1987a, 1991) have attempted to champion four major issues in clinical assessment:

1. Data versus evidence.
2. Necessity for construct validity.
3. Seven basic clinical assessment issues.
4. Appropriateness of descriptive assessment.

These are based on developments in the contemporary cognitive socialization literature, especially functionalistic perspectives of CCCE.

In 1978, using a model of *what* (knowledge of language and language acquisition) and *how* (assessment and intervention), the basic premise of that book was "to describe an individual's command of various cognitive-linguistic-communicative systems and processes—to the extent possible—

then exploit such behavior" (Muma, 1978b, p. 7). This was the beginning of my considerations of the CCCE issues from philosophical and theoretical perspectives. My current views are essentially the same but they are enunciated further with regard to new developments in the contemporary philosophical views (mentalism, constructionism, functionalism, experiential realism, experiential cognition) and theoretical perspectives (speech acts, bootstrapping, informativeness, shared meaning for events, rare-event learning, representation, representational redescription, discrepancy learning, social origins, narrative, situated mind). These views and perspectives establish construct validity for the nature of descriptive assessment and facilitation procedures in intervention. That is to say, these views and perspectives provide a bona fide rationale for holding certain clinical views and perspectives and operationally doing clinical assessment and intervention certain ways. It is this substantive base that is lacking in much traditional clinical assessment and intervention.

It is true that the clinical fields may have cited attendant philosophical views and theoretical perspectives, but such endeavors were typically perfunctory obligations for the image of scholarship rather than disciplined substantive stances. For example, Fey (1986) discussed operant theory, social learning theory, interactionist views, and transformational generative grammar theory, but what is starkly missing are the most important philosophical and theoretical influences over the past 25 years (Perera, 1994). Similarly, notice that Paul (1995) discussed models of child language disorders (mismatch model, categorical model, specific disabilities model, neuropsychological orientation, auditory perceptual deficit approach, descriptive-developmental model), but where are the philosophical and theoretical justifications for establishing a rationale for these respective models? Paul did provide a few passing comments along these lines; for example, the Illinois Test of Psycholinguistic Abilities (ITPA) model (Kirk et al., 1968), form–content–use (Bloom & Lahey, 1978), modalities model (Chapman et al., 1992; J. Miller, 1981). However, more substantial views and perspectives issuing from the cognitive socialization literature were missing.

DATA OR EVIDENCE

The distinctions between data and evidence are related to the distinctions between technicians and clinicians. Data are merely numbers open to any interpretation or dogma. It is relatively easy to compile data by using various simplistic checklists, developmental profiles, and simple, quick tests, most of which lack construct validity. Unfortunately, it is not unusual in the clinical fields to have a client's file filled with such data.

For example, Olswang and Bain (1991) discussed profiling and tracking as presumed ways of providing evidence for clinical decision making. They relied on a traditional psychometric mentality, which held that normative measures provide "necessary and sufficient" information. Even though they dutifully acknowledged that data are only as good as they are valid and reliable, they nevertheless employed data of questionable validity. The more important issue is evidence.

Before discussing the ways in which the clinical fields rely on data rather than evidence, it is useful to give a discussion about different kinds of data. Referring to Coombs' theory of data, Kaplan (1964) commented:

> The term "data" be used for observations already interpreted in some particular way . . . there are no other sorts of observations, though often the interpretation at work is far from explicit and clear. . . *Cryptic data* [are] those which, in a given state of science, are hard to make sense of in the light of the theories current at that time. Not uncommonly it is the cryptic data that provide a point of departure for significant theoretical advance. . . . On the other hand, some cryptic data turn out to be errors of observation or interpretation; they are cryptic only because there is really nothing there to be explained, save the process of observation itself. . . . Even greater importance in the history of science attaches to what might be called *invisible data*, those which are recognized as data only conjointly with the acceptance of the theory explaining them. . . . In some cases data are invisible because a scientific dogma makes for a simple refusal even to look at them: none so blind as those who will not see. . . . Whatever the scientific merit of particular findings, it cannot be denied that in general what is most responsible for invisible data is the force of preconceived opinion. (pp. 133–135)

The clinical fields have many good candidates for both cryptic and invisible data: communicative intent, categorization, and inference. The bullish use of Brown's five stages and MLUs and the Piagetian stages are others that have been tenaciously held even in the face of evidence questioning their validity. Brown (1978) urged caution about relying on the five stages because they "can only be characterized in a hypothetical way at present. . . Stages III, IV, and V did not yield up to Brown . . . any strong generalizations comparable to those of the early stages" (p. 398). Brown (1973b) also pointed out that MLU has only a limited range as an index of acquisition (1.0–4.0). Mandler (1983, 1990) raised some fundamental questions about the Piagetian stages.

For Kaplan (1964), data were assumed to be derived from theory. However, this basic tenet is commonly not so in the clinical fields. Therefore, Muma (1986a) raised the distinction between data and evidence. Data are merely observations of whatever kind that are inherently atheoretical, whereas evidence has theoretical justification and clinical relevance to a client. Perhaps the clinical fields should consider more seriously the scrutiny of valid data—evidence.

In addition to normative tests, clinical judgments provide another kind of data. Clinical judgments are deceptively complex (Goldberg, 1968). There are several issues concerning their complexity including perceptual drift, regression, multiple judgments, and naive versus sophisticated judges. Perceptual drift occurs over the course of time and many judgments. It is necessary for judges to be trained so that there is consensus about what behaviors may be indexed by particular points on a judgment scale. Thus, after necessary training, presumably judges have general agreement about the meaning of points on a scale and act accordingly in their judgments. However, over the course of time and many judgments, perceptual drifting occurs, whereby judges lose track of what the scale points index. This happens both within and between judges. Eventually, a scale loses meaning because of perceptual drift. Regression effects occur as a function of perceptual drift. That is, judgments evidence a regression toward the middle of the scale because they tend to attribute their perceptions in this way. Judges tend to deny extreme scores. A similar problem arises when judges are asked to make judgments on multiple scales. Typically, judges tend to focus on one of several scales and provide discriminate scores for a preferred scale, but the other scales evidence regression effects.

The issue concerning naive versus sophisticated judges is the issue of reliability. Contrary to intuition, naive judges tend to have higher reliabilities for clinical judgments than sophisticated judges. This is so because naive judges miss many nuances of behavior that sophisticated judges see on repeated observation. Thus, sophisticated judges tend to change their ratings in clinical judgments, whereas naive judges do not.

Evidence is data that are supportable from the relevant scholarly literature and are directly relevant to a child's repertoire of skills. Thus, evidence has continuity with appropriateness because both adhere to the same criteria: relevance to the scholarly literature and relevance to an individual's available repertoire.

In regard to CCCE, the scholarly literatures in psychology and cognitive socialization are useful. The domain of concept formation or categorization illustrates the utility of the available information. In the clinical fields, claims are made about assessing concept development by using the Boehm Test of Concept Development (Boehm, 1969, 1986) and the Bracken Basic Concept Scale (Bracken, 1986). An examination of the manuals for these tests shows that the scholarly literature on concept formation is inadequately represented, to put it mildly. Yet, there is a large scholarly literature on concept development and categorization that is missed or dismissed.

Major conceptual and theoretical advances have occurred in the cognitive socialization literature over the past two decades. Prominent in these developments is the theory of natural categories (Anglin, 1977; Heider, 1971; Rosch, 1973, 1978; Rosch & Mervis, 1975) with its use of focal and peripheral exemplars as evidence of prototypic and extended knowledge of a concept. There are other supportable theories of concept development, such as representation (Mandler, 1983, 1990), representational redescription (Karmiloff-Smith, 1992), and the theory of functional attributes for categories (K. Nelson, 1973a, 1973b, 1974), which can be extended logically to pragmatic theory in general and script theory (K. Nelson, 1981b) and shared meaning for events theory, which contributes to the situated mind (K. Nelson, 1985, 1986, 1996).

Once again there is a paradox because the clinical fields claim expertise in cognition but fail to draw adequately on the available scholarly literature on cognitive socialization by virtue of relying on the Boehm and Bracken tests of concept formation. The paradox is especially serious because claims are made about an individual's presumed conceptual abilities, but such claims are often about data rather than evidence. This, in turn, fosters dogma, authoritarianism, and hype.

Another example is the use of the PPVT–R to claim that vocabulary, or even worse, receptive language, has been assessed. When the PPVT–R is compared with the available cognitive socialization literature on vocabulary or word acquisition (Kuczaj & Barrett, 1986), it turns up embarrassingly empty (Muma, 1986b) simply because it not only fails to assess crucial issues of word acquisition such as intentional, referential, relational, and social meanings, but it even violates these issues. Yet, I have heard a prominent individual in the clinical fields who claims expertise in language acquisition ignore these problems while holding to the psychometric mentality with the silly comment, "At least the PPVT–R tells us something." Perhaps this is another version of corrosive dogma.

The second aspect of evidence is relevance to a repertoire of skills for an individual. Once again, the clinical fields are less than impressive. Returning to the quick and easy PPVT–R, a score is obtained and conclusions are made about a child's presumed vocabulary, and even more seriously about so-called receptive language. Unfortunately, there is no attempt to broach a child's word repertoire concerning intentional, referential, relational, or social meanings. Thus, there is a considerable question as to the relevance of such data to a particular individual.

This raises a question about a strange practice in the clinical fields. It is the practice of carrying out what is claimed to be an individualized assessment. Typically, an individualized assessment is carried out by administering a battery of tests to an individual. The logic is that if testing is administered to one individual at a time it constitutes individualized assessment. However, when the tests are psychometric normative tests, it is not an individualized assessment simply because an individual's available skills are subjugated to group norms. There is no attempt to ascertain repertoires of skill or other substantive issues available to a particular individual. This merely shows how subtle and pervasive the traditional psychometric mentality has become. It is well entrenched in the clinical fields.

This practice of relying on psychometric normative tests is so strongly entrenched that specialists in the clinical fields may not even recognize that it undermines the notion of individualized assessment. Olswang and Bain (1991) provided an example of this kind of assessment. Under the claim that profiling provides "a framework for charting an individual child's behaviors" (p. 257), they gave an example that shows performances on normative tests that have been subjected to normative comparisons; yet, such data do not constitute charts of "an individual child's behaviors." Indeed, the behaviors of a child had been subjugated to the psychometric norms and there was no attempt to show where an individual stood in relation to available repertoires, progress in acquisition sequences, alternative acquisition strategies, active loci of learning, and attribution of learning. Such is the psychometric mentality in the clinical fields.

To underscore this mentality, Olswang and Bain (1991) lamented about the lack of some psychometric information; however, they did not express concern about the appropriate substantive issues in the available cognitive socialization literature mentioned earlier. They said, "Unfortunately, many of the procedures employed by clinicians do not have established standard deviation information" (p. 257). Although they were concerned about standard deviations, they missed a more pervasive issue of great magnitude: the lack of construct validity for many measures used in the clinical fields and in their article. It looks like the psychometric mentality is blind or myopic because the literatures on the centrality of construct validity and substantive issues in language acquisition seem to be carelessly missed, or dismissed, under the erroneous mentality that normative tests presumably provide necessary and sufficient information.

Unfortunately, the clinical fields do not pause to consider such inadequacies; they merely administer such tests and assert that the results constitute evidence when, in fact, only data are obtained, and questionable data at that. The result is that such data may be interpreted in any way—dogma. To reiterate, data become evidence if they are supportable by the relevant scholarly literature and are relevant to a particular individual's repertoire of skills.

The basic concern is that the clinical fields may be too blind to major substantive issues in assessment. With unquestioned reliance on psychometric normative tests, the assessment process seems to have reverted to merely categorizing and labeling children. Norms were considered necessary and sufficient. It matters little if the tests or developmental profiles are incompatible with the available substantive literature.

Previously, I (Muma, 1986a) gave 10 reasons why developmental profiles lacked compatibility with the available cognitive socialization literature. In the following, I raise many questions about the value of normative tests. Again, this circumstance points to entrenchment of the psychometric mentality in the clinical fields, even at the cost of more appropriate descriptive standardized assessment procedures issuing from the available cognitive socialization literature.

Another note to underscore the myopic view of staunch believers in the psychometric normative model is the notion of standardized assessment. The traditional clinical view of standardized assessment is that such assessments must be done only by normative tests. However, this mentality is incorrect. The official interpretation of P.L. 94-142 (Martin, 1980; see Appendix A) explicitly calls for a standardized assessment that may be carried out by either formal (normative) or informal (descriptive) assessment procedures. Thus, astute clinicians could use descriptive procedures issuing from the cognitive socialization literature to assess substantive issues in CCCE.

The psychometric mentality is evidenced in another subtle but corrosive way. It has to do with the atheoretical nature of norms and the resulting lack of construct validity. The psychometric mentality assumes that norms provide necessary and sufficient information for assessment. Thus, if everyone except for one individual performs acceptably on a test, this discrepant performance is deemed necessary and sufficient to conclude that this individual is different. Indeed, I concur.

The problem arises when such differences become attributed to particular substantive domains such as vocabulary development, phonological skills, syntactic skills, and pragmatic skills. Without an underlying theory, the substantive implications of aberrant scores could be interpreted to mean virtually anything. Unfortunately, this is precisely what has happened in the clinical fields simply because so many tests lack construct validity. Performances on these tests are interpreted according to whatever notions are claimed to be assessed regardless of any incompatibilities with the available scholarly literature. In a word, the psychometric mentality in the clinical fields has become largely atheoretical, resting on the untenable premise that normative tests provide necessary and sufficient information.

Yet, scholars in the theory of science indicate that theories are indispensable because they provide appropriate explanations, predictions, and understandings (Kaplan, 1964; Kerlinger, 1973). Philosophical views and theoretical perspectives sanction professions. "It is theory that defines appropriate interpretations of the data. It is theory that provides justifiable rationale for appropriate clinical assessment and intervention. Thus, it is theory that makes things practical" (Muma, 1991, p. 230). Conversely, dogma and authoritarianism rule when reliance is not placed on theory.

I, for one, am utterly astounded that some individuals have indicated that theories may not be needed in the clinical fields (Kamhi, 1993; Perkins, 1986; Starkweather, 1992). However, Perkins has since become an advocate of theory. Notice that such perspectives reflect empirical and behavioristic traditions that are inherently atheoretical. From an empirical and behavioristic heritage, it is not surprising that these individuals have not expressed concern about:

1. The lack of construct validity for many clinical tests.
2. The need for continuity with philosophical views and theoretical perspectives in intervention.
3. A rational perspective rather than an empirical perspective of efficacy.

They are, after all, following empirical and behavioral traditions.

Kamhi (1988, 1993) mistakenly lumped Johnston's views with those that advocated atheoretical perspectives. It is disheartening to mix Johnston's (1983) message for a theoretical perspective with the preceding because she had a qualitatively different message. Yet, Johnston (1983) was right! "When we advocate the use of 'reinforcing consequent events' to effect 'abstract rule formation,' we are not combining the best of two worlds. We are building a theory that can't work" (p. 55). As indicated earlier, these are incompatible theories. Indeed, Johnston (1988) was once again the single voice that questioned whether the behaviorist notion of generalization (Connell, 1988; Kamhi, 1988) or transfer even pertains to rule learning. As Johnston (1988) and many others, notably Bowerman (1987), Macken (1987), Mandler (1983, 1988), and Ninio (1988), scholars in rule acquisition, indicate, it is an inherent contradiction to claim rule acquisition on the one hand but acknowledge that learning did not carry over, generalize, or transfer. This kind of non sequitur is commonly found in the behavioristic literature.

Another similar kind of conceptual slippage in the clinical literature is the relatively ready ease with which some terms are subtly used and misused. Notice how the following terms are used in this literature: *performance* (use) and *learning, did* and *ability, product* and *process*. Misuses of these words are common in the behavioristic literature and in the whole language literature. They are even interchanged from one sentence to the next, resulting in the misleading notion that performance is competence.

My basic point is that the cognitive socialization literature is very much committed to philosophical views and theoretical perspectives as the underpinnings of scholarship. It is this commitment that has advanced the field.

Thus, scholars such as Johnston who appreciate the significance of philosophical views and theoretical perspectives are vigilant about such violations and incompatibilities, whereas individuals who are not troubled by such matters operate with atheoretical views and perspectives. It is precisely because Perkins, Kamhi, and Starkweather apparently were oriented on behaviorism and empiricism that they did not see the value of theories and precisely because Johnston was oriented on a cognitive socialization perspective that she was concerned about philosophical and theoretical incompatibilities. Thus, theories do make a difference.

Kamhi (1993) was concerned that theories are insufficiently developed and comprehensive to address everything needed in the clinical arena. It should also be noted that theories, virtually by definition, are always provisional. However, I disagree with his bottom line: "Providing clinical services that are theoretically coherent is not only impractical, but also unrealistic" (p. 59). It is virtually a given that theories will be insufficiently comprehensive and provisional. However, they do provide an appropriate understanding and rationale that offer viable checks against dogma, authoritarianism, and hype. These functions of theoretical perspectives merit their appreciation. I would say, in contrast to Kamhi, that philosophical views and theoretical perspectives constitute the practical and realistic substantive base of the clinical fields.

Given this perspective, philosophical views and theoretical perspectives constitute the substantive base of a scholarly field and should become the substantive base of the clinical fields. Returning to the distinction between data and evidence, to reiterate, evidence is data that:

1. Are supportable by the contemporary scholarly literature.
2. Are demonstrably relevant to an individual's repertoire of skills.

To reiterate, this perspective is derived directly from the definition of appropriateness. Also, notice that this perspective may be a threat to traditional psychometric normative testing and it is consistent with various standardized descriptive procedures issuing from the cognitive socialization literature.

DESCRIPTIVE ASSESSMENT: APPROPRIATENESS

First, be assured that I regard the psychometric normative approach useful. It has appropriate applications, especially in regard to group assessments ʰ ₋ause the central premise is one of group performance, norms. I want to give this assurance simply because McCauley and Swisher (1984a) badly misrepresented my views about psychometric normative testing. Nowhere in the references of mine that they cited did I say what they attributed to me. Contrary to their claim, I indicated in the references they cited that psychometric normative tests address the problem—no problem clinical issue. Ironically enough, they followed this article with a sister article on the uses and misuses of normative tests (McCauley & Swisher, 1984b).

Second, I have consistently maintained that in the clinical arena individual differences are outstanding. In normal populations, variances are common, and often large, on virtually any significant variable. Yes, it is possible to obtain measurements with very little variance but such measurements are virtually certain to be with trivial variables. Furthermore, in clinical populations, variance is characteristically much greater than in normal populations. Even within clinical categories such as aphasia, stuttering, phonology, SLI, mental retardation, and hearing impairment, it is exceedingly difficult to find two individuals with precisely the same problem. Baumeister (1984), one of the foremost scholars in the field, indicated that the most outstanding characteristic of mental retardation is heterogeneity or individual differences. Indeed, the clinical literature is replete with studies evidencing heterogeneity. Yet, the underlying assumption of the psychometric normative test model is homogeneity, this issue is conveniently overlooked in the clinical fields.

With heterogeneity characteristic of clinical populations and homogeneity the basic underlying premise for psychometric normative testing, there is an undeniable incompatibility facing the clinical fields. Yet the clinical fields have been strangely silent about this problem and largely undaunted in the reliance on normative testing. Psychometric normative tests and developmental profiles are widely used clinically. It is not an exaggeration to say that the psychometric normative test model has become firmly entrenched in the clinical fields.

The heterogeneity–homogeneity incompatibility issue is basically passed off under the assumption that normative tests provide necessary and sufficient information for virtually any assessment. This mentality is sponsored by the logic that if everyone in a group performs on a given level with a given degree of variance, except one individual, then the group performance is the standard to which the exceptional individual should be held. This logic rings true, and indeed, it does offer a reasonable perspective for identifying a problem in the problem–no problem arena.

However, there are some very serious limitations with this logic. If the goal of clinical assessment is merely to categorize individuals with problems, something could be said for this perspective assuming that there are no other threats (i.e., content relevance, loss of assessment power, floor and ceiling effects, and reduced precision of measurement because of large variance). The result of such an assessment would be categorization and labeling, which is useful programmatically for funding and resource allocation.

However, such practices have a serious downside, which Mercer (1972a, 1972b, 1974) called the "lethal label" problem (see the three special issues of the *Harvard Educational Review*; Harvard School of Education, 1971, 1973, 1974). In short, the psychometric mentality has produced an assessment practice that merely labels individuals but does not address other major issues of clinical assessment (Muma, 1973b). More specifically and urgently, normative tests do not provide opportunities to ascertain an individual's repertoire of skills, progress in acquisition sequences, alternative strategies of learning, and active loci of learning. Such information is essentially available from descriptive procedures (Muma, 1973b) and these kinds of information are crucial for addressing other major issues of clinical assessment, namely individual differences, nature of a problem, intervention implications, and accountability or efficacy.

There are four ironies in this circumstance. First, the clinical fields are remarkably silent about these issues. Perhaps this silence is evidence that the psychometric model is truly entrenched. Second, the cognitive socialization literature offers many descriptive procedures that have the potential of estimating repertoires of skills, progress in acquisition sequences, alternative strategies of learning, and active loci of learning. The point is that the substantive literature is available for addressing the more substantial issues in clinical assessment. Third, many clinicians are not well informed about the federal policy permitting the use of descriptive assessments. Most clinicians in the field erroneously believe that P.L. 94-142 requires test scores to meet the criterion of standardized assessment for eligibility of services and evidence of accountability or efficacy.

P.L. 94-142 states explicitly that a standardized assessment is needed, but the official interpretation permits either tests or descriptive assessment (Martin, 1980; see Appendix A) of a standardized assessment. It states that either an informal (descriptive) or formal (tests) assessment may be used by a certified speech-language pathologist to meet this standard. Thus, astute clinicians aware of the descriptive procedures issuing from the cognitive socialization literature could avail themselves of these procedures and meet the requirement of a standardized assessment. Test scores are not needed. In this way the expertise of the clinical fields could be enhanced and more appropriate services rendered.

Fourth, another issue intrudes on the potential use of appropriate descriptive procedures. Simply and boldly put, it is expediency. It is widely held in the clinical fields that descriptive procedures, especially language sampling and analysis, are too time consuming to be viable options simply because there are too many clients to serve and not enough time. Therefore, there has been a rush for quick and easy tests regardless of their lack of construct validity because their norms presumably provide necessary and sufficient information. Could it be that quick and easy tests such as the PPVT–R, CELF–R, TOLD, Goldman–Fristoe, and many others are used simply because they offer expedient solutions to the assessment question?

If test scores are obtained, does it matter if these scores are of questionable value in light of what the cognitive socialization literature has to offer?

For example, does it matter in the clinical fields if the PPVT–R, Boehm–R, Bracken, and several other tests are incompatible with the literatures on word learning and concept development, respectively? The widespread use of such scores indicts the clinical fields for being committed to expediently obtained data rather than evidence.

I (Muma, 1983b, 1986a) have maintained that the expediency issue is more solvable than the advocates of testing are willing to acknowledge. The secret, of course, is training. I call my view the standing challenge. It is simply to take as much time as used for normative testing but do a descriptive assessment. This procedure will provide more information (no claim is made that the descriptive assessment is complete) and the information will be more useful for intervention than that obtained in normative testing.

This is evident in phonology. A description dealing with the following could be done (partially but sufficiently) by addressing the following issues: phonological processes, phonetic inventory, homonymy, and phonological avoidance. A descriptive assessment of grammar could also be done assuming that the sample is from a variety of contexts and is sufficiently large (on the order of 200–300 utterances) to be representative of what an individual can do (repertoire). Evidence of some grammatical problems, progress in acquisition sequences, alternative learning strategies, and active loci of learning could be obtained on a provisional basis within a relatively short time. Again, the key, of course, is training.

Evidence of this sort constitutes "assessment well done and intervention half begun." Stated differently, an assessment vested merely on expediency and data is assessment not well done and this raises a twofold problem. It yields erroneous data and raises the issue of the ethics of assessment. With erroneous data, intervention would be in jeopardy. Thus, intervention would be a waste of time and obtained gains would be misconstrued as evidence of efficacy.

Messick (1980) pointed out the ethical problem when assessment is not well done. He was concerned about assessment that lacked construct validity. Such assessment raises an ethical problem because the data become interpreted capriciously. This is an ethical dilemma because on the one hand data rather than evidence are obtained, whereas on the other hand the data carry the mantle of scholarship by virtue of a normative comparison. Thus, such data have been elevated as something to reckon with but without construct validity they are nothing more than data vulnerable to dogma. It is unethical to interpret such data as an individual's skills, capacities, or abilities without a theoretical stance that warrants such interpretations. Yet, the clinical fields seem to be either unaware or undaunted by this ethical dilemma.

Fortunately, descriptive assessments issuing from the cognitive socialization literature are well grounded on philosophical views and theoretical perspectives thereby having construct validity. Furthermore, descriptive assessments offer opportunities to ascertain available repertoires, progress in acquisition strategies, available strategies of learning, and active loci of learning. These are the substantive issues for obtaining evidence that is relevant to what an individual can do. Thus, descriptive assessment holds the potential for providing evidence rather than just data. Descriptive assessment also offers more potential than psychometric normative assessment in addressing the six basic assessment issues (Muma, 1981a, 1983b, 1986a) and in so doing it provides a satisfactory way of dealing with appropriateness.

CONSTRUCT VALIDITY

The experts in the field of what had previously been called "test and measurement"—now called "assessment and measurement"—have shown that construct validity should be established before addressing other issues of assessment. *"All measurement should be construct referenced"* (Messick, 1975, p. 957). *"All* validity is at its base some form of construct validity. . . . It *is* the basic meaning of validity" (Guion, 1977, p. 410).

The traditional view was that there were three presumed options for establishing the validity of a test or assessment procedure. The presumed options were content, criterion, and construct validity. These have been regarded as "a Holy Trinity representing three different roads to psychometric salvation. If you can't demonstrate one kind of validity, you've got two more chances!" (Guion, 1980, p. 4). However, Messick (1980) and others have shown that there are no options simply because all issues of assessment are derived from construct validity.

Validity, in general, "is the overall degree of justification for test interpretation and use" (Messick, 1980, p. 1014). The *American Psychological Association Standards for Educational and Psychological Tests* (1974) defined validity as follows: "Validity refers to the appropriateness of inferences from test scores or other forms of assessment. . . . It is important to note that validity is itself inferred, not measured." This brings home quite solidly the importance of theory for construct validity because, in science, the functions of theories are to provide appropriate inferences for explanation, prediction, and understanding (Kaplan, 1964; Kerlinger, 1973; Kuhn, 1962; Medawar, 1984). Theories only permit certain allowable inferences in explanation, prediction, and understanding. That is to say, the source of inference for construct validity in assessment should be the substantive issues from relevant theories.

Because construct validity is crucial for assessment, the obvious question is to what extent assessment in the clinical fields is predicated on construct validity. Muma and Brannon (1986) surveyed several of the most widely used language assessment tests in the clinical fields. The purpose of the survey was to ascertain the extent to which tests were predicated on construct validity. The tests surveyed were PPVT–R, ITPA, PICA, CELF, ACLC, TACL, DSS, and TOLD. Except for the ITPA, the tests did not have construct validity. In regard to the ITPA, it was based on a theoretical view of modality differences (expressive and receptive modalities) of information processing posited by Osgood (1957). This view has long since been replaced by more supportable views of information processing (Clark & Clark, 1977; Sperber & Wilson, 1986). Nevertheless, these tests are widely used in the clinical fields. Thus, the clinical fields claim expertise in language but rely on tests that lack construct validity.

A subordinate inquiry in this survey was to ascertain if the tests dealt with some substantive issues related to the contemporary theories of language acquisition. These issues included relativity, conditionality, complexity, dynamism, and ecology. These issues are discussed in the following. The surveyed tests were remarkably free of these issues also.

The survey considered the seven basic clinical assessment issues (Muma, 1981c, 1983b, 1986a): clinical complaint, problem–no problem, nature of a problem, individual differences, intervention implications, prognosis, and accountability or efficacy. These are discussed in the following. The outcome of this inquiry was that the tests were not as powerful or appropriate as descriptive procedures issuing from the cognitive socialization literature.

Finally, the survey asked if the tests were a priori or a posteriori in nature. A priori procedures are those that are prepackaged, requiring an individual to conform to specific tasks with performance compared to norms. A posteriori procedures are those that describe spontaneous intentional behavior in actual social commerce, as opposed to elicited performance on contrived tasks. A priori procedures are further removed from actual evidence of an individual's skills than a posteriori procedures. Moreover, contrived activities are imposed on an individual in a priori procedures, whereas a posteriori procedures are subject to actual social commerce. In short, a posteriori procedures may offer better opportunities to assess what an individual can do than a priori procedures simply because they are predicated on the relevant substantive literature and on what an individual actually does in social commerce. Thus, a posteriori procedures may be more appropriate than a priori procedures to assess what an individual can do with language (Beckwith, Rispoli, & Bloom, 1984). Greenfield and Smith (1976) shared the view that the a posteriori perspective may be appropriate for appreciating what an individual can do. "If we are to discover structure in, rather than to impose structure on, child language, it is useful to have a descriptive system which allows separate treatment of each element of the situation" (p. 16).

In short, the surveyed tests were remarkably weak in dealing with:

1. Construct validity.
2. The five related issues for construct validity.
3. The seven basic clinical assessment issues.
4. A posteriori evidence.

Yet, they are widely used in the clinical fields. Unfortunately, many other tests in the clinical fields are weak on similar grounds. The irony is that the available cognitive socialization literature offers many viable substantive perspectives for addressing these issues. A further irony is, of course, that expertise in language is claimed and conclusions are made about presumed verbal skills for individuals based on performances on such tests. Such tests yield data but lack evidence. To reiterate, undaunted, some technicians respond with the protectionist comment, "Well, at least they tell us something." No, this is merely a tacit admission that it is dogma, not expertise, that is operating.

Much of what is done in clinical assessment lacks construct validity. Even reviews of language tests (Darley, 1979; McCauley & Swisher, 1984a) missed the central issue—construct validity. The result is that clinical assessment may be nothing more than generating data but not much evidence. The conclusions, based on such data, are of questionable value concerning presumed language skills, capacities, or abilities.

The distinction between data and evidence is fundamentally related to construct validity. To reiterate, data are mere naked performances or numbers open to any interpretation, whereas evidence is data that are relevant to recognized theories with their attendant literatures and relevant to a repertoire of skills for an individual. Here is a fundamental problem for the clinical fields. As the preceding survey indicated, much of what is claimed in clinical assessment is little more than data gathering rather than evidence gathering.

Many assessment tests that are used clinically lack construct validity, they are atheoretical, and there is virtually no attempt to establish relevance to an individual's repertoire of skills. Yet, technicians are willing to draw conclusions about an individual's presumed abilities or capacities merely from such test data.

Indeed, the psychometric model is so strongly entrenched in the clinical fields that if a test has a norm, it is regarded as providing necessary and sufficient evidence. It does not matter if a test is not based on a recognized theory, or if it is incompatible with the relevant scholarly literature, or if it is irrelevant to an individual's repertoire of skills. Such is the psychometric mentality in the clinical fields.

Without theories to establish construct validity, assessment would be open to any interpretation of any data. For example, Semel and Wiig (1980) developed a test called the Clinical Evaluation of Language Functions (CELF; subsequently known as Clinical Evaluation of Language Foundations, or CELF–R, with different authorship) that lacks construct validity.

CELF is little more than raw empiricism whereby norms are provided for various verbal activities and conclusions are made about an individual's presumed language skills. The interpretations of performance on the CELF subtests are merely induced by the subtest labels. The fundamental issue of construct validity is simply ducked, resulting in data but not much evidence.

This problem is not localized to the CELF test. Unfortunately, it is pervasive in the clinical fields. Another example is the work of Locke (1980a, 1980b), who showed that the widely used tests of speech discrimination were incompatible with the available scholarly literature on speech discrimination.

In the Goldman–Fristoe Test (Goldman & Fristoe, 1969), pictures are named so that an inventory of sounds appearing in the initial, medial, and final positions of words could be made and a story recall task is used to obtain an elicited speech sample. There are two fundamental problems concerning construct validity with this test. First, this test is based on the faulty premise that the basic unit of speech is the phoneme. Yet, the phonological literature has shifted away from the phoneme to the syllable as the basic unit (Ferguson & Garnica, 1975; Ingram, 1976, 1989b; McDonald, 1964; Vihman & Greenlee, 1987). Furthermore, other issues have emerged, notably phonetic inventory (Ingram 1976), phonetic context (Daniloff & Hammarberg, 1973), phonological processes (Ferguson, Menn, & Stoel-Gammon, 1992; Ingram, 1989b; Vihman, 1981), phonological avoidance (Schwartz & Leonard, 1982), and homonymy (Ferguson & Farwell, 1975; Locke, 1979; Priestly, 1980; Vihman, 1981).

Second, there is a very strange issue in the Goldman–Fristoe manual, whereby literature is cited indicating that there is no medial consonant in speech because the basic unit of speech is a syllable. The medial position of syllables is always a vowel. What is strange about the manual and the test is that after acknowledging that medial consonants do not exist in syllables, the test strives to assess medial consonants in words. To make matters worse, the clinical fields seemingly go along with the test because it is widely used. This is a classic example of ignoring the relevant literature in the clinical fields.

Moreover, comparisons of spontaneous speech to elicited speech on such tests frequently yield conflicting results (Fujiki & Brinton, 1987; Prutting et al., 1975). Thus, there may be a question as to whether performance on the Goldman–Fristoe Test of Articulation is relevant to an individual's repertoire of spontaneous speech.

In summary, the experts in the field of assessment and measurement have shown that "all measurement should be construct referenced" (Messick, 1980, p. 1015). This means that in order to have appropriate inferences of an individual's capacities it is necessary to establish the relevant philosophical views and theoretical perspectives of assessment. Furthermore, assessment should be relevant to what an individual can do—a repertoire of skills. Unfortunately, most psychometric normative tests used clinically lack construct validity. Therefore, contrary to general belief, these tests do not provide necessary and sufficient evidence about what is presumably assessed.

CONSTRUCT VALIDITY: FIVE RELATED ISSUES

Construct validity should be based on an explicit philosophical view and theoretical perspective with the attendant literature. The contemporary cognitive socialization literature has established many basic principles issuing largely from the language acquisition literature that have continuity with most cognitive socialization theories and comprise a substantive base for clinical assessment and intervention. Five issues are especially important (Muma, 1978b, 1986a): relativity, conditionality, complexity, dynamism, and ecology.

Relativity

Behavior is usually not absolute but relative. That is, behavior is not present or absent but approaching and surpassing a threshold that itself may vary slightly. Behavior is not present or absent but related to a context. Behavior is usually not right or wrong but supportive or disconfirming. In all, this means that behavior is relative. The importance of relativity (Kagan, 1967; Wechsler, 1975) is that patterns of behavior are needed to infer a skill; that is, single instances or even a few instances are insufficient to warrant a claim about a skill. "We have extraordinary faith in one-shot instantiation" (Bruner, 1986, p. 51).

The notion of relativity raises the issue of attribution; that is, attribution is a relative notion also. In order to attribute a skill it may be useful to consider whether it is in preparation, attainment, or consolidation (Muma, 1983b; K. E. Nelson, 1981; Prutting, 1979). These criteria are discussed later. Rather than rely on single instances of behavior, it is necessary to rely on patterns of behavior with associated contextual information.

An issue related to relativity is the null hypothesis in research design. The null hypothesis posits that there is no difference between variables under study. What is important about the null hypothesis is that it is impossible to prove simply because a lack of performance could be due to many unknown extraneous variables. It is a basic tenet of research that the null hypothesis may be disproved but never proved. However, the logic of this view has been challenged (Rudder, 1993).

Clinically, there is a direct implication of the null hypothesis. When a child does not perform or there is no evidence of a given aspect of behavior, it is inappropriate to conclude that a child lacks a skill or competency. The lack of evidence does not permit a conclusion about a lack of a skill or competence. It is only when patterns of behavior are evidenced that inferences can be drawn about underlying skills. Thus, just as the null hypothesis cannot be proven, it is also true, for the same reason, that the lack of evidence does not permit a conclusion about presumed skills or competences. King and Goodman (1990) recognized this issue: "Too often, the reticence of minority pupils to use language with strange adults in unfamiliar settings is treated as a lack of competence" (p. 226).

In the field of mental retardation, the contrast between viewing behavior as absolute or relative is evidenced in the use of the *AAMD Adaptive Behavioral Scales* (Nihira, Foster, Shellhaas, & Leland, 1974). These scales contain rather exhaustive lists of behaviors whereby an informant is asked to rate an individual as to whether a given behavior occurs frequently, seldom, or never. A profile of such ratings is used presumably to ascertain if a particular child is adaptive. Baumeister and Muma (1975) questioned whether adaptiveness is even broached by such ratings. It seems patently obvious that such ratings are virtually meaningless because the judged behaviors are removed from the contexts in which they function. For example, it would be adaptive for a child to cry frequently in a context of persistent frustration, but it would be maladaptive to cry in a context of emotional support. To merely rate frequency of crying—or any other behavior—removed from context misses the essence of adaptiveness.

Another implication of either–or thinking is that it is incongruent with behavior. Rarely is behavior right or wrong, good or bad, or present or absent. Behavior is relative rather than absolute (Kagan, 1967). To reiterate, single instances of a behavior do not provide evidence of a skill. Because behavior is relative, it is necessary to obtain patterns of behavior from which legitimate inferences may be drawn about repertoires of skills.

Conditionality

Conditionality is about contextual influences. The contemporary cognitive socialization literature has shown that context is essential for an adequate understanding of language and communication. To reiterate, "Context is all" (Bruner, 1981, p. 172).

Fillmore (1972) identified two basic kinds of context, internal and external. Internal context is theory of the world (Palermo, 1982), possible worlds

(Bruner, 1986), or situated mind (K. Nelson, 1996) with presuppositions and implicatures needed for a particular proposition to realize communicative intent. External context includes the perception of objects, actions, events, and relationships (social, cultural) that may be coded in a message or implicated by context.

Conditionality may be appreciated from the perspective of different kinds of contexts (see chap. 6). Above all, intentional context is the nucleus of language acquisition and communication (Austin, 1962; Cazden, 1977; Grice, 1975; Halliday, 1975; Ninio & Snow, 1988; Searle, 1969, 1975; Sperber & Wilson, 1986). Intent has been regarded as the irrefutable nucleus of social commerce (Bruner, 1986; Muma, 1991).

In both assessment and intervention, the clinical fields have relied heavily on elicited verbal behavior rather than intentional behavior. Verbal performance on elicited tasks may be qualitatively different from that in spontaneous speech (Lahey, 1988; Slobin & Welch, 1971)—an issue that the clinical fields acknowledge but apparently dismiss. For example, Prutting et al. (1975) showed that grammatical errors differed between elicited and spontaneous language samples. Performances on the PPVT–R (Dunn & Dunn, 1981) or on the Goldman–Fristoe (1969) test are likely to be qualitatively different from what children do when they want to name something or talk spontaneously.

An interesting question arises: To what extent does performance on elicited tasks represent natural spontaneous (intentional) speech? Needless to say, the lack of so-called carryover from clinic performance to spontaneous speech may be, in large measure, the difference between elicited and intentional behavior.

In assessing grammatical skills, relational context is especially important. Relational context pertains to the relations between words in linguistic context. It is necessary to consider an individual's range of verbal constructions with attendant lexical variations within these constructions and variations of co-occurring structures as evidence of repertoires of grammatical skills. Children do not learn grammatical systems in isolation (McNeill, 1966), rather contextual learning takes place in the course of actually using language (Bruner, 1981, 1986). Thus, the actual use of words in relation to other words provides an understanding of relational meaning that is essential for grammatical learning.

The notion of online processing (Bates & MacWhinney, 1987; Bowerman, 1987; Maratsos, 1982; Maratsos & Chalkley, 1981) may be the utilization of relational contexts for deducing new grammatical and pragmatic relations that were not experienced directly. Moreover, contextual learning is evidenced by partial learning or developmental sequences, switching loci of learning, and loci of learning largely governed by what a child can do, or his or her repertoire (Muma, 1978b, 1986a).

The notion of repertoire may be detailed in terms of the range of available grammatical or pragmatic skills for each system of interest. However, a richer version of repertoire may be obtained by considering linguistic and referential contexts in which grammatical and pragmatic skills are evidenced.

The models of vertical and horizontal correlates in language acquisition (Bates & MacWhinney, 1987; Maratsos, 1982) offer promising ways of estimating verbal repertoires within grammatical and pragmatic contexts. A different earlier version of horizontal and vertical learning was offered by McNeill (1970). One view of vertical learning for grammatical systems would be lexical variation. Thus, if a child evidenced increased variation in the use of transitive verbs, vertical learning for this system would be evidenced. However, horizontal learning for grammatical systems would be evidenced by variations in the co-occurring systems (Harris, 1965; Muma, 1973b). For example, a child who has a rather limited set of transitive verbs but evidenced increased variation in the attendant object nominals would evidence horizontal learning for the transitive system.

In response to their concerns about the modularity notion (J. Fodor, 1983), and following Maratsos (1982), Bates and MacWhinney (1987) posited their notions of vertical and horizontal correlates in regard to form and function correlates. Correlates may be evidenced directly between forms and functions, between forms, and between functions.

In very early learning, relatively direct form–function relations are evidenced. Referring to the studies that attributed semantic cases to early one-word speech, Ninio and Snow (1988) commented, "Early one-word utterances are purely functional" (p. 15). They also said, "Our production model would predict (and much evidence confirms) that only **one** means of expression is typically found and mapped onto the communicative intent, at least during the early stages of language acquisition" (p. 13).

However, when it comes to mapping form–form and function–function relations toward achieving relational meaning (Berman, 1988; Maratsos, 1988a; Ninio, 1988; Schlesinger, 1988) and shared meaning (K. Nelson, 1985; Sperber & Wilson, 1986) for the purpose of making intentions recognizable, subsystem coalitions are needed to deal with plural form and functional relations. Turning to the transitive system whereby SVO relations, in English, become mapped grammatically, form–form relations and function–function relations are the products of several coalitions. One way of appreciating vertical correlates, in this instance, is the diversity of the transitive verbs (forms) as they map transitive notions (functions) with a relatively fixed set of object expressions. It would be expected that a child would evidence an expanded range of transitive verbs with a relatively fixed set of object noun phrases. In contrast, horizontal correlates, in this instance, may be evidenced by an increased diversity of object noun phrases with a relatively

TABLE 7.1
Illustrative Issues Attendant to the Notions of Vertical
(Form–Function) and Horizontal (Form–Form) Correlates
in Learning the Transitive (SVO) System in English

	Subject	Verb	Object
Vertical		Varied	Constant
Horizontal		Constant	Varied

fixed set of transitive verbs. This would evidence form–form correlates, which is co-occurrence (Harris, 1965; Muma, 1973b). Table 7.1 summarizes the notion of vertical and horizontal correlates.

It is one thing to merely label a referent (referential meaning), but quite a different matter to have to use the label in relation to other labels to achieve a message (relational meaning; Greenfield & Smith, 1976; Leonard, 1976). It is still another matter for a particular message to work as intended (communicative payoff; Muma, 1981c) in achieving shared meaning (K. Nelson, 1985) or mutual manifestness (Sperber & Wilson, 1986). For example, a person may have indicative skills for labeling various apples "apple." However, it is when a person can use the word *apple* in varied relations with other words within (vertical correlates) a construction (my apple, that apple, a red apple, the rotten apple, etc.) and variations of co-occurring structures (horizontal correlates; e.g., My apple is red. He ate my apple. Did someone find my apple?) that relational meaning could be attributed. When relational meaning is picked up and shared by others in the recognition of communicative intent, shared meaning becomes attained. Thus, the basic notion concerning linguistic contexts entails referential meaning, relational meaning, and shared meaning in the recognition of communicative intents.

Relational meaning goes beyond grammatical constructions and co-occurring constructions (Harris, 1965) to lexical diversity (Ninio, 1988), anaphora (Chafe, 1976; Halliday & Hansan, 1976; Lust, 1986a, 1986b), and various pragmatic devices such as those for cohesion and for conveying indirect speech acts. Coupled with the preceding discussion, there are several basic issues attendant to relational meaning: structural variation within constructions (Bloom et al., 1989), lexical variation within constructions (Ninio, 1988), varied co-occurring structures (Harris, 1965), and anaphora (Chafe, 1976). Each of these operate on different coalitions of cues and constraints (Bates & MacWhinney, 1987). It is conceivable that indirect speech acts and psychological set could also be included in accounts of relational meaning. In all, relational meaning constitutes explicit content (proposition) in the realization of communicative intents.

Anaphora refers to the function of pronominals and it was discussed in chapter 6. To reiterate, anaphora deals with sustained reference. It entails anaphoric loading, competition, and vacant anaphora. Indirect speech acts were also mentioned previously. Briefly, they are acts that on the surface convey one message but the context of a code matrix conveys a different message. For example, a person may say, "I liked the movie," but the facial code and gestures indicated that this individual did not like it. Therefore, the indirect message was that the movie was disliked.

Psychological sets constitute another dimension of effective communication. In addition to what an individual knows, the individual may have a psychological set or expectation for certain information. This is known as *canonical knowledge* in the situated mind (K. Nelson, 1996). When this expectation is challenged by virtue of discrepant information, the individual becomes alerted and attentive. However, when the psychological set is violated, an individual may become upset and essentially shut down the communication process. This is what Bruner (1986) referred to with the notion of a crossover function whereby an individual crosses over from information processing to emotional responsiveness.

These issues are summarized in Table 7.2. Such issues are virtually foreign to the clinical fields. Indeed, technicians are virtually oblivious to such issues; yet, they are essential issues for rendering appropriate clinical services in language and communication.

In summary, conditionality pertains to intentional, referential, relational, and social contexts. More on conditionality appears in chapters 2 and 4 in regard to the emergence of the situated mind. There are major questions as to whether various tests and intervention procedures in the clinical fields are supportable simply because such crucial issues are missing.

Complexity

The scholarly literature has shown that cognition, emotion, language, and communication are exceedingly complex. Yet, the clinical fields utilize quick and easy assessment measures. Even publishers frequently tout their products as providing quick and easy assessments. If the clinical fields did not buy into the quick and easy notion, publishers would not tout their products in this way, but, alas, claims of quick and easy sell in the clinical fields.

Thus, there is a paradox because the scholarly literature shows that cognition, language, and communication are very complex in nature, yet

TABLE 7.2
Basic Issues Concerning Relational Meaning

Indicative: Prerelational meaning
Vertical correlates: Lexical variation within a construction
Horizontal correlates: Varying co-occurring constructions
Anaphora: Loading, competition, vacant anaphora
Indirect speech acts: Deduced implicature

individuals in the clinical fields who claim expertise in these domains rely on simplistic, quick, and easy tests that sometimes are also claimed to be complete and accurate. The result is that data rather than evidence are usually obtained clinically. Yet, such data are regarded as evidence of an individual's abilities.

The clinical fields might be quick to say that the reason that quick and easy tests are used is because practitioners have to see so many children. However, this position is patently weak for two reasons: expediency and substance. As indicated earlier, expediency is presumably justifiable by virtue of the sheer number of individuals receiving services. The fallacy of the expediency argument is that inappropriate services become rendered. Yet, P.L. 94-142 explicitly states that individuals in need of clinical services are entitled to appropriate services rather than expedient services.

This issue can be put another way. Assume that you have an appendicitis attack that is life threatening. You are taken to a doctor who holds the expediency view that the operation you need is too time consuming and he has too many patients, so he gives you a pill to put you to sleep while you die. It is, after all, an expedient solution. It is also unethical. The point to be made is that expediency in rendering services in the health professions is a hollow, even unethical, position. Expediency is a direct threat to appropriate services and to the profession.

Given the available cognitive socialization literature, we have taken a different ploy. It is the standing challenge discussed earlier: Do whatever you do to carry out a clinical assessment using the various normative tests, developmental profiles, and checklists. Let me, or one of our trained clinicians, know how long it took for your assessment. We will take the same amount of time and carry out an assessment based on the available cognitive socialization literature. This assessment will provide more information and it will be more useful for intervention. The point is that expediency does not work on both substantive and ethical grounds. It is appropriate training that counts. Expediency merely yields data but not evidence and it raises an ugly ethical dilemma.

Dynamism

Dynamism pertains to the fluidity or elasticity of skills. The more a skill is used, the more it is available for use; the less it is used is the extent to which it lacks availability. Use begets use, lack of use means more limited skills. This is true of most skills. For example, it is well known that a person with cerebral palsy needs a bracing and physical therapy program to maintain existing motor skills, otherwise the individual may experience progressively reduced capacities for these skills. Another example is when an individual has an eye muscle imbalance or "cross-eyed" condition. With such individuals, it is necessary to put a patch over the good eye for short periods so that the poorer eye is forced to work; otherwise, the poorer eye could become functionally blind. Another example is athletes who will train to peak performances. They must maintain training or lose their peak performances. Memory is always changing as a function of use or lack of use.

Because dynamism means that behavior is always in flux or change, the clinical implication for assessment is that it is an ongoing process. The implication for intervention is that sheer talking time can be a significant issue in obtaining language.

Ecology

Ecology pertains to the relations between organisms and their environments. Human ecology pertains to the relationships of humans to their environments (Bronfenbrenner, 1979). This means that natural behavior in actual contexts should comprise the arena for assessing language and language intervention. Indeed, in England, the school language curriculum addresses human ecology by virtue of the concept of *A Language for Life* (Bullock, 1975). In another example, Donaldson (1978) showed that children perform differently on contrived tasks than natural or ecologically valid tasks that make human sense. Specifically, she showed that children who did not evidence Stage 6 in the Uzgiris and Hunt (1975) object permanence task not only evidenced this accomplishment for human sense tasks but did so much younger than was evidenced on the contrived task performances. This finding raises the question of what credence should be placed on contrived tasks such as those obtained in formal psychometric tests.

In summary, construct validity is mandatory for all assessment simply because everything else is derived from construct validity, and construct validity itself is predicated on the underlying philosophical–theoretical base. In CCCE, other issues attendant to construct validity include relativity, conditionality, complexity, dynamism, and ecology.

Perhaps another note should be added concerning the relation between construct validity and reliability. Inasmuch as everything is derived from construct validity, it should be recognized that reliability is, in a sense, subservient to construct validity. Another way of looking at this relation is that reliability is virtually meaningless without construct validity. For example, it is possible to obtain very high reliabilities for trivial issues, but is such reliability relevant to what the assessment claims to measure? More specifically, relatively high reliabilities are obtained for the PPVT–R, but do such data provide evidence of an individual's vocabulary or so-called receptive language? Because the PPVT–R misses major issues of vocabulary or word acquisition, such data are of questionable value.

PSYCHOMETRIC NORMATIVE TESTS:
INDOCTRINATION?

With the widespread reliance on psychometric normative testing in the clinical fields, a poignant question arises. To what extent should reliance be placed on psychometric normative tests? This question extends across several major issues, some of which are assumed to be both valid and immutable in the clinical fields. However, a consideration of the basic foundations of psychometric normative testing, in light of relatively recent developments in the cognitive socialization literature, not only gives pause to the validity of normative testing in the clinical fields, but raises the additional issue that these fields may have become indoctrinated to believe in such tests when it would be prudent to scrutinize them more carefully.

The basic premise of psychometric testing issued from empiricism and the Watsonian era in the early 1900s. This view held that issues should be resolved by data. The psychometric approach is an empirical stance based on the normative solution, which is to convert individual differences into a communal standard. Bateson (1980) commented that norms shift the referent from the individual to the group, "There is a jump from particular to general, from member to class" (p. 133). Norms are attractive because they constitute a portable and defensible solution to the problem of considering new instances—namely the performance of an individual. Because norms are inherently pluralistic and communal, they are heralded as a singular index freed of subjectivity, presumably capable of providing necessary and sufficient evidence of what is assessed.

Furthermore, norms were defensible on the grounds of Bayesian probability theory; that is, performance within a reasonable range of the mean (usually plus or minus two standard deviations because this range encompasses about 95% of a distribution) is attributable to what is presumably assessed by a test. Performance outside of this range should not be attributed to what is presumably assessed by a test because such performances are more likely attributable to other unknown extraneous variables. In such circumstances, tests lack sufficient assessment power for attribution.

Needless to say, psychometric normative testing is based on some weighty issues. It behooves the clinical fields to consider the extent to which these issues are credible. Consider the following limitations of psychometric norms in dealing with cognitive socialization in general and language acquisition in particular: (a) lack objectivity, (b) impose a priori categories, (c) subjugate individual differences, (d) lack necessary and sufficient information, (e) acontextual, (f) convert behavior into numbers, (g) miss language functions, (h) miss acquisition sequences, (i) miss alternative learning strategies, (j) miss loci of learning, (k) lack disciplined interpretation, (l)

TABLE 7.3
Limitations of Normative Testing in the Clinical
Fields in Dealing With Language Acquisition

Normative Tests
1. Lack objectivity.
2. Impose a priori categories.
3. Subjugate individual differences.
4. Lack necessary and sufficient information.
5. Acontextual.
6. Convert behavior to numbers.
7. Miss language functions.
8. Miss acquisition sequences.
9. Miss alternative learning strategies.
10. Miss active loci of learning.
11. Lack disciplined interpretation.
12. Provide data rather than evidence.
13. Lack construct validity.

provide data rather than evidence, and (m) lack construct validity. These issues are listed in Table 7.3.

The mere act of raising these issues may bring an outcry from those in the clinical fields simply because these fields have been silent about many of these issues and because of the apparent indoctrination for these tests. That is, if it is so that an indoctrination for psychometric testing has occurred in the clinical fields, I run the risk of being regarded as a heretic by challenging such testing on these grounds. Yet, a scholarly consideration of the issues offers an opportunity to appreciate the relative value of psychometric normative assessment.

First, the great claim for normative testing is that it is objective. To reiterate, developments in the philosophy of cognition and language have shown that there is a fundamental flaw in the objectivity claim. This claim holds that what is observed is neutral from human bias; it is presumably "clean" or truthful. The fundamental flaw is that there is no access to a "God's-eye view." Whatever is known, or done in the case of norms, is the product of human experience, not what is neutral. Said differently, whatever is known or done is inherently subjective, not objective.

Hopefully, the objectivity claim is a myth because it may have a sinister quality to it. Could the objectivity claim have a sinister function whereby an individual being assessed may become objectified by virtue of performance on a test? In this way, the professional would be psychologically removed from any humanistic factor that may otherwise come into play. This sounds very much like the lethal label problem with normative tests that Mercer (1972a, 1972b, 1974) discussed. This is another issue about which the clinical fields have been silent.

Second, normative tests use a priori categories of behavior. Performance on such tests is elicited for the categories on a test. A basic question arises concerning the relevance of a priori categories in a test: What justifies the categories on a test as being relevant to the contemporary literature and what an individual can do? From this perspective, a child merely conforms to what a test is presumably about; in contrast, descriptive procedures issuing from the cognitive socialization literature provide evidence about what an individual does in actual social commerce—assuming a representative sample—in order to infer what the individual can do.

Third, individual differences become subjugated. It is patently true that individual differences are subjugated by normative tests simply because there is no opportunity to discern an individual's repertoire of skills on a normative test. In a sense, categories of performance are imposed on individuals in normative testing; yet, no effort is made to show that the categories on a test are relevant to what an individual can do. Said differently, it is not unusual for categories on a test to be irrelevant to what an individual can do; therefore test performances merely result from imposed categories with the conclusions of questionable value. The irony, of course, is that performances on tests, when compared to the test norms, are used to draw inferences about what an individual presumably can do. The clinical fields have not faced up to this paradox.

Rather, there seem to be widespread beliefs in the clinical fields that norms provide necessary and sufficient information. Said differently, the clinical fields have been strangely silent about this fundamental issue. Perhaps this silence indexes the degree to which brute empiricism has become indoctrinated in the clinical fields.

Fourth, norms are thought to provide necessary and sufficient information. However, there are no opportunities on normative tests to estimate repertoires of skills, progress in acquisition sequences, alternative learning strategies, and active loci of learning with appropriate attribution criteria. Such information is necessary to ascertain what an individual can do with language. Thus, norms do not provide necessary and sufficient information.

Experienced clinicians and parents have questioned, intuitively, whether tests provide necessary and sufficient information. For example, "With experience, we have learned how misleading age scores could be" (Ehrens, 1993, p. 18).

Fifth, psychometric tests have norms for performances on contrived tasks. This means that such performances are removed from contextual influences (intentional meaning, referential meaning, relational meaning, shared meaning). It is what Paul (1995) regarded as decontextualized, as opposed to contextualized, assessment. Yet, these aspects of contextual influences are essential for language learning. Regarding relational contexts, Maratsos (1988a) commented, "The child internally decides that the combinatorial properties are the important defining properties for categories" (p. 35). Further, "Formal or structural categories—they are defined by use in the system itself" (p. 34). Bruner (1986) was also impressed by spontaneous coherence, "capable of imposing principles of organization that have an internal 'logic' in the sense of being principled" (p. 109).

Thus, it requires a considerable dash of mental myopia to rationalize that a priori categories on normative tests are relevant to relational knowledge available to a child in actual intended social commerce (K. Nelson, 1985, 1996; Ninio, 1988; Ninio & Snow, 1988). Said differently, what justifies the use of particular grammatical categories and relations on normative tests as valid indices of an individual's repertoire of intentional meanings, referential meanings, relational meanings, and shared meanings? Notice that advocates of normative tests are basically silent about these issues. Rather, they contend that an individual's performance compared to a norm provides necessary and sufficient information.

Sixth, behavior may be converted into numbers. This is the quantification issue that was discussed earlier. It may be useful to merely raise a fundamental question: What is gained or lost by converting behavior into numbers? In normative tests, behaviors are typically quantified in order to make a comparison to a norm. For example, the DSS procedure converts sentences into scores by giving various aspects of grammar various scores. Over a language sample of 50 utterances, an average sentence score is obtained and compared to a norm for the purpose of ascertaining if a child is within a norm or not. It may be more useful to retain the actual sentences for grammatical analysis to ascertain what an individual can do with various grammatical systems than to quantify them.

Given the inherent problems with DSS, especially pertaining to quantification, and other uses of brute empiricism (McCauley & Swisher, 1984a; Olswang & Bain, 1991), it appears that the clinical fields are indeed indoctrinated and silent about some major issues of measurement and assessment. Perhaps a comment by Kuhn (1961) pertains: "If you cannot measure, measure anyhow" (p. 164).

Seventh, normative tests rarely deal with language functions. Yet, the functionalistic movement over the past few decades has emerged as offering the greatest philosophical–theoretical continuity with the contemporary cognitive socialization literature. Language is generally held to have two basic functions: mathetic and pragmatic (Halliday, 1975; K. Nelson, 1985, 1991). These might be regarded as intrapersonal (abstraction or representation) and interpersonal (communication, social-cultural) functions, respectively (Cazden, 1966). Bloom (1973) and Gopnik (1981, 1982, 1984) also drew distinctions for early utterances between cognitive and communicative comments. In contrast, the language tests typically only address structure. Yet, the cognitive socialization literature indicates that structure is in the service of function (Bates & MacWhinney, 1987; Levy, 1988; Maratsos, 1982; K. Nelson, 1985, 1986, 1996).

Eighth, normative tests miss evidence on developmental sequences. One of the greatest contributions of the developmental cognitive socialization literature is that it has identified acquisition sequences for various aspects of language. For example, Greenfield and Smith (1976) detailed an acquisition sequence for the emergence of early semantic functions and relations and Halliday (1975) identified the emergence of communicative intents, which was elaborated further by K. Nelson (1991). Information of this kind is very useful clinically because it provides justification for appreciating what progress an individual may have made in acquiring a skill—an assessment issue— and it provides direction or goals for intervention.

Some clinicians may deny this problem by claiming that developmental profiles provide necessary and sufficient evidence of language acquisition— the traditional claim. I have addressed this fallacy elsewhere (Muma, 1986a). Briefly, this is a fallacy because there are 10 reasons why developmental profiles not only miss evidence on developmental sequences but are essentially incompatible with the relevant cognitive socialization literature. On the point of acquisition sequences, it should be appreciated that the sequences on developmental profiles rarely, if ever, portray sequences within systems. Yet, it is within-system sequences that provide the necessary information for clinical assessment and intervention. For example, the literature (Brown & Bellugi, 1964; Klima & Bellugi-Klima, 1969) has shown that the structural acquisition sequence within negation is the following:

I go, no. (S + no)
I no go. (N no V)
I won't go. (N Aux not V)

The first has negation outside of the sentence as a tag. The second has negation in the sentence but not integrated into the auxiliary system. The third has negation integrated into the auxiliary, thereby yielding a negative sentence. Functionally, the acquisition of negation has the following sequence: nonexistence, rejection, and denial (Bloom, 1970, 1973; McNeill, 1970). Information of this kind is not available from developmental profiles. Furthermore, a test merely would indicate whether a child provided a correct or incorrect form.

Ninth, the cognitive socialization literature on language acquisition has identified many different kinds of language learning strategies (Bates et al., 1988; Bloom & Lahey, 1978; Lahey, 1988; Muma, 1978b, 1981c). As indicated earlier, some children are imitators, whereas others are not (Bloom et al., 1974); some are code learners and some are message learners (Dore, 1974, 1975); some rely more on formulaic expressions, whereas others rely more on generating novel utterances (Bruner, 1981; K. Nelson, 1985); some are pronominal learners, whereas others are nominal learners (Bloom et al., 1975), and so on. Unfortunately, normative tests do not provide opportunities to identify the particular language learning strategies employed by a particular individual. Such information has considerable clinical value because language acquisition could be facilitated by exploiting available strategies and it is conceivable that acquisition could be hampered by missing or overriding such strategies (Muma, 1978b, 1986a).

Tenth, the cognitive socialization literature has provided descriptive procedures that give more or less direct evidence of active loci of learning (Muma, 1983b, 1986a). As already discussed, Bloom et al. (1974) showed that spontaneous imitations are selective. Children generally do not imitate what they know or what they do not know. Rather, they spontaneously imitate what they are actively striving to learn. Therefore, instances of spontaneous imitation are likely to contain instances of active loci of learning. The task is to identify which aspects of such utterances reflect active loci of learning. This is done by ascertaining what children can do in representative language samples and comparing the spontaneous imitations to an estimated repertoire of skills.

Sorensen and Fey (1992) recognized the value of identifying active loci of learning: "Because children normally are most likely to talk about informativeness aspects of the context, creating such contexts as the locus for learning would seem to give the child opportunities to practice new words in highly natural, communicative contexts" (pp. 320–321). Using loci of learning in this way is what I have termed communicative payoff in language intervention (Muma, 1981c, 1986a).

Psychometric normative tests do not provide opportunities to identify active loci of learning. Yet, the cognitive socialization literature has provided several ways of describing verbal behavior that identify active loci of learning. The evidence for loci of learning is descriptive in nature.

Eleventh, at some point the results of assessment must be interpreted in order for them to be used in some way. The interpretation of the data entails a subjective enterprise (Prutting, 1983). If the data are interpreted in accordance with underlying recognized philosophical views and theoretical perspectives, it would be a disciplined interpretation. However, if interpretations of the data are open to any opinion, they may be about virtually anything, thereby relegating the enterprise to dogma and diminishing appropriateness of clinical services rendered to an individual and the profession as well.

Twelfth, although it is true that norms provide a reference for appropriately interpreting a particular score in terms of aberrancy, there is a much bigger interpretation issue: the value of a particular score to the substantive domain the test presumably assesses. Several scholars in the field of assessment and measurement have made the point that data must be interpreted to become evidence. What is crucial in such interpretations is that they be disciplined—held accountable to permissible interpretations as defined by recognized philosophical views and theoretical perspectives. To reiterate, Messick (1980) defined evidence as follows: "By 'evidence' I mean both data, or facts, and the rationale or arguments that cement those facts into a justification of test-score inference" (p. 1014). According to Mitroff and Sagasti (1973), "Another way to put this is to note that data are *not* information; information is that which results from the interpretation of data" (p. 123). Kaplan (1964) said, "What serves as evidence is the result of a process of interpretation—facts do **not** speak for themselves; nevertheless, facts must be given a hearing, or the scientific point to the process of interpretation is lost" (p. 375).

Finally, all assessment must have construct validity (Messick, 1980, 1989a, 1989b). Unfortunately, the most widely used tests in the clinical fields lack construct validity (Muma & Brannon, 1986). This constitutes a major paradox because on the one hand the clinical fields claim expertise in assessing CCCE, but on the other, practitioners use tests that miss the essential issue for doing so.

It is because of such limitations with normative testing that I have advocated descriptive assessment over the past two decades or so (Muma, 1978b, 1981a, 1981b, 1981c, 1983a, 1983b, 1984a, 1984b, 1986a, 1987, 1991) predicated on the available standardized procedures in the cognitive socialization literature. These issues are underscored in clinical endeavors because individual differences are considerable. Furthermore, descriptive assessment provides the kind of information needed to appropriately address the seven basic clinical assessment issues (Muma, 1981c, 1983b, 1986a; discussed in the following). In intervention, descriptive evidence is needed to appropriately deal with facilitation, as opposed to teaching or instruction (Muma, 1978b, 1986a, 1987).

Bruner's (1986) distinctions between science and human affairs or between the paradigmatic (scientific) and narrative (humanistic) approaches to understand the world give another slant on the presumed values of norms. These distinctions may be viewed as two different modes for viewing the world: a scientific orientation and a clinical orientation.

According to Zukier and Pepitone (1984), "Scientific orientation . . . (is) concerned with general propositions—norms, and a clinical orientation . . . (is) concerned with understanding the individual case" (p. 349). The scientific or paradigmatic approach is based on Bayesian probabilities; a scientist operates by "riding with the probabilities" (Bruner, 1986, p. 89). In contrast, clinicians are committed to the so-called base rate fallacy. This fallacy is the belief that a norm is a real entity. According to Zukier and Pepitone (1984), "the base rate fallacy" is merely another rendition of "an inappropriate application of normative criteria" (p. 349).

At this point, it is necessary to make another distinction. It is the distinction between base rates that are merely frequency counts of behaviors removed from contexts and base rates that preserve contextual information. Context-free baselines may comprise an inappropriate application of normative criteria. However, contextually preserved base rates have potential for estimating repertoires of skill.

> What is clear is that the "outcomes" achieved in inference when one uses Bayesian estimates are not "reality" in contrast to an "illusion" produced by operating clinically. Subjects who go the clinical route are operating "realistically" too, but in another reality. (Bruner, 1986, p. 90)

In summary, empiricism strives to resolve issues by a reliance on data. Normative tests provide data whereby individual performance may be compared to a norm. Such comparisons were traditionally thought to be objective and to provide necessary and sufficient information for assessment. However, recent developments in the philosophy of cognition and language (Lakoff, 1987) have raised serious questions about the presumed objectivity of normative tests and at the same time they have shown that it is desirable to have disciplined subjectivity.

MUMA ASSESSMENT PROGRAM (MAP)

The Muma Assessment Program (MAP; Muma & Muma, 1979) is not a test. Rather, it is a compilation of descriptive assessment tasks derived from a variety of well-substantiated sources in the literature. For example, the Cognitive Tempo task is based on the Matching Familiar Figures Test (Kagan, 1965) and nearly 200 studies on cognitive tempo. It provides an opportunity to discern patterns of performance in terms of speed and accuracy of figure matching that could identify impulsive and reflective thinkers. Paul (1995) indicated that a reflective child may have a better prognosis for improvement than an impulsive child: "A careful, reflective child . . . is in a better position to take advantage of intervention than a hyperactive, impulsive child" (p. 49).

MAP offers opportunities to assess selected aspects of cognition, codification, and communication. MAP is based on the premise that it is only after a pattern has been established that inferences can be legitimately made about underlying systems and processes; herein lies the basis for the title of MAP. MAP is probabilistic in nature. Accordingly, it is necessary that behavioral patterns exceed chance before they can be regarded as a patterns for inferring underlying skills or capacities.

MAP has construct validity by virtue of the fact that it is derived from the available cognitive socialization literature. MAP has continuity with some, but not all, of the five issues, pertaining to the natural integrity of behavior, especially relativity. MAP also provides descriptive evidence that may be used to address the seven basic clinical assessment issues: clinical complaint, problem—no problem, nature of a problem, individual differences, intervention implications, prognosis, and accountability.

In addition to cognitive tempo, the cognitive aspects of MAP are the following: sensorimotor skills, perceptual salience, iconic—symbolic processing modes, rule—nonrule governed learning, technology of reckoning, part—whole and alternative thinking, production deficiency, and mediation deficiency. Patterns of performance for the following sensorimotor skills are sought: anticipation, causality, object permanence, deferred imitation, and alternative means. These are observed in spontaneous play rather than in contrived tasks (Donaldson, 1978). The Perceptual Salience task is derived from Caron (1969) and Odom and Guzman (1972). A series of cards containing three figures are shown that systematically vary color, size, and shape. Individuals are asked to select two. The task is to ascertain if the choices evidence patterns beyond chance for any of the variables. If so, the individual may be inordinately oriented on that variable, which could be detrimental to learning simply because rarely is a single variable sufficiently potent to dominate learning.

The Iconic—Symbolic processing task is based on the theoretical model by Bruner (1964) and Bruner, Olver, and Greenfield (1966) in which three stages of cognitive acquisition are posited and substantiated: enactive (action toward objects), iconic (perceptual awareness), and symbolic (conceptual awareness) processing. This task deals with iconic and symbolic processing, whereby individuals are asked to select two of three items on each card. Patterns of choices for color or shape would index iconic processing, whereas those for function would index symbolic processing.

The Rule—Nonrule Governed Learning task is based on the research by Kendler and Kendler (1959, 1970). Individuals are asked to pick one of two items on each card in an attempt to discern which item the clinician is "thinking of." The clinician follows a rule and provides relevant feedback for the choices of the individual. Once a pattern of choices has been established beyond chance, the rule can be attributed. Then, the information is altered to a new criterion within the variable on which the rule was derived (e.g., shift from blue to red in the color variable). The procedure continues as a measure of an individual's flexibility of thinking. On reaching a pattern beyond chance, the task is changed again so that the color variable becomes irrelevant but size becomes relevant—again another measure of flexibility of thinking.

The Technology of Reckoning task is based on the work of Bruner (1964). For variables that are relatively familiar, an individual is asked to show patterns of responses for static and dynamic variables (K. Nelson, 1973a, 1974). Dynamic variables are elaborated to include the following: intransitive, transitive, deictic, and relational.

The Part–Whole and Alternatives task is based on research by Kagan (1965) and Kagan, Rossman, Day, Albert, and Phillips (1964) on analytic and synthetic thinking. Individuals are shown a series of cards containing three pairs of items. Two pairs of items have a part–whole relationship (cow–barn, horse–barn) and one pair has an alternative relationship (cow–horse). Patterns of performance may reveal either an analytic or synthetic thinking style.

Research on production deficiency and mediation deficiency has been carried out by Corsini, Pick, and Flavell (1968), Flavell, Beach, and Chinsky (1966), and Moely, Olsen, Halwas, and Flavell (1969). Production deficiency may be evidenced by the ways in which an individual reports choices on the iconic–symbolic or part–whole and alternatives tasks. That is, after completion of each of these tasks, individuals are reminded of their choices and asked why they chose them. Some individuals are not good at verbalizing their choices; such individuals may evidence a pattern of production deficiency whereby their choices of items remain relatively constant but their verbal accounts of their choices lack congruity. Mandler (1983) put it this way: "Anglin (1977) notes that there is a fundamental distinction between the child's verbal expressions and the underlying conceptual system that supports them and that the child may know more than he or she can express in language" (p. 468).

The following kinds of responses are evidenced with production deficiency (Olver & Hornsby, 1966):

1. Nominal response (name items).
2. Thematic response (story line for the items).
3. Affect response (feeling statement).
4. Fiat response ("I don't know," shrug shoulders, etc.).
5. Perceptual intrinsic response (name a readily perceived perceptual variable such as color).
6. Perceptual extrinsic response (name an assigned perceptual variable such as size).
7. Functional intrinsic response (name a readily perceived functional attribute such as the "horse" is standing).
8. Functional extrinsic response (name an assigned functional variable such as "running" but the actual item is not running).

MAP deals with the following aspects of codification: descriptive evidence of concept–word knowledge (extended action patterns, regulation of joint attention and action, need to consider categorization, overextensions, markedness), acquisition sequence for early semantic functions and relations, active loci of learning (co-occurrence, spontaneous imitations, hesitation phenomena), alternative acquisition strategies, and phonotactic processes. MAP also deals with the following aspects of communication: communicative intent, available reference and alternative codes, code matrix, and communication game.

There is a very strange circumstance in the clinical fields concerning the MAP. This circumstance may reveal the extent to which indoctrination of psychometric testing may exist. MAP does not have norms; it is predicated on Bayesian probability theory, whereby if an individual's performance exceeds chance the obtained pattern is used for attribution. Yet, some individuals in the clinical fields do not understand that this application of probability theory has continuity with the "two standard deviations from the mean" criteria in normative testing. What is strange is that some individuals have assailed the MAP because it does not have norms. Such positions constitute tacit evidence that these individuals do not understand that patterns of performance beyond chance are as legitimate as deviations from the norm for attribution. Thus, the irony is that the clinical fields may reflect blind allegiance to psychometric normative testing. The irony is that both psychometric testing and the MAP are predicated on Bayesian probability theory but one is presumably acceptable (because it has norms), whereas the other is not (because it does not have norms).

There is a further irony in that MAP has construct validity by virtue of standardized procedures issuing from the respective research articles from which the MAP was derived. This second irony is that many if not most of the psychometric tests in the clinical fields lack construct validity. Thus, the clinical fields evidence reliance on many tests that lack construct validity but not on the MAP, which does have construct validity. Needless to say, scholarship is at issue.

Abkarian (1986, 1987) studied verbal correlates for the iconic–symbolic processing subtask of the MAP and found that what some children said about their responses lacked congruence with their actual responses (selection of pictured items). This was taken to mean that the MAP was invalid. Yet, a simple consideration of the issues reveals that such conclusions are patently silly. First, only one of six cognitive subtasks of the MAP was studied. Second, the verbal correlates of performance on the tasks were considered. The results indicate that some verbal correlates may lack congruence with the task performance, which is why verbal correlates were solicited in the MAP procedure. The MAP manual (J. Muma & D. Muma, 1979) indicates that if the verbal correlates lack congruity with the task performance, they may evidence a "production deficiency" (p. 40). Thus, rather than finding evidence against the MAP, Abkarian actually confirmed the capability of the MAP to identify production deficiency problems in accordance with the findings of Anglin (1977). Third, inasmuch as the MAP subtasks were predicated on the procedures of studies in the available cognitive literature, it would be foolhardy to indict MAP while ignoring the relevant studies from which the MAP was derived. Such selective use of the literature merely indicts capriciousness and leaves scholarship in the wake. I doubt if anyone would want to be a party to that. Furthermore, in contrast to Abkarian (1986, 1987), theses by Kelly (1976), Kramer (1976), and Vespucci (1975) provided evidence of the validity of the MAP subtasks. Nevertheless, some individuals in the clinical fields have taken the Abkarian studies as evidence that the MAP is invalid—such stances may reveal the capricious nature of scholarship in the clinical fields.

FROM NORMATIVE TO DESCRIPTIVE ASSESSMENT

When preassessment (Gallagher, 1983) and the seven basic clinical assessment issues (Muma, 1978a, 1983b, 1991) are addressed, descriptive procedures are more appropriate than psychometric normative tests in providing evidence. There is some suggestive evidence that the clinical fields appreciate the clinical value of descriptive evidence: "Formal tests do not constitute a viable starting point in the assessment of communicative behaviors. Rather, we begin by looking at the child's ability to take part in conversation" (Brinton & Fujiki, 1994, p. 61).

We (Muma, Pierce, & Muma, 1983; Muma, Webb, & Muma, 1979) surveyed training programs in speech-language pathology across the United States. The first survey showed a decided preference for normative testing, whereas the second survey showed that about two thirds of the training programs had a preference for descriptive procedures issuing from the available cognitive socialization literature. Staunch advocates of normative testing remain, but it is impressive that so many of the training programs evidenced a shift toward an increased reliance on descriptive procedures.

Undoubtedly, three other issues have restrained the shift toward descriptive procedures:

1. The normative test mentality.
2. Ignorance about available standardized descriptive procedures.
3. Ignorance about what standardized assessment means officially.

The *normative test mentality* is that such tests presumably provide necessary and sufficient information for assessment. Hopefully, once the seven basic issues of clinical assessment and the limitations of normative tests—especially their lack of construct validity—are considered, it should be abundantly clear that the normative test mentality may not be as appropriate as previously believed. Yet, the clinical fields are strangely silent about the pertinent issues.

Fortunately, ignorance about available descriptive procedures is waning; that is, more and more descriptive procedures are being used clinically, especially in the areas of pragmatics and phonology. Moreover, the primary source of information for carrying out descriptive procedures is the cognitive socialization literature rather than the behavioristic literature.

The arena of phonological assessment has led the way in this regard. Traditionally, various phoneme-oriented tests, especially the Goldman–Fristoe test (1969), have been used clinically. However, with the recognition of major developments in the phonology literature, a major shift away from normative tests to descriptive procedures has occurred. Renfrew (1966) wrote one of the most important articles for clinical assessment in phonology. She identified open syllables (unfortunately, others have detracted from her contribution by taking credit for final consonant deletion [FCD]) and several steps toward overcoming open syllables. Ingram (1976, 1989b) not only credited Renfrew appropriately but also summarized a considerable body of literature concerning phonological processes. With this literature, clinical assessment in phonology is now largely invested in descriptions of phonological processes such as vowel nuclei, reduplication, weak syllable deletion, open syllable, fronting, stopping, forward or backward coarticulation, and cluster reduction. An excellent article that provides an acquisition sequence for most of these phonological processes was written by Vihman and Greenlee (1987). Such information coupled with that concerning the phonetic inventory (Ingram, 1976), phonetic context (Daniloff, 1984; Daniloff & Hammarberg, 1973), hymonymy (Ferguson & Farwell, 1975; Locke, 1979; Priestly, 1980), and phonological avoidance (Schwartz & Leonard, 1982) offers assessment procedures that provide clinicians with appropriate ways of ascertaining what an individual can do phonologically rather than merely categorize and label a child based on test performance. This is what a posteriori assessment is about in contrast to a priori assessment.

Similarly, there are appropriate descriptive procedures for assessing what individuals can do in semantics (Greenfield & Smith, 1976; and many others), syntax (Crystal, Fletcher, & Garman, 1976; and many others), and pragmatics (Gallagher, 1991; Prutting & Kirchner, 1983, 1987; Wetherby, 1991; and many others). Moreover, the cognitive socialization literature offers ways of ascertaining progress in various acquisition sequences, which learning strategy an individual may be using, and which loci of learning may be active. The clinical fields are beginning to understand these issues and to use them in assessment.

However, notice that the assessment of developing language according to Paul (1995) in both the decontextualized and contextualized perspectives essentially miss these issues. Indeed, Paul (1995) implicitly relied on psychometric normative assessment (e.g., comprehensive list of normative tests, MLU norms, DSS norms, etc.). Moreover, notice that the test descriptors missed construct validity. For criteria-referenced language assessment, Paul (1995) provided age-based checklists, essentially subordinating performance in actual social commerce: "Informal comprehension assessment can be used to follow up standardized testing" (p. 296).

Communicative intent in actual social commerce is considered to be in the more difficult arena, whereas "more structured and less complex input from more hybrid and clinician-directed activities" (p. 297) is deemed easier and more supportive. Fey (1986) held a similar position. In order to adopt such perspectives, it would be necessary to ignore a large cognitive socialization literature (Bloom, 1991a, 1991b; Bowerman, 1987; Bruner, 1981; K. Nelson, 1985, 1986, 1996; Ninio, 1988; Ninio & Snow, 1988; among others).

The ignorance about what standardized clinical assessment officially means has been a hindrance in the shift away from a reliance on normative tests, and developmental profiles, to a reliance on descriptive procedures. To reiterate, the official (Martin, 1980) interpretation of standardized assessment in P.L. 94–142 for the field of speech-language pathology is that American Speech-Hearing-Language Association (ASHA) certified speech-language pathologists may judge eligibility for services based on either informal or formal assessments. Martin's letter to ASHA stating this official policy appears in Appendix A.

This means that descriptive procedures (informal) provide appropriate evidence in clinical assessment. This is a very important letter because there is the widespread misunderstanding in the clinical fields that test scores are required when in fact they are not. Thus, astute clinicians could use the available descriptive procedures issuing from the cognitive socialization literature to render appropriate clinical services.

I share the view expressed by Greenfield and Smith (1976):

> If we are to discover structure in, rather than to impose structure on, child language, it is useful to have a descriptive system which allows separate treatment of each element of the situation. In that way, we can trace the gradual development of a linguistic structure without assuming the presence of the total structure from the onset. (p. 16)

A priori approaches such as normative tests impose structure on a child but fail to ask which structures, indeed which functions, are available to a child in actual social commerce. Functioning in actual social commerce is "more germane than all the laboratory studies" (Brown, 1986, p. 278). Because the topic is clinical testing rather than laboratory studies, let us expand Brown's comment to include the imposed and contrived tasks of psychometric testing as contrasted with spontaneous performance in social commerce. The irony, of course, is that imposed tasks in psychometric assessments claim to measure what an individual can do in actual social commerce.

SEVEN BASIC CLINICAL ASSESSMENT ISSUES

In addition to the limitations of normative testing, behaviorism, and quantification discussed here and in chapter 2, another way of appreciating such limitations, especially for normative tests, is to compare normative tests with descriptive assessments across the seven basic clinical assessment issues (Muma, 1981a, 1983b, 1986a). These basic assessment issues are clinical complaint, problem–no problem, nature of a problem, individual differences, intervention implications, prognosis, and accountability or efficacy. They were mentioned earlier. This list of basic assessment issues is somewhat similar to the four major categories in the list of "objectives of and information from assessment" by Lahey (1988), which are existence of a problem, intervention goals, intervention procedures, and prognosis. Table 7.4 shows how adequately psychometric and descriptive approaches address the seven basic clinical assessment issues.

The bottom line is that psychometric normative tests result in data essentially because they lack construct validity and relevance to what individuals can do, whereas descriptive assessments based on the available cognitive socialization literature provide evidence precisely because they are derived from the available literature and are relevant to what individuals

TABLE 7.4
The Adequacy of Psychometric and Descriptive Approaches
in Addressing the Seven Basic Clinical Assessment Issues

Basic Clinical Issue	Psychometric	Descriptive
Clinical complaint	Yes	Yes
Problem–no problem	(Yes)	Yes
Nature of a problem	No	Yes
Individual differences	No	Yes
Intervention implications	No	Yes
Prognosis	?	?
Accountability and efficacy	(Yes)	Yes
Result	Data	Evidence

can do. Such descriptive procedures deal with representative language samples in actual social commerce.

Clinical Complaint

Both approaches deal with the clinical complaint or statement of a problem. They identify the person the complaint is about, the informant, and obtain verbatim comments about the presumed nature of a problem. The latter can be used to communicate assessment findings. That is, it is useful to use the perspective and words of an informant in discussing assessment findings.

Problem–No Problem

The problem–no problem issue is addressed by both approaches. This is the essential issue in a psychometric normative assessment. The reasoning is that if performance is within the norms for a test the conclusion is that the individual being tested is considered normal; if performance is outside of the norms, the performance is considered aberrant and the individual is thought to have a problem. Typically, scores more than two standard deviations from the mean or very low percentile scores are considered aberrant. Olswang and Bain (1991) put it this way:

> If standardized test results are available, a discrepancy of one or two standard deviations below the mean (Bloom & Lahey, 1978), or below the 10th to15th percentile (Lee, 1974; Olswang et al., 1986; Olswang et al., 1987) is suggested. Age-related performance has also been used. Crystal, Fletcher and Garman (1976) have held that in using their Language Assessment, Remediation, and Screening Procedure (LARSP), a 6-month discrepancy . . . warrants intervention. (p. 257)

However, there are other problems with age-equivalent scores that undermine their value (Carrow-Woolfolk, 1985; Lawrence, 1992; Salvia & Ysseldyke, 1988).

Unfortunately, the notion of aberrant scores raises another issue that limits the use of normative tests: the loss of assessment power that was discussed previously. Tests lose power to measure what is claimed to be measured for extreme scores. That is, the probabilities are greater that performance that leads to an extreme score is not measured by the test, but reflects other unknown extraneous variables. This is a fundamental principle in probability theory. It is strange that the clinical fields claim expertise in assessment but have been silent about the loss of assessment power for extreme scores. There is further irony in this circumstance: Most clinical criteria rely on extreme scores for the definition of aberrance. Perhaps such policies coupled with the silence about assessment power provide strong evidence of indoctrination and entrenchment of the psychometric normative model in the clinical fields.

From the psychometric model, Olswang and Bain (1991) provided a discussion of various criterion issues for deciding if intervention may be warranted. Using a data-based approach, they indicated that the following issues could be considered in making informed decisions about when children might best benefit from intervention: intra- and interindividual comparisons, profiling, dynamic assessment, and tracking and monitoring. Interindividual comparisons pertain to the normative model whereby an individual's performance is compared to a norm. Typically, such comparisons are made in reference to chronological age (CA) or mental age (MA), and even language age (LA) has been used.

The problem with the CA reference is the large amount of variance in even normal language learning, let alone larger variances in clinical populations. Brown (1973a, 1973b) and Prutting (1979) indicated that plus or minus 6 months are needed to deal with CA measurement, in early language acquisition. This is very poor precision of measurement which brings into question whether CA is a useful index. Indeed, Brown (1973a, 1973b) cautioned that rate of learning is notoriously varied, whereas sequence is highly stable. This was ample reason for him to rely on sequence rather than age: "We had not equated for age because we knew . . . that children acquire language at widely varying rates" (Brown, 1973b, p. 53). Others also are concerned about the problems with age-equivalent scores (Lawrence, 1992). Salvia and Ysseldyke (1988) said, "In our opinion, developmental scores should never be used. These scores are readily misinterpreted by both lay and professional people" (p. 92). Carrow-Woolfolk (1985) indicated, "Age-equivalent scores should not be used as a basis for determining language disorders" (p. 79).

MA is also troublesome. There is the perplexing problem of whether MA measured psychometrically carries the essential meaning of theory of the world (Palermo, 1982), possible worlds (Bruner, 1986) or situated mind (K. Nelson, 1996). There are the further problems of identifying appropriate cognitive precursors and of appreciating their relevance in language acquisition to place credence in the MA metric. Cole, Dale, and Mills (1990) recognized such problems. It may be that the mere availability of MA scores is simply too enticing to question their value.

Olswang and Bain (1991) discussed intralinguistic referencing; it is when "the language components are compared to one another, and CA and MA are omitted. A discrepancy is judged to exist, and treatment considered, if performance in any one language component is poorer than in other components" (p. 256). The nature of the comparison that Olswang and Bain had in mind was a psychometric comparison, which they detailed in their profiling notion.

I would contend that what I describe in the following sections—namely the nature of a problem and individual differences—offer better opportunities to appreciate intraindividual comparisons. Rather than force parallels between inter- (normative) and intra- (repertoire) individual comparisons, I prefer to describe an individual's estimated repertoire of skills, ascertain progress in acquisition sequences, identify alternative acquisition strategies used by an individual, and identify active loci of learning to make decisions about the need for intervention, intervention goals, and the effects of intervention. These substantive areas have more to offer in dealing with the basic clinical assessment issues than the so-called intraindividual comparison that Olswang and Bain (1991) described as "the language components compare with one another" (p. 256).

The kind of comparisons or profiling advocated by Olswang and Bain reflect the psychometric normative model. In contrast, the kind of descriptive evidence that I have advocated accords well with the available cognitive socialization literature in ascertaining what an individual can do. Thus, clinicians have an opportunity to decide which philosophical views and compatible theoretical perspectives are most appropriate because their clinical implications are very different. Needless to say, "The framework used to determine who needs therapy depends on the clinician's philosophy as well as the clinician's definition of intervention" (Olswang & Bain, 1991, p. 257).

According to Olswang and Bain (1991), the purpose of profiling is "to determine the current, independent functioning of a particular child across various domains of behavior such as cognition, motor, and language and across various components of language such as form, content, and use" (p. 257). With the belief that tests and assessment procedures used in profiling are valid and reliable, Olswang and Bain claimed that a profile provides a clear description of a child's abilities and disabilities. Inasmuch as there are many questions about the presumed validity of many clinical tests, including the tests cited by Olswang and Bain, these questions extend to the profiles that they advocate as well.

Also, their claim about "a clear description of a child's abilities and disabilities" (Olswang & Bain, 1991, p. 257) without evidence of estimated repertoires of skill and the presumption of ability measurement from test performance gives pause for what should be made of such profiles. Then, they indicated that the profiles could be used to ascertain the "overall developmental level for the child's performance in each domain" (p. 257). It should be emphasized that their conclusions are based on a psychometric normative model in which behavior is quantified and subjected to a normative metric such as CA or MA. Thus, their notion of level is CA or MA levels rather than the cognitive socialization notions of level, phase, stage, or sequence. To repeat, perhaps a more viable perspective is to actually estimate repertoires of skills, progress in acquisition sequences, alternative learning strategies, and loci of learning. This alternative is more viable because it does not carry the burden of imposed systems on a child and it is based on what a child does with language in actual social commerce. Therefore, it is ecologically more valid (Bronfenbrenner, 1979; Muma, 1981c, 1983b).

Drawing on Vygotsky's (1962) notion of zone of proximal development, Olswang and Bain (1991) discussed the notion of dynamic assessment. This kind of assessment provides evidence that a behavior is changeable. Citing Feuerstein (1979), they indicated that children have two levels of performance: actual functioning and potential functioning. Actual functioning is behavior that is available "when contextual cues and support are held to a minimum" and potential functioning is behavior that is available "when contextual cues and support are provided in order to evoke more advanced behaviors" (Olswang & Bain, 1991, p. 259). I share this perspective under the topics of the nature of a problem and attribution criteria (Muma, 1983b, 1986a, 1991).

Notice that Olswang and Bain (1991) are willing to attribute "advanced behaviors" to those found in context, whereas "less advanced" behaviors presumably are evidenced "when contextual, cues and support are held to a minimum" (p. 259). Strangely, Paul (1995) took the same position. Their notions of "contextual cues and support" are strikingly disconnected from the cognitive socialization literature because this literature supports precisely the opposite view. They contended that relevance, cues, and control are in the province of the clinician (behaviorism), whereas the cognitive socialization literature contends that the learning process is the province of the learner (Muma, 1978b, 1983b, 1986a). K. Nelson (1985), for example, would hold that behavior that is context-free would have increased difficulty. Given the importance of various contextual influences, especially intentional, referential, relational, and social-cultural contexts, in language acquisition and use, their distinction between actual and potential functioning appears to be rather capricious.

Perhaps it would be useful to consider the Piagetian criteria of preparation, attainment, and consolidation. Muma (1983b, 1986a, 1991), K. E. Nelson (1981, 1991), and Prutting (1979) found these criteria compatible with the literature on discrepancy learning and various cognitive socialization accounts. They are discussed later. Furthermore, the notion of robustness (hearty and fragile) aspects of language learning may be more appropriate (Goldin-Meadow & Mylander, 1984).

The Vygotskian notion of zone of proximal development has received acclaim as a viable notion for learning, especially in pedagogy (Bruner, 1986). Here, Olswang and Bain (1991) made a nice link between the notion of zone of proximal development and the notion of readiness to learn because both of these are psychological notions rather than a priori psychometric notions. Perhaps Bruner's (1981) notions of tuning and raising the ante for identifying how mothers operationalize the zone of proximal development in ecologically valid ways should also be considered (see Muma, 1986a, for a summary).

I want to pause on another comment that Olswang and Bain (1991) made. They said, "If intervention is provided as the child demonstrates a readiness or potential for learning, significantly effective and efficient change will occur (Olswang et al., 1986)" (p. 260). This statement has some underlying assumptions that should be raised because it is not a given that significant change will occur. Although a child may be ready to learn, it is necessary to provide appropriate opportunities for learning. What assumptions are being made about an individual's available repertoire of skills, progress in acquisition sequences, available learning strategies, active loci of learning, and intentionality? Bruner's (1981) notions of tuning and raising the ante broach the issues and Vygotsky's notion of zone of proximal development is insightful, but the pedagogical literature is a long way from knowing what to do precisely with a given individual in a given circumstance. If anything is apparent, the removal of various contextual supports, especially intentionality from the situated mind, may jeopardize learning.

Turning to behaviorism and reinforcement, Olswang and Bain (1991) discussed dynamic assessment in making the claim that a determination can be made of "the extent to which the child's behaviors can be improved or advanced" (p. 260). Kamhi (1993) accepted this notion as evidence of "the potential for change in particular language behaviors" (p. 58). Olswang and Bain (1991) claimed that options in the type of reinforcement or punishment and schedule of consequences can be used as probes to see "if the child improves performance" (p. 260). They also mentioned manipulations of modality or sensory channel (auditory or visual), presenting the stimulus several times rather than once before a response, and providing partial or total models of responses. Clearly, these notions are in the arena of peddling behavioristic notions and clearly they lack substantive continuity with the available cognitive socialization literature on language acquisition.

They then made some subtle shifts in perspective as they outlined some issues of dynamic assessment as advocated by Feuerstein (1979). The issues included:

1. Capability of learning more advanced behaviors.
2. A clinician's effort in aiding learning.
3. Transfer or generalization ability.
4. Effectiveness of teaching strategies.

The subtle shifts have to do with the words *capability, effort, ability*, and *effectiveness*. These words are pushed on the reader without appropriate criteria resulting in dogmatic statements such as, "Thus, administration of dynamic assessment procedures allows the speech-language pathologist to determine a child's ability to learn and to benefit from intervention" (Olswang & Bain, 1991, p. 260). Further, "While profiling and dynamic assessment procedures will provide speech-language pathologists with critical data for guiding their decision to treat language-impaired children, they need a method to assess the validity of these decisions" (p. 261).

The notions of tracking and monitoring were advocated to assess validity. There seems to be a non sequitur here. First, it is puzzling that earlier they claimed that dynamic assessment provides evidence of "the extent to which the child's behaviors can be improved" (p. 260) but tracking is needed to assess the validity of a decision. Perhaps this means that the former gives reason to focus on certain aspects of language in intervention and tracking gives evidence of presumed learning. Thus, they do not mean the presumed extent of improvement. Second, what is meant by critical data? I would maintain that they have not even broached the issue of critical data, if the cognitive socialization literature is to be considered. This literature indicates that the critical data include estimated repertoires, progress in acquisition sequences, alternative strategies, active loci of learning, and appropriate attribution criteria.

Olswang and Bain (1991) claimed to deal with language acquisition: "Two criteria were offered in this paper that reflect our theoretical understanding of the language acquisition literature" (p. 262). Given their previous behavioristic perspectives, the language acquisition literature apparently does not mean the cognitive socialization literature but the behavioristic literature. They used behavioristic and empirical models to deal with the issues of clinical assessment. I and others (Johnston, 1988) regard these philosophical views as incompatible with the cognitive socialization views. Bruner (1978) used the notion of corrosive dogma in regard to behavioristic claims to deal with language acquisition.

Returning to the problem–no problem issue, descriptive procedures provide evidence from the perspective of a social-cultural norm rather than a psychometric norm. That is, when complaints arise, there is a problem. This does not necessarily mean that the problem is with the individual for whom the complaint is about. For example, it is well known that young children have a phase in which they seemingly know inflections (especially plurals and tense markings), followed by a phase in which they seem to have trouble with these inflections, followed by a third phase in which these problems are overcome (Cazden, 1968; deVilliers & deVilliers, 1973, 1978; Karmiloff-Smith, 1992; Palermo & Eberhart, 1968). A similar phenomenon occurs in phonology.

It is not unusual for parents to come to the clinic when their child is in the second phase with the complaint that their child was doing well but is now "losing language." Thus, there is a problem. The problem is not with the child, but with the parents because they do not realize that their child has shifted from a vocabulary phase to a rule-governed phase resulting in an interim period of errors. Sometimes it is difficult to convince parents that this is so.

A similar circumstance often occurs in intervention in phonology. Because of phonological avoidance, it is rather common to have children in the clinic evidence an apparent increase in phonological severity as a function of intervention. What happens is that as a child becomes more comfortable in intervention, the child becomes less avoidant of speech and the true depth of errors becomes progressively evident. This may be perceived as increased severity but it actually is a sign of progress. The point is that progress may be complex and circuitous rather than linear and simplistic, especially if acquisition sequences, repertoire, alternative learning strategies, and context are considered. Notice that psychometric tests and claimed attempts to deal with efficacy are woefully short in dealing with these issues. Yet, descriptive approaches may provide appropriate evidence to address these and other issues, notably attribution criteria.

Nature of the Problem

It is one thing to obtain performance on a test but quite a different matter to understand the nature of a problem. The point is that normative tests come up short in dealing with the nature of a problem.

Descriptive evidence issuing from the cognitive socialization literature provides evidence of the nature of a problem. Descriptive procedures provide evidence for estimating repertoires of available skills, progress in acquisition sequences, alternative language learning strategies, and active loci of learning with attendant attribution criteria. With such evidence, it is possible to account for the nature of a problem at least on a provisional basis. Psychometric tests do not have these capabilities.

Appendix D gives estimated repertoires for different grammatical domains over 10 400-utterance language samples for seven normal children. For example, one participant evidenced at least one instance of 32 different structural variations, of subject nominals; she also evidenced nine structural variations, each of which had at least three lexical variations. What is impressive about such data is the fact that the relative distributions were similar across the language samples and across the children even though the MLUs varied somewhat. This suggests that the relative distributions of single and three varied (lexical variation) instances of structures may be relatively robust indices of repertoires. Furthermore, such indices were relatively robust across all of the grammatical domains, except the auxiliary system that evidenced a floor effect.

Evidence of this sort would be crucial to address the intervention principles of expansion and replacement. That is, for individuals who evidenced limited repertoires of grammatical or pragmatic skills, it would be useful to expand their repertoires. For individuals whose skills were not yet fully developed, the available repertoires would provide a baseline for replacement of subsequent skills. The point is that clinicians need to know what individuals can do in actual social commerce as estimates of available repertoires in order to establish appropriate intervention goals. Test results do not provide this kind of information.

Progress in acquisition sequences is very important for appreciating levels of acquisition and for establishing intervention goals. Strangely, the behavioristic approaches have merely considered the "failure of normal acquisition" view (see Fey, 1986; Paul, 1995). This stance was merely a behavioristic ploy for being relieved of the responsibilities of dealing with language acquisition sequences.

The notion of available alternative language learning strategies has been amply documented in the cognitive socialization literature and the clinical literature (Bloom & Lahey, 1978; Lahey, 1988; Muma, 1978b, 1986a). What is puzzling is that this issue seems to have been bypassed in some of the clinical literature (Fey, 1986; Paul, 1995). Alternative strategies of learning are trouble for behaviorism and psychometric testing, both of which advocate a singular approach to learning. Behaviorists hold that acquisition sequences are not needed because individuals in the clinic have failed the normal learning process and for the same reason there is no need to consider alternative acquisition strategies. Rather, behaviorists merely invoke technician-oriented reinforcement procedures and within-subject designs, especially multiple baselines (Fey, 1986; Paul, 1995). By doing so, the clinical fields become disconnected from the relevant scholarly literature in cognitive socialization and commit their profession to technicianship rather than clinicianship.

Needless to say, it is incumbent on clinicians to ascertain which language acquisition strategies an individual may be following so that intervention can exploit them. For example, if an individual is a referential learner (K. Nelson, 1973b), it would be necessary to orient intervention to referential learning.

Strangely enough, the clinical fields have been silent about the available literature on active loci of learning issuing from the cognitive socialization literature. Muma (1983a) summarized much of this literature. This area is much more powerful than psychometric testing simply because it provides relatively direct information about precise active loci of learning: No test can do that. For example, Bloom et al. (1974) showed that spontaneous imitation is selective. Children do not spontaneously imitate something they know or do not know. Rather, they spontaneously imitate something they are striving to learn. Astute clinicians would write down such utterances and compare them with current language samples to discover which aspects are new (active loci) and their grammatical, referential, and intentional contexts. Intervention based on such information is relevant and appropriate in the truest sense. Here is where true clinicians are to be found and effective intervention is evidenced.

Individual Differences

It is well known in the normal language acquisition literature that there are considerable individual differences. For example, Brown (1973a, 1973b) and Prutting (1979) indicated that early normal language acquisition varies greatly, on the order of plus or minus 6 months. This means that rate of learning indices such as age are too crude to be useful. To reiterate, Brown (1973a) indicated that rate of learning was notoriously varied but sequence was highly stable. This means that sequence rather than rate indices should be used in language assessment. Again, the clinical fields have missed the point because these fields have a heavy reliance on rate indices, especially age and grade levels.

Other issues pertaining to individual differences include estimated repertoire, progress in acquisition sequences, alternative strategies of learning, and active loci of learning. These were already mentioned. However, these need not be problems and they may substantiate individual differences. Again, the clinical fields are remarkably silent about estimated repertoires of verbal skills and the other attendant issues. Yet, descriptive procedures may provide evidence in these areas.

Normative tests and developmental profiles impose categories of behavior on individuals and do not actually account for what individuals can do. Consequently, psychometric normative tests and developmental profiles abrogate individual differences. There is a strangely naive view in the clinical fields concerning so-called individualized assessment. Some advocates of normative testing actually mean that when one child is tested at a time, it constitutes individualized assessment. This is very strange simply because the normative model remains and there is no attempt to ascertain what an individual can do in actual social commerce.

Intervention Implications

Performance on a normative test gives virtually no information about how to change an individual's behavior. Intervention implications are simply beyond the purview of psychometric tests.

In contrast, descriptive assessments provide useful information for setting goals in intervention. It is obvious that information about progress in acquisition sequences would be useful for establishing intervention goals. Under the premises that viable intervention principles are to expand and replace appropriate skills (Bates, 1979), it follows that both the expansion and replacement principles should be predicated on estimates of repertoires of skill, progress in acquisition sequences, alternative strategies, and active loci of learning. These kinds of information are not available from normative tests, but they may be available from descriptive assessments.

Prognosis

Prognosis is a major problem for both psychometric normative testing and for descriptive assessment. The reason that prognosis is such a problem is that learning typically occurs in spurts of unknown duration (Brown, 1973a, 1973b). There is very little evidence about when a spurt of learning will occur, how long a spurt will last, and what will be learned during the spurt—except for the research by Bloom (1990, 1991) and Bloom and Beckwith (1988, 1989), which indicated that spurts of early word learning are related to periods of neutral affect. Given the complexity of contextual learning that is part and parcel of language acquisition, it is exceedingly difficult to forecast such learning. Acquisition sequences provide stable information, but even so, we do not know when, how long, or what will be learned in a particular spurt of learning. As I said before (Muma, 1978b), the best we can do is describe what an individual can do, and is doing, and then exploit what he or she is striving to do. In this sense, the learning process is in the province of the learner. The clinician's role is that of ascertaining estimates of repertoires of skills, progress in acquisition sequences, available learning strategies, and active loci of learning, then providing contexts in which such learning may be facilitated.

Unfortunately, the prevailing practice in the clinical fields for dealing with prognosis, or more formally individualized educational plans (IEP), have relied on developmental profiles, psychometric tests (lacking construct validity), criterion testing (usually frequency counts or percentages with questionable acquisition criteria), or crudely simplistic notions such as the shift from single-word to two- or three-word utterances. I (Muma, 1986a) have given 10 reasons why developmental profiles lack support from the cognitive socialization literature. Because these issues are well known, I merely list them here. The following issues in the cognitive socialization literature raise questions about the validity of developmental profiles as indices of language acquisition: spurts of learning, highly stable sequence but notoriously varied rates of learning, processes rather than products, co-occurrence or linguistic context, grammatical systems, contextual learning, function has priority over form, language learning increments lack precision, a posteriori not a priori assessment, and heterogeneity. With the widespread use of developmental profiles to deal with IEPs, there are considerable questions about claimed expertise and appropriateness of services rendered.

The reliance on psychometric tests and criterion testing were discussed earlier and other relevant issues appear in chapter 8. As for the simplistic notion of a shift from one-word utterances to two- and three-word utterances, the problem is that this index is merely a quantitative notion, whereas a qualitative index would be more appropriate (Bloom, 1973; Greenfield & Smith, 1976). An example of a recommendation to use such quantitative indices is the following: "A prognosis might contain a statement that with intensive intervention the client will, within 1 year's time, move from single-word utterances to the production of some two- and three-word sentences" (Paul, 1995, p. 49). The quantitative perspective appears in different ways such as in Chapman et al. (1992) and in the following: "My own belief, shared by Chapman (1981), Fey (1986), and Hubbell (1981), is that the sentences children hear should, like those heard by normally developing children, be slightly longer and more advanced than those the child can currently produce" (Paul, 1995, p. 79). The cognitive socialization literature as evidenced by Bruner (1981) discusses raising the ante, whereby the parent (I insert "clinician") is sufficiently tuned to what the child (client) can do and selectively provides more advanced input. However, what is clearly different from the quantitative perspective previously cited is that more advanced input is not a quantitative issue but a qualitative one. For example, more advanced input could include longer as well as shorter utterances. More advanced but shorter utterances may include various grammatical and pragmatic mechanisms such as pronominalization, relativization, topicalization, ellipsis, noun phrase deletion, and nominal deletion.

Accountability or Efficacy

Efficacy has become a prominent issue in the clinical fields. The motivation is desirable; that is, it is desirable to be accountable for the services rendered and the effects of these services. However, the current state of affairs concerning efficacy is highly questionable and just plain muddled.

Curt Hamre and I have had many discussions about the ASHA task force and various articles on accountability. Briefly, these activities are unimpressive simply because they are single-mindedly committed to a behavioristic view and within-subject designs of dubious value. These concerns are coupled with various other concerns about lack of construct validity in tests used to deal with efficacy, nonrepresentative samples, heterogeneity of clinical populations, and inadequate evidence.

As I (Muma, 1978b) previously indicated, there is a concern that the data used to claim efficacy may be nothing more than data about the operational quality of intervention but it is likely to have little to do with actual change, or learning by the clients. This prospect is real simply because the data lack relevance to the contemporary cognitive socialization literature and relevance to what an individual can do. This enterprise comes up short in addressing the twofold criteria of evidence. Thus, the efficacy game may be nothing more than a data game lacking evidence.

I have indicated before (Muma, 1983b) that the state of the art for clinical intervention is weak on data but potentially rather impressive on rationale. That is, the available cognitive socialization literature provides good reasons—rationale—for doing intervention certain ways but because of heterogeneity and inherent ethical limitations for research design, there is a meager database to support particular ways of doing intervention, the many behavioristic studies notwithstanding. Kent (1990) also recognized that intervention approaches lack appropriate evidence. Furthermore, various attempts to establish matched CA or LA groups reflect a commitment to a psychometric model more than they provide serious evidence simply because such efforts are largely undone by heterogeneity.

Going in, efficacy is a matter of rationale goals; coming out, it is a matter of evidence (notice I did not say data). Thus, the first priority for addressing efficacy is the rationale for establishing particular intervention goals. A rationale should be derived from the philosophical views and theoretical perspectives that are supportable from the cognitive socialization literature.

Strangely, there have been many attempts to deal with efficacy (Bain & Dollaghan, 1991; Barlow, Hayes, & Nelson, 1984; Campbell & Bain, 1991; Damico, 1988; Olswang, 1993; Olswang, Thompson, Warren, & Minghetti, 1990; Parsonson & Baer, 1978; Schery & O'Connor, 1992), but there is virtual silence about the rationale issues going in. This circumstance merely shows that the clinical fields have invested the efficacy issue on the psychometric mentality, empiricism, and behavioristic perspectives. L. Miller (1993) made a similar observation: "Accountability became linked to numeric data and, for clients, test scores came to represent their thoughts, their abilities, and perhaps most important, their shortcomings" (p. 13).

The silence about issues going in is strange because such issues define the efficacy of the data obtained; that is, data obtained that are not derived from a recognized underlying philosophical view and theoretical perspective are open to any interpretation and are therefore of questionable value. For starters, data that are to be used in accounts of efficacy should be supportable by the contemporary cognitive socialization literature and should be directly relevant to what an individual can do. Such data are entitled to carry the mantle of evidence.

Fey (1986) made an intriguing comment about the presumed effectiveness of behavioristic language intervention: "There is absolutely no question that operant procedures are effective in getting children to produce new utterances that are more complex in structure than utterances produced by those same children prior to intervention" (p. 144). First, this comment merely showed his faith in and adherence to behaviorism. Second, he, like so many behaviorists, was willing to attribute learning on the basis of sheer production or usage. Yet, Bowerman (1987), Cazden (1988), Macken (1987), and others have indicated that sheer increases in use, especially elicited use, are of questionable value for attributing learning. Indeed, such behavior may even interfere with learning simply because it is acontextual. Yet, behaviorists remain undaunted and claim expertise in language acquisition. Third, in the face of so much literature to the contrary, I am utterly astounded that Fey (1986) would hold that there is "absolutely no question that operant procedures are effective" (p. 144). Thus, it matters little to Fey that the behaviorism has yielded up corrosive dogma (Bruner, 1978, 1981).

Behaviorists have turned to within-subject designs in an attempt to establish accountability or efficacy of language intervention (Fey, 1986; McReynolds & Kearns, 1983). In the multiple baseline approach, targeted behavior(s) are compared to nontargeted behavior(s) in pre- and post-baseline comparisons. If the targeted behavior(s) improved but the nontargeted behaviors remained unchanged, the improvement was deemed attributable to intervention. If both improved or neither improved intervention would be suspect. Improvement typically meant increased usage of a targeted behavior. Then, various studies that have used this approach typically perform a sleight of hand, whereby the notion of usage becomes interpreted as acquisition, learning, or facilitation (Fey, 1986; Paul, 1995).

The following issues should be considered about such ventures simply because they may be merely veiled excuses to deal with efficacy. First, the research design literature questions the appropriateness of using within-subject designs to deal with sustained effects (Ventry & Schiavetti, 1986). Second, these procedures rely on elicited rather than intentional behavior. Third, these procedures deal with acontextual language. Fourth, the criteria of presumed acquisition are questionable. Fifth, the lack of generalization from such studies is tacit evidence that appropriate learning probably did not occur. Sixth, such approaches ignore major issues of language acquisition such as sequences, alternative strategies, curvilinear functions, intentionality, partnership in actual social commerce, and so on. In all, it takes a myopic perspective to accept such arguments and ignore the relevant scholarly literature.

LANGUAGE SAMPLING

Representativeness

The goal of language sampling is to obtain a representative sample. Gallagher (1983) described three kinds of representative language samples: complete, optimal, and typical samples. A *complete sample* contains all a person can do; it gives complete evidence of the full range of grammatical and pragmatic distinctions available. Such samples are virtually unobtainable simply because it would be necessary to continuously sample an individual for months, possibly years, to sample all that is available. An *optimal sample* is one that reveals the best of what an individual can do. Such samples are also virtually unobtainable on similar grounds.

A *typical sample* is representative of one's daily use of language. Such samples are obtainable in a reasonable amount of time. However, a typical sample probably does not contain a person's full range of available skills. Thus, it is necessary to recognize some degree of sampling error. Recognition of sampling error raises two other important issues: sample size and varied sampling contexts.

Sample Size

Paul (1995) cited Lahey (1988), J. Miller (1981), and N. Nelson (1993) for recommending language sample sizes of 50 to 100 utterances and she cited Cole et al. (1989), who found that 50-utterance samples evidence about 80% of 100-utterance samples. Paul (1995) then asserted, "For efficient yet valid clinical data gathering, then, a 50-utterance sample is usually adequate" (p. 300). Lee (1974), Lee and Canter (1971), and Lee et al. (1975) relied on 50-utterance samples and Tyack and Gottsleben (1977) used 100-utterance samples.

Muma and Brannon (1986) found that the prevailing language sampling practices in the clinical fields relied on 50- or 100-utterance samples. These practices were derived apparently from Darley and Moll (1960), Johnson, Darley, and Spriestersbach (1963), McCarthy (1954), and Templin (1957). Unfortunately, these studies focused on reliabilities of response or utterance length. None of them addressed the issue of repertoires for basic grammatical systems and none were predicated on a theory of language acquisition.

Furthermore, in a survey of nearly 100 studies and clinical procedures that used such sample sizes, Muma and Brannon (1986) tried to ascertain the theoretical and empirical justifications for such practices. The results came up empty. Essentially, such practices were carried out as clinical traditions lacking appropriate theoretical and empirical justifications.

Yet, it can be assumed that relatively small samples would have relatively high sampling error rates simply because it is exceedingly difficult to package a representative sample of grammatical skills in a relatively small sample. Indeed, Gavin and Giles (1996) showed that language samples less than 175 utterances lacked adequate reliability. Furthermore, it would be exceedingly difficult to capture such samples in a sampling procedure. In contrast, large samples are likely to have relatively small sampling errors. Therefore, it is necessary to establish acceptable or tolerable sampling error rates in order to establish the size of language samples needed to obtain representative samples. Muma et al. (Appendix D) showed that with a sampling error rate of about 15% for samples of 400 utterances, it is necessary to have language samples of approximately 200 to 300 utterances to assess most grammatical domains. Inasmuch as the prevailing language sampling sizes are about 50 or 100 utterances, and such samples have excessively large error rates (55% and 40%, respectively), clinical practices, and claims of presumed validity of assessment and efficacy of intervention based on such samples are likely to be inherently flawed.

Varied Contexts

In order for a language sample to evidence a representative sample of a range of available skills, it is necessary that the sample be obtained from varied contexts. The more contextual variations reflected in the sample, the greater the likelihood of evidencing an individual's repertoire of skills. Conversely, a so-called standard sampling condition would be detrimental for obtaining a representative sample because it merely yields restricted samples.

Standard Sampling Fallacy

The issue of internal referential context or presupposition has major clinical implications, especially for the so-called standard sampling condition. The traditional empirical view was that it is necessary to have a standard sampling condition for such things as language samples. This would be conceptually sound if it were not for presupposition and implicature. However, there is no way to adequately control for presupposition and implicature by a standard sampling condition. Consequently, the control of external referents in the standard sampling condition makes no sense.

Rather, a sampling procedure should do the opposite. It should strive to vary the sampling conditions as much as possible in an attempt to estimate an individual's repertoire of grammatical and pragmatic skills. The greater the variations, the greater the opportunities to observe what a person can do. Thus, once again, theory defines what is appropriate; it defines what is practical simply because the standard sampling condition is impractical; it simply yields inappropriate data for describing what an individual can do.

Lahey (1988) indicated that standard sampling conditions lack sufficient flexibility for ascertaining what an individual can do:

> They are less flexible in the contexts observed, and restrict the language behaviors that can be observed. Standardized testing is *not* therefore, designed to provide information relevant for a *description* of a particular child's language system or his use of that system. . . . Currently, there has been a trend away

from the use of such highly structured observations (e.g., Bloom & Lahey, 1978; Leonard, Prutting, Perozzi, & Berkley, 1978; . . . Lund & Duchan, 1983; Muma, 1978b). This trend has been motivated by the desire to describe what a child knows about language as a system to be *used* for communication. Such information is needed to plan an intervention program or to specify qualitative differences between deviant and normal language. (p. 130).

Recording, Segmentation, and Transcription

There are many suggestions for recording, segmenting, and transcribing language samples. The following have been useful for us. I think the best recording is videotaping. The reason that videotaping is so useful is that tapes provide information about who is talking, available referents, ongoing events and topics, and social exchanges. Frequently, much of this information is difficult to discern from audio recordings. Unfortunately, videotaping is not readily available to most clinicians. As a compromise, I suggest writing utterances down with accompanying pertinent notes as they actually occur. This information could be supplemented by audio recordings. I definitely do not recommend relying on audio recordings alone, simply because anyone who has done this agrees there are many problems such as knowing who is talking, what the referents are, and acoustic pick-up for word endings, especially plurals and tense markers.

Segmentation is basically a decision concerning what aspects of the language sample will be attended to and what will be ignored. Thus, in a phonological assessment, grammatical and pragmatic issues are essentially ignored, whereas phonological issues become the focus of transcription. In a grammatical assessment, the phonological and pragmatic issues are held in abeyance and in a pragmatic assessment, the phonological and grammatical issues are held in abeyance. As clinicians become more skilled, they come to realize that these issues are intertwined making the segmentation decisions less categorical and more relational. In any case, a phonetic transcription is needed for a phonological assessment, a grammatical transcription is needed for a grammatical assessment, and issues of language use are needed for a pragmatic assessment.

ATTRIBUTION CRITERIA

The traditional criteria have been 80% to 100% correct performance to attribute learning.

Typically, mastery is defined operationally as 90 per cent correct usage of the form in contexts that obligate its use. The arbitrariness of the 90 per cent criterion should be acknowledged. However, this figure seems reasonable—it is high enough to indicate a near-adult level of use of the form, but it is sensitive to the fact that, under certain cognitive, linguistic, social, or emotional pressures, a child developing a new linguistic structure will occasionally make an error. (Fey, 1986, p. 123)

However, there is reason to question whether such criteria are appropriate or even detrimental. Yoder (1987) raised a poignant question, "Where are the data that tell us that 90% criterion levels are effective?" (p. 11). As indicated in chapter 4, there is reason to be concerned that having a child perform to 80% to 100% criterion may actually be detrimental because it may cause an overlearning problem.

The issue of attribution has been raised in regard to the notion of rich interpretation (Bloom, 1970, 1973):

> Rich interpretation involves assigning semantic-conceptual categories to the words in an expression based on the conditions under which expression was uttered. If certain categories are attributed some criterial number of times, then the category is considered to have psychological reality for the child. The categories assigned in rich interpretation are based on our understanding of language qua language, child language, and cognitive development. What understanding can we bring to attributions based on affect expressions? (Bloom et al., 1988, pp. 103–104)

Lee et al. (1975) suggested using 50% criteria for productions in spontaneous speech as sufficient evidence for terminating an intervention goal. The obvious question is: Where are the rational and empirical evidence that warrant this position?

The Piagetian criteria of preparation, attainment, and consolidation may be considered appropriate criteria (Muma, 1986a, 1991; K. E. Nelson, 1981, 1991; Prutting, 1979). A behavior is in preparation if it occurs infrequently, if it is context-bound, and if it is difficult to elicit. It is in attainment if it occurs relatively frequently, if it is not context-bound, and if it is relatively easy to elicit. A verbal behavior is in consolidation if it occurs relatively frequently, if it is not context-bound, if it is relatively easy to elicit, if it has lexical variation within, and if it occurs with varied co-occuring constructions.

Notice that these criteria are relative rather than absolute. For example, a demonstrative noun phrase would be considered in consolidation if it has lexical variations within (that horse, that chair, those hats, these birds, this mouse) and the co-occurring structures also vary (That horse jumped. I like that horse. Who saw that horse? That horse near the tree is mine.).

Lahey (1988) used criteria for productivity that are somewhat like preparation, attainment, and consolidation. She discussed productivity and achievement. According to Lahey, productivity could be attributed when five different utterances contained a particular construction and the construction evidenced lexically free words. She attributed this criterion to Bloom and her associates, specifically Bloom et al. (1975). Achievement referred to the use of a construction when it is expected in accordance with the adult model of use.

Another consideration for attribution criteria is robustness. Goldin-Meadow and Mylander (1984) showed that some aspects of language learning were robust or hearty, whereas other aspects were fragile. Those aspects that are relatively easily altered by available models may be regarded as fragile, whereas those that are resistant to change may be regarded as robust.

The clinical fields have not addressed issues of criteria of attribution from a cognitive socialization perspective: relative criteria vested in context. Indeed, the clinical fields have relied on behavioristic notions such as 80% to 100% and psychometric normative indices without considering an individual's estimated repertoire of skills. The irony, of course, is that these traditional clinical indices have been used to draw conclusions about an individual's presumed abilities. It is ironic simply because data of this kind result in a myopic consideration of the relevant issues.

PREGRAMMATICAL CHILD: ASSESSMENT ISSUES

Except, of course, for hearing screening, the substantive issues in assessing pregrammatical children are different from those in dealing with grammatical children. This raises the distinction between pregrammatical and grammatical children. Pregrammatical children are those who range from completely nonverbal—not talking—to those with highly limited verbalizations. Those children in the upper range of pregrammatical children actually are verbal to some extent but their verbalizations are highly restricted to formulaic, ossified, or ritualized forms and relatively few words and word combinations. When children obtain varied SVO constructions, they have entered the arena of grammatical learning (Bloom, 1973).

My view is that CCCE have such complex domains it is somewhat ludicrous to believe that they can be adequately screened. Rather, I take the position that parental intuition is sufficiently valid to warrant clinical assessment. Nevertheless, Rescorla (1989) developed what appears to be a useful screening procedure. This screening procedure is attractive because it was found to have "excellent sensitivity and specificity for the identification of language delay" (p. 587).

The substantive issues for assessing pregrammatical children include the following: presumed cognitive precursors (sensorimotor skills), symbolic play, categorization or representation (from event knowledge to narrative), explicit content, communicative intent, and affect (attachment).

Cognitive Precursors: Sensorimotor Skills

The sensorimotor skills of particular interest include object permanence, causality, deferred imitation, and anticipation. These have been widely studied. The studies in the 1970s were rather disappointing and disquieting because their results raised questions as to whether the sensorimotor skills were indeed cognitive precursors. Mandler (1979) commented on the discouraging results of these studies, "The promissory note of sensorimotor development as the key to language acquisition has remained largely unpaid. We know that the connections must be there, but how are we to dig below this surface knowledge?" (p. 374). However, as some methodological issues were settled, especially in regard to contrived as opposed to human sense tasks (Donaldson, 1978) and some substantive distinctions were made about the cognitive and communicative functions of early words (Gopnik, 1981, 1984; Gopnik & Meltzoff, 1984, 1986), the notion of sensorimotor precursors for language acquisition became supportable. These issues were discussed in chapter 4.

Symbolic Play

Similarly, early studies of the relation between symbolic play and language acquisition yielded equivocal results. However, Bates (1979) and others have provided evidence that showed that as children learn symbolic play, this knowledge also benefits language acquisition. These issues were discussed in chapter 4.

Categorization

Cognition is based on categorization. "Virtually all cognitive activities involve and is dependent on the process of categorizing" (Bruner et al., 1956, p. 246). Another way of appreciating the importance of categorization was expressed by Tyler (1969): "Life in a world where nothing was the same would be intolerable. It is through . . . classification that the whole rich world of infinite variability shrinks to manipulable size" (p. 7). It is by categorizing experiences that mental representation or abstraction is achieved. All of one's mental representations constitute a theory of the world (Palermo, 1982), Whole-Earth Catalogue (Mandler, 1983), possible worlds (Bruner, 1986), or situated mind (K. Nelson, 1996). Thus, experience defines what one's world is like.

Various theories of categorization have been posited over the past several decades. Dollard and Miller (1950) drew an important distinction be-

tween learned equivalence and learned distinctiveness in concept formation. *Learned equivalence* is when an individual regards two things as essentially equivalent when they may otherwise be considered different. For
example, a cup and a glass may, under certain conditions, be regarded as
similar because they function as containers. *Learned distinctiveness* is when
an individual regards two things as essentially different when they may
otherwise be considered the same. For example, two drinking glasses with
the same characteristics would usually be regarded as the same but they
could also be distinguished "yours" and "mine." These notions are important
because they indicate the dynamic nature of categorization. Under certain
conditions some things function one way, whereas they function in other
ways in other conditions. Therefore, the functional context is what determines how things are categorized. This means that the a priori notions of
categorization (Boehm, 1969, 1986; Bracken, 1986) miss a crucial issue of
categorization.

The theory of natural categories (Rosch, 1973, 1978; Rosch & Mervis,
1975), schema theory (Anderson, 1980; Mandler, 1978, 1988), representation
that addresses procedural and declarative knowledge (Mandler, 1983, 1990),
and representational redescription (Karmiloff-Smith, 1992) have probably
advanced the understanding of categorization more than other theories. The
essence of the theory of natural categories is that focal exemplars provide
evidence of prototypic knowledge of categories, whereas peripheral exemplars provide evidence of extended knowledge of categories by virtue of
superordinate understandings (Anglin, 1977; Mandler, 1983). These are two
important issues about categorization. Prototypic knowledge is awareness
of the core dimensions or attributes of a category (K. Nelson, 1973a, 1974).
Such knowledge is initially acquired by acting on objects thereby deducing
dynamic attributes for categories before static attributes (K. Nelson, 1973a)
and establishing procedural knowledge (Mandler, 1983). The importance of
extended knowledge as evidenced from peripheral exemplars is the realization that things may be categorized in different ways depending on intended
applications.

The essence of schema theory is that early knowledge of the world is
based on awareness of routines—schemata. This awareness is experiential
rather than categorical. Schemas contain information about events (K. Nelson, 1985, 1986). Such information is about who or what is doing something
or in a particular state. This is what Mandler (1983) regarded as procedural
knowledge and K. Nelson regarded as event knowledge.

Representation and representational redescription were discussed in
chapter 4. Therefore, there is no need to reiterate further.

In the 1950s and 1960s, there was much interest in mediation, especially
verbal mediation, in concept formation. Brown (1956) indicated that a word
is a "lure to cognition" (p. 278). Cazden (1972) indicated that a word draws

attention to another instance of a concept: "If one has no name for a phenomenon, one may not notice it" (p. 229). Gagne and Smith (1962) said that, "It would appear that requiring verbalization somehow 'forced the Ss [subjects] to think' " (p. 378). K. Nelson (1996) provided the most eloquent account of mediation to date and the neo-Vygotskian views have contributed to social–cultural mediation.

Vygotsky (1962) held that the relations between concepts and labels are bidirectional in acquisition. In spontaneous learning, a word or label serves to consolidate spontaneous inductions. Thus, a child, by virtue of previous experience, knows different balls but the label *ball* serves to consolidate these diverse notions of ball into a prototype. To reiterate, this is what Bruner (1981) called the *dubbing ceremony* and what the current literature on word capture and fast mapping is about. In scientific learning, a child is given a word, then the child hypothesizes about the nature of the word and uses available experiences to resolve these hypotheses. Thus, in spontaneous learning, a word may consolidate previous experience, whereas in scientific learning a word launches inquiries about subsequent relevant experiences. However, just as words may facilitate thought, they may also interfere with thinking.

Nevertheless, Cromer (1976) provided a nice summary of the role of language in cognition, saying, "Language is especially important in that it allows three developments to occur" (p. 306). These developments are:

1. It speeds up representation over what can be done through sensori-motor representation.
2. It provides an ability to transcend immediate space and time.
3. It provides a means for representing many things simultaneously.

According to speech act theory (Clark & Clark, 1977; Grice, 1975), mental representation that is available via categorization provides the substantive base for explicit content. This substantive base is presupposition or implicit content. A message will not work as intended if it lacks presupposition. For example, the sentence "I like Coke" will not be understood unless the listener has possible world knowledge about what Coke is and that *like* means to drink and taste. Thus, the proposition in this sentence is meaningless if a listener lacks the necessary presuppositional knowledge for it. This means that a semantic assessment should be coupled with evidence of possible worlds. Furthermore, such evidence is not provided by intelligence testing, but should be about an individual's actual available natural categories.

The theory of natural categories (Rosch, 1973, 1978) offers clinicians a useful way of assessing one aspect of possible worlds. By having individuals sort focal and peripheral exemplars of competing categories, it is possible to estimate which categories may be available to an individual and which may be insufficiently developed or disrupted.

Burger and Muma (1980) showed that individuals with aphasia who had word recall difficulties evidenced difficulties incorporating peripheral exemplars with focal exemplars for specific categories. Such evidence implicates a possible conceptual disruption underlying word use. Furthermore, individuals with aphasia who evidenced word finding difficulties also evidenced a cognitive distancing dimension in which they had more difficulty sorting pictures than objects. The new object sorting task for revealing natural categories (Muma, 1998) is currently being used in a comprehensive study of cognitive profiles for individuals with aphasia, traumatic brain injury, dementia, and SLI.

Needless to say, clinicians should assess categorization skills of pregrammatical children simply because these children may lack some basic knowledge of the world or possible worlds for word learning. Said differently, one reason that children may have limited vocabularies is that the underlying conceptual knowledge is insufficient. Assessment of categorization in accordance with available theories of concept acquisition, notably the theory of natural categories and representation, should provide clinicians with valid information in this arena.

Additionally as a part of possible worlds, clinical assessment may want to consider impulsivity, inferencing, and problem solving. These can be assessed by using some of the tasks in the MAP (Muma & Muma, 1979), specifically cognitive tempo and rule- and non-rule-governed learning. The inferencing and problem-solving tasks by Karmiloff-Smith (1984, 1992) and the Muma (1998) button-sequence task would pertain as well.

Explicit Content

Explicit content is the propositional or semantic content of a message. In the early 1970s, there were several detailed studies of the acquisition of basic semantic categories underlying messages (Bloom, 1970, 1973; Bowerman, 1973; Brown, 1973b; Schlesinger, 1971). Perhaps the Greenfield and Smith (1976) study has the most to offer clinical assessment because their data provided a developmental sequence beginning with performatives. Specifically, the acquisition sequence they identified is the following (from performative to modification): performative, indicative object, volitional object, volition, agent, action or state, object, action or state of object, dative, associated object, associated being, location, and modification of event. I found that an abridged version of this sequence is useful in clinical assessment: performative, indicative, volition, agent, action or state, object, dative, locative, and modification. The semantic functions extend to volition; the semantic relations begin with agent.

Performatives are especially important in assessing preverbal children because they comprise the means of expression that precede verbalization (Ninio, 1978, 1980). The communicative point, sounds such as "moo" to identify a cow, and displayed referents (holding a toy up to be seen by another participant) are kinds of performatives. Astute clinicians are vigilant for such events and name the referents and stay on that topic in what Muma (1981b) called communicative payoff. By doing so, children learn that performatives work as intended and they come to attend to the labels given to the referents. Then they evidence uptake of the available labels and incorporate them into their lexicon. In this way, words replace performatives. Furthermore, this whole transaction occurs in actual social commerce in the realization of communicative intent.

Clinically, a semantic analysis would describe an individual's estimated repertoire in regard to:

1. This acquisition sequence.
2. Inventory of the different kinds of semantic functions and relations.
3. An inventory of the different kinds of combinations of semantic relations.

Thus, the semantic analysis entails three fundamental issues: acquisition sequence, distribution of different kinds of semantic categories, and distribution of different combinations of semantic relations.

Notice that these notions are not well known or used in the clinical fields. Rather than address the issue of which particular semantic functions and relations are available to an individual, the clinical fields frequently turn to the notion of one- and two-word utterance. The underlying premise is a quantitative notion, namely length of utterance, when the more important issues are qualitative (Bloom, 1973; Greenfield & Smith, 1976). An example of this kind of thinking is the following: "A prognosis might contain a statement that with intensive intervention the client will, within 1 year's time, move from single-word utterances to the production of some two- and three-word sentences" (Paul, 1995, p. 49).

It should be obvious that the identification of an individual's skills with respect to acquisition sequences would have major implications for intervention. For example, children with very few words but a variety of performatives such as displayed referents, object-feature vocalizations like "moo-moo" for cow, and communicative points evidence the beginning of the acquisition sequence for semantic relations. The intervention implications are twofold, expansion and replacement (Bates, 1979) in accordance with the acquisition sequence for semantic functions and relations identified by Greenfield and Smith (1976). Therefore, it would be desirable to expand the repertoires of performatives and replace available performatives with words. For individuals who have a limited repertoire of performatives, it would be desirable to focus on embodiment (Muma, 1991; chap. 4).

Communicative Intent

The single most important issue in the cognitive socialization literature in general and speech act theory in particular is the centrality of communicative intent. As Grice (1975) indicated, the purpose of a message is to make communicative intents recognizable. This was reiterated by Sperber and Wilson (1986).

Bruner (1981) described four early innate intentions—joint attention, instrumental, affiliative, and pretense—and two major early acquired intents—indicating and requesting. I (Muma, 1986a) discussed these elsewhere. Halliday (1975) identified seven early intentions that are compatible with Bruner's list. However, Halliday's list is more detailed. Furthermore, K. Nelson (1991) provided more details than originally given by Halliday. Perhaps it is only necessary to list the early intentions here: instrumental, regulatory, interactional, personal, heuristic, imaginative, and informative. Informative comes in last. Also, these become reorganized into mathetic (cognitive) and pragmatic (communicative) intentions.

Needless to say, it behooves clinicians to inventory an individual's array of intentions to estimate what he or she can do. The intervention implications are to expand alternative ways of expressing available intentions and to add intentions that are not available. Again, it is unfortunate that much of what the clinical fields do in assessment and intervention relies on elicited rather than intentional behavior.

Affect

Given the attachment literature (Ainsworth, 1973; Bowlby, 1969, 1973; Lamb, 1977; Rutter, 1979), it behooves clinicians to orient clinical assessment on the issues of attachment, separation anxiety, and stranger anxiety. I (Muma, 1981c) described a clinical assessment procedure based on these principles. Inasmuch as it is well known, I merely make a few brief comments here.

Clinical assessment should provide young children opportunities to have ready access to a security base during both assessment and intervention. This typically means that the parent (usually the mother) should be present during assessment and intervention. With such access, young children provide representative language samples and behavior. On the other hand, in the traditional clinical model, young children are separated from their parents and administered tests and intervention programs. Such procedures are brutally insensitive and they force young children to deal with separation anxiety and stranger anxiety and leave them stripped of opportunities for attachment. This circumstance places young children in unnatural contrived circumstances that often yield atypical performance—another source of trouble for the complex issues of appropriate assessment and a lack of generalization.

Briefly, the clinical assessment–intervention procedure I recommend in view of this literature is a security-based approach for young children. In assessment, I set up a triangle in which the parent's chair, the clinician's chair, and a set of six to eight varied toys are the respective points. These are approximately 3 feet apart. The child typically begins with some form of attachment with the parent (mother). The child usually sits on the mother's lap or leans against her and surveys the clinician (stranger) and the room. During this time, the clinician talks to the mother about a typical day for her child. As the child ascertains that everything is alright, he or she releases from the security base and goes to the toys. Sometimes the child brings the toys back to the security base and plays with them at the mother's feet while establishing incidental contact by leaning against her. Other times, when an emotional stress is less eminent, the child will remain released by staying with the toys that are a few feet away. After a child shows that he or she will play with the toys and remain released from the security base, the clinician may parallel play with the toys. I have found that it is useful to make a few incidental physical contacts during such play. Then, the children tend to spontaneously join in the play. Using this procedure, it usually takes only a few minutes for the children to spontaneously play with the clinician (a stranger). The result is that a more valid language sample can be obtained than from an elicited sample. This is important because elicited samples are usually qualitatively different from spontaneous samples (Fujiki & Brinton, 1987; Prutting et al., 1975).

As for expression, early on infants rely on emotional expression to communicate. Subsequently they learn that words are more explicit means for expression of wants and desires (Bruner, 1981).

Words did not replace affect, but emerged as a new system for expressing aspects of the contents of mental states—with names of persons, objects, and actions primarily—while affect continued to express the children's feelings about those contents. (Bloom et al., 1988, p. 123)

GRAMMATICAL CHILD: ASSESSMENT ISSUES

Children who evidence varied productive lexicons and varied SVO constructions are verbal children (Berman, 1988; Bloom, 1970, 1973; Bloom et al., 1980; Bloom et al., 1988; Maratsos, 1982, 1988a). The difference between pregrammatical and grammatical children is a relative rather than an absolute difference. The difference recognizes individuals with relatively limited lexical and structural (concatenated or nondecomposable) utterances as compared to other individuals who use varied SVO constructions (Bloom, 1973). Alternatively, if varied SVO constructions are not well evidenced but a child evidences varied indirect object constructions, that would also indicate that a child is in the grammatical stage of language acquisition (Greenfield & Smith, 1976).

In order to ascertain what grammatical children can do, it is recommended that the following be done: estimate verbal repertoires, ascertain progress in acquisition sequences, identify available acquisition strategies, identify active loci of learning, assess pragmatic skills, and assess social-cultural skills. These issues should be considered with respect to appropriate attribution criteria (discussed earlier).

Repertoire

Repertoire is the range or array of available skills. This is a psychological notion that can only be inferred and estimated. Inferences and estimates of grammatical repertoires are dependent on actual instances of grammatical constructions in representative language samples from actual social commerce. Single instances may index the range of available skills, but unfortunately, they may also be misleading because some of them may not be productive. Roughly three varied instances of grammatical or pragmatic skills are sufficient to attribute productivity (Bloom et al., 1988) but not necessarily consolidation of such skills.

There is an irony of sorts in the clinical fields because rarely are true representative (spontaneous, varied contexts, sufficiently long) language samples obtained in order to ascertain what an individual can do—repertoires of skills. Rather, clinical assessments are usually based on test performances (often without construct validity) or woefully small samples (50 or 100 utterances) in standard sampling conditions and elicitation procedures (Fey, 1986; Lee, 1974; J. Miller & Chapman, 1981a; Paul, 1995; Watkins & Rice, 1991) from which conclusions are drawn about what individuals presumably can do. Inasmuch as such assessments rely on questionable normative test performances and questionable language samples to draw conclusions, there is a major question concerning validity of language assessment.

Furthermore, Paul (1995) regarded informal assessment (analysis of spontaneous speech and comprehension) as a "follow up of standardized testing" (p. 296). This view is strangely backward.

The prima facie evidence in language assessment should be derived from what individuals do with language in actual social commerce—representative samples—rather than performance on contrived tasks imposed on them. The inferences for the former are more valid and relevant than what is obtained from the latter.

As for language sample size, there is a very strange practice in the clinical fields whereby language samples of 50 or 100 utterances are deemed acceptable for ascertaining presumed grammatical skills. It is strange because a survey (Muma & Brannon, 1986) of nearly 100 studies and clinical assessment procedures advocating such procedures revealed a lack of rational and empirical evidence to warrant such samples. Thus, these practices are merely perpetuated from one clinician to another and have attained the status of a clinical tradition. What is all the more surprising is that a mundane consideration of such samples reveals how precarious clinical services are that are based on such samples. To reiterate, it is patently obvious that it would be exceedingly difficult to package a representative sample of language skills in 50 or 100 utterances. Furthermore, it would be exceedingly difficult to capture such a sample in spontaneous speech. In short, the odds are very much against obtaining representative samples of grammatical and pragmatic skills in 50 or 100 utterances. Yet, scholarship in the clinical fields has not raised these prospects. Appendix D addresses this issue and shows that language samples of 50 and 100 utterances have error rates of approximately 55% and 40%, respectively, in comparison to 400-utterance samples. Needless to say, these are excessive error rates.

Acquisition Sequences

Unquestionably, one of the major benefits from the cognitive socialization literature is the identification of acquisition sequences. These are very important for assessment because they provide an appropriate means for ascertaining where an individual is in the course of acquiring particular aspects of language. Such information is essential for establishing appropriate intervention goals and for ascertaining progress in intervention.

To reiterate, Brown (1973a, 1973b) indicated that rate of learning is notoriously varied and sequence is highly stable. He was referring to acquisition sequences within systems such as within the semantic system discussed previously. His message is that rate of learning indices such as CA, MA, MLU over 4.5, and grade level are of dubious value, possibly even inappropriate, because of excessive variances in acquisition. Rather, acquisition sequences are appropriate. Unfortunately, the clinical fields evidence a heavy reliance on CA, MA, LA, and MLU.

Progress in acquisition sequences has very important intervention implications. Such information provides appropriate goals for intervention and ways of appreciating the effects of intervention. Thus, a clinician would know what to expect next from an individual. However, it should be noted that the behavior modification literature and psychometric normative tests essentially avoid the issue of acquisition sequences by relying on 80% to 100% criteria for attribution and norms, respectively.

Some summaries of acquisition sequences are available (Bloom & Lahey, 1978; Lahey, 1988; Muma, 1978b, 1981a). Although these are useful, the literature has developed so rapidly, it would be desirable to update these sequences. Indeed, that is my next project.

Alternative Strategies

The identification of alternative language learning strategies is another major contribution of the language acquisition literature. Such strategies have very important clinical implications. In assessment, it behooves clinicians to identify the particular strategies employed by particular children so these strategies can be exploited in intervention. For example, Bloom et al. (1974) showed that some children were imitators, whereas others were not. Thus, it would be desirable to have varied imitation tasks in intervention for those individuals who evidenced this strategy, but such activities would be inappropriate for those who were not imitators.

Active Loci of Learning

Interestingly enough, the cognitive socialization literature has provided several kinds of evidence of active learning. That is, some studies have shown specific aspects of language acquisition as children strive to acquire them. These may be regarded as active loci of learning (Muma, 1983a, 1986a, 1987a, 1991).

Another interesting note about these active loci of learning is that usually a child has several active loci at one time. For example, a child might be overcoming fronting and stopping in phonology while also dealing with pluralization and tense marking in syntax, and topic sharing and topic maintenance in pragmatic skills.

It should be immediately apparent that psychometric normative tests and developmental profiles are incapable of:

1. Providing estimates of verbal repertoires.
2. Showing progress in acquisition sequences.
3. Identifying alternative acquisition strategies.
4. Identifying active loci of learning.

However, descriptive procedures issuing from the cognitive socialization literature do have the capabilities of providing these assessments. This is why psychometric normative tests are not as powerful as descriptive procedures in rendering these services, and this is why descriptive procedures are more appropriate than normative tests in addressing the seven basic clinical assessment issues. Accordingly, there has been a shift away from reliance on psychometric tests to descriptive assessment procedures (Muma, Lubinski, & Pierce, 1982; Muma & Pierce, 1980; Muma, Pierce, & Muma, 1983).

Pragmatic Skills

The issues discussed in chapter 6 as the pragmatic arena are those that should be assessed. The assessment procedure is simple and straightforward. First, observe an individual in actual social commerce with several different individuals and varied topics. Second, note those particular areas in the pragmatic arena in which the individual is awkward (e.g., topic initiation, topic sharing, adjusted messages, anaphora, deictic reference, etc.). The notes should describe specific instances as fully as possible so that the client will recollect them when they are discussed. Intervention would entail the client monitoring such behavior in himself or herself and others. The over-the-shoulder game, the barrier game, and peer modeling are very useful for altering pragmatic skills (Muma, 1978b, 1986a).

Social Skills

As Gallagher (1991) indicated, individuals with language impairments often have social difficulties as well. In assessment, it is desirable to identify an individual's circle of friends, interests, and typical activities. In intervention, these areas should be a focus for expansion.

SUMMARY

With the theme "assessment well done is intervention half begun," issues of clinical assessment were considered. With the available cognitive socialization literature and its reliance on philosophical views and theoretical perspectives, the clinical assessment perspective was predicated on the distinction between data and evidence and the reliance on descriptive assessment issuing from this literature. This kind of assessment will hopefully dethrone the expediency view of assessment that is so prevalent in the clinical fields. Appropriateness should win out over expediency if professional integrity counts!

Experts in the field of assessment and measurement have established the view that construct validity is mandatory, otherwise assessment becomes an ethical dilemma. Attendant to construct validity, relativity, conditionality, complexity, dynamism, and ecology were also discussed.

With the widespread reliance on psychometric normative tests and with developments in the literature that raise questions about the fundamental premises of such testing, it behooves clinicians to consider the value of such testing. In so doing, 12 issues were considered.

MAP was described as an example of a form of descriptive assessment derived from the cognitive socialization literature. Rather than norms, MAP provides opportunities to evidence patterns of performance beyond chance.

Alternative descriptive procedures issuing from the cognitive socialization literature offer clinicians viable opportunities to render appropriate clinical services. Appropriateness of descriptive procedures over psychometric testing can be appreciated by comparing them over the seven basic clinical assessment issues.

With these issues in mind, clinical assessments of pregrammatical and grammatical children were considered. For pregrammatical children, it is desirable to consider the following in assessing CCCE: sensorimotor skills (object permanence, causality, deferred imitation, anticipation, symbolic play), categorization (implicit content) or representation in the situated mind beginning with knowledge of events, basic semantic functions and relations (explicit content), affect (attachment), socialization, and communicative intent. For grammatical children, it is desirable to consider general cognitive skills (categorization, perceptual salience, iconic or symbolic thinking, analytic or synthetic thinking, tempo, rule learning and flexibility, problem solving and inferencing); lexical, grammatical, and pragmatic capacities (repertoire, progress in acquisition sequences, alternative acquisition strategies, and active loci of learning); and socialization.

Because these issues are vested in actual social commerce, it is usually necessary to rely on spontaneous speech in representative language samples to assess them. Thus, the goal of language sampling is representativeness. It is necessary to obtain a sufficiently large sample to be representative. The prevailing use of 50- or 100-utterance language samples results in excessively large sampling errors (on the order of 55% and 40%, respectively). It is also necessary to vary the sampling conditions to obtain representative samples. Recording, segmentation, and transcription need to be done carefully because they could have errors that threaten the validity of language sampling.

CHAPTER

8

LANGUAGE INTERVENTION: FACILITATION

The cognitive socialization literature has provided a viable substantive base for rendering assessment well done, thence intervention half begun. Thus, the cognitive socialization principles and practices in assessment should be sustained and implemented in rendering appropriate language intervention. In so doing, capricious, dogmatic, authoritarianism, and hyped clinical practices in the clinical fields would undergo careful scrutiny. In this way, the cognitive socialization literature with its attendant philosophical views and theoretical perspectives makes things practical.

Accordingly, it is desirable to establish language assessment and intervention models based on the philosophical views of mentalism, functionalism, constructionism, social origins of the mind, experiential realism and experiential cognition and several contemporary theoretical perspectives, especially those compatible with speech act theory because of its preeminence in the cognitive socialization literature (Perera, 1994). These views and perspectives provide a viable (supportable) substantive rationale for rendering clinical services certain ways.

A language assessment–intervention model with continuity between philosophical views and theoretical perspectives establishes clinical views, policies, and practices as scholarly endeavors. Such continuity provides construct validity for assessment and intervention (Muma, 1978b, 1983b, 1986a, 1987a, 1991). In short, clinical assessment and intervention are inherently philosophical and theoretical ventures, whereas empirical issues provide a substantiating function.

235

THE PARADOX

With this perspective there is a paradox in the clinical fields. On the one hand, it is desirable, indeed necessary, to establish the philosophical and theoretical substantive base of clinical endeavors. On the other hand, the clinical fields have fallen short in doing so and they have been loose with the relevant scholarly literature resulting in some major substantive disconnections; for example, reliance on behaviorism and reinforcement, blind adherence to quantification and psychometric approaches, reliance on homogeneity at the cost of heterogeneity, selective (convenient) use of the language acquisition literature, reliance on impressionism, questionable language sample sizes, capricious attribution criteria, misplaced notions of accountability or efficacy, confusions between language use and language acquisition, missing the centrality of communicative intent and the importance of actual social commerce, misused terminology, expediency supplanting appropriateness, modality orientation at the cost of the core issues of language, and reliance on authoritarian dicta and hype. Clinicians have expressed concerns about such disconnections.

With such basic issues, there is the larger issue concerning to what extent the clinical fields are scholarly and professional. On the individual level, adherents to such notions (disconnections) may want to take an introspective view of their positions, presumed expertise, and appropriateness of rendered services.

Fortunately, the cognitive socialization literature is available and it offers several promising substantive alternatives to various disconnections in the clinical fields. This literature provides a very good substantive base for a rationale for rendering appropriate clinical services. This is the potential strength of the clinical fields.

The empirical perspective is important as well. Empirical issues may substantiate or refute rational issues but the empirical perspective should never supplant rational issues. To do so opens the door again to brute empiricism, authoritarianism, dogma, and hype.

As a starting point for becoming aligned to the scholarly literature, the clinical fields need to reestablish heterogeneity as a pervasive and enduring issue. The implications of this issue are so great that virtually all of the others follow. At once, technicianship would be found wanting and clinicianship would be deemed the coin-of-the-realm of scholarship in the clinical professions. A client's repertoire of skills evidenced in actual social commerce would take precedence over test scores and capricious attribution criteria.

The current paradox is that the clinical fields claim expertise in CCCE but evidence sufficient disconnections with the relevant cognitive socialization literature to question such expertise and the value of rendered services.

For example, many behavioristic studies are available that claim to deal with language learning but are strangely silent about critical issues of language learning (see Appendix C). There seems to be a penchant to sustain behavioristic views, the psychometric normative model, and empiricism as the presumed foundations of clinical services. Yet, the literature over the past three decades has raised major questions about these perspectives. Nevertheless, the clinical fields remain largely undaunted. The paradox, then, is the extent to which these traditional clinical views and practices prevail in the face of more appropriate (viable and supportive) substantive issues. Needless to say, the clinical fields have a great deal of "cleaning up" to do in order to render appropriate clinical services, stake a legitimate claim for expertise in cognitive socialization, and establish a firm foundation for a profession.

INTERVENTION RATIONALE

The substantive base issuing from the cognitive socialization literature provides a viable rationale for clinical intervention. As a continuation of chapter 2, consider first various philosophical views. Innatism contends that individuals are uniquely wired for language acquisition. With maturation and relevant contact with one's language, acquisition transpires. The clinical implication is to enter intervention in accordance with an individual's readiness to learn and what progress an individual has made in various acquisition sequences, phases, and stages.

Mentalism and constructionism indicate that language is a mental endeavor and that acquisition is an active process derived in large measure from an individual's knowledge of the world or possible worlds with the attendant general cognitive capacities of representation, inference, and problem solving. The clinical implications are that possible worlds (representation, inference, problem solving) or situated mind (biological, cognitive, social, emotional, cultural) constitute a general substantive base for language acquisition and use. Furthermore, the active dynamic nature of cognition means that the acquisition process is essentially the province of the learner (issues of content, sequence, pacing, and intent are inherently the learner's). This means that assessment should be oriented on description (Muma, 1978b) of what an individual can do in actual social commerce (available repertoire, progress in acquisition sequences, available learning strategies, active loci of learning) rather than on performance from imposed tasks (normative tests, developmental profiles, a priori procedures) and intervention should be oriented on facilitation (Bloom & Lahey, 1978; Muma, 1978b; K. E. Nelson, 1989, 1991) in an attempt to foster what the individual is already striving to learn or is ready to learn.

Experiential realism and experiential cognition hold that experience is the basis for knowing about the world. Consequently, possible worlds is a subjective enterprise and the notion of objectivity is essentially a myth because there is no access to a "God's-eye view" of the world. Rationalism is the view that a rationale is needed to establish an appropriate view or position. This means that it is incumbent on clinicians to establish a rationale for holding certain views and taking certain actions in language intervention. Appropriate sources of rationale are recognized philosophical views and theoretical perspectives. With the contemporary philosophical views and theoretical perspectives, clinicians have an opportunity to establish a well-substantiated rationale for appropriate language intervention.

Functionalism is the view that structure is in the service of function. Accordingly, the basic functions of cognition are representation, inference, and problem solving, whereas the basic cognitive functions of language are shared representation and mediation and the basic communicative functions of language are content and intent. Content is the dynamic relation between what is coded in implicit content (proposition) and what remains in implicature (presupposition). The clinical implications are that assessment and intervention should be oriented on the basic cognitive and communicative functions, especially possible worlds or situated minds (experiential) in cognition and intent and content in communication.

Behaviorism holds that behavior is observable and that contingent relations between behaviors may be manipulated by reinforcement. This view has not held up in the cognitive socialization literature. Pinker (1988), for example, referred to "the virtual demise of classical learning theory as an explanation of language development" (p. 113). "Models of language acquisition built explicitly on assumptions of positive and negative reinforcement are no longer acceptable" (K. Nelson, 1985, p. 33). Numerous studies that claim to deal with language acquisition by employing reinforcement have, in essence, done themselves in by virtue of failing to generalize. Thus, the behavioristic view has turned up empty.

Similarly, brute empiricism has been nonproductive. Brute empiricism is the view that only empirical evidence (typically normative comparisons, frequency counts, or percentages) is needed to ascertain a skill or capacity. The problem with brute empiricism is that it is not governed by recognized theoretical perspectives, thereby establishing particular interpretations of the data. Thus, brute empiricism allows for virtually any interpretation of the data, thereby fostering dogma. These philosophical views and their respective clinical implications appear in Table 8.1.

With these philosophical views in mind, it is useful to turn to compatible theoretical perspectives for developing an appropriate intervention rationale. Based on the considerations of theoretical perspectives in chapter 2, the following perspectives are attractive: experiential realism, representation,

TABLE 8.1
Philosophical Views and Their Respective Clinical Implications

Philosophical Views	Clinical Implications
Innatism	Acquisition sequences, readiness
Mentalism	Possible worlds
Constructionism	Active learning, situated minds
Experiential realism	Subjectivity
Rationalism	Rationale
Behaviorism	(Nonproductive)
Brute empiricism	(Dogma)

representational redescription, bootstrapping, shared meaning of knowledge of events, speech acts, cohesion, situated mind, and informativeness.

Experiential realism and experiential cognition contend that what is real for an individual is the product of experience. The clinical implication is that an individual's worldly experiences, in contrast to formal instruction or imposed tasks, constitute the substantive base for cognition in general and language acquisition in particular. Representational redescription is the perspective that an individual is continually mentally redescribing possible worlds by virtue of active processing of new information. The clinical implication is that the notion of a fixed capacity (i.e., memory or concepts) is invalid. Accordingly, fixed or a priori tests with their attendant norms merely impose tasks on individuals to presumably assess available skills but they ignore performance in actual social commerce as prima facie evidence of what an individual can do.

Bootstrapping (semantic, syntactic, prosodic, pragmatic) is the perspective that the acquisition of various grammatical and pragmatic systems do not occur in isolation but rather in the context of each other in actual social commerce. The clinical implication is that it is desirable for both assessment and intervention to deal with various aspects of language in the context of other aspects in actual social commerce.

Shared meaning is the perspective that it is not only what is said but shared knowledge of an event that provides both implicit and explicit understandings of a message. Thus, shared meaning of an event constitutes a social-cultural arena for learning and using language. This is the neo-Vygotskian message (Rogoff, 1990; Wertsch, 1991). Valid assessment and intervention approaches should be oriented on actual social commerce because that is the arena of shared meaning.

Speech act theory posits that the purpose of communication is the recognition of communicative intent. The clinical implication is that both assessment and intervention should be about communicative intent in actual social commerce.

Although there is no formal theory of cohesion, there are many discussions in the cognitive socialization literature concerning how the grammatical and pragmatic systems function in a cohesive manner, thereby ridding messages of excess baggage and making communication effective. Evidently, once a system attains some level of cohesiveness it is capable of extending itself and becoming increasingly adept. Presumably, spontaneous metalinguistic and metacognitive activities provide opportunities for individuals to prune systems toward achieving increased cohesiveness.

A situated mind is the product of biological, cognitive, linguistic, emotional, social, and cultural influences (K. Nelson, 1996). From event knowledge, an individual learns about the canonical nature of social-cultural worlds. The canonical nature is that which typically happens; it is variations from canonical awareness whereby individuals become progressively more competent in acquiring a situated mind. With the onset of language, major thrusts forward occur; thus, language provides a mediating function in acquiring the situated mind toward obtaining narrative and a theoretical perspective. The intervention implication is that it is necessary to ascertain where an individual is in moving from event representation to mimesis to narrative to theory in acquiring cognitive capacities (K. Nelson, 1996). Furthermore, these issues are intentional and contextual in nature so it behooves clinicians to predicate intervention on the intentional and contextual principles of experiential cognition.

Informativeness addresses the relations between implicit and explicit information for the purpose of making communicative intent recognizable (Greenfield, 1980). Furthermore, such information may be manifest in various ways within the code matrix and it is negotiable in playing the communication game (Muma, 1975a). The clinical implication is that a message in a code matrix must be considered in relation to what is known in order to recognize communicative intent. Furthermore, the negotiable nature of communication means that the participants are actively involved in making communicative intent recognizable. Needless to say, intervention should be oriented on communicative intent. Table 8.2 shows these perspectives.

TABLE 8.2
Theoretical Perspectives and Their Clinical Implications

Theoretical Perspectives	Clinical Implications
Experiential realism	Experiential
Representational redescription	Active learning
Bootstrapping	Contextual learning
Shared meaning	Social learning
Speech acts	Recognize intent
Cohesion	Extending itself, pruning
Situated mind	Intent and context
Informativeness	Intent and negotiation

These compatible philosophical views and theoretical perspectives provide ample reason—rationale—for conceptualizing, implementing, evaluating, and revising language intervention in particular ways. It is when incompatible views and perspectives become mixed that discipline becomes trounced. "Mixed descriptions . . . are accepted uncomfortably and under what could be described as empirical and theoretical duress" (Maratsos, 1989, p. 110). A general intervention principle should be to begin with what the client can do and expand or replace those skills with skills that are warranted in accordance with the language acquisition literature, especially concerning acquisition sequences, alternative learning strategies, and active loci of learning. This principle is appropriate not only because it is oriented within available repertoires but also because it offers a motivational inducement for relative success and for extension or exploration thereafter.

A second basic intervention principle should be sheer talking time. Under the premise that an individual is an active language learner, the more he or she talks in actual social commerce the greater the opportunities for active learning (Bruner, 1981; Hoff-Ginsberg, 1987; K. Nelson, 1985, 1986; Sachs, 1983). Thus, it behooves clinicians to be sure that clients have plenty of talking in actual social commerce rather than in contrived tasks where clinicians control what, when, where, and how talking occurs.

A third basic intervention principle is communicative payoff (Muma, 1981c). When an individual strives to communicate, by whatever means possible, it behooves others to pay off a communicative attempt by making responses that strive to be most appropriate in a particular circumstance. The sheer effort to respond appropriately to a communicative attempt pays off the communicative attempt, even if the response is an errant but honest attempt to respond appropriately.

What is strikingly important about communicative payoff is that individuals typically do two things, neither of which are adequately accounted for by reinforcement theory. First, individuals tend to talk more when they receive communicative payoff. Increased talking might be construed as the result of reinforcement but reinforcement theory contends that when something is positively reinforced it will increase in frequency. Yet, individuals typically do not increase the particular utterances that were paid off; if they did then reinforcement would provide a likely account. Rather, individuals maintain their topics and continue into new topics, which is beyond the purview of reinforcement theory. Second, individuals are likely to try new things. Thus, when a communicative attempt works as intended, there is a natural tendency to try other new things. Certainly, reinforcement theory is incapable of accounting for new things.

A fourth basic intervention principle is object-based activities. Much knowledge is not only initially based on procedural knowledge issuing from person-based and object-based activities in scripts and formats of daily routines but such learning continues throughout life. Mandler (1983) commented, "The ways in which knowledge is acquired remain functionally invariant throughout life" (p. 476).

SUBSTANTIVE BASE

The following issues from the cognitive socialization literature constitute a substantive base for clinical intervention:

1. Language acquisition is "a process of cognitive socialization" (Brown, 1956, p. 247).

2. A process, phase, or systems approach is more appropriate than a products approach (Karmiloff-Smith, 1992).

3. Language learning is non-modality-specific (not the traditional notions of expressive or receptive; oral or visual) but what transpires from a cognitive-social base, notably: inference, categorization, problem solving, and intent (Clark & Clark, 1977; Karmiloff-Smith, 1992; Sperber & Wilson, 1986).

4. Internal context (possible worlds, situated mind) and external context (events) are essential aspects of coding a message of best fit (Grice, 1975; Sperber & Wilson, 1986).

5. Contextual learning (intentional, referential, relational, social, cultural), in contrast to component learning, is characteristic of language acquisition (Bruner, 1981, 1986; K. Nelson, 1985, 1986).

6. A pragmatic format provides a functional context for learning semantic, syntactic, and phonological aspects of language (Bruner, 1981; K. Nelson, 1985).

7. Language functions have priority over form (Bates & MacWhinney, 1979; Bruner, 1981, 1986; Grice, 1975; Ninio & Snow, 1988; Sperber & Wilson, 1986).

8. The essential communicative function of language is the recognition of communicative intent (Grice, 1975; Sperber & Wilson, 1986).

9. The essential cognitive functions of language are representation (Karmiloff-Smith, 1992; Mandler, 1979, 1983) and mediation (K. Nelson, 1996; Rogoff, 1990; Wertsch, 1991), culminating in possible worlds or situated minds.

10. Language acquisition is an active process. Therefore, exploitation and facilitation of active learning is appropriate (Muma, 1978b, 1983b, 1986a, 1991), in contrast to teaching and instruction.

11. The learning process is essentially the province of the learner; that is, content, sequence, pacing, and intent (Muma, 1978b).

12. The two main principles of exploitation and facilitation are expansion and replacement (Bates, 1979).

13. The substantive domains for exploitation and facilitation include estimated repertoires, progress in acquisition sequences, alternative acquisition strategies, and active loci of learning (Muma, 1978b, 1983b, 1986a).

14. The three major intervention agents are clinician parallel talk, parent participation, and peer modeling (Muma, 1983b).

15. Both cognitive and language acquisition occur in a social nexus (Bruner, 1981; Mandler, 1979; K. Nelson, 1985, 1986, 1996; Rogoff, 1990; Wertsch, 1991).

16. Metacognitive and metalinguistic activities offer powerful ways of extending learning (Karmiloff-Smith, 1992; Kretchmer, 1984; Muma, 1971a, 1978b, 1983b, 1986a; vanKleek, 1984).

These issues were discussed in previous chapters. This chapter addresses basic intervention issues derived in large measure from the basic substantive issues in the cognitive socialization literature.

INSTRUCTION OR FACILITATION

A fundamental distinction should be made between instruction or teaching approaches and facilitation approaches. This distinction was made previously (Craig, 1983; Muma, 1978b, 1983b, 1986a, 1987a). The instructional or teaching model has the implicit assumption that a teacher is presumably in control of the learning process. It is a clinician-oriented approach (Muma, 1978b, 1983b, 1986a). Fey (1986) and Paul (1995) called such orientations trainer-oriented and child-directed approaches, respectively. Issues of content (what will be learned), sequencing (the order of acquisition), pacing (rate of learning), and reinforcement are presumably in a teacher's control.

The behavioristic perspective reflects this kind of approach. Referring to behavioristic approaches, Paul (1995) commented:

> Clinician-directed (CD) approaches attempt to make the relevant linguistic stimuli highly salient, to reduce or eliminate irrelevant stimuli, to provide clear reinforcement to increase the frequency of desired language behaviors, and to control the clinical environment so that intervention is optimally efficient in changing language behavior. CD approaches tend to be less naturalistic than other approaches. (p. 65)

Perhaps we should add that such intervention approaches are typically prepackaged; thus, they are inherently a priori in nature.

Paul's comment sounds like motherhood and apple pie because it contains desirable plaudits. The implication is that these approaches are effective in some way; that is, increased use of targeted language structures is regarded as evidence of language acquisition in language intervention.

However, these intervention approaches are of dubious value—corrosive dogma—when substantive issues in the cognitive socialization literature are raised. First, notice that the notions of relevance and salience are presumably discretionary notions for the trainer or teacher. Yet, the cognitive socialization literature holds that these are psychological rather than pedagogical notions. Bruner (1981) showed that because these are psychological issues, they are in the province of the learner, and it is necessary to be tuned to what the learner can do in actual social commerce (K. Nelson, 1985, 1986, 1996) in order to deal with relevance and salience. Notice that Paul, Fey, and others have passed over this issue; this is the signature of behaviorism.

Second, the notion of reducing or eliminating irrelevant stimuli is also strangely vested in the trainer when it should be a crucial issue of the language learning context in actual social commerce (Constable, 1986; K. Nelson, 1985, 1986). Third, the notion of providing clear reinforcement to increase the frequency of desired language behaviors carries the full weight of the behavioristic perspective in the face of a tremendous cognitive socialization literature that indicates that:

1. Reinforcement has been replaced by communicative intent as a more viable account of language acquisition.
2. Frequency as a valid notion of acquisition is questionable.
3. Corrosive dogma is evident in the clinical fields by virtue of its reliance on such behavioristic perspectives to deal with language acquisition.

Fourth, to control the clinical environment for optimal efficiency in changing language behavior effectively strips away major issues of construct validity, specifically intent and context. It carries the banner of glibness by implicating hype and missing crucial aspects of a client's learning province.

Fifth, to merely place CD approaches on a presumed continuum of naturalness, following Fey (1986) is to effectively dodge the substantive issues of cognitive socialization beginning with pertinent philosophical views and theoretical perspectives that comprise the substantive rationale for doing intervention particular ways in appreciating what an individual can do—appropriateness. Such stances provide solid evidence of substantive disconnections with the cognitive socialization literature.

In contrast, facilitation approaches are based on the assumption that the learning process is an ongoing active dynamic process in actual social commerce (K. E. Nelson, 1989, 1991; Muma, 1978b, 1983b, 1986a, 1991). The role of a clinician is to facilitate what an individual is naturally striving to learn. Thus, learning is essentially the province of the learner (Muma, 1978b). Issues of content, sequencing, pacing, and intent are essentially the province of the learner. The role of the clinician is to ascertain an individual's repertoire of skills and expand or replace (Bates, 1979) these skills with other skills in accordance with acquisition sequences in the available cognitive socialization literature, available strategies of learning, and active loci of learning. This kind of approach is inherently a posteriori in nature.

Lahey (1988) distinguished between teaching and facilitation in the following way:

> If language learning is an induction, how can it be taught? One cannot, in fact, teach a child early language skills, if teaching means imparting information or knowledge. . . . The rules of language must be induced by the learner from tangible experiences with objects and events, linguistic forms, and interpersonal interactions.
>
> The person who intervenes in a child's life to aid in the language-learning process is not, then, a teacher in the traditional sense . . . but, instead, one who manipulates these tangible aspects of a child's environment in a way that facilitates the formation of these inductions. (p. 378)

To be sure that behaviorists do not jump in to claim manipulation of tangible aspects of a child's environment as a behavioral enterprise, it should be recognized that Lahey's perspective extends crucially to communicative intent with what that entails.

Thus, the behavioristic notion of facilitation (Costello, 1983; Gottlieb, 1976; Olswang & Bain, 1991; Paul, 1995) differs significantly from the cognitive socialization notion of facilitation (Muma, 1978b, 1983b, 1986a). Furthermore, Fey (1986) took a surprisingly expansive view of facilitation in that trainer-oriented, child-oriented, and hybrid intervention approaches were all regarded as facilitating. By doing so, the distinction between teaching and facilitation becomes lost—a behavioristic plight. Notice that the basic substantive issues of facilitation from the perspective of cognitive socialization—namely communicative intent, context, repertoire, progress in acquisition sequences, alternative learning strategies, and active loci of learning—are passed over or missed in both the Fey (1986) and Paul (1995) perspectives.

Drawing on competition theory, MacWhinney (1989) used *teachability* and *facilitation* interchangeably. Yet the ways that he discussed teaching potentials were somewhat compatible with the facilitation perspective; however, they could be construed as useful for behavioristic procedures:

> If language learning can be facilitated by controlling the child's diet of linguistic forms, then we can say that language is "teachable." . . . Language is indeed

teachable, as long as the teacher understands the principles of competition and the need to reinforce correct structures. (p. 63)

The clearer the input, the clearer the learning. . . . The basic message of the Competition Model to the language teacher and clinician is that language learning is based on a very richly buffered system. The system provides the child with many skills for language learning without making learning dependent on any one skill. The only principle that must be intact is the principle of competition. . . . The absence of any particular support for language learning is not critical, since the other capacities can then move in to keep the system buffered and on track. (pp. 98–99).

This pedagogical stance relies on controlled linguistic forms, principles of competition, reinforcement of correct forms, clear input, and a dynamic buffer system that may overcome deficiencies. Such notions are inviting to behaviorists simply because they fit their conceptual scheme.

However, if one is willing to appreciate the fact that the competition theory is based on the functionalistic perspective of form–function relations, then these suggestions have quite a different interpretation. Functionally speaking, the notion of controlled linguistic forms takes on the significance of the entire communicative context (K. Nelson, 1985, 1986, 1996) with the province of control in the learner rather than the teacher or clinician. Then, the other notions fall in line with reinforcement becoming replaced by intention in actual social commerce. One especially troubling notion for interpreting these issues within a functionalistic view is that "the only principle that must be intact is the principle of competition" (MacWhinney, 1989, p. 99). It could be argued from a functionalistic perspective that other principles are at least as important (i.e., intent, context, coherence).

EXPANSION AND REPLACEMENT

Bates (1979) showed that the two general principles of language acquisition are expansion and replacement. Expansion may be construed in four ways: expansion of available lexical repertoire, expansion of script repertoires, expansion of grammatical and pragmatic repertoires, and expansion of a learning strategy such that it extends to other strategies. Expansion of available lexical repertoire may be evidenced in naming or indicatives by virtue of learning new words and by virtue of extending the validity of available words. For example, a child may learn that a ball could be referred to in different ways (i.e., "ball," "it," "the big ball," "my ball," "that ball," etc.). This kind of expanded repertoire provides knowledge of one referent–many words and eventually the other side of the principle becomes realized, namely one word–many referents. Extended validity of words means that as a child discerns that the notion of "ball" extends to a variety of balls, the child comes to have prototypic knowledge (Rosch & Mervis, 1975) rather than an idiosyncratic knowledge of "ball" and such knowledge carries social and cultural meanings (K. Nelson, 1985) and thereby increased validity. The literature over the past decade has shown that such knowledge issues form varied routines in which initial words become decomposed (K. Nelson, 1985).

Expansion of available script repertoires (Constable, 1986; K. Nelson, 1981b, 1985, 1986, 1996) constitutes a means of early language acquisition. It is well known that early in language acquisition, children have social-cultural (including communication) scripts, routines, or formats that are regularly used for a purpose or intent. The importance of these scripts is that they provide the learner with event representations that comprise the corner-stones of early cognition. Scripts eventually vary (expand) in the realization of communicative intent (K. Nelson, 1985, 1986) thereby providing a means for establishing semantic knowledge and subsequently narrative. Strangely, the clinical fields have picked up on the repetitiousness of scripts as their presumed value (Duchan, 1991; Duchan, Hewitt, & Sonnenmeier, 1994). However, K. Nelson (1985, 1986) was explicit that the potency of scripts resulted not so much from their repetitiousness but their eventual variations in the realization of communicative intent.

Expansion of available grammatical and pragmatic repertoires may take place also. For example, a child may learn that a noun phrase may be as simple as "Mommy." Subsequently, knowledge of noun phrases expands to various kinds of phrase structure, derived nominals, and modified nominals. Phrase structure expansions may include: "the dog" (definite article/animate noun), "a dog" (indefinite article/animate noun), "my dog" (possessive/animate noun), "that dog" (demonstrative/animate noun), and "two dogs" (number/animate noun). Derived nominal expansions (Lees, 1965) may include: "fishing" (Ving nominal), "to fish" (toV nominal), "for him to fish" (for/to nominal), and "that he fishes" (factive nominal). Modified nominals include: "the dog that is swimming" (relative clause), "the dog in the car" (relative clause deletion), "the big dog" (adjectival), and "the dog and cat" (conjoined). Incidentally, the DSS (Lee et al., 1975) not only missed this basic arena but misconstrued some derived nominals as secondary verbs, which is very peculiar. Thus, the notion of expansion pertains to an individual's repertoire of skills for various grammatical and pragmatic systems (subject nominal system, object nominal system, auxiliary system, verbal system, adjectival system, pronominal system, anaphora, etc.).

Expansion of a learning strategy is evidenced when an individual achieves a sufficient command of a particular learning strategy so that he or she will venture into an alternative strategy. For example, Dore (1974) indicated that some learners are code learners, whereas others are message learners. As a child attains increased command over one strategy such as code learning, it is likely that he or she will venture into another related strategy such as message learning simply because the ultimate command of language entails both. Similarly, K. Nelson (1973b) showed that some children are referential learners (one word, many referents; one referent, many words), whereas other children are expressive learners (new forms come in with old functions; new functions come in with old forms). It is patently clear that as these children attain some measure of command for a particular strategy they switch to the other related strategy to achieve full command of language. Bloom (1978) showed that pronominal learners eventually entered the domain of basic determiner–noun phrase structure.

Another perspective concerning grammatical expansion is the notion of vertical as contrasted to horizontal learning of the transitive system. Some children may strive to learn the transitive system by expanding the variety of transitive verbs with a relatively limited set of object nominals (vertical correlates), whereas other children may strive to learn this system with a relatively limited set of transitive verbs but an expanding variety of object nominals (horizontal correlates). This perspective was suggested by Maratsos (1982) and elaborated by Bates and MacWhinney (1987).

Table 8.3 shows the various ways that expansion of repertoire may be achieved. What is important about this intervention perspective is that it is outside of the purview of behaviorism and normative testing.

The replacement principle is that previous skills subsequently become replaced by new skills in accordance with acquisition sequences. Bates (1979) and Ninio and Bruner (1978) substantiated this principle. The classic example of replacement is that words replace performatives for indexing referents. For example, preverbal behaviors (performatives) that function as words include the communicative point, referential displays, and noises that signify a referent ("moo" for cow, "barking" for dog, "meow" for cat, etc.). As children learn words (conventional and even nonconventional), such performatives become replaced by words. Indeed, as children learn to predicate, such constructions replace indicatives as increased explicitness becomes realized. Other kinds of replacements include modified construc-

TABLE 8.3
Different Kinds of Expansions

Lexical expansion
  (a) New words
  (b) Increased validity
Grammatical and pragmatic expansion
  (a) Expansion of available script repertoires
  (b) Expanded repertoires within systems
  (c) Expanded strategies and new strategies
  (d) Vertical and horizontal learning

---

tions replace unmodified constructions, pronominal forms replace more fully explicit forms, and shortened forms (ellipsis, noun phrase deletion, noun deletion) replace longer forms. Furthermore, conventional terms replace nonconventional terms. These kinds of replacements are summarized in Table 8.4.

Expansion and replacement comprise different kinds of intervention goals than the traditional quantitative notions such as 80% to 100% performance rates (Fey, 1986; Paul, 1995) or the performance criteria (Fey, 1986). Regarding the latter, although it is acknowledged that they were derived to some extent from the suggestions by Lee and coworkers, where is the rationale and empirical evidence that warrant these criteria? They are merely capricious notions, and they are coupled with a subtle conceptual shift from quantitative (frequency, percentage) to presumed productivity and mastery of grammatical skills (Fey, 1986).

Moreover, it should be stressed that individuals usually evidence improvement in several areas at the same time. That is, it is usual for an individual to evidence new skills in phonology, syntax, and pragmatics together and within each domain several loci of learning are frequently evidenced. Again, the behaviorists often contend that only one or two new dimensions are recommended because the learner presumably cannot handle more. This is merely a trumped up argument to align with the controlled perspective of behaviorism. For example, Paul (1995) commented, "*New forms express old functions: New functions are expressed by old forms.* This dictum . . . by Slobin (1973), tells us that when choosing targets for intervention, we must be careful to require the child to do only one new thing at a time" (p. 64). Paul is wrong. This is not a dictum—an authoritarian edict or dogmatic principle. Rather, it is a principle of language acquisition deduced by Werner and Kaplan (1963) and substantiated by Slobin (1970). Furthermore, this principle does not address the notion that language learning is confined to a single locus at a time. If anything, this principle implicates language learning with several loci at a time. That is, "new forms express old functions" is an expression of plural relations between forms and func-

TABLE 8.4
Different Kinds of Replacements

Lexical replacement
    (a) Words replace performatives.
    (b) Conventional words replace nonconventional words.
Grammatical and pragmatic replacement
    (a) Simple constructions replace indicatives.
    (b) Modified constructions replace simple constructions.
    (c) Pronominal forms replace explicit forms.
    (d) Shortened forms replace longer forms.
    (e) Conventional terms replace nonconventional terms.

tions. To controvert this principle to singular under the admonishment "We must be careful to require the child to do only one new thing at a time" comes off as a behavioral dictum inappropriately applied to a principle of cognitive socialization.

Rather, this principle is useful for language intervention. However, it is necessary to take a different interpretation that is more compatible with the cognitive socialization literature. Because new forms come in with old functions, it would be desirable to expand the use of old functions by acquiring new forms. For example, a child who may be able to express the communicative function of instrumental in limited ways would evidence acquisition by expressing this function, and other available functions, with a variety of new forms. Conversely, a child who may express particular forms in limited ways would evidence acquisition by expressing these forms, and other pending forms, with a variety of new functions. For example, "mommy" may initially function to express instrumental and regulatory functions but subsequently it could be used to express interactional, heuristic, imaginative, and informational functions. Thus, this principle has a twofold implication for the intervention principle of expansion.

INPUT STATUS

Developments in cognitive socialization have raised some fundamental issues concerning what is potentially potent input for language learning. The traditional view was that simple correct forms are needed for learning. However, the literature (Bowerman, 1987; Macken, 1987; Wexler & Culicover, 1980) has raised the prospect that positive, negative, and ambiguous exemplars may each play significant but different roles in language acquisition. Apparently, positive exemplars provide instances for rule generation, negative exemplars provide instances for rule delimitation, and ambiguous exemplars provide instances for optionally entering the learning arena to focus on those loci that are ripe for learning. Thus, virtually any utterance in social commerce has the potential, at least, of offering some prospect for learning some aspect of language.

THE THREE Ps

I have previously (Muma, 1978b, 1983b, 1986a, 1987a) indicated that the three Ps of language intervention are parallel talk, peer modeling, and parent participation. Because these are well known, the following extends the previous discussions in view of developments in the contemporary cognitive socialization literature.

Parallel Talk Strategy

When I (Muma, 1978b) first discussed the parallel talk strategy, four issues that warrant its use were given:

1. Within an individual's available repertoire of skills.
2. Deals with actual references and events.
3. Payoff of communicative intent.
4. Alternatives in form–function relations.

With the developments in the cognitive socialization literature since, it is desirable to maintain and expand these issues, especially in light of Bruner's (1975a, 1975b, 1978, 1981, 1983, 1986) notions of tuning, assistance, and child–parent partnership in language acquisition; Greenfield and Smith's (1976) notions of two-person sentences and negotiated partnership in language acquisition; and K. Nelson's (1985, 1986, 1996) notions of shared meaning of events and the situated mind. Furthermore, Gopnik (1981) indicated that parents are active participants in language acquisition coupled with cognitive development that affords readiness to avail an individual of opportunities to learn:

> The adult language provides a series of signposts that help the child find his way around uncharted cognitive territory. However, the child can only make use of the signposts that he is able to comprehend. As the child covers more cognitive ground, he can take advantage of new linguistic signposts. (p. 104)

Indeed, Hagstrom (1994) also appreciated the role of parents in language intervention.

Clinicians can provide useful signposts, or what Gleitman (1994) called the *attentional conspiracy*, by tailoring parallel talk to the specific needs and readiness capabilities of their clients. It is likely that the reason that many individuals may have difficulties with language is that they simply missed crucial opportunities to avail themselves of relevant information during a window of opportunity (Locke, 1994). If parallel talk is appropriately tuned (Bruner, 1981) to the needs of an individual, it may offer an opportunity to reopen or extend windows of opportunity.

A clinician needs an appreciation of what an individual can do (repertoire of skills), what progress an individual has made in acquisition sequences, which language learning strategies are available to an individual, and which loci of learning are active. These issues constitute, either singularly or in composite, the substantive base of the parallel talk strategy. Then, a clinician participates with a child, and probably a peer, in ongoing natural social commerce and the clinician is vigilant for relevant opportunities to parallel talk. Such opportunities may occur when the target child wants to talk or when a peer interacts with the target child. For example, when the target child says, "Him hit ball," the clinician may respond with "*He* hit ball." The locus of learning is intentionally stressed by the clinician. The contextual event that supports the utterance is maintained and the clinician's utterance is offered as a viable alternative to the child's intended utterance. Then the topic is continued to pay off the comunicative intent.

Providing utterances derived from the child's or a participating peer's utterances offer an individual opportunities to learn from within his or her own system or from a peer's system. Furthermore, such utterances have intentional, referential, and relational support and they are directly relevant to ongoing events (K. Nelson, 1985, 1986). Stress is used to highlight selected aspects of utterances that are presumably relevant to what an individual is striving to learn—loci of learning. Such loci are within a learner's representational and grammatical capabilities or are becoming so.

What is crucial is not the amount of input but its relevance to an individual's available repertoire: "Processing advantages for accented words depend on the prior development of representations of sentence semantic structure, including the concepts of focus" (Cutler & Swinney, 1987, p. 145). Indeed, relatively little input is needed if it is relevant to active loci of learning (Lightfoot, 1989; Morgan, 1989).

It is not unusual for children to adopt a new utterance immediately; and it is not unusual for children to say nothing. What is interesting about such responsiveness is that over many occasions with a variety of instances of parallel talking in varied contexts, the impact is often latent with instances culminating or stacking up to be released in a subsequent spurt of learning.

For example, many years ago we were doing the parallel talk strategy with a school-aged boy who evidenced difficulties with the pronominal system. He expressed subjects of sentences in the objective form (e.g., "Him go") and he evidenced difficulties with anaphoric loading and competing anaphoric reference. We had been carrying out the parallel talk strategy and communicative payoff strategy with relatively little immediate return for the effort over approximately a month. Then, when he and his mother came in for an intervention session, she was very excited: "You won't believe what he did last night. He was playing in our closet sorting shoes and began using pronouns, like 'Daddy's shoe—his shoe. Daddy go to work. He go to work. Mommy's shoe—her shoe, their shoes. . . . She play with baby. She play with me.' " This child seemed to be dormant, then a spurt of learning took place with remarkable speed and complexity. From then on, he had virtually no difficulty with the pronominal system. We have seen many other children go through other spurts of learning presumably induced by parallel talk focused on relevant aspects of utterances.

It is necessary for individuals to be selectively focused, otherwise grammatical and pragmatic systems do not stand a chance of being sorted out.

Individuals with learning disabilities or language impairment may not be focused on relevant information in relevant contexts.

> The trouble is that an observer who notices *everything* can learn *nothing*. . . . Indeed, not only learnability theorists but all syntacticians in the generative tradition appeal to the desirability of narrowing the hypothesis space lest the child be so overwhelmed with representational options and data-manipulative capacity as to be lost in thought forever. (Gleitman, 1994, p. 181)

Just as parents may be in partnership (Bruner, 1981; Gleitman, 1994; Greenfield & Smith, 1976) with their child in assisting language acquisition in a selective and tuned-in manner, clinicians may assume a similar role. Clinicians have two advantages that parents of language-impaired children probably do not have. First, sufficiently trained clinicians are more likely to be appropriately tuned to what an individual can do. That is, clinicians have been trained to estimate repertoires of verbal skills, ascertain progress in acquisition sequences, identify available acquisition strategies, identify active loci of learning, and employ appropriate attribution criteria. A parent may intuitively be aware of some of these issues, but a solidly trained competent clinician is ready, poised, and vigilant for opportunities to utilize these skills. Second, a clinician's expertise, by virtue of training and experience, provides a frame of reference for appreciating even subtle instances of behavior that may be overlooked by parents who may be insufficiently tuned to their child's skills or who lack a larger base of comparison to normal and clinical individuals. In short, clinicians have the available literature and experience that provide a formidable advantage over parents who may be insufficiently tuned to what their children can do.

The parent–child partnership in a well-functioning learning environment is one of active participation in which both negotiate messages in the code matrix with the central purpose of realizing communicative intent. Bruner (1981) and Gleitman (1994) indicate that both participants are in cahoots "about how the attentional conspiracy is to be set up by the mother and child" (Gleitman, 1994, p. 183). Such endeavors constitute various bootstrapping opportunities; that is, semantic (Pinker, 1984), syntactic (Gleitman, 1994), prosodic (Bedore & Leonard, 1995), and pragmatic (Bruner, 1981).

What is said by both participants is judiciously functional for social commerce in a particular circumstance. The parent is more adept, to be sure, but both are striving to communicate by whatever means possible. Indeed, the early code matrix is confined to expression (Bloom & Beckwith, 1989) with conventional codification to come. Even so, the irreducible nucleus is communicative intent.

In addition to being oriented on communicative intent, parallel talk offers a solution, of sorts, to the Wittgenstein dilemma (Bruner, 1981). This dilemma is: How is an individual to know that an object name is not the name of an attribute but the name of an object? Either prospect offers viable options. However, early on, there seems to be a disposition or propensity for young children to attend to entities and therefore regard names as entity names (Lakoff, 1987; Muma, 1991). Subsequently, they attend to attributes. What is putatively attractive about the parallel talk strategy, whether used by parents or by clinicians, is that what is said has significance about what is going on in an event (K. Nelson, 1985, 1986, 1996; Rogoff, 1990). Therefore, the meaning of what is said may be deduced from event knowledge (K. Nelson, 1986) as well as relational knowledge. The relational meanings of words in relation to other words narrows down the prospects of intended meanings. Thus, there is a double whammy in parallel talk because the meaning of utterances adheres in event knowledge and knowledge of words in relational context with each other.

After about 30 years of direct clinical practice, I have become increasingly impressed with the potencies of the parallel talk and the communicative payoff strategies. Released of the shackles of the behavioristic model in which trials to criterion are applied in a priori intervention procedures, the parallel talk and communicative payoff strategies are oriented on actual social commerce with the centrality of communicative intent, and the essence of the learning process is the province of the learner. Therefore generalization is not a problem.

We have used the parallel talk strategy successfully over many years with many clients ranging from very young to elderly and across different aspects of language (i.e., semantic, lexical, syntactic, prosodic, phonological, and pragmatic domains). The keys to its potency is neither age nor particular a priori domain. Its potency is independent of the rather capricious notions of modality cuing and frequency of use. Rather, its potency is its relevance to an individual's available repertoire, progress in acquisition sequences, available learning strategies, active loci of learning, and communicative intent in actual social commerce. Furthermore, the cognitive socialization literature provides a rationale for conceptualizing, implementing, and evaluating these intervention strategies by virtue of the contemporary philosophical views and theoretical perspectives.

Interestingly, Fey (1986) apparently picked up on the notion of the parallel talk strategy with what he called *focused stimulation*. His discussion of focused stimulation reflects the parallel talk strategy from a behaviorist perspective, but there are four fundamental differences. First and most importantly, the central issue for parallel talking, as in speech act theory—indeed communication—is exploitation of intentionality (Muma, 1978b). Second, rather than the behavioristic notion of stimulation, the underlying premise of parallel talking is that a child is an active learner. Therefore, it is incumbent on clinicians to facilitate active learning, and the most opportune way of facilitating active learning is the use of parallel talking when an individual wants to participate in actual social commerce. Third, parallel talking relies on an adequate appreciation of what an individual can do (repertoire) and how this capacity relates to progress in acquisition sequences, available strategies of learning, and active loci of learning. Fourth, the focused stimulation model utilized an a priori cyclical goal attack strategy, whereas the parallel talk strategy recognizes that the learning process is essential to the province of learning. This perspective is in keeping with the bootstrapping theory (Gleitman, 1994). These are major issues that Fey (1986) missed or glossed over in his reference to naturalness or more recently intrusiveness (Fey, Catts, & Larrivee, 1995).

Another important benefit from parallel talk that we have become increasingly aware of over the past two decades is an increase in the occurrence of self-corrections. It is fairly common for individuals to increase the amount of self-corrections subsequent to the use of the parallel talk strategy. Self-corrections are very important because they contain active loci of learning and because they provide rather direct evidence of what an individual can do. We have told our clinicians that when self-corrections, spontaneous imitations, spontaneous rehearsals or celebrations of learning, or buildups occur, they take precedence over any other goal or planned activity because they are so important to acquisition. Vigilant clinicians should pick up on such behaviors and exploit them (Muma, 1978b). Furthermore, communicative payoff should have an overriding priority for appropriate intervention.

The most common blunders that clinicians make in parallel talking are that they talk too much or they are insufficiently tuned to what a child can do. Needless to say, parallel talk facilitates language acquisition when a clinician or parent utilizes knowledge of a child's repertoire of skills, progress in acquisition sequences, available acquisition strategies, and evidence of active loci of learning. Parallel talk should be consistent with these issues and relevant to ongoing social commerce in order to provide usable input.

Peer Modeling

The theory of expression (Bloom & Beckwith, 1986, 1989) not only picked up this baton but did so by addressing social dynamics. It is abundantly clear in the cognitive socialization literature that both cognition and language acquisition are social enterprises: "Cognitive growth occurs mainly in a social nexus" (Mandler, 1979, p. 375). "Children's cognitive development is an apprenticeship—it occurs through guided participation in social activity with companions who support and stretch children's understanding of and skill in using the tools of culture" (Rogoff, 1990, p. vii). Bruner (1981) discussed the "social context of language acquisition" (p. 155). K. Nelson (1979, 1981b, 1985, 1986, 1996) provided elegant accounts of language acquisition in a social nexus. Others have also shown the importance of peer or social interaction for learning (Brenner & Mueller, 1982; Chalkley, 1982; Eckerman & Whatley, 1977; Hagstrom, 1994; Mandler, 1983; Robertson & Weismer, 1997; Rogoff, 1980; Wertsch, 1991).

Peer interaction and modeling are social arenas with great potential for facilitating language acquisition. There is a considerable literature on peer modeling. In a word, peers offer potent influences for learning in general and language learning in particular. Moreover, this arena is unique in comparison to parent–child or adult–child interactions. This uniqueness may be the key to its potency.

The literature on peer modeling has been summarized in several places (Bandura,1986; Berger, 1977; Field, 1981; Hartup, 1978; Schunk, 1987): "Modelling is a form of *social comparison* (Berger, 1977)" (Schunk, 1987, p. 149). Peer modeling is the act of comparing a peer to one's self and acting on that comparison. Thus, peer modeling is an active or volitional endeavor.

Peer modelling is predicated on perceived similarities between the observer and the peer. The observer apparently takes the attitude that if someone similar to him or her can do something it is reasonable to expect that the observer can do it also. Two key notions are entailed in this perspective:

1. Perceived similarities between the observer and peer.
2. The observed feat must be deemed worth doing or achieving.

Perceived similarity may be as simple as demographic similarities such as age, gender, physical characteristics, status, and so on. However, such issues easily slip into the background when individuals focus on perceived functional attributes for achievement.

Perceived similarity raises the spector of efficacy. That is, when an observer sees a peer accomplish something that is worth accomplishing, the observer considers the feat within his or her realm of achievement also. Thus, the achievement becomes deemed achievable by the observer. What had previously been considered unattainable may become possible, and even likely, in the context of peer modeling. Rogoff (1990) referred to appropriation as the mechanism whereby an individual strives to emulation a behavior or achievement of a peer.

Berman (1981) underscored the importance of peer modeling when she said that, "Preschool acquisition is crucially affected by peer input" (p. 181). Apparently, it is easier for children to learn from an available peer model than from an instructional model not just because language is used in a spontaneous natural way with intent and available reference supporting the utterances, but also because the repertoire of skills and the contexts of their application more closely approximate what peers can do than what competent adults can do. Thus, peers have privileged opportunities to facilitate language acquisition in ways that are likely to be qualitatively different from adult competent speakers.

Only peers have the cognitive social perspectives of their peers. It is precisely these perspectives on which much cognitive, social, and language learning transpires. Rogoff (1990) put it this way:

> Shared problem solving, in which children can participate in collaborative thinking processes, appears central to the utility of social interaction for children's development. Peers may be less skilled partners than adults in some activities, but may offer unique possibilities for discussion and collaboration when they consider each other's perspective in a balanced fashion. Peers also serve as highly available and active companions, providing each other with motivation, imagination, and opportunities for creative elaboration of the activities of their community. (p. ix)

As adults, we are merely onlookers and strive to enter this arena with the best intentions but, alas, we may be feeble in doing so. The a priori approaches not only miss the mark, but they do so in a violent way by the sheer act of imposing systems on individuals.

In language intervention, it is desirable to have children in small groups. Because heterogeneity is characteristic of clinical populations, varied skills available in the clinic can be turned into assets with which the children could facilitate each other. For example, a child having difficulties with the pronominal system may have good phonology and therefore could be a peer model for another child with phonological difficulties. A second child may have a good pronominal system; thus, the second child may be a good peer model for the first. In this way, reciprocal peer modeling can be used effectively in language intervention. As these children conduct social commerce in spontaneous play, a clinician can selectively attend to and highlight available phonological skills for one child and pronominal skills for the other.

The parallel talk strategy (Muma, 1978b) not only focuses on the intentional behaviors of a particular child but also capitalizes on the utterances and activities of peer models. Thus, as Bruner (1981), K. Nelson (1985), and others have indicated, language learning is inherently intentional and contextual in a social nexus.

Peer modeling offers an advantage from the perspective of acquisition sequences, phases, and stages of learning. Central to the notion of stages of learning is the principle of a qualitative change from one stage to another (Gleitman, 1981; Gleitman & Wanner, 1982; Ingram, 1989a; Schlesinger, 1977). If this is so, a peer model may have a qualitatively different input into the learning process than an adult model. Thus, a child who is in a similar stage of learning, or recently achieved learning in a stage that another child is striving to learn, may offer qualitative learning opportunities that may not otherwise be available from adults.

We have used peer modeling and reciprocal modeling for many years with favorable results. Indeed, peer modeling has become so beneficial that, except for very unusual circumstances, I believe that it is foolhardy not to use peer modeling. Coupled with the parallel talk strategy and parent participation, peer modeling is a formidable approach to appropriate language intervention.

Unfortunately, the behavioristic perspective of modeling lacks the rich perspective and interpretive significance discussed already. Fey (1986) and Paul (1995) regard modeling as trainer oriented or child directed, respectively. From this perspective, modeling is viewed in the following way:

> Like drill, modeling uses a highly structured format, extrinsic reinforcement, and a formal interactive context. . . . All these variations I've discussed—drill, drill play, and modelling—share the tightly structured, formal, clinician-controlled features that characterize strict behaviorist approaches to intervention. (Paul, 1995, p. 67)

Needless to say, these behavioristic perspectives belie technicianship rather than clinicianship.

Also, it should be abundantly clear that the literature on peer modeling is oriented on qualitative issues such as identification and perceived task efficacy. Thus, it matters little how much time that peer models are in activities with language-impaired individuals; rather, it is what the individuals do with the time in the activities that counts. Weiss and Nakamura (1992) found that the amount of time that potential models had with language-impaired children varied; however, the crucial issues are what they did with their time in providing usable models and what the language-impaired children did to avail themselves of potentially useful learning opportunities.

Parent Participation

Parent participation is another crucial aspect of language intervention (Hagstrom, 1994). When I was in the public schools, I had nearly 100% regular participation of the parents. As the children took part, their parents were also active partners in the learning process. I had a three-stage model of parent participation geared toward having the parents become partners in socialization and experiential development: observers, activity makers, and active participants.

It is my observation after dealing with hundreds of clients over approximately 30 years, that a high percentage of them are on the periphery of social activities and experientially limited, especially in severe cases. Accordingly, I have been asking the mothers to play an active role in enlarging the social and experiential life of their children. Specifically, mothers are asked to write a log of their child's social and experiential activities over each week. From this information, we meet with each mother and plan new activities that will expand these arenas. The mothers have been enthusiastic about this kind of participation and they often report that their child gained as much or more from this aspect of intervention as compared to the therapy sessions. Given the literatures on cognitive, social, emotional, and language acquisition, especially from the Bruner, K. Nelson, and Vygotskian perspectives, it is only reasonable to incorporate social and experiential dimensions into intervention.

As observers, the parents were given the intervention goals and it was their responsibility to observe their child in accordance with these goals. Then, we discussed their child's participation in an activity according to these goals. Thus, parents obtained regular firsthand information about the nature of intervention. They saw good days and poor days. They also appreciated the overall goals and progress toward the goals. As they became good observers, they were asked to gather data both within the intervention sessions and at home under selected circumstances. They were asked to keep a log of their child's performance for the particular goals. Clinicians should be sure to check these logs on a regular basis, not only to appreciate changes in the child's behavior but also to affirm the parents' contribution to the intervention process. Many times parental notes evidenced changes before they were seen in the intervention sessions.

As activity makers, parents were asked to generate activities that were consistent with the goals. The clinician is thus freed from the tedious job of making activities. It is my experience that the parents enjoy contributing in this way. Eventually, parents became active participants in intervention. The parents actually carry out the activities and provide needed feedback in the form of the parallel talk strategy. Then a clinician's role becomes that of maintaining intervention integrity by keeping the goals as the foremost agenda. Furthermore, the clinician maintains vigilance for desired behavioral changes. In this process, the clinician, parents, and children become partners in conceptualizing, implementing, and evaluating appropriate intervention.

Parent participation has several important side effects. First, the children generally do well with their parents present. Indeed, they want to show their parents that they can do the activities. Second, the parents understand the learning process better when they are participating. Third, parent participation has a political aspect whereby the program becomes sold to the school or hospital administration. There is nothing more powerful in the schools than a daily parade of parents coming to participate in language intervention. Fourth, typically parents want to be partners in overcoming their child's problems. Yes, there are always some parents who shy away from participation, but that is usually easily overcome as they see other parents becoming involved.

It should be stressed that the kind of intervention that we are talking about is not a drill or simple naming of picture cards and other similar elicitation tasks. The kind of activities we have been doing for the past 30 years entails natural spontaneous interaction in social commerce, usually play. In this arena, parents understand the intervention goals and children eagerly look forward to the fun things we do.

TEN TECHNIQUES

I have discussed the 10 techniques of language intervention elsewhere (Muma, 1971a, 1978b, 1983b, 1986a). They are well known so there is not much point in an extended discussion of them here. I just have some brief comments. First, the 10 techniques are correction, expansion, expatiation (simple), expatiation (complex), alternatives, completion, replacement, alternative–replacement, revision, and combination. Second, these techniques issue from a variety of sources in the cognitive socialization literature. Third, the first five techniques are child initiated, whereas the last five are clinician initiated. Fourth, their full potency arises as a child explores and varies what he or she can do with these techniques. Fifth, rather than use a priori materials, it is more desirable to base these techniques on a child's own speech thereby providing some degree of assurance that what he or she does with them is relevant to what he or she can do. Sixth, Fey (1986), Fey and Leonard (1983), and Prutting and Kirchner (1983, 1987) indicated that the cognitive, linguistic, and pragmatic problems they identified were often manifest by limited lexical, grammatical, and pragmatic systems. These 10 techniques could be used to appropriately expand an individual's command of these systems. The 10 techniques are illustrated in the following.

Correction Model. A correction is given for syntactic or referential errors. Many syntactic corrections frequently result in a child avoiding speech, so syntactic corrections should be done sparingly. Referential corrections, on the other hand, are accepted better by children.

Syntactic error
Child: Hers hat.
Clinician: Not, hers hat. Her hat.

Referential error
Child: Hers hat.
Clinician: Not hers hat. *His* hat. He is a boy.

Expansion Model. The expansion model is evidenced when an adult expands a child's utterance (Brown & Bellugi, 1964).

Child: Daddy home.
Clinician: Daddy *is* home.

Expatiation Model. Expatiation means to elaborate or broaden on (McNeill, 1966). This means to elaborate on a topic rather than syntax.

Child: My raincoat.
Clinician: Yes. Raincoats keep us dry.

Expatiation Complex Model. This model is merely a combination of expansion and expatiation in which both form (syntax) and function (topic) of a child's utterances are expanded or elaborated.

Child: Doggy bark.
Clinician: My doggy barks because he wants in.

Alternatives Model. The underlying reasons for a topic are raised.

Child: Mommy go.
Clinician: Where did Mommy go?

This model gives a child information that a message has several different meanings and intents.

Completion Model. A clinician produces some incomplete sentences derived from a child's own language sample. The child is asked to complete the utterances. The intended completions are carefully selected so a child will have opportunities to expand and vary his or her repertoire of skills in particular areas of need.

Child utterance (language sample): Doggy run.
Clinician: Doggy _____.
Child: Doggy eat. Doggy sleep. Doggy barking.

Replacement Model. A clinician produces a series of sentences derived from a child's own speech. The child is asked to take something out and replace it with something else.

Child utterance (language sample): I like big soup.
Clinician: I like hot soup.
Child: I want hot soup. I like my soup.

Alternative–Replacement Model. A clinician produces a series of alternatives that may be used to make a construction.

Child utterance (language sample): I eated.

Clinician: I
             He   eat
             We   eats
             They ate

Child: I eat. He eats. They eat.

Revision Model. A clinician produces a few utterances derived from a child's speech. The child is asked to change them.

Clinician: The dog is black. His name is Spotty. He eats popcorn.
Child: Spotty, the black dog, eats popcorn.

Combination Model. A clinician produces several utterances derived from a child's speech. The child is asked to combine them in any way he or she wishes. The combinations expand and vary one's repertoire (Mellon, 1967).

Child utterance (language sample): My doggy ate the bone.
Clinician: The dog ate a hot dog.
             The dog is big.
Child: The big dog ate a hot dog.

It is important that in the last five techniques the utterances given to a child to change are derived from the child's own speech. This gives assurance that they are relevant to his or her repertoire of skills. Once a child can provide a variety of relatively simple responses to these techniques, more complicated and silly variations should be encouraged in line with the recommendations by Mellon (1967). The more varied and silly the variations become, the more learning opportunities become available to a child within the zone of proximal development (Vygotsky, 1962) for expanding repertoires of skill. The exploration by playing with language is a metalinguistic endeavor (Kretchmer, 1984; Muma, 1981c, 1986a, 1987a; vanKleek, 1984). Table 8.5 summarizes the 10 techniques.

Such activities have great potential for effective language learning as a consequence of language play. Indeed, I devised a game to play with and explore language. It was originally published as "MAKE-CHANGE" (a game of sentence sense; Muma, 1980) but subsequently the name was changed to "The Syntax Game" because teachers thought it was a money game about making change. Nevertheless, the purpose of the game was to make a sentence, then change it under peer approval. This is a metalinguistic activity.

Fey (1986) and Paul (1995) evidently picked up on the notions of parallel talk, some of the 10 techniques (especially expansion and expatiation), and some of the active loci of learning (such as buildups and spontaneous

TABLE 8.5
A Summary of the 10 Techniques

Model	Syntax	Semantics	Functions
Child-initiated			
Correction	Errors corrected	Errors corrected	
Expansion	Available form expanded	Meaning maintained	Intent sustained
Expatiation			Topic and intent based
Expatiation-complex	Syntax expanded	Lexical variation	Intent sustained
Alternatives			Logical assumptions underlying utterances
Clinician-initiated			
Completion	Form classes	Relational meaning	
Replacement	Form classes	Relational meaning	
Alternative–Replacement	Form classes	Relational meaning	
Revision			Exploration
Combination			Exploration

self-corrections) in their views of language intervention. Evidently, these earlier contributions (Muma, 1971a, 1978b, 1983b) are becoming widespread.

PREGRAMMATICAL CHILDREN

Just as clinical assessment is different for the pregrammatical child as compared to the grammatical child, it follows that intervention differs as well. Intervention for the pregrammatical child should be oriented on expansion and replacement for:

1. General cognitive skills (especially causality, object permanence, symbolic play, categorization, impulsivity, rule-governed learning, event knowledge toward acquiring the situated mind, and inference).
2. Content (acquisition sequence for the emergence of early semantic functions and relations; Greenfield & Smith, 1976).
3. Intent (seven early intentions; Halliday, 1975).
4. Repertoire of early performatives (communicative point, displayed referents, attribution sounds for referents such as "moo" for cow).
5. Object-based (social and physical) intervention.
6. Word learning.
7. Formats and scripts.
8. Socialization.
9. Affect (stranger anxiety, separation anxiety, attachment).

The sensorimotor skills, especially object permanence, causality, and symbolic play, have been shown to be related to language acquisition. Therefore, it is desirable to provide intervention for these areas. Astute clinicians provide the following kinds of toys for intervention in these areas:

1. *Object permanence:* Pounding bench, Jack-in-the-box, peek-a-boo, blowing bubbles, postal box geometric forms are dropped in, and so on. These toys have the feature of things disappearing and then reappearing.

2. *Causality:* Pounding bench, pull–push toys, blowing and popping bubbles, fishing for prizes, and so on. These activities contain someone (agent) doing something to something (means end object).

3. *Symbolic play:* Children are allowed to select the toys they want (intent) to play with. In the course of playing, clinicians parallel talk the activities in accordance with the developmental sequence for symbolic play (function, autosymbolic, others [a, b], alternative means [a, b], and substitute objects).

Categorization, cognitive tempo, rule-governed learning (plans of action and participation), and inferencing are common in spontaneous play. What is needed from the clinician is tuned-in parallel talk that is not only sensitive to what a particular child is doing but extends the activity communally by virtue of commenting on peer play.

Following Mandler (1983), categorization is presumably the result of the hierarchical structure, which in turn is the product of procedural knowledge. For categorization, it is desirable to evidence high-utility categories. The theory of natural categories (Anglin, 1977; Rosch, 1973, 1978) and K. Nelson's distinction between dynamic and static attributes for concept formation are useful. These should be coupled with various ways of inducing categories (Muma, 1978b): demonstrate function, label items, label categories, exemplars, and peer modeling. Categorization activities may be either formal or play in which an individual finds things in a familiar context (kitchen, playground, classroom, etc.) that go together. Once things are grouped one way, children should be asked to group them another way.

The underlying premise of spontaneous play and spontaneous social commerce is intentionality. As subtle as intent is in such activities, it is exceedingly potent. During spontaneous social commerce, an abiding concern is communicative payoff (Muma, 1981c), whereby clinicians are active partners in social commerce so that they provide communicatively appropriate responses to client attempts to communicate. That is, rather than the traditional instructional model whereby the clinicians approve or reward client performances, clinicians should be active and tuned-in participants in ongoing social commerce.

Clinicians should be tuned to the client's repertoire of semantic functions and relations, progress in the acquisition sequence for this semantic domain, and available combinations of them. These constitute a major substantive base for parallel talk with the goals of expansion and replacement.

Regarding word acquisition, it would be desirable to focus on the principle of one word, many referents; one referent, many words. Initially, intervention should be object based (both social objects and physical objects) and draw on this principle as an individual uses performatives, nonconventional terms (PCFs), and conventional terms. It should be remembered that, in accordance with Vygotsky (1962), words are learned both spontaneously (fast capture, fast mapping, dubbing ceremony) and scientifically (hypothesizing about possible meanings). This means that intervention should encourage an expanded experiential base and that alternative examples of words should be available for consideration.

The expanded experiential base has cognitive, affective, social, and cultural implications and ramifications. We encourage the parents of children in the clinic to enlarge their children's world by having new experiences around their community each week. Indeed, we do this with adult aphasic and brain-injured individuals as well because they tend to be withdrawn—a compensatory activity that works against the client. We follow up on this request by asking the parents what new activities they did each week. The parents are expected to keep logs of such activities. Also, we encourage enrollment in regular nursery schools for both social and emotional development. Such participation benefits from various special ventures into the community that expand children's possible worlds.

Regarding both content and intent, in addition to the expanded experiential base, it is necessary to have intervention in which actual social commerce takes place rather than various games and activities to elicit behavior (i.e., spinner games, take-turn games, instructional activities, etc.). Because content and intent are both functions that can be expressed in a variety of ways, it is desirable to focus on the principle that new forms come in with old functions and new functions come in with old forms (Slobin, 1970).

Formats, scripts, or routines provide viable opportunities for early language acquisition. In addition to intent, they provide microcultures, usually between the mother and child, whereby the participants know the referents, roles, activities, and outcomes. Bruner (1981), Constable (1986), and K. Nelson (1985, 1986) established scripts as viable contexts for early language acquisition. In contrast to some clumsy notions about scripts that have appeared in the clinical fields (namely their presumed repetitious value), the cognitive socialization literature has shown that the potency of scripts is not so much repetition but variation coupled with intentionality (K. Nelson, 1985, 1986). Interestingly, the potency of variation may be evidenced in the degree to which children often stake a claim to their routines (Muma, 1986a). That is, children often object when others vary a familiar story, or other routine, but they find their own variations entertaining. Subsequently, children allow others to make variations.

Socialization itself constitutes an important intervention issue from early learning throughout life. Many individuals who have difficulties with language also evidence social ineptness. Consequently, it is desirable to have a period of social activities during intervention. For many years, we have divided an hour of intervention into 15- or 20-minute segments: social–language–social–language. This decision was based on the intuitive awareness that so many of the individuals with language problems also had social difficulties. Additionally, we have encouraged mothers to establish special friends for their children and to enroll their children in nursery schools to benefit from social experiences.

Gallagher (1991) provided a comprehensive review of the literature on the social bases of language acquisition. She documented the need to provide social dimensions in intervention.

Lock (1978) was concerned that "The great chasm to be bridged in both speculations on the evolution of language and those on its development is that between affective and referential communication" (p. 8). As for affect, there are two major intervention issues: role of neutral affect and attachment theory. Bloom (1990, 1991a, 1991b) showed that early on the primary means of expression is by affect and that once word learning occurs the words become the primary means of expression. Furthermore, Bloom and her colleagues found that spurts of word learning typically follow states of neutral affect. That is, when individuals are engrossed in activities of high interest, they usually are neither highly positive nor negative in affect but in a neutral state. Needless to say, intervention should be on topics of interest to a learner.

Attachment theory is also critical for learning because when individuals are in sustained states of emotional stress, learning is reduced. This literature shows that individuals operate from a security base in learning new things. That is, under conditions of stress, individuals shut down learning and seek the security base (usually physical contact with the mother). However, when individuals release from their security base, they enter the arena of learning. Thus, it is necessary for young children in intervention to have access to the security base. It has been my policy over the past two decades to have a child's parent readily available to the child during both assessment and intervention. Thus, as we engage several children in intervention activities, their parents are only a few feet away and the children are allowed to move back and forth between the activities and their parents. This not only provides the children with access to their respective security bases, but also provides the parents with direct observation and eventual participation in intervention. Said differently, after many years of providing access to the security base in this way, it has been so effective that I now consider separating the parent and child to be an act of conspiracy against the child. That is, children who do not have this access are typically more restrained, whereas those that do have this access are not only more spontaneous and assertive but also happier and they often want to show their parents new learning (celebrate new learning).

Detractors have indicated that children usually do better when their parents are not present. However, be forewarned, this is typically a defensive view whereby the notion of doing better means having more control. That is, traditional intervention typically occurs between the clinician and child with the parent absent as the clinician instructs, directs, or teaches the child what to do. In this arena, the clinician is in charge, whereas in the security base arena the province of learning is with the child. Some threatened clinicians have taken the view that the children do better without their parents present as a protective stance for themselves and their techniques. Thus, to take the child's affective state into consideration by virtue of access to the security base may be a threat to the clinician who wants control.

The issues just discussed are logical implications of the cognitive socialization literature for dealing with pregrammatical children. They make sense simply because the literature provides the necessary substantive base for justifying them. Several of these issues may also be used with grammatical children (i.e., intent, attachment, expanded repertoire, and socialization).

GRAMMATICAL CHILDREN

Because grammatical children are operating within formal grammatical and pragmatic arenas, intervention should focus on expansion and replacement of particular aspects of an individual's available grammatical and pragmatic repertoires. These repertoires afford an individual options for rendering the message of best fit and for playing the communication game (Muma, 1975a). Facilitation of the basic grammatical repertoires in actual social commerce includes subject nominals, object nominals, auxiliaries, verbals, and various grammatical operations that provide modification, elaboration, conjunction, and deletion. These should not be regarded as goals in and unto themselves, but they should be regarded as available repertoires for meeting the communicative demands of social commerce. For example, faced with a communicative obstacle in which a presumed message of best fit did not work as intended, a speaker should have recourse to alternative codes that may make desired communicative intent recognizable.

Thus, the kinds of language problems identified by Prutting and Kirchner (1983, 1987), Fey and Leonard (1983), and Fey (1986) in terms of responsiveness and assertiveness are too global. Rather, clinicians should appreciate particular lexical, grammatical, or pragmatic capabilities that afford or limit actual social commerce. Said differently, if the objective is to reduce language impairments to a normative perspective, the kinds of impairments discussed by Fey (1986) and others may be attractive. However, if heterogeneity is to be recognized and appreciated, it may be undesirable to adopt the Fey (1986) taxonomy; rather it would be more appropriate to specify (Muma, 1991) particular repertoires of skills, progress in acquisition sequences, available learning strategies, and active loci of learning with their attendant attribution criteria. Notice that the Fey (1986) and Fey, Windsor, and Warren (1995) approaches stopped short of these issues and by stopping short, the client's available skills may be essentially ignored with the subtle implication that intervention would lack a facilitative character.

Just as with the pregrammatical child, communicative payoff and sheer talking time in actual social commerce are important to facilitate language acquisition (Bloom & Lahey, 1978; Lahey, 1988; Muma, 1978b, 1986a, 1991): "Conversation is the best starting point from which to approach language impairment" (Brinton & Fujiki, 1994, p. 60). "We use conversation as the primary context of intervention" (p. 63). "Our ultimate objective is to facilitate the development of specific skills within conversational settings in a way that those skills will, in turn, enhance conversational interaction and communication" (p. 60).

In the pragmatic arena, it is desirable for intervention to incorporate the barrier game and the over-the-shoulder game (Muma, 1978b) so that individuals can see how their communication actually works. The pragmatic issues of initiating, topic development and maintenance, topic sharing, adjusted messages, coherence, preclosing, and closing should be intervention issues for individuals who are awkward at playing the communication game. Brinton and Fujiki (1994) provided a nice perspective of this arena.

SERVICE DELIVERY

Rather than face up to many of the substantive issues available in the cognitive socialization literature and the substantive failings in the traditional clinical model, some individuals have turned to alternative clinical service delivery approaches. L. Miller (1989) advocated a classroom-based model to overcome the presumed problems of the so-called traditional "pull-out" approach. She characterized the traditional approach in the following way:

> In effect, the speech clinic operated within the school; the assessment/intervention process was etiologically based; interactions took place one-to-one,

clinician to student, generally after the student was pulled out of the classroom; and the clinician's intention was to remediate speech problems, including language, which at the time was conceptualized in relatively simple fashion as vocabulary, quality of speech sounds, length, and type of sentences (L. Miller, 1976). (p. 154)

Notice that bona fide theories of learning are not raised in Miller's account of traditional practices nor in her version of the classroom-based model.

L. Miller (1989) discussed five ways in which classroom-based intervention may take place: self-contained teaching, team teaching, one-to-one intervention, consultation, and staff curriculum development. In the section concerning issues in classroom-based service delivery, Miller discussed alternative models for rendering clinical services. The models were: catch-up, stategies-based, and systems. The catch-up model was described in the following way:

Underlying the catch-up model is the assumption that the source of the problem is in the child; as a consequence, the source of the solution is also in the child (N. Nelson, 1986). If children can be taught the "right" information, they will catch up to their peers. (L. Miller, 1989, p. 160)

Citing Bashir (1987), she indicated that the problem with this model is that most children do not catch up; indeed, their problems do not go away, rather, "They are simply labelled differently (Maxwell & Wallach, 1984)" (L. Miller, 1989, p. 161).

The strategies-based model is based on the belief that strategies can be learned, generalized across content and tasks, more powerful than fact-based content, and applied appropriately. This model presumably focuses on how to learn rather than what, a distinction that I have urged (Muma, 1978b). L. Miller (1989) indicated:

Some common strategies used by successful learners are verbal mediation, rehearsal, paraphrasing, visual imagery, construction of concept networks and bridges, and building of systematic retrieval strategies (Lasky, 1985) . . . though the research literature documenting the success of strategy-based language intervention is relatively sparse to date, those who use strategy-based programs report substantial progress . . . in terms of improved grades, fewer dropouts, and higher attendance rates in school. (p. 161)

Substantial progress is not the same as significant progress; and, it implicates dogma because what may be substantial to one clinician may not be so for another. Furthermore, substantial progress was not explicitly defined in regard to the distinctions between data and evidence. The relevance of improved grades, fewer dropouts, and higher attendance rates to these strategies await substantiation. Here again, dogma is evidenced. There is also the concern that the strategies listed by Miller are not comparable to the language learning strategies identified in the cognitive socialization literature. Thus, there are two different perspectives concerning the notion of language learning strategies: a perspective of the clinical fields and a cognitive socialization perspective.

The systems-based model extends beyond a child and his or her capacities to the social and cultural systems in which a child operates (Bruner, 1981, 1990; K. Nelson, 1996; Rogoff, 1990; Wertsch, 1991). Miller's issues regarding the systems-based model are vaguely related to the much more fully enunciated systems by Muma (1971a, 1973b, 1978b, 1986a) and Prutting and Kirchner (1983, 1987). Moreover, the systems delineated by K. Nelson (1985) and Bloom and Beckwith (1988, 1989) are still more fully enunciated. Once again, the cognitive socialization literature offers a more fully developed substantive base for rendering appropriate clinical services.

Another point should be made. It is that the various issues raised, not only in intervention but throughout the book, are generally applicable with clients of all ages from infancy through adulthood. The clinical fields have made much of presumed differences for different developmental periods: infancy, preschool, early school, adolescence, and adult learners. Indeed, there is good justification for doing so. However, in taking this stance many have thrown the baby out with the wash water by thinking that principles of acquisition and intervention may not extend across age levels. Yet, this is myopic thinking. Many principles and practices are appropriate across all age levels; for example, communicative intent (communicative payoff), discrepancy learning (variation), social-cultural context, facilitation, and so on.

SUMMARY

There is a paradox in the clinical fields whereby intervention issues are generally regarded as empirical issues but the cognitive socialization literature provides a viable rationale for clinical intervention. Thus, the clinical fields have vested their efforts in an empirical solution but it is the rational solution that is most adequately supported by the cognitive socialization literature.

It is desirable to consider the intervention principles of expansion and replacement. Language intervention should include the three Ps of parallel talk, peer modeling, and parent participation. The 10 techniques offer useful intervention procedures. Issues of input status raise the prospect of different kinds of useful information for language learning.

The clinical fields have been myopic because they have missed several substantive issues in the cognitive socialization literature that are useful for language intervention. Rather than address these, the clinical fields seemed to have turned to issues of service delivery.

9

EPILOGUE

A candid view of the state of the art of language in the clinical fields reveals two sides of the coin. On the one hand, clinicians are solidly grounded on philosophical views and theoretical perspectives in the cognitive socialization literature in rendering clinical services that are specifically tailored to each individual's available repertoire. Such services meet the criteria for appropriateness. On the other hand, technicians evidence an orientation toward quick and easy approaches, dogma, hype, hearsay, anarchy, and authoritarianism; furthermore, such individuals evidence many disconnections from the scholarly cognitive socialization literature.

The contemporary cognitive socialization literature over the past four decades provides a viable substantive base for rendering appropriate clinical services in CCCE. Speech act theory is especially useful in providing a viable theoretical framework with the centrality of communicative intent.

It is from the cognitive socialization literature that I and others have urged the clinical fields to consider the following issues:

1. Cognitive socialization: CCCE.
2. Philosophical-theoretical foundation for a clinical rationale.
3. Implications of the heterogeneous nature of clinical populations.
4. Assessment: Construct validity.
5. Assessment: Seven basic issues.
6. Assessment: Viability of descriptive approaches.
7. Assessment: Discern repertoires of skill, progress in acquisition sequences, alternative strategies of learning, active loci of learning.

8. Assessment: Language sampling: Appropriate size, sampling error rates, varied conditions.

9. Assessment: Appropriate attribution criteria.

10. Intervention: Ecological validity.

11. Intervention: Facilitate active learning.

12. Intervention: Object (social and physical) and event oriented.

13. Intervention: Affect and the security base.

14. Intervention: Parallel talk strategy.

15. Intervention: Peer modeling: Socialization.

16. Intervention: Parent participation: Fostering broadened experiential base and socialization.

17. Intervention: Communicative payoff.

18. Intervention: Efficacy based on rational rather than empirical evidence.

As indicated in chapter 2, this clinical model was derived from the philosophical views and theoretical perspectives of cognitive socialization. Accordingly, it reflects the philosophical views of constructionism, functionalism, experiential realism, and experiential cognition and the theoretical perspectives of speech acts, relevance, representational redescription, informativeness, social origins of the mind, and the situated mind. In doing so, it offers a coherent clinical rationale. It is such coherence that comprises the substantive base of the field. Each clinician should have a well-grounded understanding of which particular philosophical views and theoretical perspectives establishes a clinical rationale for achieving a coherent understanding of what that clinician is thinking and doing.

Given these identified disconnections in the clinical fields, it is reasonably accurate to conclude that much of what is thought and done in the areas of CCCE is an undisciplined mixture of philosophical views and theoretical perspectives. Needless to say, there may be a need to provide in-service workshops on these topics so that technicians can become clinicians in rendering appropriate services.

In approximately 30 years of study and direct clinical services, I have become increasingly impressed with the need for a firm grounding in the cognitive socialization literature. This perspective offers the clinical fields a solid scholarly foundation and it is compatible with the need to more fully appreciate individual repertoires. The urgency of this need is underscored by the heterogeneous nature of clinical populations that haunts the clinical fields to the core.

From the onset of my professional career, I have always held it a professional responsibility to be vigilant and intelligently question the essence of the profession. To my mind such stances are scholarly responsibilities. Along the way, I have encountered individuals entrusted with the party-line narrative of the profession who dutifully held tenaciously to their cause even in the face of scholarship.

Perhaps a personal anecdote is in order. In my final semester of undergraduate school, I was in clinical practica in the public schools with a polished and highly esteemed speech-language pathologist. I was very excited about the prospect of actually rendering clinical services to real individuals under the tutelage of such a revered speech-language pathologist. My excitement was manifest in many (too many) questions to this mentor as to why assessment or intervention was a particular way and why not draw on the relevant literature that would question some views, perspectives, and practices. My interactions with her, although well-intended, were disquieting for her. Committed to her responsibility to usher me into the profession, she considered it her duty to get me in line with the profession. Needless to say, I was too much for her, resulting in a C for clinical practica, which was utterly unheard of. By the time a clinical student is placed in the final clinical practica, an A was virtually a certainty simply because such individuals had learned to conform to the professional expectations of the field. I have always cherished that C simply because it meant that penetrating inquiry has its costs in traditional institutional values but its personal benefit by virtue of being true to the clients, oneself, the literature, the profession, and scholarship was surely worth it.

Needless to say, this book is yet another series of questions about the integrity of the scholarly base of the profession. Those in the clinical fields who want to hold tight to traditional views and practices are likely to dismiss it as a C, whereas those who find the issues provocative are likely to appreciate the cognitive socialization literature and its relevance to the clinical fields.

Because it is apparent that there is an inherent conflict in the clinical fields between scholarship on the one hand and authoritarianism, elitism, hype, hearsay, and dogma on the other, it is sometimes difficult to identify the substantive pea in the academic-clinical shell game. Consequently, it is imperative for the clinical fields to be increasingly vigilant about what they profess to do, and are doing, so that scholarship is indeed a legitimate claim.

As the literature changes, I am free to change my mind about various issues—such is scholarship. Therefore, those individuals who intelligently indagate the literature and draw legitimate clinical implications are those with whom I would like to claim some measure of peership. They are the true colleagues—clinicians—and they offer the best prospects for rendering appropriate clinical services, thereby bringing us closer to the ultimate clinical compliment—desired client progress.

APPENDIX A

DEPARTMENT OF HEALTH. EDUCATION. AND WELFARE

OFFICE OF EDUCATION

WASHINGTON. D.C. 20202

MAY 30 1980

Mr. Stan Dublinske, Director
School Services Program
American Speech-Language
& Hearing Association
10801 Rockville Pike
Rockville, Maryland 20852

Dear Mr. Dublinske:

Recently, you requested a policy interpretation of the term "adversely affects educational performance" as it relates to speech impaired children. You indicated that the American Speech-Language-Hearing Association (ASHA) has received reports that some State and local educational agencies are requiring educational assessments of all speech impaired children as part of the evaluation process in order to determine their eligibility for special education and related services.

The broad issue raised in your inquiry is whether the definition of "speech impaired" in the regulations implementing the Education of the Handicapped Act, Part B (as amended by P.L. 94-142) is interpreted to mean that children with communicative disorders who have no other handicapping condition are ineligible for services as "handicapped children" unless educational assessments indicate concomitant problems in academic achievement. An interpretation is needed because "educational performance" is not specifically defined in the Part B regulations. However, the standard for determining whether a child fits into any of the categories of handicaps listed in the Act and regulations is that the impairment "adversely affects a child's educational preformance." Under Section 602(1) of the Act, a child with one of the listed impairments must need special education to be a "handicapped child". For children who need a "related service" but no other special education services, the Part B regulations in section 121a.14(a)(2) allow a State to consider that service as "special education", bringing those children within the scope of the Act.

I agree that an interpretation which denies needed services to speech impaired children who have no problem in academic performance is unreasonably restrictive in effect and inconsistent with the intent of the Act and regulations.

There is strong support in the Act and regulations for a broad construction of the term "educational performance". By its terms, the Act
affords some services (and encourages States to provide more) to infants
and preschoolers with the kinds of handicapping conditions listed in the
statute. "Speech impaired" is one of those categories of handicapping
conditions. Obviously, assessments of academic performance (through
standardized achievement tests in subject matter areas) would be inappropriate or inconclusive if administered to many such children. The meaning
of "educational performance" cannot be limited to showing of discrepancies
in age/grade performance in academic subject-matter areas.

The extent of a child's mastery of the basic skill of effective oral
communication is clearly includable within the standard of "educational
performance" set by the regulations. Therefore, a speech/language impairment necessarily adversely affects educational performance when the
communication disorder is judged sufficiently severe to require the
provision of speech pathology services to the child.

The process for determining a child's disabilities and need for educational services is described in Sections 121a.530-533 of the Part B
regulations. These evaluation and placement procedures contemplate that
the diagnosis and appraisal of communicative disorders as handicapping
conditions would be the responsibility of a qualified speech-language
pathologist. (see, also, the definition of "speech pathology" in Section
121a.13(b)(12)).

Section 121a.432 sets minimum requirements for the evaluation procedures
that public educational agencies administer.

Section 121a.532(f) indicates the possible range of areas for assessment
(i.e., health, vision, hearing, social-emotional status, general intelligence, academic performance, communicative status, and motor abilities).
However, the "comment" following this section states:

> Children who have a speech impairment as their primary handicap may
> not need a complete battery of assessments (e.g., psychological,
> physical or adaptive behavior). However, a qualified speech-language
> pathologist would (1) evaluate each speech impaired child using
> procedures that are appropriate for diagnosis and appraisal of
> speech and language disorders, and (2) where necessary, make referrals
> for additional assessments needed to make an appropriate decision.

The "multisource" requirement of Section 121a.533(a)(1) makes public agencies responsible for using information from a variety of sources in interpreting evaluation data and making placement decisions. Listed sources include: "...aptitude and achievement tests, teacher recommendations, physical condition, social or cultural background and adaptive behavior". Following this section is a "comment" which clarifies the multisource requirement in relation to speech-language children:

> Paragraph (a)(1) includes a list of sources that may be used by a public agency in making placement decisions. The agency would not have to use all the sources in every instance...For example, while all the named sources would have to be used for a child whose suspected disability is mental retardation, they would not be necessary for certain other handicapped children, such as a child who has a severe articulation disorder as his primary handicap. For such a child, the speech-language pathologist, in complying with the multi-source requirement, might use (1) a standardized test of articulation and (2) observation of the child's articulation in conversational speech. (Emphasis added.)

Any public agency requirements which impose procedures more extensive or stringent than those in the Federal regulations must be scrutinized in light of these clarifying comments. It is clear that, in establishing the existence of a speech/language impairment that is "handicapping" in Part B terms, a professional judgement is required. The basis for that judgment is the child's performance on formal and/or informal measures of linguistic competence and performance, rather than heavy reliance on the results of academic achievement testing. The impact of the child's communicative status on academic performance is not deemed the sole or even the primary determinant of the child's need for special educational services. It is the communicative status - and professional judgments made in regard to assessments of communicative abilities - which has overriding significance.

In the event that the speech-language pathologist establishes through appropriate appraisal procedures the existence of a speech/language impairment, the determination of the child's status as a "handicapped child" cannot be conditioned on a requirement that there must be a concurrent deficiency in academic performance.

It was not the intent of the Act to reduce services to handicapped children. The practice which you have brought to our attention could have that kind of negative effect. I appreciate your inquiry on behalf of children with speech/language impairment and trust that this response has made clear the Office's position on this issue.

Sincerely,

Edwin W. Martin
Acting Assistant Secretary
for Special Education & Rehabilitative Services

cc: Garry McDaniels
     Jack Jones
     Tom Irvin
     Bill Tyrrell
     Jerry Vlasak

APPENDIX B:
SCIENCE AND HUMAN AFFAIRS:
CLINICAL IMPLICATIONS

The distinctions between science and human affairs or narrative (Bruner, 1986) have far-reaching clinical implications. The basic premise of science is causality based on categorization and logic. The basic premise of narrative is intent realized in varied contexts of human affairs.

Some aspects of clinical services reflect this distinction. For example, differences in performance on tests as compared to those in actual social commerce reflect these two respective perspectives. Consequently, it is desirable to examine both perspectives in order to appreciate their potentials toward rendering appropriate clinical services.

The purposes of this appendix are to provide an overview of the distinctions between science and human affairs and to discuss their clinical implications.

SCIENCE AND HUMAN AFFAIRS

Fundamental issues have been raised in the philosophy of science regarding the distinctions between science and human affairs. These distinctions have been eloquently discussed in Bruner's (1986) classic book *Actual Minds, Possible Worlds* under the rubrics of "two modes of thought" and "possible castles." The two modes of thought are the paradigmatic or logico-scientific and the narrative modes that were translated as two possible castles: science and human affairs, respectively. Both modes of thought "trade on presupposition" (Bruner, 1986, p. 28). They are two forms of illusion with science oriented outward and narrative oriented inward (Bruner, 1986). Although an individual may be more inclined toward one mode, both are accessible. Intuitively, there seems to be a gender preference for logico-scientific thinking used more often with males and narrative with females. Parenthetically, this notion of narrative is quite different from the notion of discourse narrative, although narrative thought may be manifest in discourse. For an excellent review of discourse narrative pertaining to language-impaired individuals, see Liles (1985, 1986).

The paradigmatic or logic-scientific mode of thought strives to categorize the world and deduce logical relations. Categorization is useful, to the extent that it adequately represents reality, because it serves the purpose of reducing the complex varied world to a manageable size (Bruner et al., 1956; Mandler, 1983; Tyler, 1969). Categorization used in the service of logic is the basic premise underlying descriptive and explanatory adequacies in theory development (Kaplan, 1964; Medawar, 1984; Shapere, 1984).

The sciences were essentially launched by the establishment of taxonomies (i.e., the periodic table, the Linnaeus taxonomies of plants and animals, etc.). It is important to appreciate that the sciences proceeded productively even though these taxonomies were incomplete. This importance extends to the viability of provisional models and theories as productive enterprises (Crick, 1988). For example, it was learned that water was composed of hydrogen and oxygen well before some other elements were discovered and before the notion of heavy water was a threat to the taxonomy. Thus, the taxonomies of the sciences achieved a very important function by reducing a complex world to a manageable size; consequently, science became somewhat intolerant of variance. Bruner (1986) said that science "seeks to transcend the particular by higher and higher reaching for abstraction, and in the end disclaims in principle any explanatory value at all where the particular is concerned" (p. 13).

Principles and practices of the justice system are evidently oriented on categorization and logic. Except for motive (intent), issues of justice are based on logic (access and means). Notice the response set imposed on witnesses whereby they are asked to respond "yes" or "no" to lawyer questions, thereby making lawyers purveyors of implicature. The credibility of witnesses may be challenged by inquiries of detail rather than the gist of an event (Fillenbaum, 1966); however, except for flashbulb memory, which occurs under heightened stress (Brown & Kulik, 1977), it is the detail that becomes lost in memory over time (Loftus, 1974, 1975, 1983).

It could be that the logic of either–or thinking prunes embellishments of truth in a profitable service of justice. In this sense, jurors may attain some measure of solace concerning their actions as they respond to the categories of indictment. However, it is possible that this response set may be an injustice whereby the categorical nature of responses may miss the essence of "the vicissitudes of human intent," especially if emotional interplay is at work. Bruner (1986) recognized the trade-off between information processing and affect. With these issues, could it be that the logic of justice constitutes an instance of the imposition of science on narrative?

Categorization provides a basis for seeking logical relations in attempts to account formally for the world by virtue of theory development, and by extension to prediction and explanation, especially of the physical world via brute facts (Lakoff, 1987). In accordance with descriptive and explanatory adequacies, science proceeds to seek truth by discovering logical or causal relations between known categories:

> One mode, the paradigmatic or logico-scientific one, attempts to fulfill the ideal of a formal, mathematical system of description and explanation. It employs categorization . . . and the operations by which categories are established . . . to form a system. (Bruner, 1986, p. 12)

But, "There is a heartlessness to logic" (Bruner, 1986, p. 13). This so-called heartlessness of logic raises the fundamental distinction between science and human affairs. This distinction was eloquently put by Bruner (1986) when he indicated that causality is the irreducible "mental category" of logic and therefore of science, whereas intent is the irreducible mental category of narrative and thus of human affairs. Bruner (1986) commented, " 'Intention and its vicissitudes' constitute a primitive category system in terms of which experience is organized, at least as primitive as the category system of causality" (pp. 18–19). Table B.1 illustrates the differences between science and human affairs.

Only a brief discussion of the distinctions in Table B.1 is given here. Interested readers may turn to the literature, especially Bruner (1986), Bloom et al. (1988), K. Nelson (1985) and Sperber and Wilson (1986). The latter three do not address the distinctions between science and human affairs per se but draw on these distinctions and provide systematic considerations of the centrality of intent with its attendant issues.

TABLE B.1
Differences Between Science and Human Affairs

Science	Human Affairs
Causality	Intent
Categorization-formal	Categorization-mutual
Fully explicit	Selectively explicit
Contextualization-formulaic	Contextualization-functional
Intolerant of variation	Inherent variation
"Objective"	"Subjective"
Nonemotional	Emotional

Categorization

Although both science and human affairs deal with categorization, context, and explicitness, there are qualitative distinctions between them. The categories for the so-called "hard" sciences are formal and strive to be fully explicit even to the extent of standardized measurement, whereas the categories in human affairs are relative, functional, and negotiable in social commerce resulting in mutual manifestness (Sperber & Wilson, 1986). Lakoff (1987) used the terms *brute facts* and *institutional facts* to distinguish the categories of traditional science from those in human affairs, respectively, For example, properties of elements have specific functions for compounds, whereas knowledge of culture provides institutional facts for effective social commerce.

Explicitness

In science, parameters are explicitly measured and incorporated in formulas and calculations. However, what is psychosocially measured or calculated in human affairs is the means whereby intent may be recognized (Grice, 1975). Recognizing that intent or purpose is the essence of human affairs, all explicit acts function within the content of implicit knowledge of the world, possible worlds, or situated mind. Thus, human affairs address selective explicitness from the perspective of presupposition. An explicit message only works as intended if it provides new information in the context of old (Clark & Clark, 1977; Grice, 1975; Sperber & Wilson, 1986). For example, the comment "turn here" only works as intended if the speaker and listener regard the entailed information as needed information within the context of known information.

Context and Variance

The hard sciences notion of context is typically cast in terms of formulaic outcomes as a function of parameter manipulation. For example, a change in pressure can alter the standard reference for water freezing. The implication is that the hard sciences are intolerant of variance because in the last analysis, variance presumably can be accounted for; moreover, accountability is presumably achieved under the premise of reductionism—the ultimate account is the predicted effects of the smallest element.

A subtle but pervasive way in which reductionism has been achieved, especially in the clinical fields, is the use of contrived tasks (normative tests) in which categories of performance are imposed on individuals. With a normative comparison, such performance is regarded as evidence of the individual's competency, but, unfortunately, it lacks ecological validity (Bronfenbrenner, 1974, 1977, 1979).

In contrast, human affairs rest on the premise that intent varies as a function of context; therefore, variance is inherent in human affairs and the integrity of context must be preserved to understand how intent is functioning. Thus, reductionism may be a threat to understanding human affairs. Bruner (1986) indicated that reductionistic notions about language were nonproductive: "It has been clear that looking at language separately 'in the light' of well-formedness, of meaning, and of use was more a pedagogical convenience than a genuine intellectual undertaking" (p. 83).

Objectivity and Subjectivity: Emotionality

The distinction between objectivity and subjectivity has traditionally paralleled the differences between the so-called sciences and the humanities. However, Gould (1981), Lakoff (1987), and Prutting (1983) challenged this perspective by showing that objectivity is essentially a myth, the normative solution notwithstanding; and what may be done in both the hard sciences and the humanities is essentially subjective precisely because both are domains of human endeavors. Part of the objectivity claim for the hard sciences is the conviction that they are free of emotional involvement, whereas the humanities actually savor affect as evidenced by art appreciation. However, science limited to brute facts is not only emotionally free but downright boring; but, true scholars addressing issues of scientific merit are taken by the thrill of participation in much the same way that a poem or picture strikes the heart of the artist.

CLINICAL IMPLICATIONS

What does it matter if major issues have been raised about the nature of science and human affairs? It matters a great deal, especially for the clinical fields, simply because the clinical fields are based on principles of science on the one hand and human affairs on the other. The extent to which these principles are challenged is the extent to which basic issues in the clinical fields may need to be reconsidered.

Following Bruner (1986), there are two major implications concerning the distinctions between science and human affairs. First, the sciences are distinctly different from human affairs, with the former based on formal categorization, logic, and causality and the latter based on the importance of intent and context. Second, traditional science apparently has been imposed on human affairs at a heavy cost, especially in the clinical fields where individual differences are so evident.

Assessment

The purpose of assessment is to ascertain what an individual can do so that a diagnosis can be made, intervention goals may be established, and efficacy of intervention evaluated (Lahey, 1988; Muma, 1986a). Two basic approaches have been used to carry out such assessments: normative testing and descriptive procedures. The former reflects traditional science principles, whereas the latter reflects narrative. Both are standardized by virtue of following the procedures that warrant their use.

Construct validity is the central mandatory issue for assessment (Messick, 1989a, 1989b). *"All measurement should be construct referenced"* (Messick, 1980, p. 1015). *"All* validity is at its base some form of construct validity . . . It *is* the basic meaning of validity" (Guion, 1977, p. 410). There are two ways in which construct validity has been addressed:

1. Factor analytic and/or scaling approaches (Schiavetti, Metz, & Sitler, 1981)—renditions of categorization that eventually draw on dogma by virtue of labeling the factors and/or scales.
2. Explicit philosophical-theoretical premises (Clark & Clark, 1977; Prutting & Kirchner, 1983).

The former carries the perspective of science, whereas the latter is a more eloquent and systematic rendition of intention. Thus, in human measurement, at least, the factor analytic and scaling solutions are merely instances of the imposition of science on narrative. Furthermore, various subtests constitute yet another instance of categorization. Such notions have led to some peculiar, even silly, reductionistic practices as evidenced by the reductionistic thinking surrounding intelligence testing and worse yet their shorthand versions—vocabulary tests. Intelligence tests themselves have been offered as general indices of cognition (Kamin, 1974). Vocabulary subtests typically have relatively high correlations with overall IQ scores; thus, the vocabulary subtests are sometimes used as estimates of IQ.

What is lost in this kind of thinking is the narrative perspective. Simply, the narrative perspective is not evidenced in intelligence testing because the various tasks are contrived and the responses elicited. In a narrative perspective, systematic considerations of spontaneous behavior in actual social commerce would be the focus.

Moreover, the intelligence (vocabulary) testing perspective has two other rather serious shortcomings. First, performance on intelligence tests is tangential to the cognition of narrative. It would take a myopic view of cognition to regard intelligence test performance as a valid index of the cognitive skills of narrative. In a sense, such performance merely reflects some cognitive skills that are relatively easily packaged but they are of questionable relevance to everyday cognition. Second, performance on a vocabulary subtest is yet another step removed from an already questionable performance. If an index of determination is considered at both levels (intelligence testing and vocabulary testing) this logic would turn up shallow and unattractive.

The vanity of such thinking has already been shown (Bronfenbrenner, 1979; Donaldson, 1978). In the child development literature, Bronfenbrenner

(1979) raised the issue that much of the literature is based on contrived task performances that children had never before done in their lives and would likely not do again in their lives. Yet, such performances have been used to draw inferences and conclusions about their lives. This merely indicts the imposition of science (categorization–normative testing) on narrative. Bronfenbrenner (1979) held that evidence from one's ecology is needed to draw legitimate conclusions about what an individual can do. Brown (1986) made a similar point in referring to a study dealing with ecologically valid evidence. He commented that it "may be more germane than all the laboratory studies" (p. 278). Thus, they were implicitly recognizing the problems of the imposition of science on narrative.

Donaldson (1978) made a similar observation. She showed that some babies who did not evidence Stage 6 of the object performance subtest of the Uzgiris and Hunt (1975) scales actually evidenced object permanence under conditions of human sense. These tasks differed by virtue of one being contrived and relying on elicited performance—a science perspective—whereas the other relied on ecologically valid contexts and intention—a narrative perspective.

The imposition of science on narrative in the form of psychometric testing seems to have become institutionalized as an intellectual stupor in which test performance should not be questioned even in the face of conflicting parental intuition. However, sensitive parents are triggered by issues of narrative import. Their intuitions are intrinsically valuable. This is not to dismiss performance on psychometric tests; it merely reasserts the importance of intuition within the context of challenging the assessment power of such tests.

Unfortunately, psychometric normative tests have six major problems: questionable objectivity, questionable relevance, lack of necessary and sufficient evidence, the quantification issue, and in the clinical fields both a notorious lack of construct validity and the homogeneity–heterogeneity conflict. First, the issue of objectivity has been a long-standing cornerstone of psychometric testing. However, a serious challenge has been made as to whether objectivity is even possible. The problem with objectivity is that there is no access to a "God's-eye" view of the world (Lakoff, 1987). Therefore, whatever is done by humans in inherently subjective, the normative solution notwithstanding. Second, it is usually assumed that what is tested is relevant to what is claimed to be assessed. For example, what is measured on the PPVT–R (Dunn & Dunn, 1981) is presumably relevant to the contemporary vocabulary acquisition literature on the one hand and an individual's available vocabulary on the other. However, unfortunately, what is actually measured on this, and many other tests, lacks relevance to the available scholarly literature and to individual repertoires. The result is that data often are obtained rather than evidence (Muma, 1991). Third, another cornerstone of psychometric testing is the assumption that such tests provide necessary and sufficient information to assess what is claimed. Unfortunately, there are major questions as to whether test performance in the arena of human affairs actually yields valid data (evidence) for human affairs not only because of the distinction between data and evidence but also because the data may be unnecessary and insufficient. Fourth, the quantification issue is a complication for psychometric testing; that is, what is gained or lost when behavior becomes quantified? In language assessment, it may be a disservice to convert sentences to numbers when striving to ascertain what an individual can do. Rather, it would be more appropriate to retain the grammatical distinctions in order to ascertain which grammatical skills in which linguistic contexts may be available to an individual.

Fifth, because construct validity is notoriously missing in many tests in the clinical fields, there is the fundamental problem of whether such tests merely generate data open to virtually any interpretation or evidence that is confined to legitimate interpretations supportable by the underlying philosophical views and theoretical perspectives with the attendant literature. Sixth, the homogeneity–heterogeneity conflict is a particular problem for the clinical fields. On the one hand, psychometric tests are predicated on the homogeneity premise, but on the other hand, heterogeneity is characteristic of clinical populations. Thus, there is an inherent conflict with the use of such tests clinically.

Needless to say, these are serious issues. Unfortunately, these issues and challenges extend to an understanding of human affairs simply because of the imposition of science, by virtue of psychometric normative testing, on narrative. Said differently, if the purpose of clinical assessment is to ascertain what an individual can do, it may be more propitious to describe what he or she actually does in social commerce, from representative samples, than to impose contrived tasks with their attendant norms from which extrapolations must be made in order to broach the question of what an individual can do. Both approaches use performance to infer competence but one uses contrived tasks and normative categories, whereas the other relies on patterns of spontaneous (intentional) performance in actual social commerce as the prima facie evidence. The former is a priori in nature, whereas the latter is a posteriori in nature (Beckwith et al., 1984). For Bloom and Lahey (1978), the former approach is etic (formal, highly structured, contrived) and the latter is emic (informal, less structured, spontaneous). Thus, one rests on the notion of science and the other on narrative. These differences are listed in Table B.2.

On the surface, it would appear that a clinical profession should base its perspectives on science rather than narrative. Fundamental questions have been raised about science, but these questions pertain to human affairs to the extent that notions of science have been imposed on human affairs. The imposition of science on human affairs is clearly evident in the clinical fields.

TABLE B.2
Issues of Normative Testing Concerning the
Imposition of Science on Human Affairs

Science	Human Affairs
Causality	Intent
Objectivity	Subjectivity
Categorical: Norms (a priori)	Relevance (a posteriori)
Necessary and sufficient	Repertoire
Quantification	Preserved integrity
Construct validity: Contrived, imposed	Construct validity: Actual, natural
Homogeneity	Heterogeneity

Categories and Relevance

A fundamental question should be raised about the use of categories in either psychometric or descriptive assessment. The question is how relevant the categories are. This is a crucial issue for normative tests, especially for those tests that lack construct validity. This question can be recast for specific tests. For example, how relevant are the particular words and categories (norms) on the PPVT–R to a theory of word learning, the contemporary literature on word acquisition (Kuczaj & Barrett, 1986), and a particular individual's available words?

Typically, this question is not even raised. Yet, it is crucial for any sober claim to assess an individual's presumed abilities. Rather than face this question, staunch believers in science merely dodge the question and retort that normative tests are objective and provide necessary and sufficient information. However, these notions have also been seriously questioned and the original question remains.

Descriptive assessment, especially that derived from the contemporary cognitive socialization literature, provides a reasonably good answer to the relevance question. Because such procedures are derived from the contemporary literature, they are not only inherently relevant to this literature, but they provide standardized procedures. Furthermore, such procedures issuing from this literature are well vested in supportable philosophical views (such as functionalism, constructionism, mentalism, experiential cognition) and theoretical perspectives (such as speech acts, relevance, informativeness, shared meaning, expression, and situated mind), thereby achieving construct validity.

Because descriptive procedures use actual performance from representative samples, the issue of relevance to an individual's presumed skills is addressed inherently. Thus, whereas a priori psychometric tests may dodge the issue of relevance, it is addressed inherently by a posteriori descriptive procedures.

Objectivity

The issue of objectivity for science, and by implication for psychometric normative testing, has received increased scrutiny. Gould (1981), Lakoff (1987), and Prutting (1983) showed that objectivity is a myth of science simply because there is no access to a "God's-eye" view; whatever is known is the product of human endeavors—a subjective enterprise. Turning to psychometric testing, there is a myth about objectivity both coming in (test development) and going out (test use) simply because both are subjective enterprises. They both deal with dogma and interpretation.

Dogma is unsubstantiated opinion. A rather subtle but important example of dogma in the clinical field is the construction of language tests whereby authors make decisions about what should be on the tests and the format of the test regardless of the relevant theories with their attendant literature. Unfortunately, the clinical fields are replete with such tests (e.g., PPVT–R, TOLD, CELF–R, ACLC, DSS, etc.). In effect, the norms for these tests merely sanction the authors' dogma.

For example, the Test of Authority-Perceptual Skills (Gardner, 1985) is merely a compilation of tasks with attendant norms that presumably sanctions the claim to assess auditory-perceptual skills. Implicitly, the norms provide necessary and sufficient evidence for an objective assessment of what is claimed to be assessed. However, a consideration of the contemporary literature on memory and mental processing reveals that such tasks are questionably relevant and require dogma to sustain claims about an individual's skills, normative information notwithstanding. The claim that this is a test of auditory-perceptual skills is farfetched.

The contemporary literatures on categorization, memory, representation, and mental processing ceased relying on modality (auditory, visual, kinesthetic, haptic) perspectives a few decades ago. Clark and Clark (1977) provided a comprehensive review of this literature of language processing; they indicated that auditory information is purged from memory very early in mental processing with the bulk of the activity committed to categorization or representation, inference, and problem solving in deducing propositions for intended messages. Similarly, Tallal (1990) summarized a body of literature on presumed auditory processing, much of which was her own; she concluded that the "deficits in language-learning impaired children are specific neither to the auditory modality nor to speech perception" (p. 616). Thus, the basic premise of this test is incompatible with the contemporary scholarly literature.

Problems for this test become amplified by considering specific subtests. The Auditory Number Memory subtest has individuals recall digits forward and reversed and the Auditory Interpretation of Directions subtest is a memory for commands notion. Unfortunately, these subtests are based on two very old and inaccurate notions that memory has a fixed capacity and that it can be assessed in these ways. Blankenship (1938) and Jenkins (1974)—the latter is one of the foremost scholars in memory—showed that the fixed capacity notion of memory is false. Perhaps the title of the Jenkins article will suffice: "Remember that old theory of memory? Well, forget it."

The Auditory Word Discrimination subtest missed the relevant literature that has been reviewed by Locke (1980a, 1980b). The Auditory Processing (thinking and reasoning) subtest is another compilation of tasks lacking a substantive link with an appropriate philosophical view or theoretical perspective on thinking and reasoning; it would take a strange twist of rationalization to include such activities in a test of perceptual skills. The overall result is that performance on this test is compared to norms and conclusions are made about an individual's presumed auditory-perceptual skills. A clinician who claims expertise in this area would need to have blind allegiance and faith in the normative mentality to actually believe such tests and to lay claim to assessing an individual's skills. Thus, given the scholarly literature, one cannot help but be nonplussed by tests such as this one.

There is nothing wrong with interpretation (subjectivity) as long as it is disciplined (i.e., supportable by the contemporary scholarly literature). Thus, whatever the outcome, what is made of the data is in the last analysis an interpretation. Citing Kaplan (1964), Messick (1980) indicated, "What serves as evidence is the result of a process of interpretation—facts do not speak for themselves; nevertheless, facts must be given a hearing, or the scientific point to the process of interpretation is lost" (p. 1014).

With these considerations, objectivity is not only a myth of science but subjectivity is essential to both science and narrative. The value of subjectivity for a profession is that it is disciplined (i.e., governed by explicit philosophical views and theoretical perspectives rather than dogma).

Necessary and Sufficient

Advocates of the normative testing model rely on the premises that norms are not only objective but also provide necessary and sufficient information. The problems of relevance to the literature and relevance to an individual go to the heart of the claim about necessary and sufficient information.

Placing the individual first, because the purpose of clinical assessment is presumably to assess what an individual can do, an interesting puzzle begins to unravel regarding the necessary and sufficient claim. Under this claim, it stands to reason that a norm would be a fair index of what an individual can do. This was tested in the following way. Large representative language samples (400 spontaneous utterances) were obtained from seven normal speaking young children (see Appendix D). Descriptions were made of the arrays of different kinds of constructions for the following grammatical systems: subject nominals, object nominals, auxiliaries, verb systems, and grammatical operations. It was assumed that those constructions that were common across the language samples constituted the core or norm for a particular domain. If the sample of subjects is representative, this notion of norm could extend to the notion of a psychometric norm. If this core reflected most of what the individuals did, it was assumed that it would constitute a norm for deducing what they presumably could do. This is obviously only a pilot study about whether norms provide necessary and sufficient information to make claims about what an individual can do. However, the remarkable outcome is that all of the participants were greatly underestimated. Because all of the participants were misrepresented by virtue of underestimation, the issue about atypical participants in this study is greatly diminished, if not dismissed (one participant had a large MLU).

These data did not provide necessary and sufficient evidence of what individuals could do. For example, the core merely showed about 12 mutual constructions for the subject nominal system; yet, all of the individuals evidenced two or three times as many variations than were evidenced by the common core. Thus, the notion of norm, in principle, is questionable because the time-honored claim that norms provides necessary and sufficient information is suspect on two grounds: relevance and underestimation.

This pilot study is only suggestive, but the fallibility of the necessary and sufficient claim for normative tests has, in fact, been field tested by both parents and experienced clinicians. In dealing with several thousand parents over the years, I have been faced with those who intuitively question the validity of various tests simply because their children did not have the problems that were attributed to them by virtue of test performance. I have also seen many more children than I care to admit in which the disparity between what they could do and what test results presumably measured was a challenge to my integrity.

Quantification

Because normative tests are often based on performance scores, they carry another issue that is richly evident in science: quantification. Science evidently took Kelvin's (1891) belief to heart (cited in Hall, 1991); it was the belief that if you can express something in numbers you have achieved some measure of understanding. The inflated view is that numbers not only have captured the essence of what has been measured but captured it in such a way that data becomes positioned for manipulation. Such manipulations can extend to mathematical calculations that presumably have sufficient power to separate the chaff from the wheat.

What is achieved or lost by quantification? In language and cognition, complexity is paramount, as evidenced by context (K. Nelson, 1985, 1996). Facing complexity of context, quantification may be a great risk. The risks are great in attempting to quantitatively score language and they are no less risky in the end when CA, LA, MA, and other quantitative indices are used. Perhaps we should heed Brown's (1973b) admonition that the systems applied to observe language may actually dictate the outcomes.

The narrative view would hold, because of context and the centrality of intent, that rather than quantification it is more appropriate to preserve information about the ranges of productive grammatical and pragmatic skills and their contexts. Thus, it would be more appropriate to delineate an individual's array of structural and functional variations, evidenced in representative samples, as estimates of repertoires of grammatical and pragmatic skills than to convert them into a numerical scheme for normative comparison. Such descriptive information would be more useful than test scores for drawing conclusions about what an individual can do and what should be done in intervention. Test scores reflect the categorization–causality notion of science, whereas descriptive information reflects the functional–intentional perspective of narrative. The former is more removed and carries greater inferential risks; yet, both are aimed at arriving at a conclusion about what an individual can do.

Standard Sampling Condition

Just as there have been penetrating questions raised about the claims of objectivity and necessary and sufficient information for normative testing, the notion of the standard sampling condition is challengeable on similar grounds. In essence, the standard sampling condition is another rendition of categorization. The assumption is that if the external stimuli are held constant, variations in performance would be attributable to individuals. Thus, a comparison could be made between an individual's performance on pre- and postsamples and any change in performance, assuming representative samples, could be attributed to a particular intervention approach. Furthermore, this mentality was extended to comparisons between individuals.

If standard sampling is questioned as being too narrow to be representative of narrative, the usual defense is to call for systematic sampling in the mentality of a periodic chart. This mentality merely takes the imposition of science on narrative as the rightful given but misses the more basic issue of intent in varied context as an appropriate arena for sampling and assessment. If narrative is taken seriously, the standard sampling condition would be found wanting simply because it reduces opportunities to sample the array of skills available to an individual. Lahey (1988) recognized that the standard sampling or highly structured condition is etic or a priori in nature and restricts language that may be available to an individual:

> However, such highly structured observations are strictly etic—that is, they use preset categories for description and do not allow for other interpretations.

In addition, they are less flexible in the contexts observed, and restrict the language behaviors that can be observed.

Standardized testing is *not* therefore, designed to provide information relevant for a *description* of a particular child's language system or his use of that system. Because of this, it is *not* helpful in providing information that would lead to hypotheses about what a child is ready to learn, that is, for planning the goals of intervention. (p. 130)

Thus, Lahey was implicitly aware of the differences between science and narrative as distinguished by Bruner (1986).

The narrative perspective provides an argument against the standard sampling condition: It is necessary to sample an individual in a variety of naturally varying spontaneous conditions in order to ascertain what he or she can do. Furthermore, if intentionality and presupposition are appreciated, the standard sampling condition would be regarded as a context for misrepresentation, with respect to relevance and underestimation, of what an individual can do.

DISCIPLINE

Ironically, Bruner (1986) and other major scholars who have raised the distinctions between science and narrative have created a dilemma. On the one hand, the clinical fields strive to be scholarly and turn to science for becoming scientific. On the other hand, the model of science has not only become questioned but some of its impact on narrative appears to have been a disservice. It may be well to maintain these distinctions because they open the door to new more promising vistas for understanding the clinical fields. However, once the door has been opened, some of the cherished notions of science may come tumbling out. The door has, of course, been cracked open; it is up to us to decide if we want to slam it shut thereby not facing the issues or open the door of enlightenment to face these issues in a disciplined way. Fortunately, because these distinctions have been raised, each of us has a chance, indeed a responsibility by virtue of integrity, to consider these distinctions and their clinical implications. The basic issues are not so much science or narrative, but disciplined appreciations of both without the intrusion of one on the other. Thus, the clinical fields may achieve a disciplined understanding of science and human affairs as two distinct scholarly arenas.

APPENDIX C:
IT WORKS:
A TECHNICIAN'S CREED

When faced with penetrating concerns about various clinical practices, technicians often retort that "It works." By responding this way, they presumably become relieved of the scholarly responsibilities to deal with the issues. Consequently, scholarship becomes deflected. If such stances are pervasive across the clinical fields, there is tacit evidence that the clinical fields lack scholarship and they have become technician oriented rather than clinician oriented.

This was an abiding concern at the *1983 ASHA Conference on Training Standards* (Rees & Snope, 1983). Consequently, Resolution II-B was passed, calling for course offerings to have a strong theoretical base for the expressed purpose of circumventing technicianship and encouraging clinicianship. Thus, the implicit distinctions between technicianship and clinicianship are that the former is atheoretical, ascholarly, and based on expediency and dogma, whereas the latter is theoretical and disciplined.

Former ASHA President Fred Minifie (1996) has been concerned that scholarship is indeed losing out in the clinical fields. He held a conference of chairs of ASHA training programs. The focus of the conference was to encourage higher standards of scholarship in the profession.

Parenthetically, ASHA was formed in the Department of Psychology at the University of Iowa. Accordingly, it began with a solid scholarly foundation. Therefore, the question arises: If scholarship has eroded in the profession, how did it happen?

SCHOLARSHIP: EVIDENCE OF EROSION

Before attempting to address the issue of how it happened, it is necessary
to provide evidence that scholarship has indeed eroded. It is too easy to
point to front-line clinicians and accuse them of a lack of scholarship. It is
easy simply because these clinicians often want something practical rather
than theoretical and because they hold a master's degree as a function of
acquiring CCC certification. They are, by and large, consumers of the literature rather than contributors. So, if one wanted to rationalize the erosion of
scholarship, merely point the finger at front-line clinicians. Yet, this is hardly a
worthy indictment, nor is it substantiation. It is merely a convenient ploy.

Front-line clinicians are using clinical assessment procedures that lack
construct validity and intervention approaches that have peculiar juxta-
posed underlying theoretical perspectives, notably behavioristic notions in
the guise of mentalism and constructionism (Fey, 1986; Kamhi, 1988; Paul,
1995). These are substantive issues that surely reveal an erosion of scholarship.

In assessment, it is a scholarly responsibility to use clinical procedures
that have construct validity simply because without construct validity assessment reduces down to an ethical dilemma (Messick, 1980, 1989a, 1989b)
grounded on dogma. Unfortunately, it is easy to find assessment practices
in the clinical fields and in the clinical literature that lack construct validity
or that establish construct validity by virtue of factor analytic procedures
that are atheoretical. As for the latter, discriminate factors become identified
and then labeled whatever a test developer chooses to call them. In doing
so, they are released from interpretation from a theoretical perspective.

Several years ago, I was on an ASHA convention panel that dealt with
language assessment. As an example of a pervasive problem, I discussed
the lack of construct validity of the most widely used test in the field, the
PPVT–R (Dunn & Dunn, 1981). This test claims to assess vocabulary, and for
those who are more expansive and who are willing to follow the modality
notion, it presumably assesses receptive language. My presentation indicated that the PPVT–R failed to deal with the three most important issues
of vocabulary or word learning and use. Specifically, the PPVT–R failed to
deal with intentional meaning (it deals with elicited meaning), referential
meaning (one word, many referents; one referent, many words), and relational meaning (words in relation to other words). Mabel Rice followed my
presentation with the comment, "At least the PPVT–R tells us something."
Such comments provide tacit evidence that scholarship does not count
simply because the issues were at hand. Just like "It works" can be used to
cast aside the scholarly issues and revert to dogma, her comment had the
same potential. The panel moderator asked if I wanted to respond to Rice's
comment. The issues were at hand and dogma was looming, so I declined.

The notion that the PPVT–R may provide a useful assessment of "receptive language" is also startlingly short of scholarship. This test has already been shown to be an inadequate test of vocabulary. Indeed, Kuczaj and Barrett (1986) provided a summary of the literature on word or vocabulary acquisition. From this perspective, the PPVT–R offers a puzzling assessment of vocabulary. Furthermore, if one considers the issues attendant to language comprehension (Clark & Clark, 1977) that pertain to the construction of propositions and utilization of these propositions with reference to one's knowledge of the world (Palermo, 1971), possible worlds (Bruner, 1986), or situated mind (K. Nelson, 1996), it becomes embarrassingly silly to regard the PPVT–R as a viable measure of receptive language.

Muma and Brannon (1986) reviewed several of the most widely used language tests in the clinical fields (TOLD, CELF, DSS, PPVT–R, etc.) and found that they lacked construct validity. Subsequently, several of them were published in revised form with their manuals containing platitudes about validity, but they still lacked continuity with relevant explicit theoretical perspectives in the cognitive socialization literature.

Even reviews of these tests (Darley, 1979; McCauley & Swisher, 1984a) missed construct validity. McCauley and Swisher (1984a) asserted that construct validity was "difficult and somewhat subjective" so they dismissed it and considered 10 other subordinate psychometric criteria (p. 35). Here is more evidence of eroding scholarship.

Thus, on the one hand, the literature in test and measurement indicated that the essential issue is construct validity and that all other issues are derived from construct validity: "All measurement should be construct referenced" (Messick, 1980, p. 1015). Yet, on the other hand, reviews of clinical tests set construct validity aside in order to consider subordinate issues. This stance effectively dismisses the scholarly base of clinical assessment.

Another area that lacks construct validity is Brown's (1973b) five stages with the attendant MLU index. It is especially interesting that Brown himself provided two admonishments (Brown, 1978, 1988) to the effect that these stages have not held up. His admonishments indicate that Stages III, IV, and V are only hypothetical and should not be perpetuated because he was unable to find unifying principles across different language samples. Consequently, the major language acquisition scholars—notably Brown, Bruner, Cazden, Nelson, Snow, and others—have evidently ceased relying on Brown's five stages and MLU.

In contrast, the clinical fields remain undaunted in their reliance on Brown's five stages and MLU. Indeed, the clinical fields have basically canonized these stages and MLU (Miller & Chapman, 1981a, 1981b; Paul, 1995). Furthermore, there are several concerns about the adequacy of the Miller and Chapman (1981b) norms (Conant, 1987; Lahey, 1994; Muma, this volume).

Another common data reporting practice in the clinical fields is the misuse of percentages. Percentages should only be used when data approximate or exceed 100 instances. Yet, it is common practice, both clinically and in clinical journals, to convert instances of behavior that are well under 100 to percentages. Such practices inflate the data. Scholars are concerned about such practices simply because they yield illusionary data lacking validity.

The problem of data inflation is confounded further when pre- and post-comparisons are made to address intervention efficacy. In such instances, the inflations are disproportionate, thereby yielding data open to virtually any interpretation. The clinical fields have been silent about such matters but scholarship is vigilant about them.

Three major events have happened in the past decade that point to lowered scholarship in ASHA. These events were inbreeding that evidently reached a critical mass, turning over of the publications to applications at the cost of a theoretical base, and the call for professional doctorates.

Inbreeding is potentially destructive for a profession. It essentially restricts or confines a field to what it already knows and does and ultimately converts a profession to a political enterprise rather than a scholarly one. That is precisely the kind of comments scholars who have left the clinical fields are making (ASHA is too inbred and too political). ASHA needs influences from other disciplines to revive its own misfortunes. Bruner (personal communication, May 26, 1995) commented to me that a bona fide field of study needs critics in order to become legitimate and respectable. Without critics, politics intrude on scholarship. Evidently inbreeding in ASHA has reached a critical mass whereby scholarship has become scuttled, as evidenced by the issues raised herein, and politics has become the code of the day.

Another kind of evidence as to how scholarship has eroded in the clinical fields as a function of inbreeding is that ASHA is notoriously blind or myopic to major new developments in the scholarly literature. Three major developments have occurred in the past decade in the literature on the philosophy of cognition and language:

1. The distinction between brute and institutional facts (Lakoff, 1987).
2. The distinction between science and narrative (Bruner, 1986).
3. The emergence of the biological, cognitive, social, emotional, and cultural faceted situated mind (K. Nelson, 1996).

Lakoff (1987) drew the distinction between brute and institutional facts. Brute facts are those that are based on formal definitions, formal measurement, and quantification. Formal definitions include laws and rules, dictionary definitions, rules of conduct, and so on. Formal measurement includes such things as inches, feet, miles, pounds, tons, decibels, frequency, and so on. Quantification refers to frequency counts, assigning numerical values, and various quantitative manipulations ranging from something as simple as percentages to elaborate factor analytic procedures. Quantifications are essentially devices to make things eligible for manipulation. Thus, they are humanistic devices to tame the complexity of the world (Kaplan, 1964). However, to borrow from Bruner (1986), they are insufficiently human.

Most of the traditional literature is based on brute facts. There is inevitably the problem of appreciating the relevance of brute fact evidence for the real world. That is, after the various manipulations of the data have taken place, the real world may become so far removed that the data are of little value. This is precisely the point that Bronfenbrenner (1974, 1979) and Donaldson (1978) made.

Bronfenbrenner (1974, 1979) made the following poignant observation. Much of the literature in child development is based on tasks that children had never done before in their lives and would never do again in their lives; yet, their performances are used to draw inferences about their lives. This circumstance is incoherent. It is what Bronfenbrenner regarded as ecologically invalid.

Donaldson (1978) had essentially the same message. She indicated that performance on contrived tasks in which behavior is elicited misses the crucial intentional nature of behavior. Rather than contrived tasks, she held that it is more appropriate to ask questions that make human sense. In a similar vein, Brown (1986) commented that spontaneous language samples are "more germane than all the laboratory studies" (p. 278).

In contrast to brute facts, institutional facts are those kinds of facts that an individual learns by virtue of experience in various social and cultural institutions. Thus, an individual learns about the daily routines, or scripts, of the family institution. From these initial embodied experiences, procedural knowledge emerges (Mandler, 1983) that ultimately becomes elaborated, expanded, and reorganized into categorization or symbolization resulting in narrative thought and language of the situated mind (K. Nelson, 1996). This is the message of the cognitive socialization literature, which has much to offer the clinical fields if they can only shake loose of the traditional shackles mentioned herein.

The following are some other actual examples of this plight. Bruner (1986) drew a distinction between two modes of thought that were also regarded as two castles: science and narrative. The field of psychology has recognized the profound implications of these distinctions (Hoshmand & Polkinghorne, 1992).

Muma wrote a paper addressing the clinical implications of Bruner's distinctions between science and human affairs (narrative) and submitted it to the *Journal of Speech-Language Pathology* and the ASHA convention for

5 years running. It was rejected because it was deemed "too difficult to read. . . . The manuscript would need substantial reworking in order to be clear enough for the ideas and suggestions offered in the paper to be adequately evaluated" (J. Masterson, personal communication, May 4, 1994). Masterson indicated that science was described too narrowly and narrative was not fully described. She was obviously unaware of these perspectives of science and narrative and their significance because they were precisely those discussed by Bruner. Unfortunately for Masterson, and ultimately the clinical fields, who have parochial perspectives of science and narrative, they are likely to misunderstand these issues and their functions are the most important developments that have occurred in the philosophy of cognition and language since Piagetian psychology. To underscore the gravity of this dismissal, I sent the paper to Bruner with the editorial comments and I included some other editorial comments to the effect that my new book (this volume) was too theoretical and not practical. He responded, "I liked 'Science and human affairs' very much and I particularly liked some of the implications you drew from *Actual Minds* that I had overlooked—particularly the dilemma it has created for the clinicians" (J. Bruner, personal communication, August 18, 1993).

I told him that I intended to put this paper in an appendix in my new book, and he responded:

> I think you're right to put your paper on "Science and Human Affairs" in an appendix to your new book. . . . That is certainly an important way of keeping control over your own voice. Lots of us will be looking forward to the new book. . . . Just go on pursuing the kind of scholarship you care about: What else is there to do? (J. Bruner, personal communication, May 26, 1995)

As for the prepublication rejection comments for the book manuscript, these reviewers deemed the book to be "too theoretical and too critical." Bruner commented that that was "absurd." "What's wrong with being 'theoretical and critical'?" He authorized me to use his name and his publisher in obtaining a book publisher.

As for absurdity, here is another similar circumstance. Searle (1992), perhaps the foremost scholar on the philosophy of cognition and language, wrote a penetrating book that reviewed behaviorism, monism, dualism, materialism, constructionism, and so on. His basic conclusion was that except for constructionism, the various philosophical views considered were incoherent. With respect to different philosophical views, he used the comment "Who do we think we are?" I used that comment as the title of a paper sent to Richard Schwartz, the editor of the *Journal of Speech and Hearing Research*. This paper summarized Searle's book and position and it presented various clinical implications, especially the centrality of consciousness in assessment and intervention.

Schwartz rejected it with the claim that this area is one that is:

> close to my heart and to my own intellectual interests. Although the topic is
> a timely one and could be presented in a way that would be of interest to the
> readership of JSHR, your paper falls short of these goals in several respects.
> First, the literature on connectionist and on dynamic systems is extensive and
> complex. You have not given this topic sufficient attention to warrant its dis-
> missal. You have not provided convincing arguments against dualism or in
> favor of monism. (R. Schwartz, personal communication, May 23, 1996)

The point concerning the lack of scholarship is that this literature and this
manuscript did not discuss connectionism or dynamic systems. Furthermore, contrary to Schwartz's claimed expertise, both this literature and this
paper argued against monism. In short, Schwartz fumbled the scholarly ball.
He was once again full of himself in rejecting another paper entitled "Propo-
sitioning Propositions." Such is the caliber of scholarship in ASHA. It effectively withholds alternative views and perspectives.

Over the past decade, the conventions and publications of ASHA have
become increasingly in the grip of the technician motto "Don't give us
theory, give us hands-on practical information." It is laudable to be responsive to the needs of clinicians in the field, but to utterly strip away the
essence of the substantive foundation does more to reduce the field to
technicianship than anything else.

Another major development has been K. Nelson's (1996) account of the
emergence of the biological, cognitive, social, emotional, and cultural faceted
situated mind. The reason that this development is so important is that it
is the most eloquent account of cognitive development that brings forward
biological, mental, social, emotional, and cultural influences. Language thus
becomes subordinated to communication, which was the functionalistic
message over the past four decades and consciousness, or intentions as
specific instances of consciousness, has emerged as the central issue
(Bruner, 1986, 1990; Searle, 1992), which is the basic message of speech act
(Grice, 1975) and relevance (Sperber & Wilson, 1986) theories. By subordinating language to communication, this development gives new focus to
how possible worlds or situated minds are the products of social and cultural
influences. In doing so, this development shows that context is crucial for
any account of cognition and language. "Context is all" (Bruner, 1981, p. 172).
K. Nelson (1985, 1986, 1996) addressed several issues in appreciating contextual influences in both cognitive and language acquisition. To emphasize
the importance of social and cultural dynamics in cognitive and language
acquisition, consider the following. Possible worlds or situated minds would
be rogue in nature if it were not for the leveling effects of social and cultural
dynamics (K. Nelson, 1996; Rogoff, 1990; Wertsch, 1991).

This development has far-reaching clinical implications for the clinical
fields that strive to deal with cognition and language, indeed communica-

tion. Because context is crucial and intent is the central issue, the various acontextual activities in the clinical fields are merely peripheral to any substantive consideration of cognition and language. Thus, the widespread use of procedures and notions such as the following turn up shallow: normative tests lacking construct validity grounded on theory, developmental profiles, frequency counts as presumed evidence of acquisition, expressive and receptive language, modality processing, a priori intervention approaches, and acontextual efficacy notions. For starters, clinicians should focus on a client's social and experiential arenas as viable contexts for assessment and intervention in cognition and language. In doing so, clinicians would strive to deal with a client's repertoire, progress in acquisition sequences, alternative learning strategies, and active loci of learning. Needless to say, this development places the clinical fields on the threshold of accepting the scholarly substantive issues in the cognitive socialization literature.

The call for a professional doctorate has an interesting aspect that belies a shift from scholarship to technicianship. A PhD is a degree predicated on the philosophy of science. Curiously, most PhD-granting programs in ASHA do not provide training in the philosophy of science (Prutting, Mentis, & Myles-Zitzer, 1989). Thus, there is a very strange circumstance whereby individuals holding a PhD are presumably vested with appropriate knowledge of the philosophy of science yet they do not know this literature and profess to be scholars. By default and by definition, these individuals are already "professional" doctorates and are already committed to technicianship. The acid tests of this assertion are that the issues cited earlier are merely rationalized away by these PhDs but other PhDs who are solidly grounded in scholarship attend to the issues.

SCHOLARSHIP: HOW IT BECAME ERODED

Given the preceding debacles, it is self-evident what has happened. The onus for eroding scholarship is not on the front-line clinicians. Rather, the onus is on those individuals, either by virtue of naivete or implicit collusion, who have had opportunities to take scholarly stances but actually failed to do so, especially those vested with the convention committees and publications and those who make decisions about the nature of training programs.

Ascholarly Stance: Disdain for Theory

There is a very strange attitude about theories in the clinical fields. Technicians are prone to say, "Don't give me theory, I want something practical." Yet, it is precisely theory that makes things understood and therefore makes things practical in a scholarly arena (Muma, 1991).

The philosophy of science literature (Kaplan, 1964) indicates that theories provide prediction, explanation, and understanding. Theories are unifying constructs. They establish coherence. Philosophical views and theoretical perspectives should constitute the substantive base of a scholarly field or discipline. In doing so, theories become a clinician's best friend; theories make things useful or practical. Because theoretical perspectives are derived from recognized philosophical views, it is assumed that any scholarly discipline or profession would earnestly strive to be grounded on philosophical views and theoretical perspectives. Thus, to dismiss theory is to effectively deny scholarship and the substantive base of a field and at the same time commit it to dogma and technicianship.

Unfortunately, Kamhi (1993), Perkins (1986), and Starkweather (1992) have taken the position that theories may be dismissed in the clinical fields.

> There is a certain sense in which theoretical beliefs should influence therapy—one should have a good understanding of the disorder so as to make good judgments and choices when confronting an individual—but to allow a theoretical belief to restrain one's therapeutic practice is thoroughly irresponsible. (Starkweather, 1992, p. 95)

"Providing clinical services that are theoretically coherent is not only impractical, but also unrealistic" (Kamhi, 1993, p. 59).

Perkins (1986) held that because his physician was not oriented on theories but was successful in rendering clinical services, at least to Perkins, there was little need to be theory oriented. Fortunately, Perkins realized the weakness of this perspective and became an advocate of theories.

The obvious question is: How could such views be accepted for publication by the editors, associate editors, and reviewers? It is utterly absurd to dismiss theory and it is symptomatic of a field that is insufficiently grounded on scholarship and the philosophy of science.

In a similar vein, it would be informative to survey ASHA training programs to ascertain to what extent they are grounded on the philosophy of science. Prutting et al. (1989) surveyed ASHA training programs and found that only 3.6% of them had course work with readings in the philosophy of science—another rejection for ASHA publication. This is very serious. It means that the profession is insufficiently prepared to appreciate major substantive developments especially in the philosophical literature that pertains to the clinical fields. This is especially unfortunate because three major developments have occurred in the philosophical literature that have already had profound effects in the field of psychology (Hoshmand & Polkinghorne, 1992) and have major implications for the clinical fields; for example, Bruner (1986), Lakoff (1987), K. Nelson (1996), and Searle (1992). These were discussed earlier.

Modality Problem

There is a historical reason for how scholarship became eroded in the clinical fields: The original perspectives of language were not solidly grounded on philosophical views and theoretical perspectives. Unfortunately, ASHA's views of language were atheoretical from the start and when the early theories were offered, especially Osgood's (1957) theory of information processing that stressed modality differences, the clinical fields latched onto the modality view and held on tenaciously even in the face of other more eloquent and supportable theoretical perspectives, notably speech act theory (Austin, 1962; Clark & Clark, 1977; Grice, 1975; Searle, 1969), relevance theory (Sperber & Wilson, 1986), and shared meaning (K. Nelson, 1985, 1986, 1996).

Indeed, Clark and Clark (1977) indicated that modality information is purged very early in information processing with most of the cognitive activity in language residing in general cognition (categorization, inference, problem solving) contrary to Chomsky's notion of the language module. Furthermore, reviews of the literature on presumed auditory processing (Rees, 1981; Tallal, 1990) indicated that the difficulties with language are not modality specific: "These deficits are neither specific to speech stimuli nor confined to the auditory modality. . . . The deficit in rapid temporal analysis and production is not specific to linguistic information per se, or to the auditory modality" (Tallal, 1990, pp. 616–617).

Muma (1978b, 1986a) held that the modalities of language merely deal with rather peripheral aspects of language and the more substantial core issues in the cognitive socialization literature (cognition, codification, socialization, expression-affect, culture) are not modality specific. Thus, when the clinical fields adopted a modality stance (expressive and receptive language), they took a major step toward technicianship with a loss of attendant scholarship.

Language Sampling: Wedded to Tradition

Another historical perspective has been the clinical tradition of using 50- or 100-utterance language samples for ascertaining an individual's grammatical skills. The obvious scholarly question is what theoretical perspectives and/or empirical justifications exist for these sample sizes? Muma and Brannon (1986) surveyed over 90 studies that used such samples. The purposes of the survey were to ascertain the theoretical and empirical justifications of these samples. The survey came up empty.

Evidently, the clinical fields accept these practices merely by virtue of tradition, apparently issuing from the comments by Darley and Moll (1960) and McCarthy (1954). McCarthy (1930) regarded 50 response samples in the following way: "This number was decided upon because it would give a fairly representative sample of a child's linguistic development in a relatively short period of time, without tiring the child with a prolonged observation." Darley and Moll (1960) concluded that 50-response samples gave reliable mean length of response data but lacked reliable structural complexity scores. Thus, these comments apparently launched the prevailing clinical tradition of relying on 50-utterance samples. However, no study has shown that 50- or 100-utterance samples provide sufficient evidence of an individual's repertoire of grammatical or pragmatic skills.

On the face of it, it is patently obvious that it would be exceedingly difficult to package an individual's repertoire of grammatical skills in such small samples—even for individuals with rather limited grammars. Grammar is simply too complex for such prospects. Furthermore, it is patently obvious that it would be exceedingly difficult to capture even the most fully representative sample in a sampling procedure. Notice that the clinical fields have remained silent about these major sampling problems—save Muma (1986a, this volume) and Gavin and Giles (1996).

Several years ago, Muma et al. submitted a manuscript on language sampling and the issue of sample size to *Journal of Speech and Hearing Research*. We went several rounds with the editor, who wanted various sections rewritten and/or deleted. The end result would have gutted the article so we held steadfast and the manuscript was rejected. It now appears as Appendix D in this volume in an unadulterated form. We held to the theoretical model, attribution criteria, the cascade grammatical analysis, and the section that documented that norms do not provide necessary or sufficient information by virtue of a lack of relevance to available repertoires and underestimation. The editor had recommended that these be struck. Sometimes scholarship means holding to the philosophical stance and theoretical perspective with the attendant issues.

A major outcome of this paper was that 50-utterance and 100-utterance samples have excessively large error rates (approximately 55% and 40%, respectively). This means that clinical reports and research papers based on such samples have inordinately large errors. Furthermore, it means that the so-called efficacy studies based on such samples are likely flawed by sampling errors.

Behaviorism and Reinforcement Problem

Unfortunately, the clinical fields have been oriented on behaviorism and reinforcement theory. It is unfortunate because the clinical fields have held on tenaciously to reinforcement (Fey, 1986; Kamhi, 1988; Paul, 1995) when the major scholars of language have long since replaced reinforcement with intent as a more viable account of language acquisition. To reiterate, in addition to intent, context has emerged as a focal issue (K. Nelson, 1985, 1986, 1996): "Context is all" (Bruner, 1981, p. 172).

The following are some quotes regarding the failings of behaviorism and/or reinforcement theory in language acquisition.

Models of language acquisition built explicitly on assumptions of positive and negative reinforcement are no longer acceptable. (K. Nelson, 1985, p. 33)

The absurdity of behaviorism lies in the fact that it denies the existence of any mental states. (Searle, 1992, p. 35)

In part, the shift stems from the move away from behaviorism, with its denigration of mental events, to cognitive theories that directly focus on those events. (Mandler, 1983, p. 421)

Although many researchers were persuaded by Chomsky's arguments that the then-reigning theory of learning, behaviorism, was incapable of accounting for the acquisition of grammar. (Bowerman, 1994, p. 329)

Macken (1987) indicated that the language learning mechanism is remarkably good at discerning patterns from which a grammar may evolve and that this capacity is "*quite* unlike an empiricist reinforcement schedule" (p. 380).

In principle, such S-R analyses of language behavior can never adequately account for the acquisition and maintenance of language. (Palermo, 1971, p. 135)

These operations—which constitute the result of generative theory—cannot be accounted for, derived, from, or otherwise interpreted within the traditional psychological points of view about intellectual processes. They are particularly difficult for any theory that reduces cognition to associations between elements. (Deese, 1970, p. 42)

In reference to behaviorism, Pinker (1988) commented on "the virtual demise of classical learning theory as an explanation of language development" (p. 113).

Yoder (1987) asked a poignant question: "Where are the data that tell us that 90% criterion levels are effective?" (p. 11).

Cazden (1988) referred to the failure of studies to find evidence of reinforcement in natural language acquisition, "To put the conclusions bluntly: Reinforcement did not exist, frequency did not correlate, and expansions did not help" (p. 281).

Accordingly, major scholars have dropped notions of reinforcement and turned to intent as a more viable alternative: "Radical behaviorism is another: attributing cause and denying the role of intention in the realm of human events" (Bruner, 1986, p. 88). "More importantly, human action is intentional and thus demands interpretation" (K. Nelson, 1985, p. 37). "Everything is use" (Bruner, 1986, p. 87).

Perera (1994), the editor of the most prestigious language acquisition journal (*Journal of Child Language*), named the four most influential theories in language acquisition over the past 25 years, one of which was relevance theory, which is a new rendition of speech act theory. Behaviorism or reinforcement theory were notable for their absence.

Except for some individuals in speech-language pathology, the major scholars in language acquisition have long since dispatched such accounts (behaviorism, reinforcement) because they not only lacked construct validity and failed to generalize but they were slippery and silent about many important aspects of language acquisition. Bruner (1978) regarded behaviorism and reinforcement theory as corrosive dogma because of their silence about major issues and slipperiness for others. Chomsky (1968) had a long comment on the failings of behaviorism in general and reinforcement as its central premise.

Silence

Scholars have a commitment to ask penetrating questions. For example, why do the clinical fields rely on tests that lack construct validity? Why do the clinical fields rely on language samples of only 50 or 100 utterances? Why do the clinical fields misuse percentage and rely on quantification at the cost of context? Why have the clinical fields shied away from intent as the central issue of cognition and language when the scholarly literature over the past four decades established the centrality of intent? Why do the clinical fields continue to rely on Brown's five stages and the attendant MLUs? Why are the clinical fields not solidly grounded on the available scholarly philosophical views and theoretical perspectives? Why are the clinical fields inadequately focused on the cognitive socialization literature that provides the substantive reasons to focus on available repertoires of skills, progress in acquisition sequences, available learning strategies, and active loci of learning?

In a word, the clinical fields are silent about these and several other major issues. Silence is the signature of the uninformed and of technicians. After all, to talk about the issues may also reveal a lack of knowledge of the substantive bases of cognition and language and a lack of scholarship.

Normative Test Mentality

Another revealing perspective is the degree to which the clinical fields have been committed to the normative model. It is widely believed that if a test has norms, that is all that is needed for a valid assessment. However, the literature on test and measurement has shown that the crucial issue is construct validity (Messick, 1980).

Contrary to the understanding of many in the clinical fields, either or both formal and informal assessments are acceptable in meeting the P.L. 94–142 criteria of standardized assessment (Martin, 1980). The clinical fields should be committed to rigorous examinations of all assessment practices, both formal (normative) and informal (descriptive), to assure that such practices have solid theoretical perspectives and therefore have construct validity. In doing so, the claims that an assessment "works" or "tells us something" come up hollow simply because such claims merely license dogma. Rather, theory-based assessment confines the interpretation of the data to only particular allowable perspectives and understandings.

In addition to construct validity, the normative model has become suspect from two vantage points, shaking its very foundation, objectivity, and necessary and sufficient evidence. Heretofore, it was assumed that normative tests provide objective evidence for a particular aspect of assessment. However, Lakoff (1987) and others in the philosophy of language and cognition have raised the penetrating question as to whether it is possible to have objective evidence. In his words, it is impossible to have an objective or "God's-eye" view of the world. Both going in (test development) and coming out (test use), subjective decisions and interpretations are entailed.

Scholarship recognizes the value of both subjective and objective perspectives. Indeed, scholarship has shown that objectivity is essentially a myth (Lakoff, 1987) and that scholarship is actually dependent on disciplined subjectivity. Apparently, merely hoisting the banner of objectivity for normative tests does more to deny penetrating enquiry of scholarship than justify such tests.

In addition to objectivity, another time-honored virtue of normative tests is that they presumably provide necessary and sufficient evidence of what is being tested. The example of the PPVT–R discussed previously clearly shows that this test does not provide necessary and sufficient evidence of vocabulary and only a myopic view would consider PPVT–R performance a viable index of receptive language. Indeed, a scholarly consideration of virtually all of the tests used clinically comes up with a similar conclusion. If conclusions are to be made about an individual's presumed capacities or skills, it behooves the test developers and test users to provide evidence that such measures offer valid estimates of an individual's available repertoire. Notice that the clinical fields have been silent about this issue and have relied instead on various statistical evidence of the tests.

Thus, a test of grammatical skill should provide necessary and sufficient evidence of an individual's available repertoire. For example, DSS norms (Lee & Canter, 1971) claim to provide necessary and sufficient evidence of an individual's grammatical skills. However, there are some serious conceptual flaws with this normative assessment procedure. These flaws pertain to sampling error, grammatical domains, and quantification.

This procedure is based on 50-utterance samples. As indicated earlier, such small samples have excessive error rates. As for conceptualization of grammar, the DSS has some peculiar notions of grammar. For example, derived nominals (Lees, 1965) were regarded as secondary verbs, demonstratives were called personal pronouns, and modals and other aspects of the auxiliary system were separated from tense. There are no theories of grammar that would warrant such violations, yet the DSS has been deemed a measure of grammar. The DSS quantifies selected aspects of grammar in accordance with a parts-of-speech and levels matrix. Unfortunately, the quantification procedure followed what appears to be the traditional parts-of-speech or topological model rather than the available quantification models for sentence hierarchies (Johnson, 1965, 1966; Yngve, 1960). Consequently, the DSS merely sanctioned the authors' dogma rather than yielded a bona fide assessment of grammatical skills. Yet, the clinical fields have been silent about these problems—loss of scholarship.

Inbreeding: Revisited

Evidently the reason for such myopic stances is inbreeding with the attendant political stances. Rather than address various new developments in the literature, the clinical fields have taken a stance of preserving traditional views and practices—at a heavy cost of scholarship. A major ramification of inbreeding is politicizing, which may occur in rather subtle ways (i.e., personalizing, innuendo, and superficial comments about substantive issues).

A telling example of the latter two issues occurred when my 1986 book was reviewed in the *Asha* journal by Byrne-Saricks (1987). She lamented that my book needed more explanation of the quotations provided, and that readers needed "a great deal of knowledge about research and theories of many of the authorities to determine whether or not the statements are valid" (p. 50). The implicit assumption of this statement is that she was not willing to credit language expertise to those ASHA members who claim language expertise. Perhaps my retort clarified matters (Muma, 1987b).

In contrast, R. Brown (personal communication, October 9, 1986) made the following comment about my 1986 book: "I have been sampling it and want to congratulate you on an exceptionally well written and sensible book that seems ideal for your intended mark." J. Bruner (personal communication, December 11, 1993) wrote to me with the following comment: "I also admired your earlier book as a very sensible and clear presentation, in agreement with Roger."

Expediency

A way of rationalizing away scholarship that has become a running theme in the clinical fields is the clamor for expediency. Faced with too many clients, the clinical fields have turned to quick and easy tests and intervention approaches, without regard for whether they are relevant to the pertinent literature or an individual's available repertoire.

Expediency has been the rallying call for technicianship. Pressed with caseloads that are too large, those in the clinical fields have relinquished scholarship with quick and easy clinical services that "work." In this context, the notion that "it works" actually translates into the rationalization that a given number of clients have received services, without regard to whether the services lack validity and may be inappropriate. This is merely a sheepish plight rather than a scholarly one.

Cazden (1972) and her colleagues recognized this problem in preschool education. They pointed out that much of what is done in preschool education (and in the clinical fields) includes activities that make teachers (technicians) operational, but little consideration is given to whether what is done is philosophically or theoretically sound. Without such considerations, these activities are little more than dogma in veiled claims of expertise and professionalism.

Indoctrination: Allegiance

When scholarship is cast asunder, there is a hurry to preserve the claim for expertise and for professionalism. Such claims evidently have taken two basic forms: politics and allegiance.

I know of individuals in the clinical fields that steadfastly hold to various clinical notions and practices of the past that have long since been overcome by the literature, especially the notions of reinforcement, Brown's five stages with the attendant MLU values, and phonemes in isolation. Several of them are at major universities. What has happened is that they establish political alliances with other professionals in an effort to secure their position. They then turn to indoctrination of their students to establish a political stance for the new generation.

The indoctrination process is subtle but effective. First they peddle their wares in classes and clinically so students are subjected from the start. Then, they wage a never-ending campaign, reminding students how fierce the competition was to enter the program, implicitly indicating that the program must be one of the best. The students are actively courted personally to convey the image that Professor So-and-so is really a good person. The latter should not be construed as improper professional conduct. However, it can be easily exploited in the service of politicizing students.

Cognitive Socialization: The Saving Grace

The cognitive socialization literature, well grounded on appropriate philosophical views and theoretical perspectives, is available to provide the clinical fields a philosophically and theoretically solid substantive base for dealing with cognition and language. With this literature, the clinical fields could effectively overcome various problems mentioned earlier and turn toward increased scholarship. In doing so, technicians can become clinicians and the clinical fields could emerge from their present plight.

APPENDIX D:
LANGUAGE SAMPLING:
GRAMMATICAL ASSESSMENT

John Muma
Central Michigan University

Ana Morales, Kerri Day, Annette Tackett,
Sharon Smith, Barbara Daniel, Beverly Logue, Debra Morriss
Texas Tech University

This study addressed two basic issues of language sampling: estimated grammatical repertoires and, in view of present prevailing clinical practices, appropriate sample size.

Language samples of 400 spontaneous utterances from actual social commerce were used to ascertain estimated repertoires for the following basic grammatical systems: subject nominals, object nominals, auxiliaries, verbals, and grammatical operations. Two attribution criteria were used: single instances and three varied instances. Estimated repertoires provided evidence of vertical and horizontal learning, language learning strategies, and active loci of learning, all of which are beyond the purview of normative tests.

With a sampling error rate of about 15%, language samples should use 200 to 300 utterances to estimate most grammatical repertoires. Unfortunately, the prevailing clinical language sampling practices use 50- or 100-utterance samples. Such samples have excessively large error rates of approximately 55% and 40%, respectively, when compared to 400-utterance samples. Such large error rates are likely to make some intervention goals and some claims of efficacy inherently flawed.

GENERAL PERSPECTIVE

In general, there are two ways of doing language assessment: psychometric normative testing and descriptive assessment derived from representative language samples. Both have limitations that should be considered in clinical assessment. Psychometric normative testing should be scrutinized from the point of view of the following issues: objectivity, necessary and sufficient evidence, construct validity, quantification, standard error of measurement, and assessment power. Descriptive assessment based on language samples for estimating the grammatical repertoire should be scrutinized in regard to the following: representativeness, productivity, sampling error rate, sampling condition, elicited and spontaneous language samples, and sample size. These issues are shown in Table D.1.

ESTIMATED GRAMMATICAL REPERTOIRE

Grammatical repertoire is the range or scope of available grammatical capacities. It is a psychological notion that can be inferred or estimated from performance in representative samples of what individuals actually do in social commerce. That is, given evidence of what individuals actually do in representative language samples, it is possible to infer or estimate what the individuals can do. Thus, estimated repertoires are necessarily grounded on actual performance in representative samples. Such samples provide prima facie evidence for estimating available repertoires.

Needless to say, the key issue for estimating grammatical and pragmatic repertoires is representative language samples. Gallagher (1983) described three kinds of representative language samples: complete, optimal, and typical. A *complete* sample contains all a person can do; it is a sample that gives complete evidence of the full range of grammatical and pragmatic distinctions available to an individual. Such samples are virtually unobtainable simply because it would be impossible to sample everything a person

TABLE D.1
Issues in Dealing With Grammatical Repertoire From Language Samples

---

Productivity: Decomposition, probes and robustness, acquisition sequence, percentage, frequency, frequency with variations within and between constructions, Piagetian attribution criteria: preparation, attainment, and consolidation, and single instances (potential range) or three varied instances (decomposition).
Sampling error rate: 5%, 15%, 25%.
Sampling condition: Standardized or varied conditions.
Elicited or spontaneous samples: Centrality of communicative intent.
Sample size: Appropriateness of the prevailing practices of 50 or 100 utterances.

---

does. An *optimal* sample is one that reveals the best of what a person can do. Such samples are also virtually unobtainable on similar grounds.

A *typical* sample is representative of one's daily use of language in actual social commerce. Such samples are obtainable in a reasonable amount of time. However, typical samples, by definition, do not contain an individual's full range of available skills. Thus, it is necessary to recognize some degree of sampling error for skills available to an individual but not evidenced in typical samples. Recognition of degrees of sampling error is tied to other important issues such as productivity, sampling condition, elicited and spontaneous language samples, and sample size.

Estimates of grammatical repertoire should be based on productive grammatical capacities as opposed to those grammatical constructions evidenced in highly rehearsed or ossified utterances. That is, what an individual does should be attributable to him or her by virtue of productive constructions rather than extrapolated from highly rehearsed or nondecomposable utterances.

There are different ways of addressing productivity. One way is decomposition. If a grammatical construction is evidenced with lexical variation, it is deemed decomposable and may be attributed to an individual's grammatical capacities. For example, if an individual evidences lexical variations of the definite article and noun construction (the *hat*, the *tree*, the *dog*), it is considered productive. Also, productivity may be evidenced by probes and robustness. For example, if an individual evidences a "wh-" question, a probe may be used whereby particular wh- questions that were evidenced in spontaneous speech would be used in new contexts. Klima and Bellugi-Klima (1969) used probes to verify an individual's command of interrogative and negation constructions that occurred infrequently or were presumed to be available by virtue of more advanced constructions appearing in a language sample. A similar probe, which might be regarded as a measure of robustness, is to remove a child's grammatical construction from the original communicative context (intentional support, referential support, relational support, and pragmatic support) to see if the construction is sufficiently robust to be sustained. Slobin and Welch (1971) showed that some grammatical constructions removed from these supports in actual social commerce resulted in errors in the children's own constructions. Thus, these constructions lacked robustness (Goldin-Meadow & Mylander, 1984; Muma, 1986a). Acquisition sequence may be used to attribute productivity. That is, when individuals evidence productivity for certain grammatical capacities that are somewhat more advanced in acquisition sequences, earlier capacities may be attributed.

Frequency has been used in the clinical fields to attribute acquisition. If many instances of a construction are evidenced, that construction is likely to be deemed productive. However, there is a caution about relying merely on frequency counts: Sheer frequency may reflect highly rehearsed but nondecomposable utterances. Frequency should be tied to lexical variation within grammatical constructions and variations of co-occurring constructions to warrant attributing productivity. For example, an individual who has a high frequency of a construction but the construction lacks lexical variation within or lacks variation of co-occuring constructions (Harris, 1965; Muma, 1973a) may not yet have productive capacity for such constructions.

Related to frequency counts is the notion of percentage; for example, Brown (1973b) regarded grammatical constructions as productive if they were correct in 90% of the obligatory contexts. Lee (1974), Lee et al. (1975), and Tyack and Gottsleben (1974, 1977) also relied on percentages for attribution. Most of the behavioristic studies relied on percentages (80%–100%) to attribute acquisition. However, there is a fundamental difference between Brown's utilization of percentages and the use of percentages by the others mentioned. Brown used percentages because the instances of grammatical constructions were many from large language samples, whereas Lee and her colleagues used only 50-utterance samples, Tyack and Gottsleben used 100-utterance samples, and the samples used in most behavioristic studies were usually very small. Because relatively few instances of different constructions were obtained in small samples, the use of percentages creates two problems. First, such data became inflated. Second, when such percentages are used as pre–postintervention comparisons or comparisons between individuals, disproportionate comparisons occur that point to the fallacy of such endeavors.

The Piagetian perspectives of preparation, attainment, and consolidation may be useful for attribution of grammatical capacities. These perspectives were not offered by Piaget for attribution of language capacities but they are applicable (Muma, 1983a, 1986a, K. E. Nelson, 1981; Prutting, 1979). What is attractive about them is that they are relative and they incorporate three issues: frequency, context, and robustness. A grammatical construction is deemed in preparation if it occurs infrequently, is context bound, and is difficult to elicit. It is considered in attainment if it is relatively frequent, not context bound, and relatively easy to elicit. It is regarded as consolidated if it occurs in varied co-occurring structures.

Should a grammatical distinction be attributed if only one or a few instances are evidenced or should several varied instances be needed to claim that a particular grammatical construction is available to an individual? A few crucial instances of a construction may be sufficient to trigger learning (Freidin & Quicoli, 1989). For example, it may not be important that many instances are evidenced, so long as an essential few are evidenced (Brown & Hanlon, 1970); indeed, it is a primary tenet of learnability theory (Lightfoot, 1989; Pinker, 1984) that only a few crucial instances of a grammatical skill may be needed for learning. What makes a particular instance potent is presumably the way in which it may be cohesive with what an individual already knows. The few available instances should be intentional and provide some means of negative evidence (Bowerman, 1987) or delimitation, possibly by virtue of contextual integrity or coherence (Macken, 1987; Maratsos, 1988a, 1988b; Ninio, 1988) for revealing how language works as intended (Bruner, 1981, 1986; Ninio & Snow, 1988) rather than raw negative instantiation. The following quotes indicate the potency of a small number of instances in language acquisition when these instances evidence coherence with an individual's available grammatical system:

> She is motivated to figure out regularities in the linguistic system that surround her, for the purpose of constructing a coherent, rule-governed structure. Such work may serve the sole purpose of rendering the system intrinsically coherent. (Levy, 1988, p. 75)

> Formal or structural categories—they are defined by use in the system itself. (Maratsos, 1988a, p. 34)

> The triggering experience may be less than the total linguistic experience of a child. (Lightfoot, 1989, p. 325)

> The crucial input for language growth to take place is very small. (Lightfoot, 1989, p. 329)

> A parser is fed by a grammar, and cannot parse beyond its resources. (Valian, 1990, p. 122)

However, a single instance of a grammatical distinction may be inadequate simply because a person may be in preparation for acquiring that skill rather than attainment or consolidation. Bruner (1986) commented somewhat facetiously, "We have extraordinary faith in one-shot instantiation" (p. 51). On the other hand, it may be useful to inventory single instances of grammatical constructions as estimates of repertoires because they could index someone's imminent potential.

Watkins and Rice (1991) used three instances for attribution of grammatical skills. Bloom et al. (1989) used three varied instances of a grammatical skill to credit it to an individual. Either way, one instance or three varied instances, seemed to be useful for describing estimated grammatical repertoires.

Sampling error rate is another notion that has not been addressed in the clinical fields. Under the assumption that typical language samples are obtained in clinical assessment and that such samples do not contain all an individual knows about language or the full range of optimal performance, it is necessary to recognize the level of sampling error that should be tolerated in attributing grammatical skills. This present study generates data concerning error rates of 5%, 15%, and 25% for language samples of 400 utterances.

Under what sampling conditions should language samples be obtained? Traditionally, it was deemed necessary to sample language in a standard sampling condition. Standard sampling is predicated on the notion that an individual has equivalent opportunities to evidence grammatical capacities on pre–postintervention comparisons or when comparisons are made between individuals. It was reasoned that using the same stimuli for such comparisons assures comparable opportunities to evidence available grammatical or pragmatic capacities. On its face, such reasoning and practices reflect the traditional notion of psychometric equal potentials. However, there is a fallacy in this kind of thinking. The contemporary cognitive socialization literature makes the standard sampling condition untenable because of presupposition, possible worlds (Bruner, 1986), or situated minds (K. Nelson, 1996). Briefly, an individual's knowledge of the world changes over time and it differs from one individual to another, thereby making the control of the external context superfluous. That is, it makes little difference in sampling what individuals can do with language if the external context is held constant when the internal contexts vary. Rather, what is needed in language sampling is varied external contexts to increase the prospects of sampling the range of skills available to individuals.

Another issue that should be considered in language sampling is the distinction between elicited and spontaneous language samples. For example, the clinical fields have relied on language samples obtained from picture descriptions, talking about toys, and various probes. Such samples are the result of elicitation procedures.

> The most frequently suggested sampling contexts have focused on describing pictures, talking about toys, or responding to probes by an interviewer (Engler, Hannah, & Longhurst, 1973; Lee, 1974; Tyack & Gottsleben, 1974). (Bloom & Lahey, 1978, p. 441)

However, because communicative intent has emerged as the central issue in language acquisition, as evidenced by speech act and relevance theories (Grice, 1975; Sperber & Wilson, 1986), it is essential that representative language samples be obtained from spontaneous speech in actual social commerce.

Regarding language sample size, Muma and Brannon (1986) surveyed more than 90 research articles and clinical assessment procedures that used language samples. They found that the prevailing practices used 50 or 100 utterances. For example, Lee (1974), Lee and Canter (1971), Miller and Chapman (1981a), Watkins and Rice (1991) used 50-utterance samples, whereas Tyack and Gottsleben (1977) used 100-utterance samples to attribute gram-

matical skills to individuals: "Many have suggested 50 to 100 different utterances as a sample for clinical analysis" (Lahey, 1988, p. 294).

> Most writers (e.g., Miller, 1981; Lahey, 1988; Nelson, 1993) suggest 50 to 100
> utterances. Cole, Mills, and Dale (1989) showed that a 50-utterance sample
> yields about 80% of the information available in a sample twice as long. For
> efficient yet valid clinical data gathering, then, a 50-utterance sample is usually
> adequate. (Paul, 1995, p. 300)

There are two fundamental issues that should be raised about 50- and
100-utterance samples:

1. The likelihood that such samples are representative.
2. Capturing representative samples.

Regarding the first, what is the likelihood of packaging available grammatical
and pragmatic capacities in 50- or 100-utterance samples? From this perspective, the prospects are exceedingly slim that it is even possible to package
a repertoire of such skills in such small samples. As for the second, what
are the prospects that such samples could be caught in a sampling procedure? Again, the prospects are exceedingly slim. Even though these are
major issues, it is peculiar that the clinical fields have been silent about
them and maintained a reliance on 50 and 100 utterances. Yet, nowhere in
the clinical fields have these rational issues been raised.

In discussing some logistical issues attendant to language sampling, Lahey (1988) came perilously close to relinquishing validity for expediency
but, fortunately, she ended up on the right side. She recommended samples
of 200 or more utterances: "A sample of 200 or more different utterances
would provide a better data base" (p. 294).

The survey by Muma and Brannon (1986) not only showed that the
prevailing clinical language sampling size relied on 50 or 100 utterances, but
the survey traced the references to ascertain what justifications were given
to warrant such samples. Most studies did not give either rational or empirical justifications for such sample sizes. They merely asserted that such
samples were obtained or they cited other sources that had used such
samples. Then it became necessary to trace back to the citations that were
given in various articles or assessment procedures. This effort resulted in
the following articles that had relied on such sample sizes: Darley and Moll
(1960), Johnson et al. (1963), McCarthy (1954), and Templin (1957). McCarthy
(1930) regarded 50 responses in a language sample as a useful sample: "This
number was decided upon because it would give a fairly representative
sample of a child's linguistic development in a relatively short period of
time, without tiring the child with a prolonged observation" (p. 32).

Darley and Moll (1960) concluded that 50 response samples gave reliable mean length of response data but lacked reliable structural complexity scores. Interestingly, these studies did not address the more basic issue, which is language sample sizes needed to estimate available grammatical repertoires. Indeed, no study could be found that addressed this fundamental issue. In short, neither appropriate rational nor empirical justifications were found to warrant the use of 50- or 100-utterance samples in ascertaining available repertoires of grammatical capacities.

This study ascertains estimated grammatical repertoires for large language samples and evaluates to what extent 50- or 100-utterance samples are capable of revealing these estimated repertoires. Because Lahey (1988) recommended language samples of 200 utterances for estimating grammatical repertories, it was deemed appropriate to use much larger samples. For the present purpose, 400-utterance samples were used to estimate grammatical repertoires.

PURPOSE

This study deals with two specific issues concerning the value of language sampling in descriptive assessment. The two purposes of this study are:

1. To estimate basic grammatical repertoires from representative samples, and in so doing,
2. To ascertain needed language sample sizes in view of the prevailing clinical practices of using 50- or 100-utterance samples.

METHOD

Participants

Seven normal preschool children were the participants. Four were girls and three were boys. Their ages ranged from 2;2 to 5;2. Each child provided continuous 400-utterance spontaneous language samples from actual social commerce. The seven children provided a total of 10 400-utterance language samples of spontaneous speech as they interacted in typical social commerce with a parent at home. One individual (Peter) provided three language samples and another (Adam) provided two language samples. The samples from Peter and Adam provided opportunities to compare samples within participants, whereas all of the samples provided opportunities to make comparisons between participants. Table D.2 gives descriptive information about the participants.

TABLE D.2
A Description of the Normal Children and Their
MLUs for the Obtained 400-Utterance Language Samples

	Gender	Age	MLU
Eve	F	2;2	3.6
Nina	F	2;6	3.2
Peter1	M	2;7	4.4
Peter2	M	2;7	5.1
Peter3	M	2;11	4.1
Brad	M	3;7	6.2
Annie	F	3;8	6.4
Taylor	F	4;6	7.4
Adam1	M	4;1	4.5
Adam2	M	5;2	4.6

Note. The numbers following Peter and Adam indicate the language sampling times for each child.

All children had to have clear evidence of basic grammatical skills. Specifically, the basic grammatical relations of interest were SVO constructions (Bloom, 1973). All of the language samples for these participants evidenced varied SVO constructions.

Language Samples

Seven of the language samples were obtained from the Child Language Data Exchange System (ChiLDES; MacWhinney & Snow, 1985). Three language samples were obtained from local children.

All of the 400-utterance language samples were obtained from naturally varying spontaneous parent–child interactions in their homes. There are four major reasons for estimating grammatical repertoires from language samples in natural spontaneous social commerce. First, the key assumption underlying this study is representative samples. Representative samples are best observed in natural spontaneous social commerce. "Language is a form of communication and essentially a social interaction; its **use** can only be described in a social context—ideally one that is representative of the child's usual interactions" (Lahey, 1988, p. 131). Second, the central issue in communication is intentionality because the purpose of communication is to make intents recognizable (Clark & Clark, 1977; Sperber & Wilson, 1986). Spontaneous utterances in actual social commerce are intentional in contrast to elicited utterances. Greater confidence about representativeness can be given to spontaneous utterances with shared meaning in natural events (K. Nelson, 1985, 1986, 1996) than to elicited or spontaneous utterances in contrived events. Given this perspective, it is appropriate that language sampling be with natural spontaneous events in actual social commerce because communicative intent is richly evident in such contexts. Third, a contrived standard condition is likely to yield a more limited sample than a natural spontaneous condition. In referring to highly structured conditions, such as the standard sampling and elicitation conditions, Lahey (1988) said that they "restrict the language behaviors that can be observed" (p. 130). Because the goal is to obtain representative samples to estimate grammatical repertoires, limited samples from standard conditions would be counterproductive.

The samples were obtained from written notes supplemented by audiotape recordings. The samples obtained from ChiLDES had already been transcribed and segmented into utterances. The samples obtained locally were transcribed and segmented into utterances following similar procedures (e.g., terminal intonational contour).

A team of three trained speech-language pathologists independently transcribed and segmented the local samples and compared their efforts. There was 85% to 93% agreement for transcription and segmentation of these samples. In instances of discrepancies, they jointly listened to the tapes and resolved all discrepancies. Data were not available on the levels of agreement in transcription and segmentation of the language samples obtained from ChiLDES; however, it can be assumed that the levels were likely to be comparable to those obtained locally because they were obtained in similar circumstances and transcribed and segmented in essentially the same way.

Basic Grammatical Domains

Estimates of grammatical repertoires should be about basic grammatical domains and relations. SVO constructions contain basic grammatical relations according to Bloom (1973): "Such meaning relationships are coded in English by the BASIC GRAMMATICAL RELATIONS (subject-verb-object) of sentences" (p. 21). Thus, the study of grammatical repertoires should be with individuals who evidence varied SVO.

Because the grammatical domains within SVO may extend beyond subject–verb–object constructions, it is desirable to estimate repertoires for the basic grammatical systems rather than being confined to particular SVO constructions. Specifically, the grammatical systems entailed within SVO are subject nominals, object nominals, auxiliaries, verbals, and possibly various grammatical operations or transformations.

Grammatical Analysis

Grammatical analyses were made for the following basic grammatical systems: subject nominals, object nominals, auxiliaries, verbals, and grammatical operations. In the auxiliary system, tense marking was readily evident across all of the samples so the primary interest was the expansion of the auxiliary system beyond tense in accordance with the expansions delineated by Shatz, Hoff-Ginsberg, and Maciver (1989). The arrays of subject and object nominal constructions reflected basic phrase structure (Chomsky, 1965) and derived constructions (Lees, 1965). Animateness is a significant issue in early grammatical acquisition (Bowerman, 1976; Greenfield & Smith, 1976; Schlesinger, 1974) so descriptions of available grammatical distinctions included animateness. The arrays of verbal constructions reflected the delineations by Harris (1965). The grammatical operations reflected Chomsky's (1965) transformational operations.

Appendix A for this appendix provides the general grammatical framework for the various grammatical distinctions observed in the language samples. It should be stressed that the actual grammatical distinctions observed varied considerably from the basic distinctions in Appendix A. For example, Appendix A indicates that adjectives may modify a noun and that relative clauses may modify a noun. One of several variants involving these is the combination of a noun modified by both an adjective and a relative clause. These and other variations of the basic grammatical distinctions observed in the language samples are detailed in Tables D.4, D.5, D.6, and D.7. Such variations are to be expected simply because they reflect the generative, recursive, and derivational nature of grammar toward recognizing communicative intent. Moreover, these constructions were entered into the appendices in accordance with two criteria of attribution: at least one instance or three varied instances (+).

Grammatical Analysis: Reliability

A cascade procedure was adopted for carrying out the grammatical analyses. Each language sample was completely analyzed by a speech-language pathologist trained in grammatical analysis. Then, it was completely reanalyzed by another trained speech-language pathologist. This was followed by two different trained speech-language pathologists who compared the first two independent analyses and identified and resolved discrepancies. With this procedure, a total of 13,409 grammatical constructions were identified across the 10 400-utterance language samples. There was a 72% to 81% agreement between the first and second grammatical analyses across the language samples.

The resolution of discrepancies resulted in 368 remaining questionable constructions; thus, less than 3% of the sampled grammatical constructions remained unidentified or questionable. Moreover, the number of questionable constructions were relatively evenly distributed across all of the samples. This suggests that the samples were somewhat similar in difficulty of grammatical analyses.

RESULTS AND CONCLUSIONS

Estimated Grammatical Repertoires

The estimated repertoires were the arrays of available grammatical distinctions observed in the representative samples. Because it takes considerable space to display estimated grammatical repertoires, they appear in Tables D.4, D.5, D.6, and D.7 (see pp. 334–344). They are depicted as a function of one or three varied (+) instances of each construction. For example, Table D.4 shows that Eve had 32 different grammatical distinctions for her subject nominals; nine of these had at least three varied instances.

To facilitate reading the arrays of grammatical distinctions across these estimated repertoires, three mechanisms were incorporated. First, the grammatical distinctions delineated in Table D.3 were given letter codes (e.g., NP means noun phrase, VT means transitive verb, etc.). A full delineation of the components of these codes appears in Table D.3 (see p. 332). These codes and their combinations appear in the left margins of Tables D.4, D.5, D.6, and D.7 (see pp. 334–344). Second, an example of each observed variation of the grammatical constructions appears in the right margin of these appendices. Third, the estimated grammatical repertoires appear next to each other as a function of each observed grammatical distinction, thereby allowing for ready comparisons both within and between children.

Rather than merely listing the arrays of distinctions for each basic grammatical domain for each language sample, it may be more useful to extract some illustrative issues. Thus, the subject nominals for Eve showed the following:

1. She not only had proper nouns, definite pronouns, and indefinite pronouns, but evidenced conjoined constructions for them.
2. She evidenced a considerable array of determiner plus noun constructions for inanimate nouns but this array was relatively limited for animate nouns. This was not so for her object nominals.
3. Varied conjoined subject nominals were also evidenced more for inanimate nouns than animate nouns.

These grammatical arrays were generally similar both within and between participants. However, Taylor and Peter3 evidenced more variations in the determiner system with animate nouns than the other samples. Few derived subject nominal constructions were observed.

Regarding object nominal constructions, there was an outstanding observation that such constructions were in full bloom. That is, both within and between participants, the variations in the arrays of object nominal constructions surpassed those for subject nominals. Derived nominals and predeterminers were much more fully evidenced in object nominals than in subject nominals.

The auxiliary system was remarkably similar both within and between participants. Tense changes were so readily evident across the samples that they were not inventoried because they would have simply dominated these data. The inventoried data for modal and aspect indicate that modals were highly evident and the progressive was commonly evidenced. In contrast, "have + part" and combinations involving modals and different components of aspect were somewhat infrequent.

The verbal constructions were highly similar, both within and between participants, for BE + Adjective, BE + Noun Phrase, BE + Adverb of place, intransitive verbs, transitive verbs, and Vh verbs. Adam1, Adam2, and Annie evidenced other more complicated verbal constructions, especially dealing with conjoining, that were not so evident with the other samples.

The arrays of grammatical operations were highly similar both within and between participants for the nonderived operations. The entries in Table D.7 and including "conjoin" are nonderived. Even for the derived operations similar evidence was obtained with the exceptions of Nina, Peter1, and Peter2.

Between-participants comparisons revealed that the arrays of constructions with at least three varied instances were similar within each of the grammatical domains studied. This reveals cores of mutual grammatical distinctions shared within each grammatical domain. The cores of grammatical distinctions for each of the grammatical domains were the following:

Subject Nominals
    Noun phrase deletion
    Proper noun
    Definite pronoun
    Indefinite pronoun
    Inanimate N
    Definite article inanimate N
    Definite article adjective inanimate N
    Indefinite article inanimate N
    Indefinite article adjective inanimate N
    Possessive inanimate N
    Demonstrative inanimate N
Object Nominals
    Proper noun
    Definite pronoun
    Indefinite pronoun

> Inanimate noun
> Definite article inanimate noun
> Indefinite article inanimate noun
> Indefinite article adjective inanimate noun
> Possessive inanimate noun
> Demonstrative inanimate noun
> ToV (infinitive nominal)

Auxiliaries
> Modal
> be + ing

Verbals
> BE adjective
> BE noun phrase
> BE adverb-place
> V-Intransitive
> V-Transitive noun phrase
> V-have noun phrase

Grammatical Operations
> Do
> Not
> Yes–No
> Wh- question
> Adjective
> Particle shift
> ToV

However, the notion of a grammatical core should not be emphasized because between-participants comparisons for the arrays of constructions evidenced large variations within each grammatical domain, except for the auxiliary system. This means that each individual evidenced grammatical distinctions that extended well beyond the observed grammatical cores. Furthermore, the available distinctions varied greatly from one individual to another.

Within-participants comparisons generally showed comparable arrays of grammatical distinctions. Again, some variability was evidenced. This, of course, was to be expected simply because individuals vary what they say from one circumstance to another. Such variations confirm the point that language sampling should be sufficiently long and in varied contexts in order to sample adequately the arrays of available grammatical distinctions.

Acceptable Sampling Error Rates

Because typical samples have sampling errors in estimating repertoires of grammatical abilities, it is necessary to establish acceptable sampling error rates for dealing with such samples. Because no previous study has addressed this issue, it is addressed here from two perspectives: logical and empirical evidence.

Logically, the usual confidence levels (.01 and .05) for dealing with Type I and II errors in hypothesis testing might be used. This would mean that if more than one or five new grammatical constructions per 100 utterances, respectively, were obtained in a new sample, it would be necessary to continue sampling until fewer new distinctions were obtained. These criteria are prohibitive simply because virtually any new sample is likely to have enough new grammatical distinctions to warrant continued sampling.

Perhaps it would be useful to use 15% or 25% error rates. Such criteria could provide language samples that reveal what a child could do typically while admitting that other unidentified grammatical distinctions may be available but relatively atypical of one's performance.

Empirically, there are suggestive reasons that make the 15% criterion somewhat attractive. Bloom et al. (1974) showed that the 15% criterion was useful for distinguishing between imitators and nonimitators. Brown and Bellugi (1964) found that children respond to parental expansions by varying their own utterances in the direction of available models about 15% of the time. There is reason to believe, because of contextual learning, that this level of response to parental assistance is more potent than higher levels such as the 80% to 90% often used in the clinical fields. Indeed, Yoder (1987) asked a poignant question, "Where are the data that tell us that 90% criterion levels are effective?" (p. 11). These issues were not about language sampling, but the 15% criterion seems to be important in language learning. It may also be a useful criterion for language sampling.

Cole et al. (1989) found that 20% to 30% new information was obtained on subsequent samples. Because such findings would be large errors in sampling, they raised the issue of whether their initial samples were sufficiently large. Considering these issues, the notion of an acceptable error rate became an empirical question that could be resolved, at least on a preliminary basis, by examining the present data.

The 15% error rate was attractive both logically and empirically, but there was insufficient reason to rely on this criterion alone. Therefore, it was considered appropriate to invoke three different error rates—5%, 15%, and 25%—to ascertain needed language sample sizes with such rates. These three error rates were invoked on the 400-utterance samples.

This was done by counting the total number of structural variations for each basic grammatical domain evidenced in a sample, identifying the respective number of variations for the 5%, 15%, and 25% invoked error rates, then identifying the 10-utterance increment in the sample that from the beginning of the sample contained the needed number of structural variations. For example, Adam2 had 43 structural variations of object nominals over 400 utterances. The invoked error rates means that the last 2, 6, and 11 respective structural variations were discounted. The point in the sample whereby the remaining structural variations were evidenced constituted the size of the sample needed for a particular invoked error rate. For Adam2, 340, 250, and 210 utterances were the needed language sample sizes with invoked error rates of 5%, 15%, and 25%, respectively.

Sample Size

The first research question attempted to estimate available grammatical repertoires from 400-utterance samples. Once these estimates had been made, the issue of language sample size with attendant error rates could be addressed. Based on the structural variations obtained for estimating grammatical repertoires, it was possible to invoke error rates of 5%, 15%, and 25% on the 400-utterance samples. In doing so, the needed sample sizes under these error rates could be ascertained.

Table D.8 shows the needed language sample sizes for each of the basic grammatical domains when 5%, 15%, and 25% sampling errors are invoked, respectively. For this purpose, the number of structural variations for each basic grammatical system constituted the data. As a means of recognizing sampling variation, each language sample was analyzed in consecutive 10-utterance segments over the course of the 400 utterances. Thus, the tabled entries are in units of 10.

Entries were not made for the auxiliary system and for the verbal system for the invoked 5% error rate because the number of variations for these systems were relatively few; such entries would merely result in spurious information. These data evidenced a linear function. Larger samples were needed for the 5% sampling error rate as compared to the 15% and 25% rates. Larger samples were also needed for the 15% error rate as compared to the 25% rate.

Except for the auxiliary system, 50-utterance samples were inadequate for these error rates; furthermore, 100-utterance samples were only infrequently sufficient for some samples. Because a 25% error rate is excessive and the 5% error rate requires very large samples, the 15% error rate was considered appropriate for clinical and research purposes. In general, language sample sizes of 200 to 300 utterances are needed to adequately estimate repertoires for most grammatical domains with an acknowledged error rate of approximately 15% in comparison to 400-utterance samples.

TABLE D.8
Language Sample Sizes, According to Number of Utterances Needed for
Error Rates of 5%, 15%, and 25% According to Each Grammatical Domain

	NP1			NP2			Aux			Verbal			Operations		
	5%	15%	25%	5%	15%	25%	5%	15%	25%	5%	15%	25%	5%	15%	25%
Eve	290	250	220	380	210	160					110	110	230	170	120
Nina	250	190	130	340	290	280					120	30	50	20	20
Peter1	350	240	220	220	140	100					80	50	190	100	70
Peter2	300	240	170	340	320	200					180	80	180	80	70
Peter3	280	200	140	360	290	190					80	60	300	270	220
Brad	360	340	290	310	230	190					180	60	290	190	160
Annie	310	220	150	340	290	180					330	140	310	130	80
Taylor	390	370	230	370	320	220					280	220	360	350	280
Adam1	290	270	230	330	300	250					160	150	390	290	200
Adam2	340	250	210	350	270	160					240	230	140	70	70
Mean	316	257	199	334	266	193					176	113	244	167	129

Note. The numbers following Peter and Adam indicate the language sampling times for each child.

TABLE D.9

The Number of Construction Variations Within 50- and 100-Utterance
Samples, Respectively, Divided by the Total Number of Construction
Variations Across Each Language Sample. These Data Yield the
Success and Error Rates for 50- and 100-Utterance Samples

	NP1		NP2		Aux	Verbal		Operations	
	50	*100*	*50*	*100*		*50*	*100*	*50*	*100*
Eve	15/32	18/32	12/26	17/26		8/12	8/12	8/18	12/18
Nina	13/25	15/25	10/18	13/18		8/10	8/10	10/11	10/11
Peter1	11/22	14/22	14/20	17/20		9/13	10/13	8/13	11/13
Peter2	11/20	14/20	10/18	12/18		5/8	6/8	7/14	11/14
Peter3	8/25	12/25	13/40	21/40		8/13	11/13	12/18	15/18
Brad	6/21	7/21	12/36	17/36		6/10	7/10	11/19	12/19
Annie	10/21	12/21	14/31	16/31		5/11	6/11	14/23	16/23
Taylor	5/29	8/29	11/47	22/47		5/10	6/10	11/26	16/26
Adam1	5/21	9/21	14/33	20/33		5/13	7/13	10/21	12/21
Adam2	8/28	16/28	17/42	25/42		8/16	9/16	12/22	18/22
Totals	92/244	125/244	127/311	180/311		67/116	78/116	103/185	135/185
Success	38%	52%	41%	58%		58%	67%	56%	73%
Error	62%	42%	59%	42%		42%	33%	44%	27%

Note. The numbers following Peter and Adam indicate the language sampling times for
each child.

Adequacy of the Prevailing Practices

The second research question was about the adequacy of the prevailing
clinical practices of using 50- or 100-utterance language samples for assessing
grammatical capacities. This study indicates that 200- to 300-utterance samples are needed to adequately estimate what an individual can do grammatically. However, the prevailing language sizes use 50 or 100 utterances. Given
these results, it is apparent that there are errors, perhaps large errors, in
the prevailing practices.

Table D.9 shows the sampling success and error rates for 50- and
100-utterance samples for each basic grammatical domain. The overall sampling error rates for 50- and 100-utterance samples were very large, 55% and
40%, respectively. For example, the respective error rates for 50- and 100-ut-
terance samples for the subject nominals were 62% and 42%. This means
that research or clinical decisions based on such samples are likely to be
inherently flawed to the extent of these sampling errors.

DISCUSSION

At first glance, it appears that the notion of a grammatical core is confirmation of a descriptive norm. In a sense, it is. However, because all of the

individuals evidenced varied capacities well beyond the cores for each grammatical domain studied, the notion of a descriptive norm yielded an insufficient account of what these individuals could do. This, of course, raises a larger question concerning the degree to which normative tests may misrepresent, by virtue of underestimation, what individuals can do. A further implication is that normative tests may not be able to measure repertoires or capacities but merely sample mutual performance.

Because the individuals varied greatly from each grammatical core, it raises the importance of individual differences or heterogeneity. Heterogeneity has always been the bane of normative testing simply because such tests are based on the premise of homogeneity. Because normative tests are based on the premise of homogeneity but heterogeneity is characteristic of normal early acquisition (Brown, 1973b; Rice, 1983), there is reason to question the propriety of normative tests as presumed measures of language acquisition or use. Indeed, heterogeneity is much greater for clinical populations simply because it is very difficult to find two individuals in the same clinical category with precisely the same problem. Thus, the propriety for normative tests may be questionable in assessment for normal language acquisition, but it is more questionable for clinical populations.

Heterogeneity may be addressed in the arena of normative assessment by virtue of variance and the standard error of measurement; however, it is addressed more adequately in descriptive assessment by virtue of adducing estimates of repertoires, progress in acquisition sequences, alternative learning strategies, and active loci of learning with considerations for contextual influences and attendant attribution criteria.

No matter how one looks at it, the notion of a norm, either as a psychometric norm or a descriptive norm, as evidenced in this study, yields an incomplete, relatively inadequate assessment of what an individual can do. Moreover, norms remove behavior from contexts resulting in the baserate fallacy (Bruner, 1986). Descriptive data revealing patterns of performance in contexts provide data that are relevant to what an individual can do, evidence of repertoires. Such evidence is not only more relevant to what children can do than normative test scores but offers more clinical implications in addressing the seven basic clinical assessment issues (Muma & Muma, 1979). That is why cognitive socialization scholars have relied on descriptive evidence and clinicians have a preference for descriptive evidence in phonology (Ferguson et al., 1992; Locke, 1980a, 1980b, 1983; Vihman & Greenlee, 1987), syntax (Bloom et al., 1989; Lahey, 1988), and pragmatics (Prutting & Kirchner, 1983, 1987; Wetherby, 1991; Wetherby & Prizant, 1990).

There are some other issues that should be discussed. First, it was observed that the auxiliary and verbal systems had relatively few variations across all of the samples, 2-5 and 10-16, respectively. Perhaps these restricted variations are indicative of children relatively early in grammatical acquisition because the respective systems themselves have many more potential variations in adult language.

Second, there were many kinds of derived nominals for object nominals (Table D.5, see p. 337). Brown (1973b) reported that object nominals for verbs appear first and are elaborated before subject nominals, which would be consistent with the primary function of predicates in coding new information in the context of given information (Clark & Clark, 1977). Interestingly, many of the derived nominals (I know *what he eats.* I wish *I could stop this.*) have structural continuity with subordinating conjunctions (Don't ring the door *cause Jenny's sleeping.*), relative clauses (It was this man *that was pulling.*), and some adverbial constructions (See *how she's kinda dangling. When I get eleven,* I'm gonna have one.).

Third, detailed information about repertoires of grammatical skills coupled with lexical diversity would be useful in identifying language learning strategies, vertical and horizontal correlates of language learning, and active loci of learning. Regarding language learning strategies, K. Nelson (1973b) used language samples to show that some children are referential learners, whereas others are expressive learners. Bloom et al. (1975) showed that some individuals relied more on pronominals whereas others relied more on simple nominals in early acquisition; Bloom, Hood, and Lightbown (1974) showed that some individuals were imitators whereas others were not. Information of this sort is not available from normative tests but is available from descriptive evidence derived from language samples.

Language samples can provide evidence about vertical and horizontal correlates of language learning. There are different views of vertical and horizontal language learning (Bates & MacWhinney, 1987; Jakobson, 1960; Maratsos, 1982; McNeill, 1970). One view of vertical learning is the number of exemplars for a particular grammatical construction varies and expands. For example, an expanded number of transitive verbs may evidence vertical learning for the transitive verb system. On the other hand, horizontal learning may be evidenced when co-occurring structures (Muma, 1973a) for a target structure vary and expand. Information of this sort is only available from descriptions of language samples. For example, this study showed that Adam1 and Adam2 had more verbal constructions than the other participants. This may indicate vertical correlates if lexical variation (Ninio, 1988) is also evidenced. Interestingly, these two samples also evidenced relatively large variations for object nominal constructions which may implicate horizontal correlates as well.

The language samples also provided evidence of active loci of learning (Muma, 1983a, 1986a). Loci of learning are actual instances of active learning. For example, the language sample for Annie had several buildups and expansions (Weir, 1962) that evidenced active learning. The following three actual buildups illustrate the point:

189. Here's my purse.
190. Here's my purse that Kelcy gave me.

208. I'm just playing.
209. I'm just playing house.

230. I can just do.
231. I can just do like this.

The first buildup has pragmatic topicalization and a relative clause added resulting in utterance 190. The second buildup has an object that has an implied determiner. The third buildup has a predicate pronominalized in a vernacular. Moreover, the second and third buildups have the intensifier "just." These are all speculative loci of learning.

Pertinent constructions across her language sample provided patterns that supported the following conclusions. She had a variety of other relative clauses, including relative clause deletions, but she had few instances of topicalization and when such instances occurred disruptions were sometimes evidenced on co-occurring constructions. This implicates loci of learning for topicalization. In both of the other buildups, the intensifier appeared to be the locus of learning. Unfortunately, this is only speculative because there was insufficient evidence to place full credence in this conclusion.

The cognitive socialization literature has identified many kinds of active loci of learning (Muma, 1983b, 1986a). One type of loci of learning that was observed in these samples was double marking or buttressing. This is when a child produces a new form that is backed up with an old form. Buttressing seemed to be a provisional construction in the course of rectifying objective forms of pronouns functioning as subject nominals. Initially, a child would make the following kinds of constructions: "Me here. Them go. Him eat." Then buttressing appeared as a provisional construction whereby a new form was buttressed by an old form: "Daddy, he go." In this example, "he" is a new form because the child had previously been saying "him." The new form "he," was buttressed by an old form, "Daddy," which the child had been saying for some time. Eventually, buttressing stopped, resulting in appropriate use of subject forms of pronouns.

Another behavior could easily be confused with buttressing; it is reference clarification. A child could say, "Daddy, he go" merely to clarify who the intended referent is. However, patterns of buttressing within the context of rectifying the inappropriate use of object forms of pronouns would distinguish between buttressing and reference clarification.

Fourth, because the MLU is widely used in speech-language pathology, a special note should be made about the MLUs in this study and the available MLU norms. The range of MLUs was somewhat large for the language samples. The reported MLUs for the language samples in this study ranged from 3.2 to 7.4. Because all of the MLUs exceeded 3.0, there is reason to believe that the participants had surpassed basic grammatical relations (SVO) and were in the grammatical phase of language acquisition (Brown, 1973b; Ninio, 1988; Schlesinger, 1988).

It is well known that MLUs over 4.0 or 4.5 lose value as acquisition indices (Brown, 1973; Cazden, 1968; Cowan et al., 1967; Shriner, 1969). "The MLU measures provide an index of syntactic complexity in the child's speech at least up to Stage V (MLU in morphemes = 4.0, Brown, 1973)" (Chapman, 1981, p. 22). "MLU is a good simple index of development from about 1.0 to about 4.0" (Brown, 1973, p. 185). The reason MLUs lose value as acquisition indices is because children obtain grammatical repertoires that afford various options for constructing messages of best fit (Muma, 1975a) in the realization of communicative intents. Some options shorten or pronominalize messages, whereas others lengthen messages. Accordingly, utterance lengths over 4.0 or 4.5 are no longer good indices of learning. MLUs for 6 of the 10 language samples reached or exceeded 4.5.

These findings pertain to estimates of grammatical repertoires. Because semantic functions and relations are subsumed within grammatical relations, a similar inquiry in semantics should be carried out during the semantic period of language acquisition (Greenfield & Smith, 1976). Similar inquiries should be done in pragmatics and phonology.

Clinical Implications

Some clinicians may think that 200- to 300-utterance samples are too large to be practical. However, given the present data it is appropriate to obtain 200- to 300-utterance language samples for most grammatical analyses. Thus, an inherent conflict may arise between what is appropriate and what is practical (expedient). Such conflicts may be addressed emotionally according to the trade-off principle (Bruner, 1986), which, paraphrased, is that if a task is too complex the response to it may be an emotional response. Clinicians may hold that 200- to 300-utterance samples are too long, complex, and time consuming to be practical; therefore, they may forego what is appropriate in favor of what may be expedient and their response as to why they did so is likely to be emotional rather than rational. Scholars, on the other hand, would find the need for 200- to 300-utterance samples in contrast to the prevailing practices intellectually provocative and clinically responsible.

We have a standing challenge (Muma, 1978b, 1986a) that addresses the issue of the amount of time needed to obtain and analyze a representative language sample. The standing challenge is to take whatever time it usually takes to administer a test or battery of tests but use the time to obtain and analyze language samples. Even though there may be insufficient time to complete the task, the information obtained is more relevant to what an individual can do and more useful than a test score in deducing appropriate intervention implications.

Referring to descriptive evidence from language samples, Lahey (1988) said, "Such information is needed to plan an intervention program" (p. 130). The information is more useful because it contains patterns of behavior and information about the contexts (intentional, referential, relational, social) of the behaviors that are useful for ascertaining alternative strategies of language acquisition, evidence of vertical and horizontal correlates of language learning, and evidence of active loci of learning. Such evidence is not available from normative tests. Even though such evidence may be speculative and awaiting further substantiation, it is, nonetheless, more powerful, appropriate, and useful than test scores.

Another way of thinking about whether it is appropriate to use language sample sizes of 50 or 100 utterances with large error rates is to consider the clinical implications of the errors that ensue. Relatively small language samples (50 or 100 utterances) have relatively large error rates. Therefore, the probabilities are high that intervention goals based on such samples are inappropriate and lead to false claims of efficacy. This means that a clinician could spend an inordinate amount of time on particular goals when, in fact, by virtue of an adequate language sample, a client could provide evidence that he or she already can do at least some of the particular grammatical skills that were presumably in need of intervention; they just were not evidenced in a small sample.

Moreover, the official interpretation of P.L. 94–142 (Martin, 1980) has explicitly stated that in speech-language pathology informal (descriptive) or formal (test) information can be used by certified speech-language pathologists for a standardized assessment to establish eligibility for services and that educational needs are not required. The official federal policy supports the use of descriptive evidence and there are substantive reasons issuing from the cognitive socialization literature for using descriptive evidence. Thus, it is not true, as many speech-language pathologists believe, that a standardized assessment may only be achieved by the use of normative tests.

Descriptive assessment procedures issuing from the cognitive socialization literature provide standardized procedures for ascertaining what an individual can do. Because such procedures are derived from, and have continuity with, the contemporary philosophical views and theoretical perspectives, and most of the psychometric tests lack such substantive groundings—especially construct validity—but merely rest on brute empiricism, there is reason to place increased credence on descriptive assessment over psychometric tests (Muma, 1983a, 1986a). In all, clinicians are shifting away from a reliance on test scores to descriptive evidence.

A. *Nominal System:* Subject and Object
1. **Phrase Structure:**
   Proper Noun (Prop N): Bill, Sue, Mommy, . . .
   Indefinite Pronoun (IP): anything, anyone, . . .
   Definite Pronoun (DP): I, he, she, it, . . .
   Determiner + Noun:
   Noun-animate (Na): boy, girl, dog, . . .
   Noun-inanimate (Ni): table, chair, hat, . . .

   $$\text{Determiner} \rightarrow \text{(predet)} + \begin{bmatrix} \text{possessive} \\ \text{article} \\ \text{demonstrative} \\ \text{number} \end{bmatrix} + \text{(Postdet.)}$$

   Possessive (Poss): my, our, his, her, . . .
   Article:
     Definite article: the
     Indefinite article: Ø, a, some
     Demonstrative (Dem): this, that, these, those
   Number (#):
     Cardinal: one, two, three, . . .
     Ordinal: first, second, third, . . .
2. **Derived Nominals:**
   Quote: "No"
   ToV: to work, to run, to eat, . . .
   Ving: working, running, eating, . . .
   For/to: for him to work, for him to run, . . .
   That + S: that he works, that he runs, . . .
   What + S: what he thinks, what he wins, . . .
   Who + S: who he is, who she was, . . .
B. *Expanded Auxiliary System*
1. **Modals:** can, will, shall, may, must, could, . . .
2. **Aspect:** (have + participle) + (be + ing)
C. *Verbal System*
1. **BE system**
   BE + Adjective
   BE + Noun Phrase
   BE + Adverb of place
2. **Intransitive system:** VI
3. **Transitive system:** VT + Noun Phrase
4. **Vh system:** Vh + Noun Phrase
5. **Vb system:** Vb + Noun Phrase; Vb + Adjective
6. **Vs system:** Vs + Adjective

(Continued)

333

D. *Grammatical Operations*
1. Emphatic
2. DO
3. NOT
4. YES/NO
5. Wh?
6. Noun deletion
7. Noun Phrase deletion
8. Ellipsis
9. Adjective
10. Relative Clause
11. Iteration
12. There
13. Particle shift
14. Conjoin
15. ToV
16. **To**V
17. To**V**
18. Ving
19. For/To
20. That S
21. What S
22. Where S
23. How S
24. When S
25. If S
26. Which S
27. Why S
28. So S
29. Because S
30. Who S
31. Intensifier
32. Quote
33. Demonstration

Note. Actual instances of these, and variations of these, constructions appear in Tables D.4, D.5, D.6, and D.7.

TABLE D.4

Estimates of Repertoires of Subject Nominals for Each Language Sample

Subject Nominal Constructions	Adam (2)	Adam (1)	Taylor	Annie	Brad	Peter (3)	Peter (2)	Peter (1)	Nina	Eve	Examples From Actual Utterances
NPdel	*+	*+	*+	*+	*+	*+	*+	*+	*+	*+	Don't play it yet.
PropN	*+	*+	*+	*+	*+	*+	*+	*+	*	*+	Mommy was trying to unscrew it.
PropN & Prop N			*	*		*	*	*		*	Cathy and Becky will get better.
PropN & PropN & PropN											Caprice, Krisha and Loren go to Murphy.
PropN & DP Prop N & Prop N	*+									*	There are Cummings and you, Fraser and Colin.
DP	*+	*+	*+	*+	*+	*+	*+	*+	*+	*+	I'm gonna show you.
DP & DP		*		*						*	You and I have grape juice.
DP & PropN	*+	*+	*+	*+	*+	*+	*	*			Me and Robin are friends.
IP	*+			*+	*+	*+	*+	*+	*+	*+	This stuck together.
IP & IP & IP	*					*					That and that and that.
Na	*		*			*+	*	*	*	*	People
Na & Na						*					boys and girls
ANa			*			*	*	*	*	*	bigger boy
ANa & ANa		*									for big children and little children.
Def Na	*	*	*+		*	*+			*+	*	the baby's going in there.
Def ANa	*					*					the bigger people
Def Pos Na			*	*	*	*					The King's horses and going (gesture).
Def Na & PropN											The mailman and Bev
Indef Na	*		*	*	*	*+	*	*	*+	*+	A snake
Indef A Na	*					*	*	*		*	a cowboy doggie
Pos Na	*		*	*	*	*	*	*	*+		My daddy drived it in.
Pos Na & Indef	*					*	*		*		Her mommy and a x x x are going to eat in a plate.

(Continued)

335

Subject Nominal Constructions	Adam (2)	Adam (1)	Taylor	Annie	Brad	Peter (3)	Peter (2)	Peter (1)	Nina	Eve	Examples From Actual Utterances
DP & Pos Na	*+										Me and my freckles
Dem Na		*			*	*			*		Those people
#Na	*									*+	Two kittens
#Na & #Na										*	Five doggies and one doggy
#Na & Indef Na										*	One woman and a woman . . .
Pre Def Na			*								All the villagers are.
Pre Pos Na			*								One of your relatives lives here.
Pre Dem Na			*								All these people own them.
Pre Indef Na								*			Lots of other people on the train.
Ni	*+	*+	*	*	*	*+	*+	*+	*+	*+	crayons
A Ni	*	*	*	*	*	*	*	*	*	*	green ones down
Def Ni	*+	*+	*	*	*	*+	*+	*+	*+	*	The record stopped.
Def ANi	*				*	*+	*+	*	*+	*	The big ones go
Indef Ni	*+	*+	*	*+	*+	*+	*+	*+	*+	*+	a nickel
Indef ANi	*	*+		*+	*+	*+	*	*+	*+	*	A big bed
Indef AANi											just a little little bit
Indef ANi RelCL											there was a little bill that came in this envelope.
IndefNi IndefNi & Ni					*						some flowers, some carts and pail
IndefANi & Indef ANdel			*								some more sugar and some more
Indef Ni & Ni									*	*	a slide and steps
Indef ANi & Ni	*						*		*	*	some more spaghetti and cheese
Indef Ni & IndefNi											a frank and a banana
IndefNi & IndefNi & IndefNi											some balls and some cars and some boats
Pos Ni	*	*	*+	*+	*+	*	*+	*+	*+	*	Your hand's there
Pos ANi	*	*	*	*			*		*+	*+	my new airplane

	C1	C2	C3	C4	C5	C6	C7	C8	C9	C10	Example
Pos AAANi	*									*	my big old racing car
Dem Ni	*+	*	*	*	*	*+	*+	*+	*+	*	this car
Dem ANi	*	*	*	*	*	*					this last one is pretty
Dem AANi Rel			*	*							these little tiny envelopes that you have to send it back in
Dem A Ni Rel			*	*							that little envelope that I was in was the envelope that you
#Ni	*	*	*	*	*	*	*+	*+	*+	*	one banana
#ANi		*						*+			two big boats
#Ndel		*+	*+								Three up like that?
Poss Ndel				*	*						Yours cut?
Indef ANdel				*							Some more . . .
Pre Ni	*		*	*	*	*	*		*	*	all kinds of things
Pre Def Ni	*				*						Where's a part of the ring?
Pre ANi					*						I want some more sugar.
Pre Dem Ni						*					one of these pencils
Pre Dem Ndel	*				*						What does one of these called?
Ni & IP									*		ball and something to put ball in
Ni & Ni & IP											pies and cakes and everything
Ni & Ni							*	*			cars and cars
Ni & Ni & Ni							*	*	*	*	food and macaroni and xxx
ANi & Ni		*		*				*	*		little pies and pies
ANi & ANi				*							black ones and blue ones.
A & AANi				*							red and blue cotton candy
Pre ANi							*				long piece of chicken sandwich
Pre Indef Ni					*		*	*			What kind of bed?
What	*					*	*				What is those?
Which Ni	*					*	*				Which one is different?
ToV									*+		To put on your back if you have a safety pin.
Ving											Playing a banjo is good exercise for your thumb.
For/to											A bone for the dogs to eat
* At least one instance	28	21	29	21	21	25	20	22	25	32	
+ At least three varied instances	8	9	6	6	8	11	10	11	13	9	

337

TABLE D.5
Estimates of Repertoires of Object Nominals for Each Language Sample

Object Nominal Constructions	Adam (2)	Adam (1)	Taylor	Annie	Brad	Peter (3)	Peter (2)	Peter (1)	Nina	Eve	Examples From Actual Utterances
Prop N	*	*	*	*+	*+	*	*+	*+	*	*+	Lady name is *Gloria*
Prop N & Prop N					*			*		*	That for *Fraser and Colin*
DP	*+	*+	*+	*+	*+	*+	*+	*+	*+	*+	I did *it.*
DP & DP		*	*								He made *me and you.*
DP & Prop N		*								*	I can't see *you and Fraser.*
IP	*+	*+	*+	*+	*+	*+	*+	*+	*+	*+	You got *one.*
Na	*	*	*	*	*	*				*	They are *rabbits.*
ANa	*	*	*			*					This is for *big children.*
AANa	*									*	It look like *little Black Sambo.*
Def Na	*			*	*	*+	*		*	*	Put *the kids* on the roof.
Def A Na		*		*	*	*				*	I'll need *the baby puppy* my Bible.
Def Pos Na						*				*	That's not *the baby's cow.*
Def # Na								*			Is those *the two cow?*
Def ANa & DefNa			*							*+	It looks like *the little girl and the daddy.*
Indef Na	*+		*		*	*	*		*+	*+	This is *a cow.*
Indef Na & Indef Na											He had *a Swifty and a Blackie.*
Indef ANa	*	*+		*		*+		*	*		He's *a funny fish.*
Indef AANa		*									He is *a little naughty baby.*
Indef Ni & Na						*					Let's put in *a doll or people.*
Pos Na	*		*	*	*	*	*		*+		That's *his horse.*
Pos A Na										*	That *my gingerbread man.*
Na & Prop N						*			*		I like you and not *my mom and dad.*
Dem Na	*		*		*						I can stand *that horse* up now.
Dem AaNa		*	*	*							Look at *that humungus shark.*
Dem Na Rel			*								It was *this man that was pulling.*

338

Category	Example
# Na	I have just one kid.
Na Na & Na & IP	All we talked about was deer, sharks, and rabbits and all
Pred Def Na & DefNa & Def Ni	God made all the spirits and the birds and the trees.
Ni	Can I watch TV?
Ni & Ni	A grabby boat is for shirts and things in there.
Ni & Ni & Ni	Food and chicken and bones, they want to eat.
ANi	I want more tapioca.
A & ANi	They like brown and yellow ones.
Def Ni	I'm gonna play with the ball.
Def Pos Ni	She borrowed the King's sword.
Def ANi	Turn the other page.
Def ANdel	He's gonna go and scare the other.
Indef Ni	I have a holster.
Indef ANi	This is a bad one.
Indef AANi	Is this a big red case?
Indef ANi & ANi	She has a black tail and black tail.
Indef ANi Rel CL	You wanna see a funniest one you ever saw?
Indef Ni Rel CL	That would be a tower which would be that big.
Indef Ni & Ni	Want some rice and spaghetti?
Indef Ni & Indef Ni	She doesn't have a sword and a hat.
Pos Ni	Build something with my blocks.
Pos ANi	Wanna see my new camera?
Pos & Pos Ni	I'm writing Jonathan and Kelcip's name.
Pos Ni & Ni	I have his arms and legs.
Dem Ni	You use this pen.
Dem ANi	Is it that noisy train?
Dem AANi	See that little black thing.
#Ni	These are two motorboats.
#AANdel	This is two big front.
#Ndel	I give him two each day.

(Continued)

TABLE D.5
(Continued)

Object Nominal Constructions	Adam (2)	Adam (1)	Taylor	Annie	Brad	Peter (3)	Peter (2)	Peter (1)	Nina	Eve	Examples From Actual Utterances
Pre Ni	*		*	*	*	*	*	*		*	Kathy has some of these.
Pre Def Ni	*+	*	*			*		*			Where's all of the ring?
Pre Def ANi	*										It's all the different colors.
Pre Def Pos Ni			*								I just got delivered out of the postman's hand.
Pre Dem Ni	*	*	*								Make eight of these oranges.
Pre Dem AANi Rel CL	*			*	*						I'm one of those big big envelopes in here.
Pre Pos Ni	*		*	*							It's all of their land.
Pre Pos ANi	*									*	Want some your grape juice?
Pre Pos N Rel	*										I'm gonna have some of my crayons that I'm gonna bring home.
Pre Dem Ndel											I wanna play with both of these.
Pre Ni & Pre Ni	*										Make 8 of bananas and 8 of these.
Pos Ndel					*+	*					Put yours down.
Indef Pos Ndel										*	Let me see a lady's

Structure	1	2	3	4	5	6	7	8	9	10	Example
Indef AA Ndel					*						I just need *a little more*.
Indef A Ndel	*										It just had *a little*.
Pre Dem Ndel & Indef ANi					*						I want *some more of this and some more sugar*.
"Quote"	*+		*	*+	*						I say *"no"*.
To V	*+	*+	*+	*+		*+	*+				I like *to play in water*.
To V	*		*			*+	*				What song you want *hear*?
ToV & V		*									I like *to stand up in water and go down in it too*.
Ving			*	*+	*+						I love *swimming*.
That S	*+	*+	*+	*+	*	*				*	I wish *I have a banjo like that*.
What S	*+	*+	*	*	*	*					I know *what he eats*.
Who S			*								How do you know *who in the world sent it to you*?
How S	*+	*+	*	*+		*					See *how she's kind of dangling*.
When S	*	*	*	*	*						*When I get eleven*, I'm gonna have one.
Where S			*		*	*					Know *where'd is it*?
If S	*+	*	*	*	*						*If you keep on going*, it's gonna get bigger.
Why S		*	*								Do you know *why*?
Because S			*	*		*					Don't ring the door *cause Jenny's sleeping*.
So S del			*								I think *so*.
* At least one instance	43	33	47	32	36	35	18	20	18	26	
+ At least three varied instances	15	13	7	15	9	6	9	9	10	10	

TABLE D.6
Estimates of Repertoires of Auxiliaries and Verbals for Each Language Sample

	Adam (2)	Adam (1)	Taylor	Annie	Brad	Peter (3)	Peter (2)	Peter (1)	Nina	Eve	Examples From Actual Utterances
Auxiliary Constructions											
Modal	*+	*+	*+	*+	*+	*+	*+	*+	*+	*+	Nobody *can* see him.
Be ing	*+	*+	*+	*	*	*+	*+	*+	*+	*+	*I'm going* on the rainbow.
be ing		*+	*+	*	*	*+	*+	*+	*+	*+	I'm working
be ing							*		*		He's have vitamin C.
have part		*+	*+	*							I've *seen* this church before.
have part		*	*					*			It stopped raining.
Modal be ing											Her hair *won't be sticking* up like a pig.
* At least one instance	2	3	5	5	3	3	4	4	4	3	
+ At least three varied instances	2	3	4	1	1	3	3	3	3	3	
Verbal Constructions											
Be Adjective	*+	*+	*+	*+	*+	*+	*+	*+	*+	*	That's *funny*
Be adjective								*+			
Be adjective	*								*	*	Sara *awake.*
BE Noun Phrase	*+	*+	*+	*+	*+	*+	*+	*+	*+	*+	He's a *funny* fish.
BE Noun Phrase	*+	*+	*		*	*		*	*+	*+	You're not. All the villagers *are.*

342

Construction	C1	C2	C3	C4	C5	C6	C7	C8	C9	C10	Example
BE Noun Phrase	*	*+				*	*		*+	*+	That *Gloria*
BE Adv-pl	*+	*	*+	*+	*+	*+	*+	*+	*+	*+	Two motor boats gonna *be there.*
BE *Adv-pl*			*	*		*					It's on my bed. It *is.*
BE Adv-pl	*	*+	*+	*+	*+	*+	*+	*+	*+	*+	He's *gone.*
VI	*+	*+	*+	*+	*+	*+	*+	*+	*+	*+	This baby *crying.*
VI particle	*				*+						I'm gonna *hang on.*
VT Noun Phrase	*+	*+	*+	*+	*+	*+	*+	*+	*+	*+	I *want my car.*
VT Noun Phrase deletion	*	*+	*	*	*	*+	*+	*	*+	*+	I *forgot.*
VT particle Noun Phrase	*+	*	*+		*	*					*Stand it up* in here.
Vh Noun Phrase	*+	*	*+	*+	*+	*+	*+	*+	*+	*+	They *have their hats on.*
Vh Noun Phrase del			*	*	*	*					I never *have.*
VI & VT Noun Phrase			*								I *goed* and *watched* T.V.
Vb Adjective	*+	*+		*	*	*				*	Cathy and Becky *will get better.*
Vb Noun Phrase			*	*							*Was just getting into autumn.*
Vs Adjective		*	*					*			He *look sleepy.*
Vs particle Adjective										*	That *looks like papa.*
VI & VT & VI	*										It *grows and grows and grows.*
VT NPdel & VT NPdel	*										You have to *squeeze and squeeze.*
VT NPdel & VT NPdel & NPdel	*										We gonna *squeeze and squeeze and squeeze.*
T particle & VT NPdel		*									It's gonna *mix up and break.*
* At least one instance	16	13	11	11	10	13	12	8	10	12	
+ At least three varied instances	8	7	7	7	6	8	8	7	8	8	

TABLE D.7

Estimates of Repertoires of Grammatical Operations for Each Language Sample

Grammatical Operations	Adam (2)	Adam (1)	Taylor	Annie	Brad	Peter (3)	Peter (2)	Peter (1)	Nina	Eve	Examples From Actual Utterances
DO	*+	*+	*+	*+	*+	*	*+	*	*+	*	Do you want some?
DO		*	*+	*+	*+				*+		How _ this goes with?
NOT	*+	*+	*+	*+	*+	*+	*+	*+	*+	*+	I *can't* find some.
YES/NO	*+	*+	*+	*+	*+	*+	*+	*+	*+	*+	Would you do this?
Wh?	*+	*+	*+	*+	*+	*+	*+	*+	*+	*+	*What* is this?
Noun deletion	*				*+					*	Yours cut?
Noun Phrase deletion	*+	*+	*+	*+	*+	*+	*+	*+	*+	*+	Push these up?
Ellipsis	*	*+	*+	*+	*+	*		*		*	We didn't
Adjective	*+	*+	*+	*+	*+	*+	*+	*+	*+	*+	I made *good* road.
Rel Cl.		*	*+	*+	*+			*+		*	Where's her skirt *that goes right here?*
Iteration			*+	*+	*+	*	*+	*+			It's Monday.
There	*+	*+	*			*				*	*There's* the man.
Part Shift	*+	*+	*	*+	*+	*+	*	*+	*+	*	I gonna put me all these rubber bands *on.*
Conjoin	*+	*+	*+	*+	*+	*+	*+		*+	*+	*You and I* have grape juice.

										Examples
ToV	*+	*+	*+	*+	*+	*+	*+	*+		*+	I love *to swim.*
ToV	*+		*+	*		*		*		*+	Want *to?*
ToV	*		*+		*+				*		I want *play* with that.
Ving	*	*+	*	*+	*+			*		*	Here we go *cleaning the city up.*
For/to	*+	*+	*+	*+	*+	*				*+	A bone *for the dogs to eat.*
That S	*+	*+	*+	*+	*	*	*		*		I wish *I could stop this.*
What S	*+	*+	*+	*	*	*	*		*		I know *what's in there.*
Where S	*	*	*	*	*						This is *where you open it.*
How S	*+	*+	*+	*+	*		*			*+	I know *how I got 'em down.*
When S	*+	*	*	*		*				*	I get bigger and bigger *when you do that.*
If S	*+	*	*+	*+	*						*If you put upside down,* it be hard to get in.
Which S	*	*	*								*Which one I didn't pick?*
Why S	*	*+	*								You know *why?*
So S			*	*							I'm combing his hair *so it won't be sticking up like a pig.*
Because S				*							It couldn't be a church *cause a church is bigger.*
Who S			*		*						How do you know *who in the world send it to you?*
Intensifier			*								It *just* had a little there.
Quote	*		*	*		*	*				I say, "No".
Demonstration			*		*						She's going *(demonstration)*
* At least one instance	22	21	26	22	19	18	14	13	11	18	
+ At least three varied instances	15	16	14	17	14	8	9	8	10	8	

REFERENCES

Abbeduto, L., & Benson, G. (1992). Speech act development in nondisabled children and individuals with mental retardation. In R. Chapman (Ed.), *Processes in language acquisition and disorders* (pp. 257–278). St. Louis, MO: Mosby Yearbook.

Abkarian, G. (1986). Measuring iconic-symbolic classification: It doesn't MAP out. *Journal of Childhood Communication Disorders, 19*, 139–156.

Abkarian, G. (1987). Clinical evaluation of children's classification behavior. *Journal of Communication Disorders, 20*, 219–232.

Acredelo, L. (1978). Development of spatial orientation in infancy. *Developmental Psychology, 14*, 224–234.

Ainsworth, M. (1973). The development of infant-mother attachment. In B. Caldwell & H. Ricciuti (Eds.), *Review of child development research 3* (pp. 1–95). New York: Russell Sage Foundation.

American heritage dictionary: New college edition. (1976). Boston: Houghton-Mifflin.

American Psychological Association, American Educational Research Association, & National Council on Measurement in Education. (1974). *Standards for educational and psychological tests.* Washington, DC: American Psychological Association.

Anderson, J. (1980). Concepts, propositions, and schemata: What are the cognitive units? *Nebraska Symposium of Motivation, 28*, 121–162.

Anderson, J. (1983). *The architecture of cognition.* Cambridge, MA: Harvard University Press.

Anglin, J. (1977). *Word, object and concept development.* New York: Norton.

Aram, D., Ekelman, B., & Nation, J. (1984). Preschoolers with language disorders: 10 years later. *Journal of Speech and Hearing Research, 27*, 232–244.

Ashley, M., & Krych, D. (1995). *Code of conduct.* Bakersfield, CA: Centre for Neuro Skills.

Athey, I. (1970). *Theories of language development and their relation to reading.* St. Petersburg, FL: National Reading Conference.

Atkinson, M. (1992). *Children's syntax: An introduction to principles and parameters theory.* Oxford, England: Blackwell.

Atkinson, R., & Shiffrin, R. (1968). Human memory: A proposed system and its control processes. In K. Spence & J. Spence (Eds.), *The psychology of learning and motivation* (pp. 89–195). New York: Academic.

Austin, J. (1962). *How to do things with words.* New York: Oxford University Press.

Baddeley, A. (1994). Working memory: The interface between memory and cognition. In D. Schacter & E. Tulving (Eds.), *Memory systems: 1994* (pp. 351–368). Cambridge, MA: MIT Press.

Bain, B., & Dollaghan, C. (1991). The notion of clinically significant change. *Language, Speech, and Hearing Services in Schools, 22,* 264–270.

Bandura, A. (1986). *Social foundations of thought and action: A social cognitive theory.* Englewood Cliffs, NJ: Prentice-Hall.

Barlow, D., Hayes, S., & Nelson, R. (1984). *The scientist practitioner: Research and accountability in clinical and educational settings.* New York: Pergamon.

Bashir, A. (1987). *Language and the curriculum.* Workshop presented at the Language Learning Disabilities Institute, Emerson College, Boston.

Bates, E. (1979). *The emergence of symbols.* New York: Academic Press.

Bates, E., Bretherton, I., & Snyder, L. (1988). *From first words to grammar: Individual differences and dissociable mechanisms.* New York: Cambridge University Press.

Bates, E., & MacWhinney, B. (1979). A functionalist approach to the acquisition of grammar. In E. Ochs & B. Schieffelin (Eds.), *Developmental pragmatics* (pp. 167–214). New York: Academic Press.

Bates, E., & MacWhinney, B. (1987). Competition, variation and language learning. In B. MacWhinney (Ed.), *Mechanisms of language acquisition* (pp. 157–194). Hillsdale, NJ: Lawrence Erlbaum Associates.

Bateson, G. (1980). *Mind and nature: A necessary unity.* Toronto: Bantam.

Baumeister, A. (1984). Some methodological and conceptual issues in the study of cognitive processes with retarded people. In P. Brooks, R. Sperber, & C. McCauley (Eds.), *Learning and cognition in the mentally retarded* (pp. 1–38). Hillsdale, NJ: Lawrence Erlbaum Associates.

Baumeister, A., & Muma, J. (1975). On defining mental retardation. *Journal of Special Education, 9,* 293–306.

Beckwith, R., Rispoli, M., & Bloom, L. (1984). Child language and linguistic theory: In response to Nina Hyams. *Journal of Child Language, 11,* 685–687.

Bedore, L., & Leonard, L. (1995). Prosodic and syntactic bootstrapping and their clinical applications: A tutorial. *American Journal of Speech-Language Pathology, 4,* 66–72.

Berger, S. (1977). Social comparison, modeling, and perseverance. In J. Suls & R. Miller (Eds.), *Social comparison processes: Theoretical and empirical perspective* (pp. 209–234). Washington, DC: Hemisphere.

Berko, J. (1958). The child's learning of English morphology. *Word, 14,* 150–157.

Berman, R. (1981). Language development and language knowledge: Evidence from the development of Hebrew morphophonology. *Journal of Child Language, 8,* 609–626.

Berman, R. (1988). Word class distinctions in developing grammars. In Y. Levy, I. Schlesinger, & M. Braine (Eds.), *Categories and processes in language acquisition* (pp. 45–72). Hillsdale, NJ: Lawrence Erlbaum Associates.

Bever, T. (1970). The cognitive basis for linguistic structures. In J. Hayes (Ed.), *Cognition and the development of language* (pp. 279–362). New York: Wiley.

Bever, T. (1992). The logical and extrinsic sources of modularity. In M. Gunnar & M. Maratsos (Eds.), *Modularity and constraints in language and cognition* (pp. 179–212). Hillsdale, NJ: Lawrence Erlbaum Associates.

Black, I. (1995). Trophic interactions and brain plasticity. In M. Gazzaniga (Ed.), *The cognitive neurosciences* (pp. 9–18). Cambridge, MA: MIT Press.

Blankenship, A. (1938). Memory span: A review of the literature. *Psychological Bulletin, 35,* 1–25.

Block, N. (1992). [Book cover comment]. In J. Searle, *The rediscovery of the mind.* Cambridge, MA: MIT Press.

Bloom, L. (1970). *Language development: Form and function in emerging grammar.* Cambridge, MA: MIT Press.

Bloom, L. (1973). *One word at a time: The use of single-word utterances before syntax.* The Hague: Mouton.

Bloom, L. (1978). *Readings in language development.* New York: Wiley.

Bloom, L. (1990). Developments in expression: Affect and speech. In N. Stein, B. Leventhal, & T. Trabasso (Eds.), *Psychological and biological approaches to emotion* (pp. 215–245). Hillsdale, NJ: Lawrence Erlbaum Associates.

Bloom, L. (1991). Representation and expression. In N. Krasnegor, D. Rumbaugh, R. Schiefelbusch, & M. Studdert-Kennedy (Eds.), *Biological and behavioral foundations for language development* (pp. 117–143). Hillsdale, NJ: Lawrence Erlbaum Associates.

Bloom, L. (1993). *The transition from infancy to language: Arguing the power of expression.* New York: Cambridge University Press.

Bloom, L., & Beckwith, R. (1986). *Intentionality and language development.* Unpublished manuscript, Columbia University Teachers College, New York.

Bloom, L., & Beckwith, R. (1988). *Intentionality and language development.* Unpublished manuscript, Columbia University Teachers College, New York.

Bloom, L., & Beckwith, R. (1989). Talking with feeling: Integrating affective and linguistic expression in early language development. *Cognition and Emotion, 3,* 313–342.

Bloom, L., Beckwith, R., Capatides, J., & Hafitz, J. (1988). Expression through affect and words in the transition from infancy to language. In P. Baltes, D. Featherman, & R. Lerner (Eds.), *Life-span development and behavior* (Vol. 8, pp. 99–127). Hillsdale, NJ: Lawrence Erlbaum Associates.

Bloom, L., Hood, L., & Lightbown, P. (1974). Imitation in language development: If, when, and why. *Cognitive Psychology, 6,* 380–420.

Bloom, L., & Lahey, M. (1978). *Language development and language disorders.* New York: Wiley.

Bloom, L., Lifter, K., & Hafitz, J. (1980). Semantics of verbs and the development of verb inflection in child language. *Language, 56,* 386–412.

Bloom, L., Lightbown, P., & Hood, L. (1975). Structure and variation in child language. *Monographs of the Society for Research in Child Development, 40*(Serial No. 160).

Bloom, L., Rispoli, M., Gartner, B., & Hafitz, J. (1989). Acquisition of complementation. *Journal of Child Language, 16,* 101–120.

Bobrow, D., & Norman, D. (1975). Some principles of memory schemata. In D. Bobrow & A. Collins (Eds.), *Representation and understanding: Studies in cognitive science* (pp. 131–150). New York: Academic Press.

Boehm, A. (1969). *Boehm Test of Basic Concepts.* New York: Psychological Corporation.

Boehm, A. (1986). *Boehm Test of Basic Concepts–Revised.* New York: Psychological Corporation.

Bollinger, R., & Stout, C. (1976). Response-contingent small-step treatment: Performance-based communication intervention. *Journal of Speech and Hearing Disorders, 41,* 40–51.

Bowerman, M. (1973). *Early syntactic development.* New York: Cambridge University Press.

Bowerman, M. (1976). Semantic factors in the acquisition of rules for word use and sentence construction. In D. Morehead, & R. Morehead (Eds.), *Normal and deficient child language* (pp. 99–180). Baltimore: University Park Press.

Bowerman, M. (1982). Reorganizational processes in lexical and syntactic development. In E. Wanner & L. Gleitman (Eds.), *Language acquisition: The state of the art* (pp. 319–346). New York: Cambridge University Press.

Bowerman, M. (1987). Commentary: Mechanisms of language acquisition. In B. MacWhinney (Ed.), *Mechanisms of language acquisition* (pp. 443–466). Hillsdale, NJ: Lawrence Erlbaum Associates.

Bowerman, M. (1990). Mapping thematic roles onto syntactic functions: Are children helped by innate "linking rules"? *Journal of Linguistics, 28,* 1253–1289.

Bowerman, M. (1994). Learning a semantic system: What role do cognitive predispositions play? In P. Bloom (Ed.), *Language acquisition: Core readings* (pp. 329–363). Cambridge, MA: MIT Press.

Bowlby, J. (1969). *Attachment and loss: Vol. I. Attachment.* New York: Basic Books.

Bowlby, J. (1973). *Attachment and loss: Vol. II. Separation.* New York: Basic Books.

Bracken, B. (1986). *Bracken concept development program.* San Antonio, TX: Psychological Corporation.

Braine, M. (1988). Modeling the acquisition of linguistic structure. In Y. Levy, I. Schlesinger, & M. Braine (Eds.), *Categories and processes in language acquisition* (pp. 217–260). Hillsdale, NJ: Lawrence Erlbaum Associates.

Brenner, J., & Mueller, E. (1982). Shared meaning in boy toddlers' peer relations. *Child Development, 53,* 380–391.

Brentano, F. (1966). *The true and the evident* (R. Chrisholm, I. Politzer, & K. Fischer, trans.). New York: Humanities Press.

Bretherton, I., Bates, E., McNew, S., Shore, C., Williamson, C., & Beeghly-Smith, M. (1981). Comprehension and production of symbols in infancy: An experimental study. *Developmental Psychology, 17,* 728–736.

Bretherton, I., McNew, S., Snyder, L., & Bates, E. (1983). Individual differences at 20 months: Analytic and holistic strategies in language acquisition. *Journal of Child Language, 10,* 293–320.

Brigance, A. (1978). *Inventory of early development.* North Villerica, MA: Curriculum Associates.

Brinton, B., & Fujiki, M. (1994). Ways to teach conversation. In J. Duchan, L. Hewitt, & R. Sonnemeier (Eds.), *Pragmatics* (pp. 59–71). Englewood Cliffs, NJ: Prentice-Hall.

Britton, B., & Pellegrini, A. (Eds.). (1990). *Narrative thought and narrative language.* Hillsdale, NJ: Lawrence Erlbaum Associates.

Bronfenbrenner, U. (1974). Developmental research, public policy, and the ecology of childhood. *Child Development, 45,* 1–5.

Bronfenbrenner, U. (1977). Toward an experimental ecology of human development. *American Psychologist, 32,* 513–531.

Bronfenbrenner, U. (1979). *The ecology of human development.* Cambridge, MA: Harvard University.

Brown, R. (1956). Language and categories: Appendix. In J. Bruner, J. Goodnow, & G. Austin (Eds.), *A study of thinking* (pp. 247–312). New York: Wiley.

Brown, R. (1958a). How shall a thing be named? *Psychological Review, 65,* 18–21.

Brown, R. (1958b). *Words and things.* New York: The Free Press.

Brown, R. (1973a). Development of the first language in the human species. *American Psychologist, 28,* 97–106.

Brown, R. (1973b). *A first language: The early stages.* Cambridge, MA: Harvard University Press.

Brown, R. (1977). Introduction. In C. Snow & C. Ferguson (Eds.), *Talking to children* (pp. 1–27). New York: Cambridge University Press.

Brown, R. (1986). *Social psychology* (2nd ed.). New York: The Free Press.

Brown, R. (1988). Roger Brown: An autobiography in the third person. In F. Kessel (Ed.), *The development of language and language researchers* (pp. 395–404). Hillsdale, NJ: Lawrence Erlbaum Associates.

Brown, R., & Bellugi, U. (1964). Three processes in the child's acquisition of syntax. *Harvard Educational Review, 34,* 133–151.

Brown, R., Cazden, C., & Bellugi-Klima, U. (1969). The child's grammar from I to III. In J. Hill (Ed.), *Minnesota symposia on child psychology* (Vol. 2, pp. 28–73). Minneapolis: University of Minnesota Press.

Brown, R., & Hanlon, C. (1970). Derivational complexity and order of acquisition in child speech. In J. Hayes (Ed.), *Cognition and the development of language* (pp. 11–55). New York: Wiley.

Brown, R., & Kulik, J. (1977). Flashbulb memories. *Cognition, 5,* 73–99.

Bruner, J. (1964). The course of cognitive growth. *American Psychologist, 19,* 1–15.

Bruner, J. (1973). *Beyond the information given.* (J. Anglin, Ed.). New York: Norton.

Bruner, J. (1975a). From communication to language—A psychological perspective. *Cognition, 3,* 255–288.

Bruner, J. (1975b). The ontogensis of speech acts. *Journal of Child Language, 2*, 1–19.

Bruner, J. (1978). Foreword. In A. Lock (Ed.), *Action, gesture and symbol* (pp. vii–viii). New York: Academic Press.

Bruner, J. (1981). The social context of language acquisition. *Language & Communication, 1*, 155–178.

Bruner, J. (1983). *Child's talk: Learning to use language.* New York: Norton.

Bruner, J. (1986). *Actual minds, possible worlds.* Cambridge, MA: Harvard University Press.

Bruner, J. (1990). *Acts of meaning.* Cambridge, MA: Harvard University Press.

Bruner, J., Goodnow, J., & Austin, G. (1956). *A study of thinking.* New York: Science Editions.

Bruner, J., Olver, R., & Greenfield, P. (1966). *Studies in cognitive growth.* New York: Wiley.

Bullock, S. A. (1975). *A language for life.* London: Her Majesty's Stationery Office.

Burger, R., & Muma, J. (1980). Cognitive distancing in mediated categorization in aphasia. *Journal of Psycholinguistic Research, 9*, 355–365.

Buttrill, J., Nizawa, J., Biemer, C., Takahashi, C., & Hearn, S. (1989). Serving the language learning disabled adolescent: A strategies-based model. *Language, Speech, and Hearing Services in Schools, 29*, 185–204.

Byrne-Saricks, M. (1987). Book review: Language acquisition: A functionalistic perspective (1986). *Asha, 29*, 7, 50.

Camarata, S., & Schwartz, R. (1985). Production of action words and object words: Evidence for a relationship between semantics and phonology. *Journal of Speech and Hearing Research, 28*, 323–330.

Campbell, T., & Bain, B. (1991). How long to treat: A multiple outcome approach. *Language, Speech, and Hearing Services in Schools, 22*, 271–276.

Carey, S. (1982). Semantic development: The state of the art. In E. Wanner & L. Gleitman (Eds.), *Language acquisition: The state of the art* (pp. 347–389). New York: Cambridge University Press.

Carmichael, L., Hogan, H., & Walter, A. (1932). An experimental study of the effect of language on the reproduction of visually perceived form. *Journal of Experimental Psychology, 11*, 567–574.

Caron, A. (1969). Discrimination shifts in three year olds as a function of dimensional salience. *Developmental Psychology, 1*, 333–339.

Carrow-Woolfolk, E. (1985). *Test for Auditory Comprehension of Language–revised.* Allen, TX: DLM Teaching Resources.

Cazden, C. (1966). Subcultural differences in child language: An interdisciplinary review. *Merrill-Palmer Quarterly, 12*, 185–219.

Cazden, C. (1968). The acquisition of noun and verb inflections. *Child Development, 39*, 433–448.

Cazden, C. (1972). *Child language and education.* New York: Holt, Rinehart & Winston.

Cazden, C. (1975). Play with language and metalinguistic awareness: One dimension of language experience. In C. Winsor (Ed.), *Dimensions of language experience* (pp. 3–19). New York: Agathon Press.

Cazden, C. (1977). The quest of intent. In M. Lewis & L. Rosenblum (Eds.), *Interaction, conversation, and the development of language* (pp. 309–313). New York: Wiley.

Cazden, C. (1988). Environmental assistance revisited: Variation and functional equivalence. In F. Kessel (Ed.), *The development of language and language researchers* (pp. 281–298). Hillsdale, NJ: Lawrence Erlbaum Associates.

Chafe, W. (1976). Givenness, contrastiveness, definiteness, subjects, topics, and point of view. In C. Li (Ed.), *Subject and topic* (pp. 25–55). New York: Academic.

Chalkley, M. (1982). The emergence of language as a social skill. In S. Kuczaj (Ed.), *Language development* (Vol. 2). Hillsdale, NJ: Lawrence Erlbaum Associates.

Chalupa, L. (1995). The nature and nurture of retinal ganglion cell development. In M. Gazzaniga (Ed.), *The cognitive neurosciences* (pp. 37–50). Cambridge, MA: MIT Press.

Chapman, R. (1981). Exploring children's communicative intents. In J. Miller (Ed.), *Assessing language production in children* (pp. 111–138). Baltimore: University Park Press.

Chapman, R., & Kohn, L. (1978). Comprehension strategies in two- and three-year-olds: Animate agents or probable events? *Journal of Speech and Hearing Research, 21*, 746–761.

Chapman, R., Streim, N., Crais, E., Salmon, D., Strand, E., & Negri, N. (1992). Child talk: Assumptions of a developmental process model for early language learning. In R. Chapman (Ed.), *Processes in language acquisition and disorders* (pp. 3–19). St. Louis, MO: Mosby Yearbook.

Chomsky, N. (1957). *Syntactic structures.* The Hague: Mouton.

Chomsky, N. (1965). A transformational approach to syntax. In J. Fodor & J. Katz (Eds.), *The structure of language* (pp. 211–245). Englewood Cliffs, NJ: Prentice-Hall.

Chomsky, N. (1968). *Language and mind.* New York: Harcourt, Brace, Jovanvich.

Chomsky, N. (1980). *Rules and representations.* New York: Columbia University Press.

Chomsky, N. (1986). *Knowledge of language: Its nature, origin, and use.* New York: Praeger.

Clark, H., & Clark, E. (1977). *Psychology and language.* New York: Harcourt, Brace, Jovanovich.

Cole, K., Dale, P., & Mills, P. (1990). Defining language delay in young children by cognitive referencing: Are we saying more than we know? *Applied Psycholinguistics, 11*, 291–302.

Cole, K., Mills, P., & Dale, P. (1989). Examination of test–retest and split-half reliability for measures derived from language samples of young handicapped children. *Language, Speech, and Hearing Services in Schools, 20*, 259–268.

Conant, S. (1987). The relationship between age and MLU in young children: A second look at Klee and Fitzgerald's data. *Journal of Child Language, 14*, 169–173.

Connell, P. (1986). Teaching subjecthood to language-disordered children. *Journal of Speech and Hearing Research, 29*, 481–492.

Connell, P. (1988). Induction, generalization, and deduction: Models for defining language generalization. *Language, Speech, and Hearing Services in Schools, 19*, 282–291.

Connell, P. (1990). Linguistic foundations of clinical language teaching: Grammar. *Journal of Speech Language Pathology and Audiology, 14*, 25–36.

Constable, C. (1986). The application of scripts in the organization of language intervention contexts. In K. Nelson (Ed.), *Event knowledge: Structure and function in development* (pp. 205–230). Hillsdale, NJ: Lawrence Erlbaum Associates.

Corsini, D., Pick, A., & Flavell, J. (1968). Production deficiency of nonverbal mediators in young children. *Child Development, 39*, 53–58.

Costello, J. (1983). Generalization across settings: Language intervention with children. In J. Miller, D. Yoder, & R. Schiefelbusch (Eds.), *Contemporary issues in language intervention* (ASHA Reports, No. 12, pp. 275–297). Rockville, MD: American Speech-Language-Hearing Association.

Cowan, P., Weber, J., Hoddinott, B., & Klein, T. (1967). Mean length of a spoken response as a function of stimulus, experimenter, and subject. *Child Development, 38*, 191–203.

Craig, H. (1983). Applications of pragmatic language models for intervention. In T. Gallagher & C. Prutting (Eds.), *Pragmatic assessment and intervention issues in language* (pp. 101–128). San Diego, CA: College-Hill Press.

Craik, F., & Lockhart, R. (1972). Levels of processing: A framework for memory research. *Journal of Verbal Learning and Verbal Behavior, 11*, 671–684.

Crais, E. (1992). Fast mapping: A new look at word learning. In R. Chapman (Ed.), *Process in language acquisition and disorders* (pp. 159–185). St. Louis, MO: Mosby Yearbook.

Crick, F. (1988). *What mad pursuit.* New York: Basic Books.

Cromer, R. (1974). Receptive language in the mentally retarded: Processes and diagnostic distinctions. In R. Schiefelbusch & L. Lloyd (Eds.), *Language perspectives: Acquisition, retardation, and intervention* (pp. 237–268). Baltimore: University Park Press.

Cromer, R. (1976). The cognitive hypothesis of language acquisition for child language deficiency. In R. Schiefelbusch (Ed.), *Normal and deficient child language* (pp. 283–333). Baltimore: University Park Press.

Crowder, R. (1982). The demise of short-term memory. *Acta Psychologica, 50*, 291–323.

Cruickshank, W. (1972). Some issues facing the field of learning disabilities. *Journal of Learning Disabilities, 5*, 380–387.

Crystal, D. (1987). Towards a "bucket" theory of language disability: Taking account of interaction between linguistic levels. *Clinical Linguistics and Phonetics, 1*, 7–22.

Crystal, D., Fletcher, P., & Garman, M. (1976). *The grammatical analysis of language disability.* New York: Elsevier.

Cutler, A., & Swinney, D. (1987). Prosody and the development of comprehension. *Journal of Child Language, 14*, 145–167.

Daniloff, R. (1984). *Articulation assessment & treatment issues.* San Diego, CA: College-Hill Press.

Daniloff, R., & Hammarberg, R. (1973). On defining coarticulation. *Journal of Phonetics, 1*, 239–248.

Darley, F. (1979). *Evaluation of appraisal techniques in speech and language pathology.* Reading, MA: Addison-Wesley.

Darley, F., & Moll, K. (1960). Reliability of language measures and size of language samples. *Journal of Speech and Hearing Research, 3*, 166–173.

Deese, J. (1970). *Psycholinguistics.* Boston: Allyn & Bacon.

Dennett, D. (1978). *Brainstorms.* Montgomery, VT: Bradford Books.

Deregowski, J. (1977). Pictures, symbols and frames of reference. In G. Butterworth (Ed.), *The child's representation of the world.* New York: Plenum.

deSaussure, G. (1915). *Course in general linguistics.* New York: McGraw-Hill.

deVilliers, J., & deVilliers, P. (1973). A cross-sectional study of the acquisition of grammatical morphemes. *Journal of Psycholinguistic Research, 2*, 267–278.

deVilliers, P., & deVilliers, J. (1978). *Language acquisition.* Cambridge, MA: Harvard University.

Dickinson, D. (1984). First impressions: Children's knowledge of words gained from a single exposure. *Applied Psycholinguistics, 5*, 359–373.

Dollaghan, C. (1987). Fast mapping in normal and language impaired children. *Journal of Speech and Hearing Disorders, 52*, 218–222.

Dollard, J., & Miller, N. (1950). *Personality and psychotherapy.* New York: McGraw-Hill.

Donaldson, M. (1978). *Children's minds.* New York: Norton.

Donnellan, K. (1981). Intuitions and presuppositions. In P. Cole (Ed.), *Radical pragmatics.* New York: Academic Press.

Dore, J. (1974). A pragmatic description of early development. *Journal of Psycholinguistic Research, 3*, 343–350.

Dore, J. (1975). Holophrases, speech acts, and language universals. *Journal of Child Language, 2*, 21–40.

Duchan, J. (1991). Everyday events: Their role in language assessment and intervention. In T. Gallagher (Ed.), *Pragmatics of language: Clinical practice issues* (pp. 11–42). San Diego, CA: Singular.

Duchan, J., Hewitt, L., & Sonnenmeier, R. (1994). *Pragmatics.* Englewood Cliffs, NJ: Prentice-Hall.

Dunn, L., & Dunn, L. (1981). *Peabody Picture Vocabulary Test–Revised.* Circle Pines, MN: American Guidance Service.

Eckerman, C., & Whatley, J. (1977). Toys and social interaction between infant peers. *Child Development, 48*, 1645–1656.

Ehrens, T. (1993). Tests: A significant difference? *American Journal of Speech-Language Pathology, 2*, 17–19.

Emslie, H., & Stevenson, R. (1981). Pre-school children's use of the articles in definite and indefinite referring expressions. *Journal of Child Language, 8*, 313–328.

Engler, L., Hannah, E., & Longhurst, T. (1973). Linguistic analysis of speech samples: A practical guide for clinicians. *Journal of Speech and Hearing Disorders, 38*, 192–204.

Ferguson, C. (1977). New directions in phonological theory: Language acquisition and universals research. In R. Cole (Ed.), *Current issues in linguistic theory* (pp. 247–300). Bloomington: Indiana University Press.

Ferguson, C. (1978). Learning to pronounce: The earliest stages of phonological development in the child. In F. Minifie & L. Lloyd (Eds.), *Communicative and cognitive abilities—Early behavioral assessment* (pp. 273–298). Austin, TX: PRO-ED.

Ferguson, C., & Farwell, C. (1975). Words and sounds in early language acquisition. *Language, 51,* 419–439.

Ferguson, C., & Garnica, O. (1975). Theories of phonological development. In E. Lenneberg & E. Lenneberg (Eds.), *Foundations of language development* (pp. 149–180). New York: Academic.

Ferguson, C., Menn, L., & Stoel-Gammon, C. (1992). *Phonological development: Models, research, and implications.* Monkton, MD: York Press.

Festinger, L. (1957). *A theory of cognitive dissonance.* New York: Harper & Row.

Feuerstein, R. (1979). *The dynamic assessment of retarded performers.* Baltimore: University Park Press.

Fey, M. (1986). *Language intervention with young children.* San Diego, CA: College-Hill Press.

Fey, M., Catts, H., & Larrivee, L. (1995). *Language intervention: Preschool through the elementary years.* Baltimore: Brookes.

Fey, M., & Leonard, L. (1983). Pragmatic skills of children with specific language impairments. In T. Gallagher & C. Prutting (Eds.), *Pragmatic assessment and intervention issues in language* (pp. 65–82). San Diego, CA: College-Hill Press.

Fey, M., Windsor, J., & Warren, S. (1995). *Language intervention: Preschool through the elementary years.* Baltimore: Brookes.

Field, T. (1981). Early peer relations. In P. Strain (Ed.), *The utilization of classroom peers as behavior change agents* (pp. 1–30). New York: Plenum.

Fillenbaum, S. (1966). Memory for gist: Some relevant variables. *Language and Speech, 9,* 217–227.

Fillmore, C. (1972). Subjects, speakers, and roles. In D. Davidson & G. Jarman (Eds.), *Semantics of natural language* (2nd ed., pp. 1–24)). Boston: Reidel.

Fischer, K. (1980). A theory of cognitive development: The control and construction of hierarchies of skills. *Psychological Review, 87,* 476–531.

Fivush, R., & Hudson, J. (1990). *Knowing and remembering in young children.* New York: Cambridge University Press.

Flavell, J. (1968). *The development of role-taking and communication skills in children.* New York: Wiley.

Flavell, J. (1971). Stage-related properties of cognitive development. *Cognitive Psychology, 2,* 421–453.

Flavell, J. (1982). Structures, stages, and sequences in cognitive development. In W. Collins (Ed.), *Minnesota symposia on child psychology* (Vol. 5, pp. 1–28). Hillsdale, NJ: Lawrence Erlbaum Associates.

Flavell, J. (1985). *Cognitive development.* Englewood Cliffs, NJ: Prentice-Hall.

Flavell, J., Beach, D., & Chinsky, J. (1966). Spontaneous verbal rehearsal in a memory task as a function of age. *Child Development, 37,* 283–299.

Fodor, J. (1983). *The modularity of mind: An essay on faculty psychology.* Cambridge, MA: MIT Press.

Fodor, J., & Crain, S. (1987). Simplicity and generality of rules in language acquisition. In B. MacWhinney (Ed.), *Mechanisms of language acquisition* (pp. 35–64). Hillsdale, NJ: Lawrence Erlbaum Associates.

Folger, M., & Chapman, R. (1978). A pragmatic analysis of spontaneous imitations. *Journal of Child Language, 5,* 25–39.

Frege, G. (1952). On sense and reference. In P. Greach & M. Block (Eds.), *Translations from the philosophical writings of Gottlob Frege.* Oxford, UK: Blackwell. (Original work published 1892)

Freidin, R., & Quicoli, C. (1989). Zero-stimulation for parameter setting. *Behavioral and Brain Sciences, 12,* 338–339.

Fujiki, M., & Brinton, B. (1987). Elicited imitation revisited: A comparison with spontaneous language production. *Language, Speech, and Hearing Services in Schools, 18,* 301–311.

Furth, H. (1984, May). *A school for thinking for deaf children.* Paper presented at the Spring Conference, May, Texas Tech University, Lubbock.

Gagne, R., & Smith, E. (1962). A study of the effects of verbalization on problem solving. *Journal of Experimental Psychology, 63,* 12–18.

Gallagher, T. (1977). Revision behavior in the speech of normal children developing language. *Journal of Speech and Hearing Research, 20,* 303–318.

Gallagher, T. (1981). Contingent query sequences with adult–child discourse. *Journal of Child Language, 8,* 51–62.

Gallagher, T. (1983). Pre-assessment: A procedure for accommodating language use variability. In T. Gallagher & C. Prutting (Eds.), *Pragmatic assessment and intervention issues in language* (pp. 1–28). San Diego: College-Hill Press.

Gallagher, T. (Ed.). (1991). *Pragmatics of language: Clinical practice issues.* San Diego, CA: Singular.

Gallagher, T., & Darnton, B. (1978). Conversational aspects of the speech of language disordered children: Revision behaviors. *Journal of Speech and Hearing Research, 21,* 118–135.

Gallistel, C. (1995). The replacement of general-purpose theories with adaptive specializations. In M. Gazzaniga (Ed.), *The cognitive neurosciences* (pp. 1255–1268). Cambridge, MA: MIT Press.

Gardner, M. (1985). *Test of Auditory-Perceptual Skills.* San Francisco: Children's Hospital of San Francisco.

Garner, W. (1966). To perceive is to know. *American Psychologist, 21,* 11–19.

Garvey, C. (1975). Requests and responses in children's speech. *Journal of Child Language, 2,* 41–63.

Garvey, C. (1977). *Play.* Cambridge, MA: Harvard University Press.

Garvey, C. (1979). Contingent queries and their relations in discourse. In E. Ochs & B. Schieffelin (Eds.), *Developmental pragmatics* (pp. 363–372). New York: Academic Press.

Gathercole, S., & Baddeley, A. (1989). Evaluation of the role of phonological STM in the development in children: A longitudinal study. *Journal of Memory and Language, 28,* 200–213.

Gathercole, S., & Baddeley, A. (1990). Phonological memory deficits in language-disordered children: Is there a causal connection? *Journal of Memory and Language, 29,* 336–360.

Gavin, W., & Giles, L. (1996). Sample size effects on temporal reliability of language sample measures of preschool children. *Journal of Speech and Hearing Research, 39,* 1258–1262.

Gee, J. (1991). Memory and myth: A perspective on narrative. In A. McCabe & C. Peterson (Eds.), *Developing narrative structure* (pp. 1–25). Hillsdale, NJ: Lawrence Erlbaum Associates.

Geschwind, N. (1965a). Disconnexion syndromes in animals and man. *Brain, 88,* 237–294.

Geschwind, N. (1965b). Disconnexion syndromes in animals and man. *Brain, 88,* 585–644.

Gillespie, P., Miller, T., & Fielder, V. (1975). Legislative definitions of learning disabilities: Roadblocks to effective service. *Journal of Learning Disabilities, 8,* 61–67.

Gleitman, L. (1981). Maturational determinants of language growth. *Cognition, 10,* 103–114.

Gleitman, L. (1994). The structural sources of verb meanings. In P. Bloom (Ed.), *Language acquisition: Core readings* (pp. 174–221). Cambridge, MA: MIT Press.

Gleitman, L., & Wanner, E. (1982). Language acquisition: The state of the art. In E. Wanner & L. Gleitman (Eds.), *Language acquisition: The state of the art.* New York: Cambridge University Press.

Glucksberg, S. (1966). *Symbolic processes.* Dubuque, IA: Brown.

Goldberg, L. (1968). Simple models or simple processes? Some research on clinical judgments. *American Psychologist, 23,* 483–496.

Goldin-Meadow, S., & Mylander, C. (1984). Gestural communication in deaf children: The effects and noneffects of parental input on early language development. *Monographs of The Society of Research in Child Development* (Serial No. 207).

Goldman, R., & Fristoe, M. (1969). *Goldman–Fristoe Test of Articulation.* Circle Pines, MN: American Guidance Service.

Goldstein, H. (1984). Effects of modeling and connected practice on generative language learning of preschool children. *Journal of Speech and Hearing Disorders, 49,* 389–398.

Goodman, K. (1967). Reading: A psycholinguistic guessing game. *Journal of the Reading Specialist, 6*, 126–135.

Goodman, K. (1986). *What's whole in whole language?* Portsmouth, NH: Heinemann.

Gopnik, A. (1981). Development of non-nominal expressions in 1–2-year-olds: Why the first words aren't about things. In P. Dale & D. Ingram (Eds.), *Child language* (pp. 93–104). Austin, TX: PRO-ED.

Gopnik, A. (1982). Words and plans: Early language and the development of intelligent action. *Journal of Child Language, 9*, 303–318.

Gopnik, A. (1984). The acquisition of gone and the development of the object concepts. *Journal of Child Language, 9*, 303–318.

Gopnik, A., & Meltzoff, A. (1984). Semantic and cognitive development in 15- to 21-month-old children. *Journal of Child Language, 11*, 495–514.

Gopnik, A., & Meltzoff, A. (1986). Relation between semantic and cognitive development in the one-word stage: The specificity hypothesis. *Child Development, 57*, 1040–1053.

Gottlieb, G. (1976). *The roles of experience in the development of behavior and the nervous system. Studies on the development of behavior and the nervous system: Neural and behavioral specificity.* New York: Academic Press.

Gould, S. (1981). *The mismeasure of man.* New York: Norton.

Greenfield, P. (1980). Going beyond information theory to explain early word choice: A reply to Roy Pea. *Journal of Child Language, 7*, 217–221.

Greenfield, P., & Smith, J. (1976). *Communication and the beginnings of language.* New York: Academic Press.

Grice, H. (1975). 'Logic and conversation.' In P. Cole & J. Morgan (Eds.), *Syntax and semantics: Vol. 3. Speech acts* (pp. 41–58). New York: Seminar Press.

Gropen, J., Pinker, S., Hollander, M., & Goldberg, R. (1994). Affectness and direct objects: The role of lexical semantics in the acquisition of verb argument structure. In P. Bloom (Ed.), *Language acquisition: Core readings* (pp. 285–328). Cambridge, MA: MIT Press.

Guess, D., Keogh, W., & Sailor, W. (1978). Generalization of speech and language behavior. In R. Schiefelbusch (Ed.), *Bases of language intervention* (pp. 373–396). Baltimore: University Park Press.

Guess, D., Sailor, W., Rutherford, G., & Baer, D. (1968). An experimental analysis of linguistic development: The productive use of the plural morpheme. *Journal of Applied Behavioral Analysis, 1*, 297–306.

Guion, R. (1977). Content validity: Three years of talk—What's the action? *Public Personnel Management, 6*, 407–414.

Guion, R. (1980). On trinitarian doctrines of validity. *Professional Psychology, 11*, 385–398.

Gunnar, M., & Maratsos, M. (1992). *Modularity and constraints in language and cognition.* Hillsdale, NJ: Lawrence Erlbaum Associates.

Hagstrom, F. (1994). Therapy at home: Vygotskian perspectives on parental involvement. *Clinical Communication Disorders, 4*, 237–245.

Hall, S. (1991). *Basic biomechanics.* Toronto: Mosby Yearbook.

Halliday, M. (1975). Learning how to mean. In E. Lenneberg & E. Lenneberg (Eds.), *Foundations of language development: A multidisciplinary approach* (pp. 239–266). New York: Academic Press.

Halliday, M., & Hansan, R. (1976). *Cohesion in English.* London: Longman.

Harris, Z. (1965). Co-occurrence and transformation in linguistic structure. In J. Fodor & J. Katz (Eds.), *The structure of language: Readings in the philosophy of language* (pp. 155–210). Englewood Cliffs, NJ: Prentice-Hall.

Hart, B., & Risley, T. (1975). Incidental teaching of language in the preschool. *Journal of Applied Behavior Analysis, 8*, 411–420.

Hartup, W. (1978). Children and their friends. In H. McGurk (Ed.), *Issues in childhood social development* (pp. 130–170). London: Methuen.

Harvard School of Education. (1971). *Challenging the myths: The schools, the blacks, and the poor.* Cambridge, MA: Harvard Educational Review.

Harvard School of Education. (1973). *The rights of children* (Special issue: Part 1). Cambridge, MA: Harvard Educational Review.

Harvard School of Education. (1974). *The rights of children* (Special issue: Part 2). Cambridge, MA: Harvard Educational Review.

Hegde, M., & McConn, J. (1981). Language training: Some data on response classes and generalization to an occupational setting. *Journal of Speech and Hearing Disorders, 46,* 353–358.

Hegde, M., Noll, M., & Pecora, R. (1979). A study of some factors effecting generalization of language training. *Journal of Speech and Hearing Disorders, 44,* 301–320.

Heider, E. (1971). "Focal" color areas and the development of color names. *Developmental Psychology, 4,* 447–455.

Heibeck, T., & Markman, E. (1987). Word learning in children: An examination of fast mapping. *Child Development, 58,* 1021–1034.

Heshusius, L. (1989). The Newtonian mechanistic paradigm, special education, and contours of alternatives: An overview. *Journal of Learning Disabilities, 22,* 403–415.

Hester, P., & Hendrickson, J. (1977). Training functional expressive language: The acquisition and generalization of five-element syntactic responses. *Journal of Applied Behavior Analysis, 10,* 316.

Hoff-Ginsberg, E. (1987). Topic relations in mother–child conversation. *First Language, 7,* 145–158.

Hoshmand, L., & Polkinghorne, D. (1992). Redefining the science–practice relationship and professional training. *American Psychologist, 47,* 55–66.

Hubbell, R. (1981). *Children's language disorders: An integrated approach.* Englewood Cliffs, NJ: Prentice-Hall.

Hudson, J., & Fivush, R. (1990). Introduction: What young children remember and why. In R. Fivush & J. Hudson (Eds.), *Knowing and remembering in young children* (pp. 1–8). New York: Cambridge University Press.

Huttenlocher, J. (1974). The origins of language comprehension. In R. Solso (Ed.), *Theories in cognitive psychology: The Loyola symposium* (pp. 331–368). New York: Wiley.

Ingram, D. (1976). *Phonological disability in children.* New York: Elsevier.

Ingram, D. (1989a). *First language acquisition: Method, description and explanation.* New York: Cambridge University Press.

Ingram, D. (1989b). *Phonological disability in children* (2nd ed.). New York: Elsevier.

Jackendoff, R. (1983). *Semantics and cognition.* Cambridge, MA: MIT Press.

Jakobson, R. (1960). Concluding statement: Linguistics and poetics. In T. Sebeok (Ed.), *Style in language* (pp. 350–377). Cambridge, MA: MIT Press.

Jenkins, J. (1974). Remember that old theory of memory? Well, forget it! *American Psychologist, 29,* 785–795.

Johnson, N. (1965). The psychological reality of phrase structure rules. *Journal of Verbal Learning and Verbal Behavior, 4,* 469–475.

Johnson, N. (1966). The influence of associations between elements of structural verbal responses. *Journal of Verbal Learning and Verbal Behavior, 5,* 369–374.

Johnson, W., Darley, F., & Spriestersbach, D. (1963). *Diagnostic methods in speech pathology.* New York: Harper & Row.

Johnston, J. (1983). Discussion: Part I: What is language intervention? The role of theory. In J. Miller, D. Yoder, & R. Schiefelbusch (Eds.), *Contemporary issues in language intervention* (ASHA Reports No. 12, pp. 52–60). Rockville, MD: ASHA.

Johnston, J. (1988). Generalization: The nature of change. *Language, Speech, and Hearing Services in Schools, 19,* 314–329.

Just, M., & Carpenter, P. (1992). A capacity theory of comprehension: Individual differences in working memory. *Psychological Review, 99,* 122–149.

Kagan, J. (1965). Reflectivity-impulsivity and reading ability in primary grade children. *Child Development, 36,* 609–628.

Kagan, J. (1967). On the need for relativism. *American Psychologist, 22,* 131–142.

Kagan, J. (1968). On cultural deprivation. In D. Glass (Ed.), *Environmental influences* (pp. 211–350). New York: Russell Sage Foundation.

Kagan, J. (1969). Continuity in cognitive development during the first year. *Merrill-Palmer Quarterly, 15,* 101–119.

Kagan, J. (1970). The determinants of attention in the infant. *American Scientist, 56,* 298–306.

Kagan, J. (1971). *Change and continuity in infancy.* New York: Wiley.

Kagan, J., & Lewis, M. (1965). Studies of attention in the human infant. *Merrill-Palmer Quarterly, 11,* 95–127.

Kagan, J., Rossman, B., Day, D., Albert, J., & Phillips, W. (1964). Information processing in the child. Significance of analytic and reflective attitudes. *Psychological Monographs, 78*(578), 1–37.

Kaiser, A., Alpert, C., & Warren, S. (1987). Teaching functional language: Strategies for language intervention. In M. Snell (Ed.), *Systematic instruction of persons with severe handicaps* (3rd. ed., pp. 247–272). Columbus, OH: Merrill.

Kamhi, A. (1988). A reconceptualization of generalization and generalization problems. *Language, Speech, and Hearing Services in Schools, 19,* 304–313.

Kamhi, A. (1993). Some problems with the marriage between theory and clinical practice. *Language, Speech, and Hearing Services in Schools, 24,* 57–60.

Kamhi, A., Catts, H., & Davis, M. (1984). Management of sentence production demands. *Journal of Speech and Hearing Research, 27,* 329–337.

Kamin, L. (1974). *Science and the politics of I.Q.* Hillsdale, NJ: Lawrence Erlbaum Associates.

Kaplan, A. (1964). *The conduct of inquiry: Methodology for behavioral science.* San Francisco: Chandler.

Karmiloff-Smith, A. (1984). Children's problem solving. In M. Lamb, A. Brown, & B. Rogoff (Eds.), *Advances in developmental psychology* (Vol. 3, pp. 39–90). Hillsdale, NJ: Lawrence Erlbaum Associates.

Karmiloff-Smith, A. (1992). *Beyond modularity.* Cambridge, MA: MIT Press.

Karmiloff-Smith, A. (1994). Innate constraints and developmental change. In P. Bloom. (Ed.), *Language acquisition* (pp. 563–590). Cambridge, MA: MIT Press.

Karmiloff-Smith, A., & Inhelder, B. (1974/1975). If you want to get ahead, get a theory. *Cognition, 3,* 195–212.

Kelly, G. (1976). *Two developmental cognitive processes: Performance at the preschool level.* Unpublished masters thesis, State University of New York, Buffalo.

Kendler, H., & Kendler, T. (1959). Reversal and nonreversal shifts in kindergarten children. *Journal of Experimental Psychology, 58,* 56–60.

Kendler, H., & Kendler, T. (1970). Developmental processes in discrimination learning. *Human Development, 13,* 65–89.

Kent, R. (1990). The fragmentation of clinical service and clinical science in communicative disorders. *NSSLHA, 17,* 4–16.

Kerlinger, F. (1973). *Foundations of behavioral research* (2nd ed.). New York: Holt, Rinehart & Winston.

Kessen, W. (1962). "Stage" and "structure" in the study of children. *Monographs of the Society for Research in Child Development, 27.*

King, K., & Goodman, K. (1990). Whole language: Cherishing learners and their language. *Language, Speech, and Hearing Services in Schools, 21,* 221–227.

Kirk, S., McCarthy, J., & Kirk, W. (1968). *The Illinois test of psycholinguistic abilities* (Rev. ed.). Urbana: University of Illinois Press.

Klee, T., & Fitzgerald, M. (1985). The relation between grammatical development and mean length of utterance in morphemes. *Journal of Child Language, 12,* 251–269.

Klima, E., & Bellugi-Klima, U. (1969). Syntactic regularities in the speech of children. In D. Reibel & S. Schane (Eds.), *Modern studies in English* (pp. 448–466). Englewood Cliffs, NJ: Prentice-Hall.

Kramer, S. (1976). *Performance of four year old iconic and four year old symbolic processors on reversal and nonreversal set shifts.* Unpublished masters thesis, State University of New York, Buffalo.

Kretschmer, R. (1984). Metacognition, metalinguistics, and intervention. In K. Ruder & M. Smith (Eds.), *Developmental language intervention* (pp. 209–230). Austin, TX: PRO-ED.

Kripke, S. (1972). Naming and necessity. In D. Davidson & G. Harman (Eds.), *Semantics of natural language* (pp. 253–355). Boston: Reidel.

Kuczaj, S. (1982). Children's overextensions in comprehension and production: Support for a prototype theory of object word meaning acquisition. *First Language, 3,* 93–105.

Kuczaj, S., & Barrett, M. (1986). *The development of word meaning.* New York: Springer-Verlag.

Kuhn, T. (1961). The function of measurement in modern physical science. *ISIS, 52,* 161–193.

Kuhn, T. (1962). *The structure of scientific revolutions.* Chicago: University of Chicago Press.

Labov, W. (1970). The study of language in its social context. *Studium Generale, 23,* 30–87.

Labov, W., & Waletzky, J. (1967). Narrative analysis. In J. Helm (Ed.), *Essays on the verbal and visual arts* (pp. 12–44). Seattle: University of Washington Press.

Lahey, M. (1988). *Language disorders and language development.* New York: Macmillan.

Lahey, M. (1994). Grammatical morpheme acquisition: Do norms exist? *Journal of Speech and Hearing Research, 37,* 1192–1194.

Lakoff, G. (1987). *Women, fire, and dangerous things: What categories reveal about the mind.* Chicago: University of Chicago Press.

Lamb, M. (1977). The development of mother–infant and father–infant attachments in the second year of life. *Developmental Psychology, 13,* 637–648.

Lasky, E. (1985). Comprehending and processing of information in clinic and classroom. In C. Simon (Ed.), *Communication skills and classroom success: Therapy methodologies for language-learning disabled students* (pp. 113–132). San Diego, CA: College-Hill Press.

Lawrence, C. (1992). Assessing the use of age-equivalent scores in clinical management. *Language, Speech, and Hearing Services in Schools, 23,* 6–8.

Lee, L. (1974). *Developmental sentence analysis: A grammatical assessment procedure for speech and language clinicians.* Evanston, IL: Northwestern University Press.

Lee, L., & Canter, S. (1971). Developmental sentence scoring: A clinical procedure for estimating syntactic development in children's spontaneous speech. *Journal of Speech and Hearing Disorders, 36,* 315–340.

Lee, L., Koenigsknecht, R., & Mulhern, S. (1975). *Interactive language development teaching.* Evanston, IL: Northwestern University Press.

Lees, R. (1965). *The grammar of English nominalizations.* Bloomington: Indiana University Press.

Leonard, L. (1976). *Meaning in child language.* New York: Grune & Stratton.

Leonard, L. (1982). The nature of specific language impairment in children. In S. Rosenberg (Ed.), *Handbook of applied psycholinguistics* (pp. 295–327). Hillsdale, NJ: Lawrence Erlbaum Associates.

Leonard, L. (1983). Discussion. Part II: Defining the boundaries of language disorders in children. In J. Miller, D. Yoder, & R. Schiefelbusch (Eds.), *Contemporary issues in language intervention* (ASHA Reports No. 12, pp. 183–195). Rockville, MD: American Speech-Language-Hearing Association.

Leonard, L. (1987). Is specific language impairment a useful construct? In S. Rosenberg (Ed.), *Advances in applied psycholinguistics. I. Disorders of first language development* (pp. 1–39). New York: Cambridge University Press.

Leonard, L. (1989). Language learnability and specific language impairment in children. *Applied Psycholinguistics, 10,* 179–202.

Leonard, L., Prutting, C., Perozzi, J., & Berkley, R. (1978). Nonstandardized approaches to the assessment of language behaviors. *Asha, 20,* 371–379.

Levy, Y. (1988). The nature of early language: Evidence from the development of Hebrew morphology. In Y. Levy, I. Schlesinger, & M. Braine (Eds.), *Categories and processes in language acquisition* (pp. 73–98). Hillsdale, NJ: Lawrence Erlbaum Associates.

Lewis, M. (1970). *Attention and verbal labeling behavior: A study in the measurement of internal representations.* Princeton, NJ: Educational Testing Service.

Lightfoot, D. (1989). The child's trigger experience: Degree-0 learnability. *Behavioral and Brain Sciences, 12*, 321–375.

Liles, B. (1985a). Cohesion in the narratives of normal and language disordered children. *Journal of Speech and Hearing Research, 28*, 123–133.

Liles, B. (1985b). The production and comprehension of narrative discourse in normal and language disordered children. *Journal of Communication Disorders, 18*, 409–428.

Limber, J. (1976). Unraveling competence, performance and pragmatics in the speech of young children. *Journal of Child Language, 3*, 309–318.

Lock, A. (Ed.). (1978). *Action, gesture and symbol.* New York: Academic.

Locke, J. (1979). Homonymy and sound change in the child's acquisition of phonology. In N. Lass (Ed.), *Speech and language: Advances in basic research and practice* (pp. 258–282). New York: Academic Press.

Locke, J. (1980a). The inference of speech perception in the phonologically disordered child. Part I: A rationale, some criteria, the conventional tests. *Journal of Speech and Hearing Disorders, 45*, 431–444.

Locke, J. (1980b). The inference of speech perception in the phonologically disordered child. Part II: Some clinically novel procedures, their use, some findings. *Journal of Speech and Hearing Disorders, 45*, 445–468.

Locke, J. (1983). Clinical phonology: The explanation and treatment of speech sound disorders. *Journal of Speech and Hearing Disorders, 48*, 339–341.

Locke, J. (1994). Gradual emergence of developmental language disorders. *Journal of Speech and Hearing Research, 37*, 608–616.

Loftus, E. (1974). Reconstructing memory: The incredible eyewitness. *Psychology Today, 8*, 116–119.

Loftus, E. (1975). Leading questions and the eyewitness report. *Cognitive Psychology, 7*, 560–572.

Loftus, E. (1983). Silence is golden. *American Psychologist, 38*, 564–572.

Lund, N., & Duchan, J. (1983). *Assessing children's language in naturalistic contexts.* Englewood Cliffs, NJ: Prentice-Hall.

Lust, B. (1986a). *Studies in the acquisition of anaphora* (Vol. I). Boston: Reidel.

Lust, B. (1986b). *Studies in the acquisition of anaphora* (Vol. II). Boston: Reidel.

Lyons, J. (1977). *Semantics* (Vol. 1). New York: Cambridge University Press.

Macken, M. (1987). Representation, rules, and overgeneralization in phonology. In B. MacWhinney (Ed.), *Mechanisms of language acquisition* (pp. 367–397). Hillsdale, NJ: Lawrence Erlbaum Associates.

MacWhinney, B. (1989). Competition and teachability. In M. Rice & R. Schiefelbusch (Eds.), *The teachability of language* (pp. 63–104). Baltimore: Brookes.

MacWhinney, B., & Snow, C. (1985). The Child Language Data Exchange System. *Journal of Child Language, 12*, 271–296.

Mandler, J. (1978). A code in the node: The use of a story schema in retrieval. *Discourse Processes, 1*, 14–35.

Mandler, J. (1979). Commentary: A trilogue on dialogue. In M. Bornstein & W. Kessen (Eds.), *Psychological development from infancy* (pp. 373–382). Hillsdale, NJ: Lawrence Erlbaum Associates.

Mandler, J. (1983). Representation. In P. Mussen (Series Ed.), & J. Flavell & E. Markman (Vol. Eds.), *Handbook of child psychology: Vol. 3. Cognitive development* (4th ed., pp. 420–494). New York: Wiley.

Mandler, J. (1988). How to build a baby: On the development of an accessible representational system. *Cognitive Development, 3*, 113–136.

Mandler, J. (1990). A new perspective on cognitive development in infancy. *American Scientist, 78*, 236–243.

Maratsos, M. (1976). *The use of definite and indefinite reference in young children: An experimental study in semantic acquisition.* Cambridge, UK: Cambridge University Press.

Maratsos, M. (1982). The child's construction of grammatical categories. In E. Wanner & L. Gleitman (Eds.), *Language acquisition: The state of the art* (pp. 240–266). New York: Cambridge University Press.

Maratsos, M. (1988a). The acquisition of formal word classes. In Y. Levy, I. Schlesinger, & M. Braine (Eds.), *Categories and processes in language acquisition* (pp. 31–44). Hillsdale, NJ: Lawrence Erlbaum Associates.

Maratsos, M. (1988b). Crosslinguistic analysis, universals, and language acquisition. In F. Kessel (Ed.), *The development of language and language researchers* (pp. 121–152). Hillsdale, NJ: Lawrence Erlbaum Associates.

Maratsos, M. (1989). Innateness and plasticity in language acquisition. In M. Rice & R. Schiefelbusch (Eds.), *The teachability of language* (pp. 105–126). Baltimore: Brookes.

Maratsos, M., & Chalkley, M. (1980). The internal language of children's syntax. In K. Nelson (Ed.), *Children's language* (Vol. 2). New York: Gardner.

Martin, E. (1980). [Correspondence to ASHA (Stan Dublinske) regarding the official interpretation of P. L. 94-142]. Washington, DC: U.S. Department of Health, Education, and Welfare.

Masterson, J., & Kamhi, A. (1992). Linguistic trade-offs in school-age children with and without language disorders. *Journal of Speech and Hearing Research, 35*, 1064–1075.

Maxwell, S., & Wallach, G. (1984). The language-learning disabilities connection: Symptoms of early language disability change over time. In G. Wallach & K. Butler (Eds.), *Language-learning disabilities in school-age children* (pp. 15–32). Baltimore: Williams & Wilkins.

McCabe, A., & Peterson, C. (1991). *Developing narrative structure.* Hillsdale, NJ: Lawrence Erlbaum Associates.

McCall, R., & Kagan, J. (1969). Individual differences in the infant's distribution of attention to stimulus discrepancy. *Developmental Psychology, 2*, 90–98.

McCarthy, D. (1954). Language development in children. In L. Carmichael (Ed.), *Manual of child psychology* (pp. 492–630). New York: Wiley.

McCarthy, D. A. (1930). The language development of the preschool child. *Institute of Child Welfare Monograph Series No. 4.* Minneapolis: University of Minnesota Press.

McCauley, R., & Demetras, M. (1990). The identification of language impairment in the selection of specifically language-impaired subjects. *Journal of Speech and Hearing Disorders, 55*, 468–475.

McCauley, R., & Swisher, L. (1984a). Psychometric review of language and articulation tests for preschool children. *Journal of Speech and Hearing Disorders, 49*, 34–42.

McCauley, R., & Swisher, L. (1984b). Use and misuse of norm-referenced tests in clinical assessment: A hypothetical case. *Journal of Speech and Hearing Disorders, 49*, 338–348.

McClelland, J., & Rumelhart, D. (Eds.). (1986). *Parallel distributed processing: Explorations in the microstructure of cognition.* Cambridge, MA: MIT Press.

McCune-Nicolich, L. (1975). (Stages of symbolic play reported as non-dated). Pragmatics and symbolic play. In P. Dale & D. Ingram (Eds.), *Child language* (pp. 151–174). Baltimore: University Park Press.

McCune-Nicolich, L. (1977). Beyond sensorimotor intelligence: Assessment of symbolic maturity through analysis of pretend play. *Merrill-Palmer Quarterly, 23*, 89–101.

McCune-Nicolich, L. (1981a). The cognitive basis of relational words in the single word period. *Journal of Child Language, 8*, 15–34.

McCune-Nicolich, L. (1981b). Toward symbolic functioning: Structure of early pretend games and potential parallels with language. *Child Development, 52*, 785–797.

McDonald, E. (1964). *Articulation testing and treatment: A sensory-motor approach.* Pittsburgh, PA: Stanwix House.

McNeill, D. (1966). Developmental psycholinguistics. In F. Smith & G. Miller (Eds.), *The genesis of language* (pp. 15–84). Cambridge, MA: MIT Press.

McNeill, D. (1970). *The acquisition of language: The study of developmental psycholinguistics.* New York: Harper & Row.

McReynolds, L., & Kearns, K. (1983). *Single-subject experimental designs in communication disorders.* Austin, TX: PRO-ED.

Medawar, P. (1984). *The limits of science.* New York: Harper & Row.

Mellon, J. (1967). *Transformational sentence combining: A method for enhancing the development of syntactic fluency in English composition* (Harvard Research & Development Center on Educational Differences Report No. 1). Cambridge, MA: Harvard University.

Menyuk, P. (1964). Alternation of rules of children's grammar. *Journal of Verbal Learning and Verbal Behavior, 3,* 480–488.

Menyuk, P., & Looney, P. (1972a). A problem of language disorder: Length versus structure. *Journal of Speech and Hearing Research, 15,* 264–269.

Menyuk, P., & Looney, P. (1972b). Relationships among components of the grammar in language disorder. *Journal of Speech and Hearing Research, 15,* 395–406.

Mercer, J. (1972a). *Labeling the mentally retarded.* Berkeley: University of California Press.

Mercer, J. (1972b). The lethal label. *Psychology Today, 6,* 44–47, 95–97.

Mercer, J. (1974). A policy statement on assessment procedures and the rights of children. *Harvard Educational Review, 44,* 125–142.

Mervis, C., & Pani, J. (1980). Acquisition of basic object categories. *Cognitive Psychology, 12,* 496–522.

Messick, S. (1975). The standard problem: Meaning and values in measurement and evaluation. *American Psychologist, 30,* 955–966.

Messick, S. (1980). Test validity and the ethics of assessment. *American Psychologist, 35,* 1012–1027.

Messick, S. (1989a). Meaning and values in test validation: The science and ethics of assessment. *Educational Researcher, 18,* 5–11.

Messick, S. (1989b). Validity. In R. Linn (Ed.), *Educational measurement* (3rd ed., pp. 13–103). New York: American Council on Education/Macmillan.

Miller, G. (1956). The magical number seven, plus or minus two: Some limits on our capacity for processing information. *Psychological Review, 63,* 81–97.

Miller, J. (1981). *Assessing language production in children: Experimental procedures.* Needham Heights, MA: Allyn & Bacon.

Miller, J., & Chapman, R. (1981a). *Assessing language production in children: Experimental procedures.* Baltimore: University Park Press.

Miller, J., & Chapman, R. (1981b). The relation between age and mean length of utterance in morphemes. *Journal of Speech and Hearing Research, 24,* 154–161.

Miller, L. (1976). *The influence of psycholinguistics on the speech pathologist's view of language acquisition.* Unpublished doctoral dissertation, University of Colorado, Boulder.

Miller, L. (1989). Classroom-based language intervention. *Language, Speech, and Hearing Services in Schools, 20,* 153–169.

Miller, L. (1993). Testing and the creation of disorder. *American Journal of Speech-Language Pathology, 2,* 13–16.

Minifie, F. (1996, April). *The future of the discipline.* Paper presented at the Council of Graduate Programs in Communication Sciences and Disorders, San Diego, CA.

Mitroff, I., & Sagasti, F. (1973). Epistemology as general systems theory: An approach to the design of complex decision-making experiments. *Philosophy of Social Science, 3,* 117–134.

Moely, B., Olsen, F., Halwas, T., & Flavell, J. (1969). Production deficiency in young children's clustered recall. *Developmental Psychology, 1,* 26–34.

Morgan, J. (1989). Learnability considerations and the nature of trigger experiences in language acquisition. *Behavioral and Brain Sciences, 12*, 352–353.

Mulac, A., & Tomlinson, C. (1977). Generalization of an operant remediation program for syntax with language delayed children. *Journal of Communication Disorders, 10*, 231–243.

Muma, J. (1971a). Language intervention: Ten techniques. *Language, Speech, and Hearing Services in Schools, 5*, 7–17.

Muma, J. (1971b). *Parent–child development center: Conceptualization, program, evaluation.* Birmingham, AL: Parent–Child Development Center.

Muma, J. (1973a). Language assessment: Some underlying assumptions. *Asha, 15*, 331–338.

Muma, J. (1973b). Language assessment: The co-occurring and restricted structures procedure. *Acta Symbolica, 4*, 12–29.

Muma, J. (1975a). The communication game: Dump and play. *Journal of Speech and Hearing Disorders, 40*, 296–309.

Muma, J. (1975b). [Review of R. Schiefelbusch & L. Lloyd (Eds.), Language perspectives: Development, retardation, and intervention]. *Asha, 18*, 371–373.

Muma, J. (1977a). Language intervention strategies. *Language, Speech, and Hearing Services in Schools, 8*, 107–125.

Muma, J. (1977b). *Make-change: A game of sentence sense.* Austin, TX: Learning Concepts.

Muma, J. (1978a). Connell, Spradlin and McReynolds: Right but wrong! *Journal of Speech and Hearing Disorders, 43*, 549–552.

Muma, J. (1978b). *Language handbook: Concepts, assessment, intervention.* Englewood Cliffs, NJ: Prentice-Hall.

Muma, J. (1980). *MAKE-CHANGE (A game of sentence sense).* Boston: New York Times Teaching Resources.

Muma, J. (1981a). Language: A new era. *Journal of Childhood Communication Disorders, 5*, 70–72.

Muma, J. (1981b). Language: A new era. *Journal of Childhood Communication Disorders, 5*, 83–89.

Muma, J. (1981c). *Language primer for the clinical fields.* Austin, TX: PRO-ED.

Muma, J. (1983a). Assessing loci of linguistic learning. *Australian Journal of Human Communication Disorders, 11*, 37–50.

Muma, J. (1983b). Speech-language pathology: Emerging clinical expertise in language. In T. Gallagher & C. Prutting (Eds.), *Pragmatic assessment and intervention issues in language* (pp. 195–214). San Diego, CA: College-Hill Press.

Muma, J. (1984a). Clinical assessment: New perspectives. In K. Ruder & M. Smith (Eds.), *Developmental language intervention* (pp. 57–80).

Muma, J. (1984b). Semel and Wiig's CELF: Construct validity? *Journal of Speech and Hearing Disorders, 49*, 101–104.

Muma, J. (1985). No news is bad news. *Journal of Speech and Hearing Disorders, 50*, 290–293.

Muma, J. (1986a). *Language acquisition: A functionalist perspective.* Austin, TX: PRO-ED.

Muma, J. (1986b). Review: Kuczaj, S., & Barrett, M. (Eds.), The development of word meaning. *Asha, 29*, 8, 47.

Muma, J. (1987a). Functionalism: Clinical implications. *NSSLHA Journal, 15*, 106–119.

Muma, J. (1987b). Response to Byrne Savichs' review of language acquisition: A functionalistic prospective. *Asha, 28*, 70.

Muma, J. (1991). Experiential realism: Clinical implications. In T. Gallagher (Ed.), *Pragmatics of language* (pp. 229–247). San Diego, CA: Singular.

Muma, J. (1993). The need for replication. *Journal of Speech and Hearing Research, 36*, 927–930.

Muma, J. (1994). Letter: Silverman and Lenhard survey. *Asha, 36*, 2, 70.

Muma, J. (1998). Muma Object Sorting Task and Muma Button Sequence Task (experimental editions). Unpublished manuscript, Central Michigan University.

Muma, J., Adams-Perry, M., & Gallagher, J. (1974). Some semantic properties in sentence perception. *Psychological Reports, 35*, 23–32.

Muma, J., & Brannon, C. (1986, November). *Language sampling.* Miniseminar presented at the American Speech-Language-Hearing Association Convention.

Muma, J., Lubinski, R., & Pierce, S. (1982). Language assessment: Data or evidence. *Speech and Language, 7*, 135–147.

Muma, J., & Muma, D. (1979). *Muma assessment program (MAP).* Lubbock, TX: Natural Child.

Muma, J., & Pierce, S. (1980). Language intervention: Data or evidence? *Topics in Language and Learning Disabilities, 1*, 1–11.

Muma, J., Pierce, S., & Muma, D. (1983). Language training in ASHA: A survey of substantive issues. *Asha, 35*, 35–40.

Muma, J., Webb, P., & Muma, D. (1979). Language training in speech pathology and audiology: A survey. *Asha, 21*, 467–473.

Muma, J., & Zwycewicz-Emory, C. (1979). Contextual priority: Verbal shift at seven? *Journal of Child Language, 6*, 301–311.

Nelson, K. (1973a). Some evidence for the cognitive primacy of categorization and its functional basis. *Merrill-Palmer Quarterly, 19*, 27–39.

Nelson, K. (1973b). Structure and strategy in learning to talk. *Monographs of The Society for Research in Child Development, 38*(Serial No. 149).

Nelson, K. (1974). Concept, word, and sentence: Interrelations in acquisition and development. *Psychological Review, 81*, 267–285.

Nelson, K. (1978). How young children represent knowledge of their world in and out of language. In R. Siegler (Ed.), *Children's thinking: What develops?* (pp. 255–273). Hillsdale, NJ: Lawrence Erlbaum Associates.

Nelson, K. (1981a). Individual differences in language development: Implications for development and language. *Developmental Psychology, 17*, 170–187.

Nelson, K. (1981b). Social cognition in a script framework. In J. Flavell & L. Ross (Eds.), *Social cognitive development* (pp. 97–118). New York: Cambridge University Press.

Nelson, K. (1985). *Making sense: The acquisition of shared meaning.* New York: Academic Press.

Nelson, K. (1986). *Event knowledge: Structure and function in development.* Hillsdale, NJ: Lawrence Erlbaum Associates.

Nelson, K. (1991). Event knowledge and the development of language functions. In J. Miller (Ed.), *Research on child language disorders* (pp. 125–142). Austin, TX: PRO-ED.

Nelson, K. (1996). *Language in cognitive development.* New York: Cambridge University Press.

Nelson, K., & Gruendel, J. (1981). Generalized event representations: Basic building blocks of cognitive development. In M. Lamb & A. Brown (Eds.), *Advances in developmental psychology* (Vol. 1, pp. 131–158). Hillsdale, NJ: Lawrence Erlbaum Associates.

Nelson, K. E. (1981). Toward a rare-event cognitive comparison theory of syntax acquisition. In P. Dale & D. Ingram (Eds.), *Child language* (pp. 229–240). Austin, TX: PRO-ED.

Nelson, K. E. (1989). Strategies for first language teaching. In M. Rice & R. Schiefelbusch (Eds.), *The teachability of language* (pp. 263–310). Baltimore: Brookes.

Nelson, K. E. (1991). On differentiated language-learning models and differentiated interventions. In N. Krasnegor, D. Rumbaugh, R. Schiefelbusch, & M. Studdert-Kennedy (Eds.), *Biological and behavioral determinants of language development* (pp. 399–428). Hillsdale, NJ: Lawrence Erlbaum Associates.

Nelson, N. (1986). Individual processing in classroom settings. *Topics in Language Disorders, 6*, 13–27.

Nelson, N. (1989). Curriculum-based language assessment and intervention. *Language, Speech, and Hearing Services in Schools, 20*, 170–184.

Nelson, N. (1993). *Childhood language disorders in context: Infancy through adolescence.* Columbus, OH: Merrill.

Newell, A. (1992). Precis of unified theories of cognition. *Behavioral and Brain Sciences, 15*, 425–492.

Nihira, K., Foster, R., Shellhaas, M., & Leland, H. (1974). *AAMD Adaptive Behavior Scale.* Washington, DC: American Association of Mental Deficiency.

Ninio, A. (1978). The achievements and antecedents of labelling. *Journal of Child Language, 5,* 1–16.

Ninio, A. (1980). Ostensive definition in vocabulary teaching. *Journal of Child Language, 7,* 565–573.

Ninio, A. (1988). On formal grammatical categories in early child language. In Y. Levy, I. Schlesinger, & M. Braine (Eds.), *Categories and processes in language acquisition* (pp. 99–120). Hillsdale, NJ: Lawrence Erlbaum Associates.

Ninio, A. (1995). Expression of communicative intents in the single-word period and the vocabulary spurt. In K. Nelson & Z. Reger (Eds.), *Children's language* (Vol. 8). Hillsdale, NJ: Lawrence Erlbaum Associates.

Ninio, A., & Bruner, J. (1978). The achievements and antecedents of labeling. *Journal of Child Language, 5,* 1–15.

Ninio, A., & Snow, C. (1988). Language acquisition through language use: The functional sources of children's early utterances. In Y. Levy, I. Schlesinger, & M. Braine (Eds.), *Categories and processes in language acquisition* (pp. 11–30). Hillsdale, NJ: Lawrence Erlbaum Associates.

Ninio, A., Snow, C., Pan, B., & Rollins, P. (1994). Classifying communicative acts in children's interactions. *Journal of Communication Disorders, 27,* 157–187.

Odom, R., & Guzman, R. (1972). Development of hierarchies of dimensional salience. *Developmental Psychology, 6,* 271–287.

Olswang, L. (1993). Developmental speech and language disorders. *Asha, 35,* 42–44.

Olswang, L., & Bain, B. (1991). When to recommend intervention. *Language, Speech and Hearing Services in Schools, 22,* 255–263.

Olswang, L., Bain, B., Rosendahl, P., Oblak, S., & Smith, A. (1986). Language learning: Moving performance from a context-dependent to -independent state. *Child Language Teaching and Therapy, 2,* 180–210.

Olswang, L., Stoel-Gammon, C., Coggins, T., & Carpenter, R. (1987). *Assessing linguistic behaviors: Assessing prelinguistic and early linguistic behaviors in developmentally young children.* Seattle: University of Washington Press.

Olswang, L., Thompson, C., Warren, S., & Minghetti, N. (1990). *Treatment efficacy research in communication disorders.* Rockville, MD: American Speech-Language-Hearing Foundation.

Olver, P., & Hornsby, R. (1966). On equivalence. In J. Bruner & P. Olver (Eds.), *Studies in cognitive growth* (pp. 68–85). New York: Wiley.

Osgood, C. (1957). Motivational dynamics of language behavior. *Nebraska Symposium on Motivation.* Lincoln: University of Nebraska Press.

Palermo, D. (1971). Is a scientific revolution taking place in psychology? *Science Studies, 1,* 135–155.

Palermo, D. (1982). Theoretical issues in semantic development. In S. Kuczaj (Ed.), *Language development* (Vol. 1). Hillsdale, NJ: Lawrence Erlbaum Associates.

Palermo, D., & Eberhart, W. (1968). On the learning of morphological rules: An experimental analogy. *Journal of Verbal Learning and Verbal Behavior, 7,* 337–344.

Parsonson, B., & Baer, D. (1978). A tale of two paradigms. In T. Kratchwill (Ed.), *Single subject research: Strategies for evaluating change* (pp. 101–108). New York: Academic Press.

Paul, R. (1995). *Language disorders from infancy through adolescence.* St. Louis, MO: Mosby Yearbook.

Perera, K. (1994). Editorial: Child language research: Building on the past, looking to the future. *Journal of Child Language, 21,* 1–7.

Perkins, W. (1986). Functions and malfunctions of theories in therapies. *Asha, 28,* 31–33.

Peters, A. (1983). *The units of language acquisition.* Cambridge, UK: Cambridge University Press.

Piaget, J. (1952). *The origins of intelligence in children.* New York: International Universities Press.

Piaget, J. (1964). *The child's construction of reality.* New York: Basic Books.

Pinker, S. (1984). *Language learnability and language development.* Cambridge, MA: Harvard University Press.

Pinker, S. (1988). Learnability theory and the acquisition of a first language. In F. Kessel (Ed.), *The development of language and language researchers* (pp. 97–120). Hillsdale, NJ: Lawrence Erlbaum Associates.

Poplin, M. (1988). The reductionistic fallacy in learning disabilities: Replicating the past by reducing the present. *Journal of Learning Disabilities, 21,* 389–400.

Popper, K. (1972). *Objective knowledge: An evolutionary approach.* London: Oxford University Press.

Prelock, P., & Panagos, J. (1981). The middle ground in evaluating language programs. *Journal of Speech and Hearing Disorders, 46,* 436–437.

Priestly, T. (1980). Homonymy in child phonology. *Journal of Child Language, 7,* 413–427.

Prizant, B., & Wetherby, A. (1989). Enhancing language and communication in autism: From theory to practice. In G. Dawson (Ed.), *Autism: Nature, diagnosis, and treatment* (pp. 282–309). New York: Guilford.

Prizant, B., & Wetherby, A. (1990). Toward an integrated view of early language, communication and socioemotional development. *Topics in Language Disorders, 10,* 1–16.

Prutting, C. (1979). Process. *Journal of Speech and Hearing Disorders, 44,* 3–40.

Prutting, C. (1982). Pragmatics as social competence. *Journal of Speech and Hearing Disorders, 47,* 123–133.

Prutting, C. (1983). Scientific inquiry and communicative disorders: An emerging paradigm across six decades. In T. Gallagher & C. Prutting (Eds.), *Pragmatic assessment and intervention issues in language* (pp. 247–266). San Diego, CA: College-Hill Press.

Prutting, C., Epstein, L., Beckman, S., Dias, I., & Gao, X. (1989). *Inquiry into and tampering with nature: A clinical perspective.* Unpublished manuscript, University of California at Santa Barbara.

Prutting, C., Gallagher, T., & Mulac, A. (1975). The expressive portion of the N.S.S.T. compared to a spontaneous language sample. *Journal of Speech and Hearing Disorders, 40,* 40–49.

Prutting, C., & Kirchner, D. (1983). Applied pragmatics. In T. Gallagher & C. Prutting (Eds.), *Pragmatic assessment and intervention issues in language* (pp. 29–64). San Diego, CA: College-Hill Press.

Prutting, C., & Kirchner, D. (1987). A clinical appraisal of the pragmatic aspects of language. *Journal of Speech and Hearing Disorders, 52,* 105–119.

Prutting, C., Mentis, M., & Myles-Zitzer, C. (1989). *Philosophy of science: A template for understanding our science.* Unpublished manuscript, University of California at Santa Barbara.

Putnam, H. (1975). *Mind, language and reality.* New York: Cambridge University Press.

Pylyshyn, Z. (1980). Computation and cognition: Issues in the foundations of cognitive science. *Behavioral and Brain Sciences, 3,* 111–132.

Quine, W. (1978, November 23). Other worldly. *New York Review of Books,* 25.

Ramer, A. (1976). Syntactic styles in emerging language. *Journal of Child Language, 3,* 49–62.

Rees, N. (1973). Auditory processing factors in language disorders: The view from Procrustes' bed. *Journal of Speech and Hearing Disorders, 38,* 304–315.

Rees, N. (1981). Saying more than we know: Is auditory processing disorder a meaningful concept? In R. Keith (Ed.), *Central auditory and language disorders in children* (pp. 94–120). San Diego, CA: College-Hill Press.

Rees, N., & Snope, J. (1983). National conference on undergraduate, graduate, and continuing education. *Asha, 25,* 49–59.

Renfrew, C. (1966). Persistence of the open syllable in defective articulation. *Journal of Speech and Hearing Disorders, 31,* 370–373.

Rescorla, L. (1989). The Language Development Survey: A screening tool for delayed language in toddlers. *Journal of Speech and Hearing Disorders, 54,* 587–599.

Rescorla, L., & Goossens, M. (1992). Symbolic play development in toddlers with expressive specific language impairment (SLI-E). *Journal of Speech and Hearing Research, 35*, 1290–1302.

Rice, M. (1983). Contemporary accounts of the cognition/language relationship: Implications for speech-language clinicians. *Journal of Speech and Hearing Disorders, 48*, 347–359.

Rice, M., Buhr, J., & Nemeth, M. (1990). Fast mapping word-learning abilities of language-delayed preschoolers. *Journal of Speech and Hearing Disorders, 55*, 33–42.

Rice, M., & Wexler, K. (1996). Toward tense as a clinical marker of specific languge impairment in English-speaking children. *Journal of Speech and Hearing Research, 39*, 1239–1257.

Ringel, R., Trachtman, L., & Prutting, C. (1984). The science in human communication sciences. *Asha, 26*, 33–37.

Robertson, S., & Weismer, S. (1997). The influence of peer models on the play scripts of children with specific language impairment. *Journal of Speech, Language, and Hearing Research, 40*, 49–61.

Rocissano, L., & Yatchmink, Y. (1983). Language skill and interactive patterns in premature born toddlers. *Child Development, 54*, 1229–1241.

Rogers-Warren, A., & Warren, S. (1980). Mands for verbalization: Facilitating the display of newly taught language. *Behavior Modification, 4*, 361–382.

Rogoff, B. (1990). *Apprenticeship in thinking: Cognitive development in social context.* New York: Oxford University Press.

Rosch, E. (1973). Natural categories. *Cognitive Psychology, 4*, 328–350.

Rosch, E. (1978). Principles of categorization. In E. Rosch & B. Lloyd (Eds.), *Cognition and categorization* (pp. 27–48). Hillsdale, NJ: Lawrence Erlbaum Associates.

Rosch, E., & Mervis, C. (1975). Family resemblances: Studies in the internal structure of categories. *Cognitive Psychology, 7*, 573–605.

Rudder, C. (1993). The falsification fallacy. *Studies in Philosophy and Education, 12*, 179–199.

Russell, B. (1905). On denoting. *Mind, 14*, 479–493.

Rutter, M. (1979). Maternal deprivation, 1972–1978: New findings, new concepts, new approaches. *Child Development, 50*, 283–305.

Sachs, J. (1983). Talking about there and then: The emergence of displaced reference in parent–child discourse. In K. E. Nelson (Ed.), *Children's language* (Vol. 4, pp. 1–28). Hillsdale, NJ: Lawrence Erlbaum Associates.

Salvia, J., & Ysseldyke, J. (1988). *Assessment in special and remedial education* (4th ed.). Boston: Houghton-Mifflin.

Schacter, D. (1992). Understanding implicit memory: A cognitive neuroscience approach. *American Psychologist, 47*, 559–569.

Schacter, D., & Tulving, E. (Eds.). (1994). *Memory systems 1994.* Cambridge, MA: MIT Press.

Schank, R., & Abelson, R. (1977). *Scripts, plans, goals and understanding.* Hillsdale, NJ: Lawrence Erlbaum Associates.

Schank, R., Collins, G., Davis, E., Johnson, P., Lytinen, S., & Reiser, B. (1982). What's the point? *Cognitive Science, 6*, 255–275.

Scherer, N., & Olswang, L. (1984). Role of mother's expansions in stimulating children's language production. *Journal of Speech and Hearing Research, 27*, 387–395.

Schery, T., & O'Connor, L. (1992). The effectiveness of school-based computer language intervention with severely handicapped children. *Language, Speech, and Hearing Services in Schools, 23*, 43–47.

Schiavetti, N., Metz, D., & Sitler, R. (1981). Construct validity of direct magnitude estimation and interval scaling of speech intelligibility: Evidence from a study of the hearing impaired. *Journal of Speech and Hearing Research, 24*, 441–445.

Schlesinger, I. (1971). Production of utterances and language acquisition. In D. Slobin (Ed.), *The ontogensis of grammar* (pp. 63–101). New York: Academic Press.

Schlesinger, I. (1974). Relational concepts underlying language. In R. Schiefelbusch & L. Lloyd (Eds.), *Language perspectives: Acquisition, retardation, and intervention* (pp. 129–152). Baltimore: University Park Press.

Schlesinger, I. (1977). The role of cognitive development and linguistic input in language acquisition. *Journal of Child Language, 4,* 153–170.

Schlesinger, I. (1988). The origin of relational categories. In Y. Levy, I. Schlesinger, & M. Braine (Eds.), *Categories and processes in language acquisition* (pp. 121–144). Hillsdale, NJ: Lawrence Erlbaum Associates.

Schunk, D. (1987). Peer models and children's behavioral change. *Review of Educational Research, 57,* 149–174.

Schwartz, R., & Leonard, L. (1982). Do children pick and choose? An examination of phonological selection and avoidance in early lexical acquisition. *Journal of Child Language, 9,* 319–336.

Searle, J. (1969). *Speech acts: An essay in the philosophy of language.* Cambridge, UK: Cambridge University Press.

Searle, J. (1975). Indirect speech acts. In P. Cole & J. Morgan (Eds.), *Syntax and semantics* (Vol. 3, pp. 59–82). New York: Academic Press.

Searle, J. (1977). A classification of illocutionary acts. *Language in Society, 5,* 1–23.

Searle, J. (1979). The classification of illocutionary acts. In J. Searle (Ed.), *Expression and meaning* (pp. 1–29). Cambridge, UK: Cambridge University Press.

Searle, J. (1983). *Intentionality: An essay in the philosophy of mind.* Cambridge, UK: Cambridge University Press.

Searle, J. (1992). *The rediscovery of the mind.* Cambridge, MA: MIT Press.

Semel, E., & Wiig, E. (1980). *Clinical evaluation of language functions.* Columbus, OH: Merrill.

Shapere, D. (1984). Objectivity, rationality, and scientific change. *Philosophy of Science Association, 2,* 637–663.

Shapiro, H. (1992). Debatable issues underlying whole-language philosophy: A speech-language pathologist's perspective. *Language, Speech, and Hearing Services in Schools, 23,* 308–311.

Shatz, M., Hoff-Ginsberg, E., & Maciver, D. (1989). Induction and the acquisition of English auxiliaries: The effects of differentially enriched input. *Journal of Child Language, 16,* 121–140.

Sherry, D., & Schacter, D. (1987). The evolution of multiple memory systems. *Psychological Review, 94,* 439–454.

Shriner, T. (1969). A review of mean length of responses as a measure of expressive language development in children. *Journal of Speech and Hearing Disorders, 34,* 61–67.

Sigel, I. (1971). Language of the disadvantaged: The distancing hypothesis. In C. Lavatelli (Ed.), *Language training in early childhood education* (pp. 60–78). Urbana: University of Illinois Press.

Sigel, I., & Cocking, R. (1977). Cognition and communication: A dialectic paradigm for development. In M. Lewis & L. Rosenblum (Eds.), *Interaction, conversation, and the development of language* (pp. 207–226). New York: Wiley.

Simon, H. (1974). How big is a chunk? *Science, 183,* 482–488.

Sinclair, H. (1969). Developmental psycholinguistics. In D. Elkind & J. Flavell (Eds.), *Studies in cognitive development* (pp. 315–336). New York: Oxford University Press.

Sinclair, H., & Bronckart, J. (1972). SVO—A linguistic universal?: A study in developmental psycholinguistics. *Journal of Experimental Child Psychology, 14,* 329–348.

Slobin, D. (1970). *Suggested universals in the ontogenesis of grammar* (Working Paper No. 32). Stanford University: Language Behavior Research Laboratory.

Slobin, D. (1973). Cognitive prerequisites for the development of grammar. In C. Ferguson & D. Slobin (Eds.), *Studies of child language development* (pp. 175–208). New York: Holt, Rinehart & Winston.

Slobin, D., & Welch, C. (1971). Elicited imitation as a research tool in developmental psycholinguistics. In C. Lavatelli (Ed.), *Language training in early childhood education* (pp. 170–185). Urbana: University of Illinois Press.

Smith, F. (1971). *Understanding reading: A psycholinguistic analysis of reading and learning to read.* New York: Holt, Rinehart & Winston.

Snow, C., & Tomasello, M. (1989). Data on language input: Incomprehensible omission indeed! *Behavioral and Brain Sciences, 12,* 357–358.

Sorensen, P., & Fey, M. (1992). Informativeness as a clinical principle: What's really new? *Language, Speech, and Hearing Services in Schools, 23,* 320–328.

Sperber, D., & Wilson, D. (1986). *Relevance: Communication and cognition.* Cambridge, MA: Harvard University Press.

Squire, L. (1994). Declarative and nondeclarative memory: Multiple brain systems supporting learning and memory. In D. Schacter & E. Tulving (Eds.), *Memory systems 1994* (pp. 203–232). Cambridge, MA: MIT Press.

Sroufe, L., & Waters, W. (1976). The ontogenesis of smiling and laughter: A perspective on the organization of development in infancy. *Psychological Review, 83,* 173–189.

Starkweather, W. (1992). Responses and reactions to Hamre, "Stuttering prevention II: Progression." *Journal of Fluency Disorders, 17,* 95–106.

Stoel-Gammon, C., & Cooper, J. (1984). Patterns of early lexical and phonological development. *Journal of Child Language, 11,* 247–272.

Strawson, P. (1950). On referring. *Mind, 59,* 320–344.

Strohner, J., & Nelson, K. (1974). The young child's development of sentence comprehension: Influence of event probability, nonverbal context, syntactic form, and strategies. *Child Development, 45,* 564–576.

Sylva, K., Bruner, J., & Genova, P. (1976).The role of play in the problem-solving of children 3–5 years old. In J. Bruner, A. Jolly, & K. Sylva (Eds.), *Play: Its role in development and evolution* (pp. 244–261). New York: Basic Books.

Tallal, P. (1990). Fine-grained discrimination deficits in language-learning impaired children are specific neither to the auditory modality nor to speech perception. *Journal of Speech and Hearing Research, 33,* 616–617.

Tallal, P. (1991). Back to the future: Research on developmental disorders of language. In J. Miller (Ed.), *Research on child language disorders* (pp. 399–408). Austin, TX: PRO-ED.

Tattershall, S. (1987). Mission impossible: Learning how a classroom works before it's too late! *Journal of Childhood Communication Disorders, 2,* 181–184.

Templin, M. (1957). *Certain language skills in children* (Monograph No. 26). Minneapolis: University of Minnesota Press.

Thal, D., & Tobias, S. (1992). Communicative gestures in children with delayed onset of oral expressive vocabulary. *Journal of Speech and Hearing Research, 35,* 1281–1289.

Thal, D., Tobias, S., & Morrison, D. (1991). Language and gesture in late talkers: A one year follow-up. *Journal of Speech and Hearing Disorders, 34,* 604–612.

Toch, T. (1992, September 14). Nu waz for kidz tu lern rdn, rtn. *U.S. News & World Report,* pp. 75–76.

Tulving, E. (1972). Episodic and semantic memory. In E. Tulving & M. Donaldson (Eds.), *Organization of memory* (pp. 382–403). New York: Academic Press.

Tulving, E. (1995). Memory: Introduction. In M. Gazzaniga (Ed.), *The cognitive neurosciences* (pp. 751–754). Cambridge, MA: MIT Press.

Tyack, D., & Gottsleben, R. (1974). *Language sampling, analysis and training: A handbook for teachers and clinicians.* Palo Alto, CA: Consulting Psychologists Press.

Tyack, D., & Gottsleben, R. (1977). *Language sampling, analysis and training: A handbook for teachers and clinicians* (Rev. ed.). Palo Alto, CA: Consulting Psychologists Press.

Tyler, S. (1969). *Cognitive anthropology.* New York: Holt, Rinehart & Winston.

Uzgiris, I., & Hunt, J. (1975). *Assessment in infancy: Ordinal scale of psychological development.* Chicago: University of Illinois Press.

Valian, V. (1990). Logical and psychological constraints on the acquisition of syntax. In L. Fraiser & J. deVilliers (Eds.), *Language processing and language acquisition* (pp. 119–146). Boston: Kluwer Academic.

vanKleek, A. (1984). Metalinguistic skills: Cutting across spoken and written language and problem-solving abilities. In G. Wallach & K. Butler (Eds.), *Language learning disabilities in school-age children* (pp. 128–154). Baltimore: Williams & Wilkins.

VanRiper, C. (1954). *Speech correction: Principles and methods.* Englewood Cliffs, NJ: Prentice-Hall.

Ventry, I., & Schiavetti, N. (1986). *Evaluating research in speech pathology and audiology* (2nd ed.). New York: Macmillan.

Vespucci, P. (1975). *Two developmental cognitive processes: Performance at the kindergarten level.* Unpublished master thesis, State University of New York, Buffalo.

Vihman, M. (1981). Phonology and the development of the lexicon: Evidence from children's errors. *Journal of Child Language, 8,* 239–264.

Vihman, M., Ferguson, C., & Elbert, M. (1987). Phonological development from babbling to speech: Common tendencies and individual differences. *Applied Psycholinguistics, 7,* 3–40.

Vihman, M., & Greenlee, M. (1987). Individual differences in phonological development: Ages one and three years. *Journal of Speech and Hearing Research, 30,* 503–521.

Vygotsky, L. (1962). *Thought and language.* Cambridge, MA: MIT Press.

Wallach, G., & Miller, L. (1988). *Language intervention and academic success.* San Diego, CA: College-Hill/Little Brown.

Wanner, E. (1988). The parser's architecture. In F. Kessel (Ed.), *The development of language and language researchers* (pp. 79–96). Hillsdale, NJ: Lawrence Erlbaum Associates.

Warden, D. (1976). The influence of context on children's use of identifying expressions and references. *British Journal of Psychology, 67,* 101–112.

Warren, S., McQuarter, R., & Rogers-Warren, A. (1984). The effects of mands and models on the speech of unresponsive, language delayed, preschool children. *Journal of Speech and Hearing Disorders, 47,* 42–52.

Waterson, N. (1984). *Phoneme segments in child phonology: How valid is the concept?* Paper presented at the Third International Congress for the Study of Child Language, Austin, TX.

Watkins, R., & Rice, M. (1991). Verb particle and proposition acquisition in language-impaired preschoolers. *Journal of Speech and Hearing Research, 34,* 1130–1141.

Weaver, C. (1985). Parallels between new paradigms in science and in reading and literacy theories: An essay review. *Research in the Teaching of English, 19,* 298–316.

Wechsler, D. (1975). Intelligence defined and undefined: A relativistic appraisal. *American Psychologist, 30,* 135–139.

Weir, R. (1962). *Language in the crib.* The Hague: Mouton.

Weiss, A., & Nakamura, M. (1992). Children with normal language skills in preschool classrooms for children with language impairments: Differences in modeling styles. *Language, Speech and Hearing Services in Schools, 23,* 64–70.

Wells, G. (1981). *Learning through interaction.* New York: Cambridge University Press.

Werner, H., & Kaplan, B. (1963). *Symbol formation.* New York: Wiley.

Wertsch, J. (1991). *Voices of the mind, a sociocultural approach to mediated action.* Cambridge, MA: Harvard University Press.

Wetherby, A. (1991). Profiling pragmatic abilities in the emerging language of young children. In T. Gallagher (Ed.), *Pragmatics of language* (pp. 249–282). San Diego, CA: Singular.

Wetherby, A., & Prizant, B. (1990). *Communication and symbolic behavior scales—Research edition.* Chicago: Riverside.

Wexler, K., & Culicover, P. (1980). *Formal principles of language acquisition.* Cambridge, MA: MIT Press.

White, S. (1965). Evidence for a hierarchical arrangement of learning processes. In L. Lipsett & C. Spiker (Eds.), *Advances in child development and behavior* (pp. 187–220). New York: Academic Press.

Wiig, E., & Semel, E. (1980). *Language assessment and intervention for the learning disabled.* Columbus, OH: Merrill.

Winner, E. (1979). New names for old things: The emergence of metaphoric language. *Journal of Child Language, 6,* 469–492.

Winner, E., Engel, M., & Gardner, H. (1980). Misunderstanding metaphor: What's the problem? *Journal of Experimental Child Psychology, 30,* 22–32.

Wittgenstein, L. (1953). *Philosophical investigations.* New York: Macmillan.

Yngve, V. (1960). A model and an hypothesis for language structure. *Proceedings of the American Philosophical Society, 108,* 275–281.

Yoder, D. (1987). Would you tell me please, which way I ought to walk from here: Wonderland or looking-glass? *NSSLHA Journal, 15,* 5–15.

Zukier, H., & Pepitone, A. (1984). Social roles and strategies in prediction: Some determinants of the use of base rate information. *Journal of Personality and Social Psychology, 47,* 349.

Zwitman, D., & Sonderman, J. (1979). A syntax program designed to present base linguistic structures to language-disordered children. *Journal of Communication Disorders, 2,* 323–335.

AUTHOR INDEX

SUBJECT INDEX